The NAKED COMMUNIST

by W. Cleon Skousen

Published by
Ensign Publishing
P.O. Box 298
Riverton, UT 84065
www.skousen2000.com

Eleventh Edition

Designed by Keith Eddington
Illustrated by Arnold Friberg

"THE CONFLICT BETWEEN COMMUNISM AND FREEDOM IS THE PROBLEM OF OUR TIME. IT OVERSHADOWS ALL OTHER PROBLEMS. THIS CONFLICT MIRRORS OUR AGE, ITS TOILS, ITS TENSIONS, ITS TROUBLES, AND ITS TASKS. ON THE OUTCOME OF THIS CONFLICT DEPENDS THE FUTURE OF ALL MANKIND."

George Meany
President, AFL-CIO

PREFACE

One of the most fantastic phenomena of modern times has been the unbelievable success of the Communist conspiracy to enslave mankind. Part of this has been the result of two species of ignorance—ignorance concerning the constitutional requirements needed to perpetuate freedom, and secondly, ignorance concerning the history, philosophy and strategy of World Communism.

This study is designed to bring the far-flung facts about Communism into a single volume. It contains a distillation of more than one hundred books and treatises—many of them written by Communist authors. It attempts to present the Communist in his true native elements, stripped of propaganda and pretense. Hence, the title, "The Naked Communist."

Students in the western part of the world have a tendency to shy away from the obscure complexity of Communism because they have a feeling they are groping about in a vacuum of unknown quantities. It therefore became the author's objective many years ago to try and clarify these concepts so that they could be more readily understood and thereby become less frightening. The most terrifying of all human fears is "fear of the unknown" and consequently it seemed highly desirable to disarm the Communist revolutionists of any such supreme advantage by spreading before the student the whole picture of Marxism which is simply "modern materialism in action."

A panoramic study of Communism might easily degenerate into a long list of dates, names, and platitudes without helping the student to gain a genuine understanding of the history and philosophy of Marxism. Therefore, in this study, an attempt has been made to present Communism as the living, breathing, vibrating force in the earth which it really is. The political development, the philosophy, the economic theory and the big names in World Communism have all been presented in their historical setting.

Since an ever increasing number of disillusioned Communist officials have fled from behind the Iron Curtain, it has been possible to remove much of the mystery which formerly obscured a correct understanding of the Marxian-disciplined mind. This study therefore presents the Marxian civilization without reference to its propaganda claims but within the realm of reality where, during each passing day, millions of human beings are vicariously learning for the rest of the race the true meaning of life under Communism.

To those who have never taken occasion to study the past one hundred years of Marxism, this presentation may at first seem somewhat harsh. But that is because the exposed seams of Communism are inherently harsh. Marx designed it that way. From a comfortable armchair in a cloistered study it is sometimes difficult for a student to catch the spirit and substance of Communism in action. But the Korean veteran, the Iron Curtain refugee, the returning ambassador from Moscow—these who have felt the physical and psychological impact of World Communism—may count this study underdrawn and overconservative.

The reader should be warned that the complex nature of Communism prevents some of this material from being geared to rapid reading. Sometimes whole volumes have been digested into a few paragraphs. It will be helpful to the reader if sufficient time is taken to explore rather thoroughly the technical or philosophical chapters before proceeding. To help the reader identify the most significant points in the text, a list of preliminary questions is presented at the beginning of each chapter. While seeking to be brief, the author hopes he has not been obscure.

There are many to whom I am indebted for assistance, suggestions and technical data used in connection with the preparation of this work. Since the writing and much of the research was completed while I was a member of the faculty of Brigham Young University I received much valuable help from the members of the faculty as well as the administrative staff. I am also indebted to several of my former associates in the FBI with whom I studied Communist philosophy, Communist subversion and Communist espionage during my sixteen years with that organization.

The impressive vignette illustrations heading each chapter throughout this book are the work of the famous American artist, Arnold Friberg. They exemplify his ability to condense a complex idea into a simple, forceful, pictorial symbol. His magnificent gallery of Biblical paintings which he did for Cecil B. DeMille's production of "The Ten Commandments" has been widely acclaimed during their worldwide tour of exhibition. I am proud to have the text of these pages enhanced by the talented hand of such a good friend.

Another close associate, Keith Eddington, is responsible for the striking jacket and impressive design of this book.

The tedious task of typing the manuscript and reams of research data for the project was capably performed by Velora Gough Stuart and Louise Godfrey.

The bulk of the credit for the final completion of the work should go to my wife who efficiently managed the affairs of eight robust offspring while their father completed the research and writing for the manuscript. I am deeply grateful to all those who contributed time, skill and encouragement to bring the work to final fruition.

W. CLEON SKOUSEN
Salt Lake City, Utah, November 1, 1958

Preface to the Eleventh Edition

The generous acceptance of this book by the public has been both encouraging and gratifying. In this edition, as in several of the others, I have included some new material in order to keep the study up to date.

W. CLEON SKOUSEN
Salt Lake City, Utah, January 1, 1962

CONTENTS

III

The Communist Approach
to the Solution of World Problems — 43

IV

A Brief Critique
of the Communist Approach to World Problems — 61

V

The Rise of the Revolutionary Movement in Russia — 89

VI

How Russia Became a Communist World Power — 109

VII

Communism in the United States — 131

VIII

Communism and World War II — 155

IX

Communist Attacks on the Free World
During the Post-War Period — 177

X

Communism Under Khrushchev — 209

Historical Photographs

FIVE VITAL QUESTIONS

1

What Do the Defenders of Communism Say? — 289

PEACEFUL COEXISTENCE

ILLEGAL OPERATIONS

REVOLUTIONARY VIOLENCE

WAR AND PEACE

THE COMMUNIST INTERNATIONAL

DIPLOMATIC INTRIGUE

ETHICS AND MORALS

THE BIBLE

RELIGION

INDIVIDUAL FREEDOM AND CIVIL LIBERTIES

EDUCATION

LABOR

HOMO MARXIAN

The Rise of the Marxist Man

It is a terrible and awesome thing when a man sets out to create all other men in his own image. Such became the goal and all consuming ambition of Karl Marx. Not that he would have made each man equal to himself; in fact, it was quite the contrary. The image he hoped to construct was a great human colossus with Karl Marx as the brain and builder and all other men serving him as the ears and eyes, feet and hands, mouth and gullet. In other words, Marx surveyed the world and dreamed of the day when the whole body of humanity could be forced into a gigantic social image which conformed completely to Marx's dream of a perfect society.

To achieve his goal, Marx required two things. First, the total annihilation of all opposition, the downfall of all existing governments, all economies and all societies. "Then," he wrote, "I shall stride through the wreckage a creator!" The second thing he needed was a new kind of human being.

He visualized a regimented breed of Pavlovian men whose minds could be triggered into immediate action by signals from their masters. He wanted a race of men who would no longer depend upon free will, ethics, morals or conscience for guidance. Perhaps, without quite realizing it, Marx was setting out to create a race of human beings conditioned to think like criminals.

Producing such a race had been the dream of power-hungry men for more than 4000 years. Nimrod had projected the design, Plato polished it, Saint Simon sublimated it—now Marx materialized it.

Today this breed of criminally conditioned man walks the earth in sufficient numbers to conquer countries or continents, to change laws and boundaries, to decree war or peace. He might well be called *Homo-Marxian*—the Marxist Man. He has made it terribly clear that he intends to become the man of the twentieth century.

Homo-Marxian is frightening and puzzling to the rest of humanity because a criminally conditioned mind does not respond the way normal people expect.

For example, if a well meaning person invited a professional criminal into his home for dinner the shifty eyed guest would be likely to survey the fine variety of choice foods, the expensive silverware and shiny goblets, and completely miss the warm sincerity and friendship which the host was trying to convey. In fact, the criminal mind would probably conclude that his host was not only soft hearted but soft headed. Eventually, he would get around to deciding that such a weak man could not possibly deserve so many fine things. Then he would spend the rest of the evening figuring out how he could return in the darkness of the night and relieve his host of all his bounteous treasures.

Anyone familiar with the history of Communist leadership during the past one hundred years will immediately recognize this same kind of mind at work. The flagrant abuse of U.S. friendship and generosity during World War II is typical.

Homo-Marxian puzzles all those who try to work with him because he seems irrational and therefore unpredictable. In reality, however, the Marxist Man has reduced his thinking to the lowest common denominator of values taken from nature in the raw. He lives exclusively by the jungle law

Marxist Man

of selfish survival. In terms of these values he is rational almost to the point of mathematical precision. Through calm or crisis his responses are consistently elemental and therefore highly predictable.

Because Homo-Marxian considers himself to be made entirely of the dust of the earth, he pretends to no other role. He denies himself the possibility of a soul and repudiates his capacity for immortality. He believes he had no creator and has no purpose or reason for existing except as an incidental accumulation of accidental forces in nature.

Being without morals, he approaches all problems in a direct, uncomplicated manner. Self-preservation is given as the sole justification for his own behavior, and "selfish motives" or "stupidity" are his only explanations for the behavior of others. With Homo-Marxian the signing of fifty-three treaties and subsequent violation of fifty-one of them is not hypocrisy but strategy. The subordination of other men's minds to the obscuring of truth is not deceit but a necessary governmental tool. Marxist Man has convinced himself that nothing is evil which answers the call of expediency. He has released himself from all the confining restraints of honor and ethics which mankind has previously tried to use as a basis for harmonious human relations.

History is demonstrating that because of his mental conditioning, Homo-Marxian is probably the most insecure of all men in his feelings. Since he believes himself to be an accidental phenomenon in a purposeless universe, he has an insatiable appetite to bring all things under his total domination. He admits that until this is done he cannot feel secure. Not only must he conquer the human race, but he has assigned himself the task of conquering matter, conquering space, and conquering all the forces of cosmic reality so as to bring order out of natural chaos. He must do this, he says, because man is the only creature in existence which has the accidental but highly fortunate capacity to do intelligent, creative thinking. He believes that since Homo-Marxian is the most advanced type of man, he must accept the responsibilities of a supreme being. He is perfectly sincere in his

announcement that Homo-Marxian proposes to become the ultimate governor and god of the earth and then of the universe.

Under the impact of such sweeping theoretical ambitions,
many non-Marxists have been caught in the emotional tide of
this ideological fantasia and have allowed themselves to be
carried along in the current toward the shores of what they
hoped would be a promised land of man-made godliness. However, in recent years a growing number of these pilgrims have
risked life itself to come back to reality. Each one returns
with the same story. Homo-Marxian was found to behave
exactly like the graduate creature from the jungle which he
believes himself to be. He regards all others with fearful
suspicion and responds to each problem as though his very
existence were at stake. Although he demands the right to
rule humanity, he disdainfully rejects the most basic lessons
learned during thousands of years of human experience. Returning pilgrims bear one witness: Homo-Marxian has
reversed the direction of history. He has turned man against
himself.

It is in this historical crisis that man finds himself today.
Marxist Man could not have come upon the earth at a more
illogical time. In an age when technological advances have
finally made it feasible to adequately feed, clothe and house
the entire human race, Marxist Man stands as a military threat
to this peaceful achievement. His sense of insecurity drives
him to demand exclusive control of human affairs in a day
when nearly all other peoples would like to create a genuine
United Nations dedicated to world peace and world-wide prosperity. Although man can travel faster than sound and potentially provide frequent, intimate contacts between all
cultures and all peoples, Marxist Man insists on creating iron
barriers behind which he can secretly work.

Marxist Man makes no secret of his ultimate objectives.
He is out to rule the world. Because Homo-Marxian is still
an adolescent he knows he cannot devour the whole human
race in one greedy gulp. Therefore, he must be satisfied with
one chunk at a time. As we shall see later, he has adopted
an orderly "time-table of conquest" which he is following

with a deadly fixation. According to Communist prophecy, time is running out on the free world.

This dilemma leaves the unconquered portion of frightened humanity with only three possible courses of future action:

1. *They can meekly capitulate.*
2. *They can try to co-exist.*
3. *They can set about to pull the blustering bully down.*

As far as this writer is concerned there is absolutely no question whatever as to the course of action free men must ultimately take. In fact, it is the only choice the law of survival allows. Surely no man who has felt the throbbing pound of freedom in his veins could countenance capitulation as a solution. And no man who knows what lies behind the lethal Communist program of "co-existence" would dare accept that proposal as a long range solution.

What then remains?

Several years ago while serving with the FBI this writer became aware that the experts on Marxism have known for a long time that there are definite ways to stop Communism cold. Furthermore, if free men move in time, *this can be done without a major war!* That is why this book was written. It was written under the persuasion that modern men would be foolish indeed if they accepted the phenomenon of Homo-Marxian as a permanent fixture in the earth.

There are well established and easily understood historical reasons why every legitimate influence should be brought to bear on the removal of this roadblock from the pathway of normal human advancement. This must be done for the sake of Homo-Marxian as well as for the rest of humanity. He is the victim of a man-made experiment, trapped in his own self-perpetuating cycle of human negation. As long as free men are the prevailing majority in the earth there is a very good chance of breaking this cycle. To do so, however, free men must achieve an intelligent and dynamic solidarity at least as strong as the illusory but firmly fixed purposes of Homo-Marxian.

6   At the conclusion of this study there are listed a number
of policies which, if used in time, could remove the roadblock
that Marxist Man has thrown across the pathway of the race.
These policies are solutions which automatically spring out of
an understanding of the history, philosophy and ultimate
objectives of Marxism. They are also the cold hard facts which
have grown out of our bitter experiences in attempting to
deal with Marxist Man.

If enough people will study the problem and move across
the world in one vast united front it is entirely possible that
the race can celebrate the close of the Twentieth Century with
this monumental achievement:

Freedom in our time for all men!

I

The Founders of Communism

In this chapter we shall try to become acquainted with two men. The first is Karl Marx, the originator of Communism, and the second is Friedrich Engels, his collaborator. We shall try to present their lives the way the Communists present them—not as the soft, visionary social reformers which so many text books seem anxious to describe, but rather as the two-fisted, power hungry revolutionists which their closest followers found them to be. Although presented in brief summary, this chapter attempts to include sufficient details so that the student of Communism can answer these questions:

Why do Marxist writers call their founder a "genius" yet frankly admit he was "a violent, quarrelsome, contentious man, a dictator and a swashbuckler"?

Was Marx well educated? What was his nationality? Where did he do most of his revolutionary writing?

AUTHOR'S NOTE: *Because this book was written for high school seniors as well as college students and members of the armed forces, the author has deliberately avoided the use of research references such as ibid., and op. cit., lest they prove confusing.*

The Naked Communist

How was it that Marx never acquired a profession, an office, an occupation or a dependable means of livelihood?

How did Engels differ from Marx?

What were the six principal goals which Marx and Engels set forth in the *Communist Manifesto?*

Why did Marx believe one of his first tasks was to "dethrone God"? Why did he think his book, *Capital,* would change the world?

Why did Marx fail in his two attempts to create organizations for the promotion of world revolution?

London, 1853

On a chilly, foggy day in 1853, a British government official stood in the drizzling rain before the doorway of a human hovel in the heart of London's slums. He knocked and after a short delay was admitted. As the officer entered the room thick clouds of smoke and tobacco fumes billowed about his head causing him to choke and cough while his eyes watered. Through the haze he saw the proprietor of the slum dwelling, a barrel-chested man with disheveled hair and a bushy beard. The man greeted the officer in a strong German accent, offered him a clay pipe and then motioned him toward a broken-backed chair.

If the officer had not known better he would never have guessed that the bushy-bearded man who sat before him was a graduate of a university with a Ph.D. degree. Nor that the wife who had just hustled the children into a back room was the daughter of a German aristocrat. Yet such was the case. This was the residence of Dr. and Mrs. Karl Marx.

At the moment Karl Marx was a political fugitive—having been driven from Germany, France and Belgium. England had granted him domicile along with other revolutionary leaders from the Continent and for this Marx was grateful. It gave him a lifelong base from which to continue his revolutionary work.

On this particular day the presence of the officer was no

The Founders of Communism

cause for alarm. It was the routine check which the British Government made on all political exiles living in England. Nor was the officer hostile. He found the Marxes strange but interesting people who could engage in very lively conversation on world problems while sitting blissfully in a domestic environment of incomprehensible confusion. The officer later included his puzzled observations concerning the Marxes in his official report:

"(Marx) lives in one of the worst, therefore one of the cheapest, neighborhoods in London. He occupies two rooms. The room looking out on the street is the parlor, and the bedroom is at the back. There is not one clean or decent piece of furniture in either room, but everything is broken, tattered and torn, with thick dust over everything and the greatest untidiness everywhere. In the middle of the parlor there is a large old-fashioned table covered with oilcloth. On it there are manuscripts, books and newspapers, as well as the children's toys, odds and ends and his wife's sewing-basket, cups with broken rims, dirty spoons, knives and forks, lamps, an ink-pot, tumblers, some Dutch clay-pipes, tobacco ashes—all in a pile on the same table. . . . But all these things do not in the least embarrass Marx or his wife. You are received in the most friendly way and cordially offered pipes, tobacco and whatever else there may happen to be. Eventually a clever and interesting conversation arises which makes amends for all the domestic deficiencies."[1]

Thus we are introduced to one of the most dramatic personalities to cross the pages of history during the nineteenth century. And one who would have a greater impact dead than alive. Biographers would grapple with the enigma of Marx's life. At one moment Marx would be called "the greatest genius of this age," and a moment later even his disciples would feel forced to call him "a violent, quarrelsome, contentious man, a dictator and a swashbuckler, one at feud with all the world and continually alarmed lest he should be unable to assert his superiority."[2]

---

[1] *Wilson, Edmund*, "TO THE FINLAND STATION," *pp. 217-218.*
[2] *Ruhle, Otto*, "KARL MARX," *pp. 209, 308.*

Such were the contradictory, surging forces of human dynamics which found expression in the turbulent personality of Karl Marx.

The Early Life of Karl Marx

Karl Marx first saw the light of day at Treves, Germany, May 5, 1818. He certainly had no need to apologize for his progenitors. For many generations his male ancestors on both sides had been outstanding scholars and distinguished rabbis. However, the father of Karl Marx decided to break the ties of the past both religiously and professionally. He withdrew his family from the local synagogue to join the congregation of a local protestant faith and then reached out after professional recognition as a practicing attorney. Karl Marx was six years of age when the traditional moorings of the family were thus uprooted, and some biographers of Marx attribute his rejection of religion in later years to the conflicts which this sudden change in his life precipitated.

In elementary school young Karl revealed himself to be a quick, bright scholar. He also revealed a quality which would plague him the rest of his life—his inability to keep a friend. Seldom, in all of Marx's writings, do we find a reference to any happy boyhood associations. Biographers say he was too intense, too anxious to dominate the situation, too concerned about personal success, too belligerent in his self-assertiveness, to keep many friends. However, Karl Marx was not lacking in sentiment and genuine hunger for affection. At 17, when he began his university career, the letters which he wrote to his parents occasionally unveiled deeply sentimental, woman-like feelings. Here is an example:

"In the hope that the clouds which hang over our family will gradually disperse; that I shall be permitted to share your sufferings and mingle my tears with yours, and, perhaps, in direct touch with you, to show the profound affection, the immeasurable love, which I have not always been able to express as I should like; in the hope that you, too, my fondly and

The Founders of Communism

eternally loved Father, bearing in mind how much my feelings have been storm-tossed, will forgive me because my heart must often have seemed to you to have gone astray when the travail of my spirit was depriving it of the power of utterance; in the hope that you will soon be fully restored to health, that I shall be able to clasp you in my arms, and to tell you all that I feel, I remain always your loving son, Karl."

Such expressions must have puzzled the elder Marx. Throughout his career as a father he was never able to counsel or cross this hot-tempered son without precipitating an emotional explosion. The letters of Karl Marx make frequent reference to the violent quarrels between himself and his parents; the letters from Karl's parents complain of his egoism, his lack of consideration for the family, his constant demands for money and his discourtesy in failing to answer most of their letters.

Marx as a Young Man

It was in the fall of 1835 that Marx entered the University of Bonn to study law. This was a hectic year. He scandalized his parents by joining a tavern club, running himself deeply in debt and almost getting himself expelled for "nocturnal drunkenness and riot." His studies were most unsatisfactory and he threatened to become a professional poet instead of a lawyer. In the summer of 1836 he fought a duel and received a wound over the eye. It was finally decided that it would be better for the University of Bonn if Karl Marx transferred to some other university. The elder Marx heartily agreed. Karl was sent to Berlin.

It was at the University of Berlin that the intellectual forces in Karl Marx became sinews and the whole pattern of his life began to take shape. Although he complied with his father's wishes and studied law, it was a half-hearted camouflage to cover up his avid exploration of philosophy. In the midst of this exploration his father died and Marx immediately came out in the open with his announcement that he would seek an academic career. He wanted to occupy a chair of philosophy at some university. Marx chose for his doctoral dissertation: "The Difference Between the Natural Philosophy of Democritus and of Epicurus."

In this study he favored the materialism of Epicurus because it allowed for an energizing principle in matter. He thought that if matter were auto-dynamic it would do away with the need for a Creator, a designer or a governing force in the universe. The anti-religious sentiments of Marx found further expression in his thesis when he chose for its motto the cry of Prometheus: "In one word— I hate all the gods!" During this period of intellectual incubation three things dominated the thinking of Karl Marx: his desire to discover a philosophy of nature; his desire to completely repudiate all forms of religion; his desire to win the hand of the daughter of Baron von Westphalen.

While Marx was at the University of Berlin he fell in with a left-wing school of Hegelians who were followers of the German philosopher, Georg Wilhelm Hegel. At the moment their whole energy was consumed by a desire to liquidate Christianity. David Friedrich Strauss had published his *Life of Jesus* in 1835 and shocked all Germany with his contention that the Gospels were not true historical documents but were merely myths which he believed evolved from the communal imagination of early Christians. A close associate of Marx, Bruno Bauer, wrote on the same theme in 1840 under the title, *Historical Criticism of the Synoptic Gospels.* In this book he claimed the Gospels were forgeries. He said Jesus had never existed, that he was a figure of fiction and therefore Christianity was a fraud.

At this point Bauer and Marx decided they would boldly publish a *Journal of Atheism,* but the magazine lacked financial sponsorship and died in gestation.

Nevertheless, the anti-Christian campaign gained another eloquent protagonist named Ludwig Feuerbach who came out in 1841 with his *Essence of Christianity.* He not only ridiculed Christianity but presented the thesis that man is the highest form of intelligence in the entire universe. This

The Founders of Communism

exotic flash of speculation fascinated Marx. He had written the same idea into his thesis for a doctorate. Marx had bluntly said it is necessary "to recognize as the highest divinity, the human self-consciousness itself!"

The government's reaction to this anti-Christian campaign took a serious turn, therefore Marx decided it would not be prudent to present his thesis to the University of Berlin where he had been studying. His friend, Bruno Bauer, suggested that he go to the University of Jena. Marx followed this suggestion and consequently received his degree of Doctor of Philosophy from that institution in April, 1841.

Shortly afterwards, however, a leveling blow wiped out his passionate ambition to become a professor of philosophy at some German university. This resulted from the fact that Marx collaborated with Bauer in writing a pamphlet which was vigorously investigated because of its revolutionary flavor. When the Prussian officials identified the authors, Bauer was summarily dismissed from the University of Bonn and Marx was assured that he would never be allowed to teach at any university in Germany.

Now the revolutionary spirit flamed high in Marx; somehow he must start a movement to remake the world. However, to succeed in such a task he felt he must have the companionship of Jenny von Westphalen, the attractive and popular daughter of a German aristocrat who lived in Marx's hometown. For seven years he had corresponded with her. One of his letters made it clear that if she married him she would become the wife of a revolutionary. Said he: "Jenny! If we can but weld our souls together, then with contempt shall I fling my glove in the world's face, then shall I stride through the wreckage a creator!"[3]

In June, 1843, the wedding took place. At the time the bridegroom was unemployed and Jenny von Westphalen soon discovered that this was to be a permanent characteristic of their entire married life. Karl Marx never acquired the slightest comprehension of the responsibilties which a hus-

---

[3] *Wilson, Edmund*, "TO THE FINLAND STATION," *p. 115.*

band assumes as the head of a family. Nevertheless, Jenny von Westphalen remained loyal and devoted to Karl Marx under circumstances which would have crushed a woman of weaker mettle. After the marriage they had a five month honeymoon following which they went to Paris, where Marx hoped to collaborate in publishing a revolutionary organ called *The Franco-German Year Books*. The publication collapsed after its first issue and Marx spent the next fifteen months in the pleasant task of "studying and writing."

This was to be the pattern of his whole life. In later years while his family was starving he could be found at the library devoting himself to the interesting but, for him, completely unremunerative study of higher mathematics. Voltaire referred derisively to the breed of men who cannot run their own families and therefore retreat to their attics so that from there they can run the whole world. Marx seemed to fit this pattern. Although he seemed physically indolent, Marx was actually capable of prodigious quantities of intellectual work if it dealt with a subject which interested him. Otherwise, he would not stir. As a result of these personal characteristics, Marx never did acquire a profession, an office, a regular occupation or a dependable means of livelihood. Concerning this phase of his career a friendly biographer states:

"Regular work bored him, conventional occupation put him out of humor. Without a penny in his pocket, and with his shirt pawned, he surveyed the world with a lordly air. . . . Throughout his life he was hard up. He was ridiculously ineffectual in his endeavors to cope with the economic needs of his household and family; and his incapacity in monetary matters involved him in an endless series of struggles and catastrophies. He was always in debt; was incessantly being dunned by creditors. . . . Half his household goods were always at the pawnshop. His budget defied all attempts to set it in order. His bankruptcy was chronic. The thousands upon thousands which Engels handed over to him melted away in his fingers like snow."[4]

---

[4] *Ruhle, Otto, "KARL MARX," pp. 383-384.*

The Founders of Communism

This brings us to the only close friend Karl Marx ever had—Friedrich Engels.

Friedrich Engels

In many ways Engels was the very opposite of Karl Marx. He was tall, slender, vivacious and good natured. He enjoyed athletics, liked people and was by nature an optimist. He was born in Barmen, Germany, November 28, 1820, the son of a textile manufacturer who owned large factories both in Barmen, Germany, and in Manchester, England. From his earliest youth Engels chafed under the iron discipline of his father, and he learned to despise the textile factories and all they represented. As he matured it was natural that he should have lined himself up with the "industrial proletariat."

For the son of a bourgeois businessman, young Engels had a surprisingly limited education; at least it did not include any extensive university training. But what he lacked in formal training he supplied through hard work and native talent. He spent considerable time in England and learned both English and French with such facility that he succeeded in selling articles to liberal magazines of both languages.

Biographers have emphasized that while the hearty and attractive Engels differed in personal traits from the brooding, suspicious Marx, nevertheless, the two of them followed an identical course of intellectual development. Engels, like Marx, quarreled bitterly with his father, took to reading Strauss's *Life of Jesus,* fell in with the same radical left-wing Hegelians who had attracted Marx, became an agnostic and a cynic, lost confidence in the free-enterprise economy of the Industrial Revolution and decided the only real hope for the world was Communism.

Engels had been an admirer of Marx long before he had a chance to meet him. It was in August, 1844, that he traveled to Paris for the specific purpose of visiting Marx. The magnetic attraction between the two men was instantaneous. After ten days both men felt it was their destiny to work together. It was during this same ten days that Marx converted Engels from a Utopian Communist to an outright revolutionist. He convinced Engels that there was no real hope for humanity in the idealism of Robert Owen or Saint-Simon but that conditions called for a militant revolution to overthrow existing society. Engels agreed and proceeded back to Germany.

Six months later Marx was expelled from France, along with other revolutionary spirits, and took up residence in Brussels, Belgium. Here Marx and Engels wrote *The Holy Family,* a book designed to rally around them those Communists who were willing to completely disavow any connection with the so-called "peaceful reforms" of philanthropy, Utopianism or Christian morality. The red flag of revolution was up and Marx and Engels considered themselves the royal color-guard.

The strange relationship which rapidly developed between Marx and Engels can be understood only when it is realized that Engels considered it a privilege to be associated with such a genius as Marx. Among other things, he counted it an honor to be allowed to assume responsibility for Marx's financial support. Shortly after Marx was expelled from France, Engels sent him all the ready cash in his possession and promised him more: "Please take it as a matter of course that it will be the greatest pleasure in the world to place at your disposal the fee I hope shortly to receive for my English literary venture. I can get along without any money just now, for my governor (father) will have to keep me in funds. We cannot allow the dogs to enjoy having involved you in pecuniary embarrassment by their infamous behavior."

This new partnership between Marx and Engels gave them both the courage to immediately launch an International Communist League based on the need for a violent revolution. They planned to use the workers in Germany and France as the backbone for their new political machine but this proved

The Founders of Communism

bitterly disappointing. After spending several months among the French workers Engels castigated them because they "prefer the most preposterous day-dreaming, peaceful plans for inaugurating universal happiness." He told Marx that the tinder for a revolution in France was nonexistent. Having thus failed in their plan to build their own revolutionary organization, Marx and Engels decided to take over one that was already in existence. In August, 1847, they succeeded in gaining control of the "Workers' Educational Society" in Brussels. This immediately gave them prestige among reform organizations in Europe. It also gave them the first opportunity to extend their influence in England. At this point Marx and Engels would have been surprised to know that England rather than the Continent would become the headquarters for their revolutionary work.

The Communist Manifesto

During November, 1847, word came from London that the "Federation of the Just" (later known as the Communist League) wanted Marx and Engels to participate in their second congress as representatives of the Communist organizations in Brussels. Marx and Engels not only attended the congress but practically took it over. By staying up most of the night laying their plans and by using shrewd strategy at each of the meetings, they succeeded in getting the congress to adopt all of their basic views. Marx and Engels were then commissioned to write a declaration of principles or a "Manifesto to the World." They returned to Brussels and immediately set to work with Marx pouring into the text his passionate plea for a revolution. When they were through they had announced to mankind that the new program of International Communism stood for: 1. the overthrow of capitalism, 2. the abolition of private property, 3. the elimination of the family as a social unit, 4. the abolition of all classes, 5. the overthrow of all governments, and 6. the establishment of a communist order with communal ownership of property in a

The Naked Communist

classless, stateless society. To accomplish this, the Communist Manifesto was crystal clear as to the course to be taken:

"In short, the Communists everywhere support every revolutionary movement against existing social conditions. Let the ruling classes tremble at a Communist revolution. The proletarians have nothing to lose but their chains. They have a world to win. Working men of all countries, unite!"

The Revolution of 1848

The red glare of revolution came much sooner than either Marx or Engels had anticipated. In February, 1848, while the ink on the Communist Manifesto was still drying, the revolutionary spirit of the French proletariat united with the resentment of the bourgeoisie against Louis Philippe and a violent uprising ensued which drove the Emperor from the country. Immediately afterwards a provisional government was set up which included members of the Communist League, who promptly summoned Marx to Paris. Marx was flushed with excitement when he arrived at the French capitol armed with full authority from the Communist League headquarters to set up the international headquarters in Paris and to engineer the revolutions in other countries from there.

Marx learned that the intoxicating success of the uprising in France had induced the radical element in the provisional government to send "legions" into surrounding countries. Their purpose was to launch an uprising in each country and build the revolution into one magnificent conflagration. Although this was precisely what Marx had been advocating for several years, he suddenly sensed that such a campaign at the present moment might backfire and cause them to lose the support of the masses in those countries where legions were sent. Nevertheless, the plan was adopted and the first legions were marched off to Germany. Marx soon followed and began publishing a revolutionary periodical in his native tongue called the *Rheinische Zeitung*.

The revolutionary leaders soon discovered that Marx was

The Founders of Communism

a propaganda liability. This became painfully evident when
he was sent with other members of the Communist League to
organize the workers in the Rhine Valley. Marx, when asked
to address the German Democratic Congress, badly bungled
this golden opportunity. Carl Schurz says: "I was eager to
hear the words of wisdom that would, I supposed, fall from
the lips of so celebrated a man. I was greatly disappointed.
What Marx said was unquestionably weighty, logical and
clear. But never have I seen any one whose manner was more
insufferably arrogant. He would not give me a moment's consideration to any opinion that differed from his own. He
treated with open contempt everyone who contradicted him. . . .
Those whose feelings he had wounded by his offensive manner
were inclined to vote in favor of everything which ran counter
to his wishes . . . far from winning new adherents, he repelled
many who might have been inclined to support him."[5]

From the beginning the revolution in Germany had been
anemic and by May 16, 1849, it had reached a state of in-
glorious collapse. Marx was given twenty-four hours to quit
the country. He stayed just long enough to borrow funds and
print the last edition of his paper in red ink and then hastened
away to find refuge in France.

But France was no refuge. Marx arrived in Paris penni-
less and exhausted, only to find that the Communist influence
in the new Republic had wilted and died. The National Assembly was in the hands of a monarchial majority.

As soon as possible he fled from France, leaving his family
to follow later because he was destitute of funds. He decided
to make his permanent exile in London.

The End of the Communist League

Although Marx had to cram his family into a cheap, one-
room apartment in the slums of London, he felt sufficiently

---

[5] *Ruhle, Otto, "KARL MARX," pp. 157-158.*

satisfied with their well-being to immediately concentrate his attention once again on the task of reviving the fires of the revolution. In spite of this spirit of dedication, however, Marx's effort to lead out did more harm than good. His agitating spirit always seemed to create splinters and quarrels in the ranks of his confederates and before long he had practically cut himself off from his former associates. The Central Committee was taken out from under his influence and transferred to Cologne. There it remained until 1852 when all Communist leaders in Germany were arrested and sentenced to heavy prison terms for revolutionary activity. Marx did everything in his power to save his estranged comrades. He gathered documents, recruited witnesses and proposed various legal arguments which he thought might help, but in spite of all this yeoman service the verdicts of "guilty" pulled out of active revolutionary service every one of the party leaders then on trial. This sounded the death knell for the Communist League.

The Family of Karl Marx

From this time on the Marx family lived in London in the most extreme poverty. A peculiar combination of emotions was expressed by Marx in his correspondence during this period. On the one hand he expressed soulful concern for the welfare of his wife and children. He confessed in a letter to Engels that the "nocturnal tears and lamentations" of his wife were almost beyond endurance. Then, in the same letter he blithely went about explaining how he was spending his whole time studying history, politics, economics and social problems so as to figure out the answers for all the problems of the world.

In 1852 his little daughter, Francisca, died. Two years later marked the passing of his young son, Edgar, and two years after that a baby died at birth.

A few paragraphs from a letter written by Mrs. Marx indicates the amazing loyalty of this woman who saw her half-

The Founders of Communism

fed children dying around her while their father spent days and nights in the British Museum library.

"Let me describe only one day of this life, as it actually was. . . . Since wet-nurses are exceedingly expensive here, I made up my mind, despite terrible pains in the breasts and the back, to nurse the baby myself. But the poor little angel drank in so much sorrow with the milk that he was continually fretting, in violent pain day and night. Since he has been in the world, he has not slept a single night through, at most two or three hours. Of late, there have been violent spasms, so that the child is continually betwixt life and death. When thus afflicted, he sucked so vigorously that my nipple became sore, and bled; often the blood streamed into his little mouth. One day I was sitting like this when our landlady suddenly appeared. . . . Since we could not pay this sum (of five pounds) instantly, two brokers came into the house, and took possession of all my belongings—bedding, clothes, everything, even the baby's cradle and the little girls' toys, so that the children wept bitterly. They threatened to take everything away in two hours. (Fortunately they did not.) If this had happened I should have had to lic on the floor with my freezing children beside me. . . .

"Next day we had to leave. It was cold and rainy. My husband tried to find lodging, but as soon as he said he had four children no one would take us. At length a friend helped us. We paid what was owing, and I quickly sold all my beds and bedding in order to settle accounts with the chemist, the baker, and the milkman."[6]

Thus the years passed. Literally hundreds of letters were exchanged between Engels and Marx and nearly all of them refer in one place or another to money. Engels' letters characteristically contain this phrase: "Enclosed is a post office order for five pounds," while Marx's epistles are shot through with exasperated passages such as: "My mother has positively assured me that she will protest any bill drawn on her." "For ten days we have been without a sou in the house."

[6] *Ruhle, Otto,* "KARL MARX," *pp. 202-204.*

"You will agree that I am dipped up to my ears in petty-bourgeois pickle."

At one point in this bitter existence there seemed to be a sudden ray of hope. During a particularly desperate period when Engels could give no relief, Marx made a trip to Holland where a prosperous uncle generously handed him one hundred and sixty pounds. This was enough to put Marx on his financial feet, pay off his debts and give him a new start. But with money in his pocket, Marx decided to take a tour of Germany. He visited his mother in Treves, proceeded to Berlin, undertook a number of drinking excursions with his old friends, had himself photographed and generally played the role of a gentleman of leisure. Two months later he returned home. Frau Marx welcomed her tourist husband thinking that now bills could be paid, clothing and furniture could be purchased and better rooms rented. She was horrified to learn that practically nothing remained of the hundred and sixty pounds.

The Founding of the First International

In 1862 a great international exhibition was held in London to proudly parade the industrial achievements of nineteenth century capitalism. The promoters of the exhibition were desirous of creating an atmosphere of international good will and therefore invited all countries to not only submit displays but also to send representatives of their workers to exchange ideas and good will with the workers of other countries who would be in attendance.

The British labor leaders, who had been gaining strength since 1860, considered this an excellent time to set up an international workers' organization. They therefore took every opportunity to make firm friends with labor leaders from Italy, Germany, France, Poland and Holland. In due time they were able to establish a permanent "International" with headquarters in London. One of the leaders of this movement was a tailor named Eccarius who had formerly been a

The Founders of Communism

right hand man to Marx during the days of the Communist League. As soon as the new movement began to catch on, Marx was invited by Eccarius to participate.

Immediately Marx began to assert himself—but within bounds. This was the lesson he had partially learned from the failure of the Communist League. The new organization was called the International Workingmen's Association and is frequently referred to as the First International. As long as Marx restrained himself he was able to exercise considerable influence among the labor leaders from the various countries. By careful maneuvering behind the scenes he was able to get nearly all of his ideas adopted in preference to weaker, more peaceful programs suggested by "social-minded reformers." But all of this seemed mealy-mouthed and unnatural to Marx. He admitted to Engels he had been forced to make compromises in order to keep peace:

"My proposals were all adopted by the sub-committee. Only one thing, I had to pledge myself to insert in the preamble to the rules two phrases about 'duty' and 'right'; also about truth, morality and justice—but they are all so placed that they cannot do any harm. . . . It will be some time before the reawakened movement will permit the old boldness of speech. We must be strong in the substance, but moderate in the form."[7]

In spite of this determination to be "moderate," however, it was not long before the true feeling of Marx rumbled to the surface. He was concerned about two things: first, the need to create a hard core of disciplined revolutionists who could inflame the workers of the major industries in all countries with a will to act, and secondly, the need to eliminate any who might threaten Marx's leadership in this new movement. What Marx was contemplating was a party purge.

The first to feel the force of the new campaign was the German labor leader, Herr von Schweitzer. All students of Marx and Engels seem to agree that both of them were completely without mercy when it came to dealing with a

---

[7] *Ruhle, Otto, "KARL MARX," pp. 248-249.*

comrade who was marked for party liquidation. The broadside of propaganda which they launched against Schweitzer alleged that he was working for Bismarck, the Iron Man of Germany. Although this was pure fabrication, nothing would have been more devastating to Schweitzer's reputation. Even today some historians use Marx's charges as a basis for the claim that Schweitzer was a traitor to the cause of labor.

Another party pillar to fall under the purge was Mikhail Bakunin, the first Russian to become interested in revolutionary activities. He escaped from a Russian prison and had taken up residence in Geneva. Bakunin became so enthusiastic in advocating Marx's principles that certain elements of the labor movement began gravitating toward his leadership. This was fatal. Marx immediately set out to destroy him. The technique was the same as that used against Schweitzer except that Marx and Engels charged Bakunin with being an agent of the Russian Czar. This had a ruinous effect for awhile. Then they spread a charge which later proved to be completely false—that Bakunin had embezzled 25,000 francs. Finally, to administer the coup de grace, Marx succeeded in getting the International to oust Bakunin from the Association. By this act Marx secretly felt he had destroyed the last man who might seriously threaten his leadership. What Marx did not know was the fact that in spite of this abuse, Bakunin would remain loyal to Marx's precepts, even translate Marx's books into Russian and thereby plant seeds which would ultimately bring the first nation in the modern world under a Communist dictatorship.

However, Mark's anxiety to purge the International of all his personal enemies created such violent suspicion, distrust and party dissension that it brought about the organization's total destruction. In fact, the end of the First International came close on the heels of Bakunin's expulsion. The trade unions in England began to abandon the cause of international revolution and the workers' groups on the Continent began ignoring the mandates of the Association. Finally, on September 8, 1873, the last congress of the International Workingmen's Association was held at Geneva and Marx found that

The Founders of Communism

the thirteen delegates who finally agreed to attend had to be practically "dug up out of the ground." For all practical intents and purpose, the First International was dead.

Marx Writes a Book to Change the World

Much of Marx's motivation in trying to make the International Workingmen's Association a great world movement was his desire to put into practice the very theories he was struggling to put down on paper. For several years he had pampered his two pet projects—the International and his "book." Both projects drained him of his normal physical strength. This permitted an old liver ailment to flare up again and before long he was suffering from a rash of boils which threatened to cover his entire body. Ill health was to plague him the remainder of his days. In a letter to Engels he poured out his complaints against the pain and disappointment he was suffering:

"To my extreme disgust, after being unable to sleep all night I discovered two more first-class boils on my chest." Later he wrote, "I am working now like a drayhorse, seeing that I must make the best use of all the time available for work, and the carbuncles are still there, though they are now giving me only local trouble, and are not interfering with my brain." After a particularly severe attack he wrote: "This time it was really serious—the family did not know how serious. If it recurs three or four times more, it will be all up with me. I have wasted amazingly, and am still damnably weak, not in the head, but in the trunk and limbs. . . . There is no question of being able to sit up, but, while lying, I have been able, at intervals, to keep digging away at my work."[8]

The "work" to which Marx refers was the research and preparation of the first volume of *Capital*. Marx was convinced that a revolution would never succeed unless the working masses had a revolutionary philosophy of history,

---

[8] *Ruhle, Otto*, "KARL MARX," *p. 262.*

economics and social progress. He wrote *Capital* in order to show why the violent overthrow of the present order was not only justified but inescapable. Elsewhere, we shall examine the theories of Marx, but at this point it is sufficient to point out that Marx looked upon the writing of this book as an unpleasant mission which had to be completed before international communism could germinate and flourish.

During 1865, when Marx was striving to prepare a final copy of his first volume for the printer, he told Engels he wanted to "finish it off quickly, for the thing has become a perfect nightmare to me." He occasionally enjoyed periods of respite from his illness and finally wrote to Engels: "As regards the damned book, this is how the matter stands. It was finished in the end of December." Engels assured Marx that the pain and suspense of getting the book completed were as great a trial to him as they were to Marx. He wrote: "The day the manuscript goes to press, I shall get gloriously drunk!"

It was not until March, 1867, that all the revisions were finally completed and Marx set out for Germany to have the book published in his native tongue. In a short time it began to be distributed.

But when *Capital* appeared in the book stalls it was far from the literary triumph which Marx and Engels had both expected. Its line of reasoning was entirely too finely drawn for the working masses and far from persuasive among intellectual reformers. It remained for the intellectuals of another generation to make *Capital* the principal excuse for their attack on the existing order of things.

The Closing Years

By 1875 Marx had little satisfaction to draw from his life of struggle. The International had disintegrated around him and the book which was written to justify his policies was gathering dust in the bookstores across the Continent. Marx continued writing two more volumes but the flame was

The Founders of Communism

going out in him. After Marx's death, it would remain the task of Engels to publish the second volume in 1885 and the third volume in 1894.

The closing years for Karl Marx were sterile, lonely ones. In abject defeat he turned to the bosom of his family. Always there would be Jenny to give comfort and consolation. But the Marx children bore the scars of their upbringing. When Marx interfered with the courtship of his daughter, Eleanor, she entered a free-love union with Edward Aveling and, following a most wretched existence with him, committed suicide. Another daughter, Laura, married a renegade doctor and later died with him in a suicide pact.

By 1878 Marx had abandoned practically every aspect of his work. His rock-ribbed self confidence had been shattered. Labor leaders ignored him, reformers ridiculed him. His words carried little weight, either at home or abroad.

Thus, his morale was at the breaking point when the toll of time struck down his only kindred spirit outside of Engels —Frau Marx. This gentle, aristocratic and long-suffering companion died of cancer December 2, 1881. Thirteen months later, Marx's favorite daughter, Jenny, also suddenly died. Thereafter, Engels noted that Marx, the man, was as well as dead. He survived his daughter, Jenny, by only two brief months. On March 14, 1883, at 2:45 in the afternoon, he died while sitting alone in his chair.

Three days later six or seven persons followed the casket of Karl Marx to Highgate cemetery in London and there his one abiding friend, Friedrich Engels, read a funeral oration. It was the kind of oration Marx would liked to have heard. It granted him in death what Marx was never granted in life —an unequivocal tribute of glowing praise.

Epilogue

Thus ended the dynamic, turbulent and restless career of Karl Marx. By all standards it was a pathetic life, filled with burning ambition, constant frustration and continuous failure. Whether seen from the viewpoint of friend or foe, perhaps the real tragedy of Marx's life can be found in the fact that for some amazing reason he almost instinctively planted the seeds of self-destruction in any project he promoted.

One cannot pore over the almost endless products of his pen—the weighty, complex books or the reams of sniping, feverish correspondence without feeling that Karl Marx projected into Communism the very essence of his own nature. His resentment of political authority expressed itself in a ringing cry for universal revolution. His refusal or inability to compete in a capitalistic economy wrung from him a vitriolic denunciation of that economy and a prophecy that its destruction was inexorably decreed. His deep sense of insecurity pushed him to create out of his own imagination a device for interpreting history which made progress inescapable and a Communist millennium unavoidable. His personal attitude toward religion, morals and competition in everyday existence led him to long for an age when men would have no religion, morals or competition in everyday existence. He wanted to live in a classless, stateless, noncompetitive society where there would be such lavish production of everything that men, by simply producing according to their apparent ability, would automatically receive a superabundance of all material needs.

Another characteristic of Marx which he shared with his intellectual off-spring—Communism—is that both must be viewed from a distance to be admired, even by friends. It is for this reason that biographers often treat Marx as though he were two persons. From a distance they might feel to admire his theories but upon close contact Marx becomes a different entity. Thus, Bakunin could call Marx the "supreme economic and socialist genius of our day" and then give the following evaluation of Marx, the man:

"Marx is egotistical to the pitch of insanity. . . .

"Marx loved his own person much more than he loved his friends and apostles, and no friendship could hold water against the slightest wound to his vanity. . . . Marx will never

The Founders of Communism

forgive a slight to his person. You must worship him, make
an idol of him, if he is to love you in return; you must at
least fear him if he is to tolerate you. He likes to surround
himself with pygmies, with lackeys and flatterers. All the
same, there are some remarkable men among his intimates.
In general, however, one may say that in the circle of Marx's
intimates there is very little brotherly frankness, but a great
deal of machination and diplomacy. There is a sort of tacit
struggle, and a compromise between the self-loves of the various persons concerned; and where vanity is at work there is
no longer place for brotherly feeling. Every one is on his
guard, is afraid of being sacrificed, of being annihilated.
Marx's circle is a sort of mutual admiration society. Marx is
the chief distributor of honours, but is also the invariably
perfidious and malicious, the never frank and open, inciter to
the persecution of those whom he suspects, or who had the
misfortune of failing to show all the veneration he expects.
As soon as he has ordered a persecution there is no limit to the
baseness and infamy of the method."

The acid of boiling intolerance which Marx frequently
poured down on the heads of his followers may be partially
explained by his own complete certainty that the theories he
had concocted were infallible gems of cosmic truth. In his
heyday of abounding strength Marx often bowled over his
opposition with mountain-moving declarations of supreme
self-confidence:

"Historical evolution is on your side," he shouted to his
followers. "Capitalism, brought into being by the laws of
historical evolution, will be destroyed by the inexorable working of these same laws. The bourgeoisie, the business manager of the capitalist system, appeared on the stage of history
with that system, and must make its exit when that system
walks off the stage. You, proletarians, keep capitalism going
by your labour, and maintain the whole of bourgeois society
by the fruits of your industry. But socialism will be a necessary organic outcome of capitalism, the essence of the latter
being implied in the essence of the former. With the end of

capitalism, comes the beginning of socialism as a logical consequence. You proletarians, as a class, being the incorporators of the forces and tendencies which will do away with capitalism, must necessarily make an end of the borgeoisie. You merely need, as a class, to fulfill the evolution which your mission calls on you to fulfill. *All you need is to will!* History makes this as easy as possible for you. You need not hatch out any new ideas, make any plans, discover a future State. You need not 'dogmatically anticipate the world.' You need merely put your hands to the task which is awaiting you. The means by which you will do it are to be found in the unceasing, purposive, consistent fighting of the class struggle, whose crown will be the victory of the social revolution."

When Marx died there was little to suggest to him in his closing hours that he yet would be remembered for the thing he had striven unsuccessfully to produce—a genuine revolution. While Western Europe wrote off revolutionary violence as a mere phase of Nineteenth Century social reform, a great slumbering giant in Eastern Europe was about to be rudely awakened by Marx's revolutionary call to arms. This, of course, was Russia.

Before studying the revolution in Russia, we must turn to a brief review of the theories which Karl Marx and Friedrich Engels left as a legacy to the disciples of World Communism. In these theories may be found the explanation for many things in the Russian Revolution and in subsequent Communist activities which otherwise might be difficult or impossible to understand.

II

The Appeal of Communism

"How could a great scientist or anyone with so much education fall for Communism?" During the past 20 years this question has echoed around the land with each fresh exposure of Red espionage. It has been amazing to many people to discover that Communism appeals to certain educated individuals because it includes an intriguing "philosophy of nature." In this philosophy Communism does seem to explain the origin and development of everything in existence—life, planets, galaxies, evolution, even human intelligence. To those who have not previously delved into philosophy these concepts sometimes prove infatuating and persuasive. Therefore, in this chapter we shall deal with them.

Perhaps this material may prove to be difficult reading. However, the theories of Communism will be far easier to digest in this brief, concentrated form than they would be if the student attempted to spend several months digging them out of far-flung, technical treatises in Communist literature.

Every student should pursue his studies of Marxism until he has discovered the answers to such questions as these:

What is the Communist "law of opposites"? What is the "law of negation"? Explain the "law of transformation."

How does the Communist philosopher explain the origin of life? Does the universe have a designer or a purpose?

What is meant by the Communist concept that everything is the result of accumulated accident?

Does Communism have a god? What did Feuerbach say man's god really is?

Who did Marx say must remake the world?

How did Marx and Engels justify the use of violence?

What is the basic fallacy in the Communist "law of opposites"?

What is the inherent fallacy in the "law of negation"?

What is the weakness in the "law of transformation"?

The Case for Communism

The influence of Marx and Engels has continued in the earth, not simply because they were against so many things but primarily because they stood *for* something. In a word, they promised to satisfy humanity's two greatest needs: the need for universal peace and the need for universal prosperity.

The very fact that Communism offered a millennium for all the distracted, dissatisfied and unhappy people in the world assured it a hearing, not merely by under-privileged workers, but by many of the aristocracy, many of the wealthy, and many of the political and economic theorists.

When these people began hearing *how* Marx and Engels were going to achieve universal peace and universal prosperity they began dividing into clear-cut camps for or against Communism. One group insisted that Communism was worth a try in spite of the blood bath it would bring to humanity (after all, what is one more war if it is the gateway to permanent peace?). The other camp insisted that Communism is a complete repudiation of every decent human attribute. It would summarily forfeit all the gains which men have made through centuries of struggle.

What, then, is the case for Communism?

In this chapter we shall attempt to reduce Communist

thought to its basic formula. The student will become imme- **33**
diately aware that Marx and Engels dealt with much more
than violent revolution and Communist economics.   In fact,
they developed a framework of ideas designed to explain everything in existence. This philosophy is the pride and joy of
every modern Communist intellectual and therefore deserves
careful scrutiny.

The Communist Philosophy of Nature

To begin with, the basic Communist idea is that everything in existence can be explained by one thing—*matter*.
Beyond matter there is nothing. Matter is the total explanation for atoms, solar systems, plants, animals, man, psychic
consciousness, human intelligence and all other aspects of
life. Communist philosophy maintains that if science can
get to know all there is to know about matter, we will then
know all there is to know about everything.[1] Communism has
therefore assigned to science the monumental task of making
man totally omniscient—of knowing all truth—but has limited
the investigation to one reality—*matter*. Matter is conclu-
sively accepted as the beginning and the end of all reality.

Communist philosophy then sets forth to answer three
questions:

What is the origin of energy or motion in nature?

What causes galaxies, solar systems, planets, animals and
all kingdoms of nature to constantly increase their numerical
quantity?

What is the origin of life, the origin of species and the
origin of consciousness and mind?

Marx and Engels answered all of these questions with
their three laws of matter:

THE LAW OF OPPOSITES—Marx and Engels started with
the observation that everything in existence is a combination

---

[1] *Engels, Friedrich,* "LUDWIG FEUERBACH," *International Publishers,*
N. Y., 1934, p. 31.

34 or unity of opposites.[2] Electricity is characterized by a positive and negative charge. Atoms consist of protons and electrons which are unified but contradictory forces. Each organic body has qualities of attraction and repulsion. Even human beings find through introspection that they are a unity of opposite qualities—selfishness and altruism, courage and cowardice, social traits and anti-social traits, humbleness and pride, masculinity and femininity. The Communist conclusion is that everything in existence "contains two mutually incompatible and exclusive but nevertheless equally essential and indispensable parts or aspects."[3]

Now the Communist concept is that this unity of opposites in nature is the thing which makes each entity auto-dynamic and provides the constant motivation for movement and change. This idea was borrowed from Georg Wilhelm Hegel (1770-1831) who said: "Contradiction (in nature) is the root of all motion and of all life."[4]

This, then, introduces us to the first basic observation of Communist dialectics. The word "dialectics" has a very special meaning to Communists. It represents the idea of *conflict* in nature. The beginning student of Communist philosophy can better understand the meaning of dialectics if he substitutes the word "conflict" each time "dialectics" appears.

So at this point the student is expected to understand that each thing in the universe is in a state of motion because it is a parcel made up of opposite forces which are struggling within it. This brings us to the second law of matter.

THE LAW OF NEGATION—Having accounted for the origin of motion and energy in the universe, the Communist writers then set about to account for the tendency in nature to constantly increase the numerical quantity of all things. They decided that each entity tends to negate itself in order to reproduce itself in greater quantity. Engels cited the case of the barley seed which, in its natural state, germinates and

---

[2] *Conze, E.*, "DIALECTICAL MATERIALISM," *London, N.C.L.C. Society 1936, p. 35.*
[3] *Conze, E.*, "DIALECTICAL MATERIALISM," *pp. 51-52; See also Engels, Friedrich*, "SOCIALISM: UTOPIAN AND SCIENTIFIC," *pp. 47-48.*
[4] *Quoted by V. Adoratsky*, "DIALECTICAL MATERIALISM," *pp. 26-27.*

out of its own death or negation produces a plant. The plant
in turn grows to maturity and is itself negated after bearing
many barley seeds. Thus, all nature is constantly expanding
through dying. The elements of opposition which produce
conflict in each thing and give it motion also tend to negate
the thing itself; but out of this dynamic process of dying the
energy is released to expand and produce many more entities
of the same kind.[5]

Having accounted for numerical increase in the universe,
the Communist philosophers then set about to account for all
the different creations in nature.

THE LAW OF TRANSFORMATION—This law states that a
continuous quantitative development by a particular class often
results in a "leap" in nature whereby a completely new form
or entity is produced.[6] Consider, for example, the case of the
paraffin hydrocarbons:

"Chemistry testifies to the fact that *methane* is composed
of one atom of carbon and four atoms of hydrogen. Now, if
we add to methane another atom of carbon and two more atoms
of hydrogen (a mere quantitative increase since these are the
elements already composing the methane) we get an entirely
new chemical substance called *ethane*. If we add another atom
of carbon and two more atoms of hydrogen to the ethane, we
get *propane*, an entirely different chemical substance. Another
quantitative addition of an atom of carbon and two atoms of
hydrogen results in a fourth chemical substance, *butane*. And
still another quantitative addition of an atom of carbon and
two more atoms of hydrogen results in a fifth chemical substance, *pentane*."[7]

The Marxist philosophers immediately concluded that this
is the clue to the "Creative Power" in nature. Matter is not
only auto-dynamic and inclined to increase itself numerically,
but through quantitative accumulations it is also inherently
capable of "leaps" to new forms and new levels of reality.

---

[5] *Engels, Friedrich*, "ANTI-DUHRING," *p. 138.*
[6] *Engels, Friedrich*, "ANTI-DUHRING," *p. 145.*
[7] *McFadden, Charles J.*, "THE PHILOSOPHY OF COMMUNISM," *p. 50; see
also C. Porter*, "THE CARBON COMPOUNDS," *p. 10.*

Marx and Engels now felt they had not only found an explanation for the "origin of species," but that they had discovered a thrilling explanation for the greatest mystery of all: What is Life?

The Origin of Life, Consciousness and Mind

On the basis of this principle the Communist philosophers decided that the phenomenon of life was the product of one of these leaps. Engels stated that the complex chemical structure of matter evolved until albuminous substance was formed, and from this albuminous substance life *emerged.* In fact, he insisted that just as you cannot have matter without motion, so also you cannot have albumin without life. It is an inherent characteristic of albumin—a higher form of motion in nature.

Engels also suggested that as soon as life emerged spontaneously from albuminous substance, it was bound to increase in complexity. Dialectical Materialism is an evolutionary philosophy. However, the Communist does not believe that new forms in nature are the result of *gradual* change but that quantitative multiplication builds up the momentum for a "leap" in nature which produces a change or a new specie.

The Communist believes that incidental to one of these leaps, the phenomenon of consciousness emerged. The creature became aware of the forces which were playing upon it. Then at an even higher level another form of life appeared with the emerging capacity to work with these impressions— to arrange them in associations—and thus mind emerged as an intelligent, self-knowing, self-determining quality in matter. However, matter is primary, mind is secondary. Where there is no matter there is no mind—therefore, there can be no soul, no immortality, no God.

With the setting down of the Law of Transformation the Communist philosophy of nature became complete. The Dialectical Materialists felt that a great intellectual contribution had been made to man's understanding of the universe.

Engels, Friedrich, "ANTI-DUHRING," pp. 78, 85.

The Appeal of Communism

Through these laws they decided they had shown: 1. Matter is a unity of opposites which creates a conflict that makes it auto-dynamic and self-energizing; therefore matter does not need an outside source of power for its manifestation of motion; 2. Through its pattern of constant negation or dying, nature tends to multiply itself and fill the universe with an orderly development or increase without requiring any guiding intelligence; and 3. Through the Law of Transformation matter is capable of producing new forms without the need of any creative or directing power outside of itself.

Engels boasted that by discovery of these laws "the last vestige of a Creator external to the world is obliterated."[9]

From this brief summary, it will be seen that the Communist intellectual believes that everything in existence came about as a result of ceaseless motion among the forces of nature. Everything is a product of accumulated accident. There is no design. There is no law. There is no God. There is only matter and force in nature.

As for man, the Communist philosopher teaches that he is a graduate animal—an accident of nature like all other forms of life. Nevertheless, man is supposed to have the accidental good fortune to possess the highest intelligence in existence. This is said to make him the real god of the universe. This is precisely what Ludwig Feuerbach had in mind when he said: "The turning point of history will be the moment man becomes aware that the only God of man is man himself."

This will account for the almost passionate zeal of Communist leaders to destroy all forms of religion and the worship of God. Nicholai Lenin declared: "We must combat religion—this is the ABC of materialism, and consequently of Marxism." When Karl Marx was asked what his objective in life was, he said, "To dethrone God and destroy capitalism!" However, it is interesting to observe that having denounced God, the scriptures, morals, immortality, eternal judgment, the existence of the spirit and the sanctity of individual human life, the dialectical materialists turned to the worship of themselves.

---

[9] *Engels, Friedrich.* "ANTI-DUHRING," *p. 18.*

They decided that man is the epitome of perfection among nature's achievements and therefore the center of the universe.

But if man is supposed to have the highest intelligence in existence then it becomes his manifest duty to remake the world. Naturally, Marx believed this task was the inescapable responsibility of the Communist leaders since they are the only ones who have a truly scientific understanding of social and economic progress. Marx and Engels accepted the fact that the remaking of the world will have to be a cruel and ruthless task and that it will involve the destruction of all who stand in the way. This is necessary, they said, in order to permit the Communist leadership to wipe out the social and economic sins of human imperfection in one clean sweep and then gradually introduce a society of perfect harmony which will allow all humanity to live scientifically, securely and happily during all future ages.

However, before striking out on such a bold course, the founders of Communism realized they would have to develop a whole new approach to morals and ethics for their followers. Lenin summarized it as follows: "We say that our morality is wholly subordinated to the interests of the class struggle of the proletariat."[10] In other words, whatever tends to bring about the Communist concept of material betterment is morally good, whatever does not is morally bad. This concept is simply intended to say that "the end justifies the means." It is not wrong to cheat, lie, violate oaths or even destroy human life if it is for a good cause. This code of *no* morals accounts for the amoral behavior on the part of Communists which is frequently incomprehensible to non-Communists.

A Brief Critique of the
Communist Philosophy of Nature

From experience it has been observed that a newly converted Communist frequently acquires a feeling of omniscient

---

[10] *Lenin, V. I.,* "RELIGION," *p. 47.*

The Appeal of Communism

superiority over his unconverted fellow men. He feels that at last the universe is laid out before him in a simple, comprehensible manner. If he has never wrestled with philosophical problems before he is likely to be overwhelmed by the infatuating possibility that through Dialectical Materialism man has finally solved all of the basic problems necessary to understand the universe. In this state of mind the student will often drop his attitude of critical inquiry. He will invite indoctrination in heavy doses because of his complete assurance that he has at last discovered Truth in its ultimate form.

There are many things, however, which the alert student will immediately recognize as fallacies in the Communist philosophy of nature. Take, for example, the Law of Opposites. This law proclaims that all matter is a unity of opposites, and that out of the opposition manifested by these contradictory elements, energy is derived. This is supposed to explain the origin of motion. But two contradictory elements would never come together in the first place unless they *already had energy in themselves.* Contradictory forces in nature are found to have energy independent of each other. Bringing them together simply unifies energy or motion already in existence. Therefore, as philosophical scholars have pointed out, the Communist Law of Opposites does not explain motion; *it presupposes it!*[11]

As one author facetiously put it: "Two inert elements could no more produce a conflict and create motion than a thousand dead Capitalists and a million dead Communists could produce a class war."

It will be recalled that the second law of matter according to the Communists is the Law of Negation. This is the principle that the contradictory forces in an entity tend toward its own negation but, through the process of dying, these forces of motion are released into an even more extended development. Thus, a barley seed germinates and is negated to produce a plant which, in turn, is negated to produce a quan-

---

[11] *For an extended discussion of this problem see* "THE PHILOSOPHY OF COMMUNISM," *by Dr. Charles McFadden, pp. 177-184.*

tity of new seeds. In this manner the numerical increase in nature is accounted for.

But as Dr. McFadden points out in his *Philosophy of Communism*, the Law of Negation explains nothing. It merely describes a phenomenon in nature. True, the plan of nature is to reproduce itself in ever-expanding quantities, but the demise or negation of a parent is not necessarily related in any way to its power to reproduce itself. The growth and demise of any being goes forward whether it reproduces itself or not, and some beings reproduce over and over again before any negation takes place.

Furthermore, the first and second laws of matter leave the Communist philosopher in the position of arguing that motion and life are not only auto-dynamic, self-creating and spontaneous but that the development of a barley seed into a plant and the reproduction of many barley seeds by the plant is the result of accumulated accident. Engels deplored the possibility of being left in this position and frankly agreed that there is "law, order, causality and necessity in nature."[12] Nevertheless, he would not admit the possibility of intelligent design in nature but said the barley seed produces a plant and the plant produces more barley seeds because *the nature of the thing demands it.*[13] Why does the thing demand it? No matter how the point is obscured by philosophical terminology, the student will have little difficulty detecting that Engels is arguing that blind, uncomprehending forces of mechanical motion in nature are capable of ordering themselves to produce intricate things which are designed in advance to achieve a *pre-determined end.* What, for example, is there about a barley seed which would demand that it negate itself and produce a plant? And by what rule of reason can the Dialectical Materialist account for the fact that a germinated barley seed always produces a certain kind of plant and nothing else?

The authorities point out that Engels developed a pattern of thought that led to conclusions which even he recognized

[12] *Quoted by V. I. Lenin in* "MATERIALISM AND EMPIRO-CRITICISM," p. 125.
[13] *Engels, Friedrich,* "ANTI-DUHRING," p. 79.

The Appeal of Communism

could not be demonstrated in nature and therefore he retreated behind obscure generalities which the student finds nebulous and intangible.

The third law—the Law of Transformation—also describes a phenomenon in nature but fails to account for it. It confirms that in nature we discover widely separated species with distinguishing qualities and characteristics. But while some of these "leaps" can be produced with certain inorganic substances simply by quantitative accumulation (as in the paraffin hydrocarbons) it does not explain how the new qualities are produced. Furthermore, when this same principle is used to explain life as spontaneously emerging in albuminous substances, the Communist philosopher is defiantly flying in the face of all scientific experience. The universal demonstration of nature is the fact that only life begets life. It has not been possible to produce life synthetically or spontaneously either in the laboratory or in nature.

These basic weaknesses in Communist philosophy were the factors which ultimately convinced Whittaker Chambers (an American espionage agent for the Communists) that he had been deceived. In spite of the heavy terminology of Communist dialectics he finally became convinced that blind, uncomprehending material forces in nature could never produce —regardless of the time allowed—the highly complex things which man finds all around him.

As students of the problem have often pointed out: "The odds against nature, of itself *happening* to produce an organ of such complexity as the eye, with its thousands of infinitesimal parts combined in exactly the manner required for vision, are mathematically almost incalculable. But the eye is only one of the many complex parts of the human body. The chances against nature producing precisely that material organization found in each of the other organs and glands is equally great. But this is not all. For, in man, all of these organs and glands are organized into a perfect functional unit. And man is only one of the countless species of nature, inanimate and animate, each one of which possesses a similar marvelous organization of its most minute parts."

The Naked Communist

42

It was this kind of thinking which finally awakened Whittaker Chambers to the realization that the realities around him were much more complex and profound than the Communist explanation of "motion in matter" could begin to satisfy or account for. Thus, he began his retreat from the philosophy of Communism.

The great tragedy of Communism, however, is the fact that its founders did not stop at the so-called "harmless speculation" of Dialectical Materialism. They determined to permeate every aspect of human existence with the principles which they felt they had discovered. Therefore, they promoted a new approach to history, economics, politics, ethics, social planning and even science. In the Communist Manifesto Marx and Engels admitted that critics of Communism could say that it "abolishes eternal truths, it abolishes all religion, and all morality, instead of constituting them on a new basis; it therefore acts in contradiction to all past historical experience."[14]

Because more than a third of the earth's population is now being subjected to the terrifying "plan of action" which the Communist founders believed should be forced upon all mankind for their ultimate good, we will try to discover how Communism proposes to solve the world's problems.

---

[14] *Marx and Engels*, "COMMUNIST MANIFESTO," *Authorized English Translation, p. 40.*

III

The Communist Approach to the Solution of World Problems

Now we come to the part of Communism with which more people are familiar. At least, more people have heard about the Communist plan of action than the Communist philosophy of nature which we have just covered. Here are some questions that every student of Communism should be able to answer concerning the Marxist solution to world problems:

Why did Marx and Engels think they had discovered an inexorable law in history which made it possible for them to predict the course of future human development?

What is "Economic Determinism"? What is the "Activist Theory"? According to Marx and Engels is there any such thing as "free will"? Can men choose the kind of society in which they will live or are they victims of material forces which surround them?

How did Marx and Engels explain human progress as a product of class struggle?

What is the Communist theory of private property? Why is it considered a curse?

How did Marx and Engels account for the origin of the State? Why did they think it was "unnatural"?

How did they account for the origin of religion, morals and jurisprudence?

What was supposed to be accomplished during the Communist "Dictatorship of the Proletariat"?

Why do the Communists say "socialism" is only a temporary stage of human progress?

How did they propose to develop a civilization which would consist of a classless, stateless society?

The Communist Interpretation of History

Today very few people have had occasion to sit down with a professional Communist and listen to his views. Should such an occasion arise the student would receive the immediate impression that a Communist has a reverential regard for the record of man's past. This is because Marx and Engels thought their studies of the past had led them to discover an "inexorable law" which runs through all history like a bright red thread. They further believed that by tracing this thread it is possible to predict with positive assurance the pattern of man's progress in the future.

What did Marx and Engels discover during their study of history? First of all they decided that self-preservation is the supreme instinct in man and therefore his whole pattern of human conduct must have been governed by an attempt to wrest the necessities of life from nature. It is a dialectical process—man against nature. This led them to a monumental conclusion: all historical developments are the result of "Economic Determinism"—man's effort to survive. They said that everything men do—whether it is organizing a government, establishing laws, supporting a particular moral code or practicing religion—is merely the result of his desire to protect whatever mode of production he is currently using to secure the necessities of life. Furthermore, they believed that if some

The Communist Approach

revolutionary force changes the mode of production, the dominant class will immediately set about to create a different type of society designed to protect the new economic order.

"Does it require deep intuition to comprehend that man's ideas, views and conception, in one word, man's *consciousness,* changes with every change in the conditions of material existence. . . . What else does the history of ideas prove than that intellectual production changes in character in proportion as material production is changed?"[1]

To appreciate their point of view, it is necessary to understand Marx and Engels' mechanistic conception of the way the human mind works. They said that after the brain receives impressions from the outside world, it automatically moves the individual to take action (this is their Activist Theory). They did not believe knowledge could be acquired without motivating the owner to do something about it. For example, when men became aware that slavery was a satisfactory way to produce crops, construct buildings and enjoy various kinds of services, this knowledge moved the dominant class to create a society which protected the interest of the slave owners. And in modern times Marx and Engels believed that the bourgeois or property class have done the same thing by instinctively creating a society to protect their capitalistic interests. As they said to the bourgeois in the Communist Manifesto:

"Your very ideas are but the outgrowth of conditions of your bourgeois production and bourgeois property, just as your jurisprudence (system of law) is but the will of your class, made into law for all, a will whose essential character and direction are determined by the economic conditions of existence of your class."[2]

From this it will be seen that Marx and Engels did not believe that men could arbitrarily choose any one of several forms of society but only that one which promotes the prevailing mode of production. The very nature of man's materialis-

---

[1] *Marx-Engels,* "COMMUNIST MANIFESTO," *p. 39.*
[2] *Marx-Engels,* "COMMUNIST MANIFESTO," *p. 35.*

tic make-up requires him to do this. "Are men free to choose this or that form of society? By no means."[3] According to Marx the thing which we call "free will" is nothing more nor less than an awareness of the impelling forces which move an individual to action; in taking action he is not free to change the course his very nature dictates.

"Communism has no idea of freedom as the possibility of choice, of turning to right or left, but only as the possibility of giving full play to one's energy when one has chosen which way to turn."[4]

In other words, human minds receive knowledge of existing economic circumstances and "choose" to turn in the direction which is necessary to preserve the current mode of production. They are then free only in the sense that they are moved to decide that they will expend vast quantities of energy in building a superstructure of government, morals, laws and religion which will perpetuate these basic economic circumstances. At the foundation of all activities of society lies "Economic Determinism." "The mode of production in material life determined the general character of the social, political and spiritual processes of life."[5]

Marx and Engels now felt they had discovered something much more vital to human welfare than simply a philosophical explanation of history. In fact, they believed they had identified Economic Determinism as the basic *creative force* in human progress. Having made this important discovery they felt that if they could somehow force upon mankind the influence of a highly perfected system of economic production it would automatically produce a highly perfected society which, in turn, would automatically produce a higher type of human being. In other words, they would reverse the Judaic-Christian approach which endeavors to improve humanity in order to improve society. Here again they were reaffirming their conviction that human beings are not the creators of society but its products: "The final causes of all social changes and

[3] *Marx, Karl*, "POVERTY OF PHILOSOPHY," *p. 152.*
[4] *Berdyaev, N.*, "VITAL REALITIES," *p. 175.*
[5] *Marx, Karl*, "CONTRIBUTION TO CRITIQUE OF POLITICAL ECONOMY," *p. 11.*

The Communist Approach

political revolution are to be sought, not in men's brains, not in man's insight into eternal truth and justice . . . but in the economics of each particular epoch."[6]

Therefore, Marx and Engels advocated a change in economic structure as the only valid way of improving society and refining the intellectual make-up of humanity. But how can a new, improved system of production and distribution be introduced among men? What historical procedure has Economic Determinism unconsciously followed to bring mankind to its present state of advancement?

Human Progress Explained in Terms of Class Struggle

Marx and Engels answered their own question by deciding that from earliest times the mode of production and the means of distribution have always produced two basic classes of people: those who owned the means of production and thereby became exploiters, and those who owned nothing and therefore had to sell or trade their physical labor to survive. The element of conflict between these two groups was identified by Marx and Engels as the basic force in history which has prompted the evolution of society toward ever-ascending levels of achievement.

"The history of all hitherto existing society is the history of class struggles. Freeman and slave, patrician and plebeian, lord and serf, guildmaster and journeyman, in a word, oppressor and oppressed, stood in constant opposition to one another, carried on an uninterrupted . . . fight that each time ended either in a revolutionary reconstitution of society at large or in the common ruin of the contending classes."[7]

Here again Marx and Engels were applying the principles of Dialectics. All past societies have been a combination of opposite force or classes—the exploiters and the exploited.

---

[6] *Engels, Friedrich,* "SOCIALISM—UTOPIAN AND SCIENTIFIC," *p. 54.*
[7] *Marx-Engels,* "THE COMMUNIST MANIFESTO," *p. 12.*

The clash between them has always generated the dynamic force which has propelled society into some new development. The transition, they noted, was often accompanied by revolution and violence.

But must the course of human events always follow this never-ending cycle of clashes between the two opposing classes of society? Must there always be revolution to produce new orders which in turn are destroyed by revolution to produce others? Marx and Engels visualized a day when there would be unity among men instead of opposition, peace instead of war. Such a hope, of course, violated their own theory of dialectics which says nothing in nature can be at rest—everything is a unity of opposing forces. Nevertheless, Marx and Engels reasoned that since they had discovered the inexorable law of history with its self-improving device of class struggle, they would use one final, terrible class struggle for the purpose of permanently eliminating the thing which had caused all past conflicts in society. What is this one terrible feature of all past societies which has caused selfishness, jealousy, class struggle and war? Marx and Engels thought all of these things could be traced to one root—*private property*. If they used a final revolutionary class uprising to overthrow private property, it would mean that class struggle would become unnecessary because there would be nothing to fight over!

The Communist Theory
Concerning Private Property

Why do Communists believe that private property is the root of all evil?

Engels wrote that in primitive times he believed all people followed the principle of common ownership of everything except the most personal belongings such as clothing and weapons. Then he felt that the domestication of land and flocks resulted in certain men producing more commodities than they required for themselves, and therefore they began

The Communist Approach

exchanging these surplus items for other commodities which they lacked. He said these commodities used in exchange were naturally identified with the person who possessed them and thus the concept of private property was born.[8]

Engels then postulated that those who owned the land or other means of production would obviously reap the major profit from the economic resources of the community and ultimately this would place them in a position to hire other men to do their work. They would be able to dictate wages, hours and conditions of labor for their employees, thereby insuring their own freedom and social status while exploiting the toiling class. Therefore, said Engels, out of private property blossomed class antagonism with its entourage of camp followers: greed, pride, selfishness, imperialism and war. He said private property also had led to the necessity of creating the State.

The Communist Theory of the Origin of the State

Engels decided that when the non-property class had been exploited to the point where there was danger of revolt, the dominant class created an organ of power to maintain "law and order," that is, a system of laws to protect the private property and advantages of the exploiting class. This new order, he said, is the State.

"The state, then, is . . . simply a product of society at a certain stage of evolution. It (the creation of any kind of government) is the confession that this society has become hopelessly divided against itself, has entangled itself in irreconcilable contradictions which it is powerless to banish."[9]

Therefore the State is designed to postpone the day of judgment. Government is the "instrument of power"—the unnatural appendage to society—which is created for the ex-

---

[8] *See Friedrich Engels*, "THE ORIGIN OF THE FAMILY, PRIVATE PROPERTY AND THE STATE."
[9] *Engels, Friedrich*, "THE ORIGIN OF THE FAMILY, PRIVATE PROPERTY AND THE STATE," *p. 206*.

press purpose of protecting the privileged class and the private property it possesses from the just demands of the exploited class. Marx and Engels reasoned that if they somehow could eliminate private property, it would do away with class struggle, and then the state would no longer be necessary and it would gradually wither away.

The Communist Theory of the Origin and Economic Significance of Religion

Marx and Engels further believed that another great evil has grown out of private property—the exploitation of religion. They recognized, of course, that probably the roots of religion were established long before the institution of private property. However, they felt that since religion was not of divine origin it must have grown out of the frantic efforts of early man to explain the forces of nature and man's psychic experiences such as dreams. When private property emerged as the foundation of society, they believed religion was seized upon as a device to put down the rebellion of the exploited class.

According to Marx it was the property class who wanted their workers to be taught humility, patience and long-suffering; to endure the wrongs heaped upon them with the hope that justice would be meted out "in the next life." He said religion was made to serve as an opiate for the oppressed. The workers were told to "judge not" but to remain passive and dutiful toward their masters. "Religion is the sigh of the oppressed creature, the sentiment of a heartless world, as it is the spirit of spiritless conditions. It is the opium of the people."[10]

This explains the presence of vigorous anti-religious campaigns in the Communist program: "One of the most important tasks of the cultural revolution affecting the wide

---

[10] "SELECTED ESSAYS OF MARX," *p. 16.*

The Communist Approach

masses is the task of systematically and unswervingly combating religion—the opium of the people."[11] "There can be no doubt about the fact that the new state of the U.S.S.R. is led by the Communist Party, with a program permeated by the spirit of militant atheism."[12] "Have we suppressed the reactionary clergy? Yes, we have. The unfortunate thing is that it has not been completely liquidated."[13]

The Communist Theory of the Origin and Economic Significance of Morals

Up to this point Marx and Engels felt they had established that the evil of private property is responsible for the origin of class antagonisms, the creation of the State and the exploitation of religion. Now they attached a similar explanation to the origin and economic significance of morals. Engels and Marx denied that there could be any eternal basis for the moral standards of "right and wrong" set up in the Judaic-Christian code. Lenin summarized their ideas when he said: "In what sense do we deny ethics, morals? In the sense in which they are preached by the bourgeoisie, which deduces these morals from God's commandments. Of course, we say that we do not believe in God. We know perfectly well that the clergy, the landlords, and the bourgeoisie all claimed to speak in the name of God, in order to protect their own interests as exploiters. We deny all morality taken from superhuman or non-class concepts. We say that this is a deception, a swindle, a befogging of the minds of the workers and peasants in the interests of the landlords and capitalists."[14]

The Marxists believe that "Thou Shalt Not Steal" and "Thou Shalt Not Covet" are examples of the dominant class trying to impose respect for property on the exploited masses

---

[11] "PROGRAM OF THE COMMUNIST INTERNATIONAL," *International Publishers, New York, 1936, p. 54.*
[12] *Yaroslavsky, E.,* "RELIGION IN THE USSR," *p. 59.*
[13] *Stalin, Joseph,* "LENINISM," *Vol. I, p. 387.*
[14] *Lenin, V. I.* "RELIGION," *pp. 47-48.*

who cannot help but covet the wealth and property of their masters. As Engels said: "Thou shalt not steal. Does this law thereby become an eternal moral law? By no means."[15] They called such teachings "class" morality—a code designed to protect the property class.

But in rejecting the Judaic-Christian code of morals, Engels tried to represent that Communism was merely moving up to a higher level where human conduct will be motivated exclusively by the needs of society: "We say that our morality is wholly subordinated to the interest of the class-struggle of the proletariat."[15] But in spite of this attempt to delicately obscure the true significance of Communist moral thought, Engels could not prevent himself from occasionally unveiling the truth of what was in his mind: "We therefore reject every attempt to impose on us any moral dogma whatever. . . ."[16] In other words, Communism undertakes to replace Judaic-Christian morals with a complete absence of morals. That this was exactly what later Communists deduced from the teachings of their leaders is demonstrated in the words of a modern American Marxist: "With him (the Communist) the end justifies the means. Whether his tactics be 'legal' or 'moral' or not, does not concern him, so long as they are effective. He knows that the laws as well as the current code of morals are made by his mortal enemies. . . . Consequently, he ignores them insofar as he is able, and it suits his purposes. He proposes to develop, regardless of capitalist conceptions of 'legality,' 'fairness,' 'right,' etc., a greater power than his capitalist enemies have. . . ."[17]

So now Marx and Engels had completed their original purposes in making an intensive study of history. They felt they had successfully explained the origin of the various institutions in society by showing that all of these were the product of Economic Determinism, and they felt they had traced to its source the cause of strife, inequity and injustice among men—private property. Only one task now remained

[15] *Lenin, V. I.,* "RELIGION," *p. 47.*
[16] *Friedrich Engels quoted in the* "HANDBOOK OF MARXISM," *p. 249.*
[17] *Foster, William Z.,* "SYNDICALISM," *p. 9.*

The Communist Approach

for the master architects—to apply this knowledge to a "plan of action" which would permanently solve the economic, political and social ills of all mankind.

The Communist Plan of Action

As Marx and Engels analyzed modern civilization they concluded that capitalistic society is rapidly reaching that point where a revolution is inevitable. This is the way they reasoned: After the overthrow of feudalism the capitalistic society came into being. At first it consisted primarily of individuals who owned their own land or their own workshops. Each man did his own work and reaped the economic benefits to which he was entitled. Then the industrial revolution came along and the private workshop was supplanted by the factory. Products no longer came from the private workshop but from the factory where the united effort of many individuals produced the commodity. Engels said manufacturing thereby became *social* production rather than private production. It was therefore wrong for private individuals to continue owning the factory because the factory had become a social institution. He argued that no private individual should get the profits from something which many people were required to produce.

"But," critics asked, "do not the workers share in the profits of the factory through their wages?"

Marx and Engels did not believe that wages were adequate compensation for labor performed unless the workers received *all the proceeds* from the sale of the commodity. Since the hands of the workers produced the commodity they believed the workers should receive all the commodity was worth. They believed that the management and operation of a factory were only "clerical in nature" and that in the near future the working class should rise up and seize the factories or means of production and operate them as their own.

"But does not the investment of the capitalist entitle him to some profit? Without his willingness to risk considerable wealth would there be any factory?"

Marx and Engels answered this by saying that all wealth is created by the worker. Capital creates nothing. Marx and Engels believed that the reason certain men have been able to accumulate wealth is because they have taken away the fruits of the worker in the form of interest, rent or profits. They said this was "surplus value" which had been milked from the labor of men in the past and should be confiscated from the capitalists by the workers of the present.

Marx and Engels now dared to predict the ultimate trend of development in modern capitalistic civilization. They said that just as private workshops had been taken over by the factory, so the small factory would be taken over by the big combine. They said the monopoly of capital would continue until it was concentrated in the hands of fewer and fewer men while the number of exploited workers would grow proportionately. And while a few were becoming richer and richer the exploited class would get poorer and poorer. They predicted that the members of the so-called middle class who own small shops and businesses would be squeezed out of economic existence because they could not compete with the mammoth business combines. They also predicted that the government would be the instrument of power which the great banks and industrial owners would use to protect their ill-gotten wealth and to suppress the revolt of the exploited masses.

In other words, all levels of society were being forced into the opposing camps of two antagonistic classes—the exploiting class of capitalistic property owners and the bitterly exploited class of the propertyless workers.

They further predicted that the revolutionary explosion between these two classes would be sparked by the inevitable advancement of technological improvements in capitalistic industry. The rapid invention of more and more efficient machines was bound to throw more and more workers out of employment and leave their families to starve or perhaps survive on a bare subsistence level. In due time there would be sufficient hatred, resentment and class antagonism to motivate the workers in forming militant battalions to overthrow

The Communist Approach

their oppressors by violence so that the means of production and all private property could be seized by the workers and operated for their own advantage.

It is at this point that Communists and Socialists take different forks of the road. The Socialists have maintained from the beginning that centralized control of all land and industry can be achieved by peaceful legislation. Marx denounced this as a pipe dream. He held out for revolution. Nevertheless, he was quick to see some advantage in pushing forward any legislation which concentrated greater economic power in the central government. But he did not look upon such minor "victories of the Socialists" as anything more than a psychological softening up for the revolution which was to come.

Marx was particularly emphatic that this revolution must be completely ruthless to be successful. It must not be a "reform" because reforms always end up by "substituting one group of exploiters for another" and therefore the reformers feel "no need to destroy the old state machine; whereas the proletarian revolution removes all groups of exploiters from power and places in power the leader of the toilers and exploited . . . therefore it cannot avoid destroying the old state machine and replacing it by a new one."[18]

Marx further justified the use of violence to bring about the new society because he felt that if moral principles were followed the revolution would be abortive. He pointed to the failure of the Socialist Revolution in France during 1871: "Two errors robbed the brilliant victory of its fruit. The proletariat stopped half-way: instead of proceeding with the 'expropriation of the expropriators,' it was carried away with dreams of establishing supreme justice in the country. . . . The second error was unnecessary magnanimity of the proletariat: *instead of annihilating its enemies, it endeavored to exercise moral influence on them.*"[19]

Marx attempted to soften the blow of his doctrine of

---

[18] *Quoted from* "PROBLEMS OF LENINISM," *by Joseph Stalin, pp. 16-17.*
[19] *Marx, Karl,* "THE CIVIL WAR IN FRANCE," *p. 80.*

violence by stating that he would be perfectly satisfied if the capitalistic state could be transformed into a Communist society by peaceful means; however, he pointed out that this would be possible only if the capitalists voluntarily surrendered their property and power to the representatives of the workers without a fight. He logically concludes that since this is rather unlikely it must be assumed that revolutionary violence is unavoidable.

Marx and Engels were also convinced that the revolution must be international in scope. They knew that all countries would not be ready for the revolution at the same time, but all Marxist writers have emphasized the "impossibility of the complete and final victory of socialism in a single country without the victory of the revolution in other countries."[20]

The Dictatorship of the Proletariat

Since they now believed a revolution was inevitable, the next question Marx and Engels asked was this: Should they wait for it to come in the normal course of events or should they take steps to promote the revolution and speed up the evolution of society toward Communism? Marx and Engels decided that it had become their manifest duty to see that the revolution was vigorously promoted. Why prolong the suffering? The old society was doomed. In the light of the principles discovered by Marx and Engels perhaps the race could be saved a dozen generations of exploitation and injustice simply by compressing this entire phase of social evolution into a single generation of violent readjustment.

They felt it could be done in three steps: *First*, by wiping out the old order. "There is but one way of simplifying, shortening, concentrating the death agony of the old society as well as the bloody labor of the new world's birth—Revolutionary Terror."[21] *Second*, the representatives of the working

[20] "PROGRAM OF THE COMMUNIST INTERNATIONAL," pp. 34-35.
[21] Quoted from the "NEUE RHEINISCHE ZEITUNG," by J. E. LeRossignol in "FROM MARX TO STALIN," p. 231.

class must then set up a Dictatorship of the Proletariat. **57**
Joseph Stalin described the things which must be accomplished during this period of the dictatorship:

1. *Completely suppress the old capitalist class.*
2. *Create a mighty army of "defense" to be used "for the consolidation of the ties with the proletarians of other lands, and for the development and the victory of the revolution in all countries."*
3. *Consolidate the unity of the masses in support of the Dictatorship.*
4. *Establish universal socialism by eliminating private property and preparing all mankind for the ultimate adoption of full Communism.*[22]

Third, the final step is the transition from socialism to full Communism. Socialism is characterized by state ownership of land and all means of production. Marx and Engels believed that after awhile when class consciousness has disappeared and there is no further resistance to be overcome, the state will gradually wither away and then property will automatically belong to all mankind "in common." Later Lenin explained how the Dictatorship of the Proletariat would pave the way for this final phase. He said the dictatorship would be "an organization for the systematic use of violence by one class against the other, by one part of the population against another. . . . But, striving for Socialism, we are convinced that it will develop further into Communism, and, side by side with this, there will vanish all need for force, for the subjection of one man to another, of one section of society to another, since people will grow accustomed to observing the elementary conditions of social existence without force and without subjection."[23]

Even in the latter stages of Socialism, Lenin visualized a world without courts, lawyers, judges, rulers, elected representatives or even policemen. All these would be swept down into the limbo of forgotten and useless appendages which

---

[22] *Stalin, Joseph,* "PROBLEMS OF LENINISM," *pp. 26-27.*
[23] *Lenin, V. I.,* "IMPERIALISM: THE STATE AND REVOLUTION," *p. 187.*

characterized the old order of decadent capitalism. Lenin said the spontaneous homogeneity of the socialized masses would make all the machinery of the old order superfluous. He felt that the new society would even change human nature until resistance to the communal society would become "a rare exception and will probably be accompanied by such swift and severe punishment (for the armed workers are men of practical life, not sentimental intellectuals, and they will scarcely allow anyone to trifle with them), and very soon the necessity of observing the simple, fundamental rules of everyday social life in common will have become a *habit*. The door will then be open for the transition from the first phase of communism to the higher phase (full Communism)."[24]

The Classless, Stateless Society Under Full Communism

All Marxists fervently hope that the new society will produce the changes in human nature which are necessary before full Communism can become a reality. Individuals must forget that there was ever a time when income could be secured from the mere ownership of property or from productive labor. In other words, wages will be abolished. They must forget that some people once received very large incomes while others received small ones. They must lose any hope of a graduated pay-scale for differences in productivity or service. They must forget all about differences in skill, training, and mental or physical abilities. They must come around to the notion that, if man does the best he can in the best type of work for which he is fitted, he is just as good and just as deserving of income as any other man regardless of differences in productivity and output. This is the Communist promise that, *"Each will produce according to his ability and each will receive according to his need."* He must give up his old profit-motive incentive and become socially minded

---

[24] *Lenin, V. I.*, "IMPERIALISM: THE STATE AND REVOLUTION," *p. 759.*

The Communist Approach

so that he will work as hard as he can for the benefit of society as a whole and at the same time be content to receive, as a reward for his work, an amount of income based on his needs in consumption.

Marx and Engels presumed that under such a system the output of production would be so tremendous that they could dispense with markets, money and prices. Commodities would be stockpiled at various central places, and all individuals who worked would be entitled to help themselves on the basis of their needs. Marx and Engels felt there would be no particular incentive to take more than was needed at any one time because, due to the superabundance of commodities, the worker could replenish his desires at will. Services were likewise to be dispensed at convenient places and individuals could call for these services as they felt they were needed.

Under these pleasant circumstances, the Marxist writers explain, the government machinery of the State will no longer be necessary:

"Only Communism renders the state absolutely unnecessary, for there is no one to be suppressed—'no one' in the sense of a class, in the sense of a systematic struggle with a definite section of the population. We are not Utopians (believing that society can function on a sublime level of perfection), and we do not in the least deny the possibility and inevitability of excesses on the part of individual persons, nor the need to suppress such excesses. But, in the first place, no special machinery, no special apparatus of repression is needed for this: *this will be done by the armed people itself,* as simply and as readily as any crowd of civilized people, even in modern society, parts a pair of combatants or does not allow a woman to be outraged. And, secondly, we know that the fundamental social cause of excesses . . . is the exploitation of the masses, their want and their poverty. With the removal of this chief cause, excesses will inevitably begin to 'wither away.' We do not know how quickly and in what succession, but we know that they will wither away. With their withering away, the state will also wither away."[25]

---

[25] *Burns, E.,* "HANDBOOK OF MARXISM," *p. 747.*

The Naked Communist

It is significant that Communist theory treats the proletariat as though it were a unique branch of the human race. The proletariat is assumed to be a special breed which would almost automatically blossom into pleasant, efficient social-economic living if it could just be liberated from oppressive government. The government is presumed to be nothing more than the tool of an oppressive class of capitalists and consequently, if the capitalist class were destroyed, the need for any kind of government would be obliterated. The Communist leaders have always felt confident that when the proletariat takes over it will not want to oppress anyone and therefore the need for government will be nonexistent.

It is also worthy of note that Lenin wanted the proletariat to be an "armed people." This prospect did not frighten Lenin at all. He had unmitigated confidence that the members of the proletariat would never abuse their power as the capitalists had done. Furthermore, Lenin assumed that the proletariat had the instinctive capacity to recognize justice on sight. Not only would they use their weapons to put down any nonsocial acts in the community by spontaneous "mass action," but Lenin believed they would genuinely and heroically suppress any selfish, nonsocial tendencies in themselves. They would have acquired the "habit" of living in a communal social order and would have grown "accustomed to observing the elementary conditions of social existence without force and without subjection."

Lenin then says that with the machinery of government gone and with the Communist pattern of a classless, stateless society established throughout the world, finally "it becomes possible to speak of freedom!"[26]

---

[26] *Burns, E.,* "HANDBOOK OF MARXISM," *p. 745.*

IV

A Brief Critique of the
Communist Approach to World Problems

The modern student of history and economics will have little difficulty discovering for himself where Communist theory departs from the most elementary aspects of reality.

Disciples of Marx look upon the theories of Communism as the most penetrating analysis of history ever made by man, but many scholars look upon the whole Communist framework as more or less the product of the times in which Marx and Engels lived. The writings of these men clearly reflect a studied attempt to reconcile the five great influences of their generation, which they tried to bring together in one single pattern of thought. The influences which left their mark on the minds of Marx and Engels were:

First, *the violent economic upheaval of their day.* This is believed to have made Marx and Engels over-sensitive to the place of economics in history.

Second, *the widespread popularity of the German philosopher, Georg Wilhelm Hegel.* His theory of "Dialectics" was adopted by Marx and Engels with slight modification to explain all phenomena of nature, the class struggle and the inevitable triumph of a future proletariat society.

Third, *the anti-religious cynicism of Nineteenth Century Materialism.* This led them to try to explain everything in existence in terms of one single factor—matter. They denied intelligent design in the universe, the existence of God, the divinity of religion and the moral precepts of Judaic-Christian teachings.

Fourth, *the social and economic ideals of Utopian Communism.* Marx and Engels decided they wanted a communal society, but they felt it had to be a controlled society; they therefore abandoned the brotherhood principle of the Utopians and declared that Communism could only be initiated under a powerful dictatorship.

Fifth, *the revolutionary spirit of the Anarchists.* Marx and Engels promised two things which appealed to the Anarchists—the use of violent revolution to overthrow existing powers, and eventually the creation of a classless, stateless society.

It is because of these five important influences that the student of Communism will find it to be a vast conglomerate, designed, it would seem, to be all things to all people.

Communism as a By-Product of the Industrial Revolution

Marx and Engels were born in the midst of the Industrial Revolution. Before this revolution four out of every five citizens were farmers, but by the time Marx and Engels were ready for college the mass migration of farmers to the industrial centers was reaching the proportions of a flood tide. The resulting concentration of the population created slum-ridden cities which, in turn, contributed to disease, violence and vice. It was a chain-reaction which grew out of the amazing new machine-age. Pioneers of the Industrial Revolution looked upon machines as the pounding, pumping, inanimate

A Brief Critique

monsters that would eventually liberate mankind from the
slavery of "bare-subsistence" economics, but the negative
critics saw in them only the problems they created—dislocation of the population, maladjustment for the individual, the
family and the community, and finally, the inhuman treatment
of the men, women and children who served industry.

Thus, Marx and Engels, like many others, felt a violent
reaction to the times in which they lived. Because it was a
period of economic upheaval, perhaps it is understandable that
they should have reached the conclusion that economic forces
constitute the cruel and ruthless iron hand which has guided
the course of all human history. It is at this point that we
begin our critique of Communist theory.

The Communist Interpretation of History

FALLACY 1—The first fallacy of Communism is its attempt
to over-simplify history. Marx and Engels attempted to
change history from a fluid stream, fed by human activities
from millions of tributaries, into a fixed, undeviating, predetermined course of progress which could be charted in the
past and predicted for the future on the basis of a single,
simple criterion — economics. Obviously economics have
played a vital and powerful role in human history but so have
climate, topography, access to oceans and inland waterways,
mechanical inventions, scientific discoveries, national and
racial affinities, filial affection, religion, desire for explanatory
adventure, sentiments of loyalty, patriotism and a multitude
of other factors.

A number of modern Communists have admitted that
history is molded by all of these different influences, but they
have insisted that Marx and Engels intended to include all of
them in their Economic Determinism; because all of these
things directly or indirectly affect the economic life of humanity. However, the writings of Marx and Engels fail to reflect
any such interpretation. Even if they did, the modern Marxist
would still be in difficulty because if Economic Determinism is

intended to include every influence in life then the Communist formula for interpreting history would be: "Everything determines everything." As a basis for interpreting history this would be absurd.

Another group of modern Communists has tried to extricate Marx and Engels from the narrow confines of Economic Determinism by suggesting that economic circumstances do not *absolutely* determine the course of human history but merely *condition* men to follow after a particular trend in social development.[1] But this, of course, while coming closer to the truth, presumes a variable element of free will in the making of history which Marx and Engels emphatically denied. In fact, Economic Determinism in the absolute, fixed and undeviating sense, is the very foundation for the prediction of Marx and Engels that society must follow an inevitable course of development from capitalism to socialism and from socialism to Communism. This is what they meant when they said of capitalism: "Its fall and the victory of the proletariat are equally inevitable."[2]

Furthermore, when any modern Marxist attempts to argue that the course of human progress is not fixed and inevitable he destroys the entire justification for the Communist Revolution—that violent upheaval which Marx said was the "**one** way of simplifying, shortening, concentrating the death agony of the old society."[3] There is no excuse for the use of lethal violence to concentrate and simplify the death of the old society unless the death of that society is, in fact, inevitable. That was the heart of Marx's argument. His excuse for revolution falters if it is admitted that the death of the old society is merely one of several possibilities and not necessarily inevitable. Likewise, his excuse is exploded if it is shown that the present society is not dying at all but is actually more robust than ever before and seems to be contributing more to the welfare of mankind with each passing generation.

---

[1] See *Shirokov-Mosley*, "A TEXTBOOK OF MARXISM," *p. 22.*
[2] *Marx and Engels*, "COMMUNIST MANIFESTO," *p. 29.*
[3] *Marx, quoted by J. E. LeRossignol in* "FROM MARX TO STALIN," *p. 321.*

A Brief Critique

So the Communist interpretation of history on the basis
of Economic Determinism turns out to be a weak and brittle
reed even in the hands of its defenders. The disciples of
Marx have recognized its weaknesses and tried to patch it up
but the patches have only created new splinters in the already
frail, dry straws of Communist logic.

FALLACY 2—Marx and Engels not only over-simplified
history, but they relied on a second fallacy in order to justify
the first. They said that the human mind is incapable of moral
free will in the sense that it makes a choice in directing the
course of history. Marx and Engels believed that material
circumstances force the human mind to move in a certain direction and that man does not have the free will to resist it. This
sounds like the teachings of the Nineteenth Century Mechanistic Materialists who claimed that the brain is somewhat like
a passive wax tablet which receives impressions from the
outside world and then responds automatically to them; but
Marx and Engels did not want to be identified with this school
of thought. They therefore said the run-of-the-mill materialists had made a mistake. The brain is not passive like a wax
tablet but is an active embodiment which not only receives impressions from the outside world but has the ability to digest
those impressions through a process of analysis and synthesis.
Then came the joker.

They declared that after the brain has digested its impressions of the outside world it always decides to do *whatever
is necessary for the preservation of the individual in the light
of material circumstances*. In their own subtle way they were
simply saying that man is the victim of his material environment. By a slightly different line of thinking they had reached
exactly the same conclusions as the mechanistic materialists
whom they had repudiated.

It will be recalled from the previous chapter that Marx
and Engels identified the thing we call "free will" as being
nothing more nor less than a conscious awareness of the materialistic forces which impel the individual to act. This conscious awareness of "natural necessity" makes men think they
are choosing a course of action, when, as matter of fact, they

are simply watching themselves follow the dictates of material circumstances.

Once again it will be seen that Marx and Engels oversimplified. The complexities of human behavior cannot be explained simply in terms of "necessary" responses to material circumstances. Often men defy material circumstances to satisfy numerous other motivations such as the desire for self-expression, the moving power of a religious conviction, the drive of a moral sense of duty, the satisfying of personal pride or the realizing of a personal ambition.

This fallacy—the refusal to recognize man's moral agency and the power to make a choice—is fatal to Marxism. It is the initial error on which a multitude of other fallacies are built. When Communism says the human mind is the absolute victim of material circumstances and that human history is merely the unavoidable response of human beings to physical conditions, it must demonstrate these claims with examples. Note how this fallacy compounds itself as Marx and Engels attempt to use it in explaining the structure of society.

The Communist Explanation of Society

FALLACY 3—First of all, Marx and Engels said the form of society is automatically determined by the economic conditions which motivate the dominant class in any particular age. As Marx put it: "Are men free to choose this or that form of society for themselves? By no means. Assume a particular state of development in the productive forces of man and you will get a particular form of commerce and consumption. Assume a particular stage of development in production, commerce and consumption and you will have a corresponding social structure, a corresponding organization of the family, of orders or of classes, in a word, a corresponding civil society. Presuppose a particular civil society and you will get particular political conditions which are only the official expression of civil society."[4]

---

[4] *Marx, Karl, "*POVERTY OF PHILOSOPHY,*" pp. 152-153.*

A Brief Critique

It seems inconceivable that Marx and Engels could have allowed wishful thinking to so completely obscure the facts of history that they would have convinced themselves that when a certain type of production exists a certain type of society must exist also. In ancient times the mode of production remained the same for centuries while society ran the gamut of almost continuous change. Historians and economists have pointed out that if history demonstrates anything at all it is the fact that there is no direct relation between mode of production and the form society will take. Let us see why.

The Origin of the State

FALLACY 4—Marx and Engels believed that the State (any form of sovereign government) is an unnecessary appendage to society which the dominant class creates to forcibly preserve its interests and suppress the uprising of the exploited class. Marx and Engels did not believe any government in any age represented the interests of all of the people or even the welfare of a majority of the people. In the Communist Manifesto they said: "The executive (branch) of the modern State is but a Committee for managing the common affair of the whole bourgeoisie (property class)."[5]

Sociologists, psychologists, historians and political scientists point out that not by any stretch of imagination can government be called an *appendage* to society because it is the very heart of group living. This is true because society cannot exist unless it is governed by some degree of authority, and the presence of authority in society constitutes "government." Man is by nature a social and political being, and therefore the creation of governments to direct the members of the community toward their common welfare is simply an inherent expression of the very nature of man. Therefore a stateless society (a civilization without a government) which

---

[5] *Marx and Engels, "THE COMMUNIST MANIFESTO," p. 15.*

Marx and Engels vigorously advocated would be an unorganized mob. *It would be no society at all.*

FALLACY 5—Marx and Engels also encounter difficulty when the form of the State is explained as an inevitable outgrowth of some particular form of economic circumstances. If this were true then the same mode of production would always produce the same essential form of government. Let us take a look at the history of ancient Greece and ancient Rome. In both of these nations the fundamental mode of production was slavery. According to the Marxian explanation the form of these governments should have remained approximately the same so long as the mode of production (slavery) remained in effect. But contrary to Marxian expectations we find both these governments passing through many changes even though the mode of production did not change. In Athens there was a succession of hereditary monarchies, followed by the aristocratic and democratic republics, then the despotism of the thirty tyrants and finally democracy was established once again. In Rome there was first an elective royalty followed by the aristocratic and democratic republics, and then came the absolute monarchy under the Caesars. These are typical of the incidents in history where the form of the government has changed while the mode of production has remained the same.

Now let us illustrate the fallacy of this Communist theory another way. If the form of the State is fixed by Economic Determinism, then the form of the State should change when the mode of production changes. But this seldom happens. Take the history of the United States for instance. The form of the U.S. Government has remained essentially the same since its founding. Was the government different in the slave-economy of the south than the industrial economy of the north? Did the government in the south change after slavery was abolished? The mode of production changed, the form of government did not. In other words, men can create any form of government they wish without reference to the prevailing mode of production. There are many historical examples which clearly refute this important Communist concept.

A Brief Critique

FALLACY 6—In connection with the creation of the State, the Communists also maintain that a code of laws is developed to protect the exploiting class; further, that if the mode of production changes the code of laws will have to be reformulated to foster the specific new mode of production. Logically, this would mean that each time there is a revolutionary change in the mode of production there will have to be a revolutionary change in the system of law. In no instance should the same code of law be capable of serving nations which are under different modes of production.

Once again history throws confusion on Communism when this theory is applied to specific situations. One of the best examples is the history of the Western World where radical changes in methods of production have often been followed by no more than minor alterations in the various codes of law. Modern capitalistic society throughout Europe and America is, in general, governed by codes of law which are founded on the same fundamental principle as those which prevailed centuries before the Industrial Revolution. In England the Common Law was developed during the days of a feudal economy. The overthrow of Feudalism only strengthened the Common Law, and it was further strengthened after the Industrial Revolution. In America the abolition of slavery did not overthrow the fundamental legal code of either the states or the nation. These are simple examples of the rather obvious historical fact that there is no essential dependence between society's method of production and the code of laws which it chooses to create.

What Is Religion?

FALLACY 7—Communism further alleges that religion is not of divine origin but is simply a man-made tool used by the dominant class to suppress the exploited class. Marx and Engels described religion as the opiate of the people which is designed to lull them into humble submission and an acceptance of the prevailing mode of production which the dominant class desires to perpetuate. Any student of history would agree that there have been times in history when unscrupulous individuals and even misdirected religious organizations have abused the power of religion, just as all other institutions of society have been abused at various times. But it was not the abuse of religion which Marx and Engels deplored so much as the very existence of religion. They considered it a creation of the dominant class, a tool and a weapon in the hands of the oppressors. They pointed out the three-fold function of religion from their point of view: *first,* it teaches respect for property rights; *second,* it teaches the poor their *duties* towards the property and prerogatives of the ruling class; and *third,* it instills a spirit of acquiescence among the exploited poor so as to destroy their revolutionary spirit.

The fallacy of these allegations is obvious to any student of Judaic-Christian teachings. The Biblical teaching of respect for property applies to rich and poor alike; it admonishes the rich to give the laborer his proper wages and to share their riches with the needy. Time and again the Old Testament denounces the selfish rich because "the spoil of the poor is in your houses. What mean ye that ye beat my people to pieces, and grind the faces of the poor? saith the Lord."[6]

The New Testament denunciation of the selfish rich is just as pointed: "Go to now, ye rich men, weep and howl for your miseries that shall come upon you. . . . Behold, the hire of the laborers who have reaped down your fields, which is of you kept back by fraud, crieth: and the cries of them which have reaped are entered into the ears of the Lord of Sabaoth."[7] "It is easier for a camel to go through the eye of a needle, than for a rich man to enter into the kingdom of God."[8]

As to the allegation of the Communist that religion makes men passive, we have only to observe that the dynamic power of religious convictions is precisely what prevents a soundly

---

[6] *Isaiah 3:14-15.*
[7] *James 5:1-6.*
[8] *Matthew 19:24.*

A Brief Critique

religious person from accepting Communist oppression and Communist mandates. A person practicing the teachings of the Judaic-Christian philosophy will not lie or steal on command. He will not shed innocent blood. He will not participate in the diabolical Communist practice of genocide—the systematic extermination of entire nations or classes.

It is clearly evident from the numerous Communist writings that what they fear in religion is not that it makes religious people passive to the dominant class but that it *prevents* them from becoming passive to Communist discipline. Deep spiritual convictions stand like a wall of resistance to challenge the teachings and practices of Communism.

Furthermore, the Communist sees in the dynamic ideology of Judaic-Christian teachings a force for peace which cuts through the vitals of Communism's campaign for worldwide revolution. As Anatole Lunarcharsky, the former Russian Commissar of Education declared: "We hate Christians and Christianity. Even the best of them must be considered our worst enemies. They preach love of one's neighbor and mercy, which is contrary to our principles. *Christian love is an obstacle to the development of the Revolution.* Down with love of our neighbor! What we want is hate. . . . Only then can we conquer the universe."[9]

The Communist Theory of Morals

FALLACY 8—Communist writers likewise maintain that the Judaic-Christian code of ethics is "class" morality. By this they mean that the Ten Commandments and the ethics of Christianity were created to protect private property and the property class. To show the lengths to which Communist writers have gone to defend this view we will mention several of their favorite interpretations of the Ten Commandments. They believe that "Honor thy Father and thy Mother" was

---

[9] *Quoted in U. S. Congressional Record, Vol. 77, pp. 1539-1540.*

created by the early Hebrews to emphasize to their children the fact that they were the private property of their parents. "Thou shalt not kill" was attributed to the belief of the dominant class that their bodies were private property and therefore they should be protected along with other property rights. "Thou shalt not commit adultery" and "Thou shalt not covet thy neighbor's wife" were said to have been created to implement the idea that a husband was the master of the home and the wife was strictly private property belonging to him.

This last line of reasoning led to some catastrophic consequences when the Communists came into power in Russia. In their anxiety to make women "equal with men" and prevent them from becoming private property, they degraded womankind to the lowest and most primitive level. Some Communist leaders advocated complete libertinism and promiscuity to replace marriage and the family. Excerpts from a decree issued in the Soviet of Saralof will illustrate the point: "Beginning with March 1, 1919, the right to possess women between the ages of 17 and 32 is abolished . . . this decree, however, not being applicable to women who have five children. . . . By virtue of the present decree no woman can any longer be considered as private property and all women become the property of the nation. . . . The distribution and maintenance of nationalized women, in conformity with the decision of responsible organizations, are the prerogative of the group of Saralof anarchists. . . . All women thus put at the disposition of the nation must, within three days after the publication of the present decree, present themselves in person at the address indicated and provide all necessary information. . . . *Any man who wishes to make use of a nationalized woman must hold a certificate* issued by the administrative Council of a professional union, or by the Soviet of workers, soldiers or peasants, attesting that he belongs to the working class. . . . Every worker is required to turn in 2% of his salary to the fund. . . . Male citizens not belonging to the working class may enjoy the same rights provided they pay a sum equivalent to 250 French francs, which will be turned over to the public fund. . . . Any women who by virtue of the present

A Brief Critique

decree will be declared national property will receive from the public fund a salary equivalent to 575 French francs a month. . . . Any pregnant woman will be dispensed of her duties for four months before and three months after the birth of the child. . . . One month after birth, children will be placed in an institution entrusted with their care and education. They will remain there to complete their instruction and education at the expense of the national fund until they reach the age of seventeen. . . . All those who refuse to recognize the present decree and to cooperate with the authorities shall be declared enemies of the people, anti-anarchists, and shall suffer the consequences."[10]

Another document which illustrates the kind of "liberation" which women received under the Communist version of morality is contained in a decision handed down by a Soviet official in which he said: "There is no such thing as a woman being violated by a man; he who says that a violation is wrong denies the October Communist Revolution. To defend a violated woman is to reveal oneself as a bourgeois and a partisan of private property."[11]

Only one other thought need be added concerning the Communist allegation that Judaic-Christian morals represent a "class" morality. That is the fact that not only is it quite simple to illustrate that such an allegation is untrue but it is also quite simple to illustrate that the most perfect example of "class" morality on the face of the earth today is Communism. Of the 180,000,000 people in Russia, only about 3,000,000 are members of the Communist party. This small ruling minority ruthlessly compels the remainder of the people to accept its decision as to what is good and what is bad. Communist morals follow a simple formula. Anything which promotes the communist cause is good, anything which hinders

[10] *Quoted by Gabriel M. Roschini in his article,* "CONTRADICTIONS CONCERNING THE STATUS OF WOMEN IN SOVIET RUSSIA," *which appears in* "THE PHILOSOPHY OF COMMUNISM," *by Giorgio La Pira and others, Fordham University Press, New York, 1952, pp. 97-98.*

[11] "OUTCHIT GAZETA," *October 10, 1929. Quoted by Charles J. McFadden in* "THE PHILOSOPHY OF COMMUNISM," *pp. 292-293 and note.*

it is bad. Upon examination, that philosophy turns out to be a code of opportunism and expediency, or a code of no morals at all. Anyone who does not conform to the dictates of the Party as to what is good for Communism and what is not, is subjected to the most severe penalties under Articles 131 and 133 of the Soviet Constitution. Thus, the perfect example of "class" morality, which the Marxists attribute to the Judaic-Christian code, is to be found right in the Communist plan of action itself.

The Communist Theory of Class Struggle

FALLACY 9—The next fallacy is the claim of Marx and Engels that they had discovered the secret of human progress. This was identified by them as "class struggle."

As the student will recall, they said that when men became aware that slavery was a satisfactory mode of production, they built a society designed to protect the rights of the slave owner. They further believed that if this state of affairs had never been challenged the mode of production by slavery would have become a permanent fixture and society likewise would have been fixed. But Marx and Engels found, as do all students of history, that the economic order passed from slavery to feudalism and then from feudalism to capitalism. What caused this? They decided it was class struggle. They decided the slaves overthrew their masters and created a new mode of production based on feudalism. A society was then developed to protect this mode of production until the serfs overthrew their lords and set up a mode of production characterized by free-enterprise capitalism. Modern society, they said, is to protect capitalism.

Critics declare that Marx and Engels apparently ignored some of the most obvious facts of history. For example, the decay and overthrow of ancient civilizations such as Egypt, Greece and Rome had nothing to do with slaves rising up against their masters: "The slaves of those days were for the most part subservient, abject, and helpless creatures, whose

A Brief Critique

occasional murmurings and rebellions were suppressed with horrible cruelty. Those were not class struggles of the imaginary Marxian type and did not bring the transition to feudalism. Engels himself says that toward the end of the Roman Empire slaves were scarce and dear; that the *latifundia*, which were great agricultural estates based on slave labor, were no longer profitable; that small-scale farming by colonists and tenants was relatively lucrative; and that, in short, 'slavery died because it did not pay any longer.' Then came the barbarian invasion, the downfall of Rome, and the establishment of feudalism as the result of the conquest of a higher civilization by a lower and not through the alleged driving force of a class struggle."[12]

Similar historical problems exist for Marx and Engels in connection with the transition of society from feudalism to capitalism.

FALLACY 10—Not only does Communism fail in its attempt to account for past progress on the basis of class struggle, but it also fails in its prediction that class antagonism would increase under capitalism in the future. One hundred years have failed to develop the two violently antagonistic classes which Marx and Engels said were inevitable.

Communist agitators have done everything in their power to fan the flame of artificial class-consciousness in the minds of the workers, but the basic struggle between labor and capital has not been to overthrow capitalism but to get the workers a more equitable share of the fruits of capitalism. For example, during the past twenty years labor has attained a higher status in the United States than ever before. The Communists tried to seize leadership in this reform trend, but the more the workers earned the more independent they became—not only by asserting their rights in relation to their employers but also in discharging the *Communist agitators from labor union leadership*. Workers did not respond to the Communist call to overthrow capitalism, and Communist writers have admitted this with some bitterness.

---

[12] *LeRossignol, J. E.*, "FROM MARX TO STALIN," *pp. 152-153.*

At the same time, both governmental and industrial leaders generally developed the philosophy that strong buying power in labor is essential to keep the wheels of industry moving. Labor therefore came closer to assuming its proper role as an integral part of capitalism than ever before. This trend leaves Communism completely undone because such a development makes labor an indispensable part of capitalism rather than its class-conscious enemy.

FALLACY 11—Another Communist premise which has failed is the assumption that under capitalism all wealth would be gradually monopolized until a handful of men would own everything and the exploited, propertyless class would be the overwhelming majority of mankind. Instead of growing, however, the propertyless proletariat actually have been decreasing under capitalism. Marx wrote his massive tome on *Capital* while he was living in the most abject poverty. He looked upon the proletariat as those who were living under conditions similar to his own—people who had absolutely no property and no capital interests. Today, in the highly-developed capitalistic nation of the United States, the only people who could be classed as proletariat under Marx's definition would be those who own no land, have no savings deposits, no social security, no retirement benefits, no life insurance, no corporate securities and no government bonds, for all these represent the ownership of productive wealth or of money funds over and beyond the immediate needs of consumption. Such a class of propertyless proletariat does exist in the United States just as there has been one in all nations and in all ages, but the significant thing is that the proletariat in the United States is such a small minority that Marx would scarcely want to claim it. Under American capitalism wealth has been more widely distributed among the people than in any large nation in secular history. This has reduced the propertyless class which Marx had in mind to little more than a fringe of the population.

In contrast to this we find that the country which really does have the majority of its population in a class of propertyless proletariat is the Motherland of Communism where the

A Brief Critique

Dictatorship of the Proletariat has been in force for over thirty-five years!

FALLACY 12—Marx's theory on wages also collapsed with the passing of time. He assumed that technological developments would make machines more and more efficient and therefore throw so many men out of work that they would compete for jobs until wages would become more and more meager. Technological development has actually created more jobs than it has destroyed and, except during intervals of depression, the long-range trend in capitalism has been to get closer and closer to the economic dream of "full-employment."

FALLACY 13—Since Marx believed that wages would become smaller and smaller he assumed that the only possible way to attain an adequate living would be by owning property. That is why he said the possession of property was the one thing which distinguished the proletariat from the exploiting class. This conclusion was another major error. Today some individuals may readily receive $10,000 a year for the sale of their labor services while others live on incomes of $2,500 derived from the ownership of property. In such cases it would certainly seem ludicrous to call the first group proletariat and the second group exploiting bourgeoisie. Under capitalism the ownership of property is certainly not the only means of gaining adequate economic independence.

FALLACY 14—Marx and Engels also failed in trying to predict what would happen to the middle class under capitalism. They said the middle class would be forced to follow the dismal process of sinking back into the propertyless class so that ultimately there would be just two violently antagonistic classes—the capitalists and the propertyless proletariat. The very opposite happened. Economists have made studies which show that the middle class (consisting of people who are neither extremely prosperous nor exceptionally poor) has been rapidly growing. As a group the members of the middle class have increased in number, in wealth and in proportion to the rest of the population.[13]

---

[13] *Blodgett, Ralph E.,* "COMPARATIVE ECONOMIC SYSTEMS," *p. 735.*

The Naked Communist

78

FALLACY 15—Another fallacy in Communism is the theory that class struggle leads to "necessary progress." In this theory Marx and Engels attempted to apply the dialectics of their philosophy which say that out of struggle between two opposing forces an inescapable new evolutionary advancement is made. This fails to explain the unprogressiveness which has characterized many nations for centuries—nations such as India, China, Egypt, Arabia and the populations in East Asia.

It also fails to explain one of the most obvious facts of history, namely, the *retrogression* of civilizations. The whole pattern of human experience shows that nations rise to a summit of power and then pass through moral and intellectual decay to lose their cultural standing and economic predominance. This is vastly easier to demonstrate in history than the theory that class struggle has lifted man through an ever-ascending series of stages called "necessary progress."

FALLACY 16—Finally, the failure of class struggle to explain the past also failed Marx and Engels when they tried to predict what would happen in their own lifetime. They said that Communism would come first in those countries which were most highly capitalistic because the class struggle would become more sharply defined as capitalism increased. On this basis they thought Communism would come first in Germany.[14] A few years later Marx shifted his prediction to England.[15]

It was ironical that Communism (at least the Dictatorship of the proletariat) should first come to Russia—a nation which in economic matters was one of the least developed among all the countries in Europe. Furthermore, Communism came as a coup in Russia, not through any class struggle on the part of the workers. It came through the conspiratorial intrigue of V. I. Lenin, who was encouraged by the German High Command to go into Russia during the closing months of World War I and use a small, hard core of revolutionaries to seize the provisional government which had but recently forced the Tzar to abdicate and was at the moment representing the

---

[14] *Marx and Engels, "THE COMMUNIST MANIFESTO," p. 58.*
[15] *Marx is quoted by M. D'Arcy in "CHRISTIAN MORALS," p. 172.*

A Brief Critique

working class, as much as anyone else, in setting up a democratic constitution.

Communism therefore did not come to Russia as the natural outcome of class struggle but like any other dictatorship—by the military might of a small minority. This brings us to the fallacy of the "Dictatorship of the Proletariat."

The Dictatorship of the Proletariat

FALLACY 17—This proposed monopoly of political and economic power was designed to do many things for the good of humanity, but experience has proven them to be false dreams. For example, the Dictatorship of the Proletariat was designed to spread the enjoyment of wealth among the people by abolishing private property and putting all means of production in the hands of the government. Why did they want to do this? They said it was to prevent all property and wealth from falling into the hands of private capitalists. But what happened when the Communists attempted to do this in Russia? It destroyed what little division of wealth there was and sent the economy hurtling back in the direction of feudalism—an economic system under which a few privileged persons dispense the necessities of life by arbitrary determination while at the same time dictating the way in which all important phases of life shall be lived by the citizens. The folly of Marx and Engels was in failing to distinguish the difference between the *right* of private property and the *abuse* of private property. They were going to get rid of the abuse by abolishing the right. The problem of humanity has not been the right to own private property but how to provide an equitable distribution of property rights so that many people could enjoy them. Therefore, Communist theory does not solve the problem because of the simple fact that putting all property back under the supervision of the hirelings of a dictatorship launches a trend toward monopoly of property rather than toward a wider distribution of its enjoyment.

FALLACY 18—The Dictatorship of the Proletariat was

also designed to compensate each man for work performed rather than for wages earned. But by abolishing wages in favor of labor certificates, Communist leaders were simply abandoning the prevailing medium of exchange. After the Communist revolution in Russia it was found that this idea forced that nation to resort to a primitive barter system. The whole idea was so disastrous that it had to be abandoned after a few months. The Communists learned that the problem of *equalizing wages* is not solved by abolishing wages *per se.*

FALLACY 19—The Dictatorship of the Proletariat was also intended to permit the creation of a huge "defense" army which would help "liberate" the proletariat in other nations until finally the Dictatorship would cover the entire earth.

This veiled attempt to obscure the imperialistic ambitions of Communist leaders for world conquest is still employed. Their armies are always described as being for "defense" and the victims of their aggression as being "liberated." Recent world history has provided a tragic commentary on the role of Communist liberation.

FALLACY 20—The Dictatorship of the Proletariat was further expected to give the Communist leaders time to demonstrate to the masses the effectiveness of their plan so as to insure a unity of support for "full communism" which was soon to follow. The Communist Dictatorship in Russia has had no such power to persuade. In fact, the violence which was authorized for use against the capitalist class has had to be turned loose with equal fury on the proletariat or working class so that today the masses have been reduced to a state of numb and fearful acquiescence rather than a "unity of support" for the Communist cause.

The Stateless, Classless Society Under Full Communism

FALLACY 21—The Communist dream of a great new "one world" of the future is based on the belief that a regime of violence and coercion under the Dictatorship of the Proletariat

A Brief Critique

would permit the establishment of a society which would produce a new order of men who would acquire the *habit* of observing what Lenin called the "simple fundamental rules of every-day social life in common." The fallacy of this hope lies in Communism's perverted interpretation of human behavior. It assumes, on the basis of Dialectical Materialism, that if you change things *outside* of a man this automatically compels a change on the *inside* of the man. The inter-relation between environment on the outside and the internal make-up of man is not to be disputed, but environment only *conditions* man, it does not *change his very nature.* For example, just as men will always laugh, eat, propagate, gravitate into groups and explore the unknown, so likewise they will always enjoy the pleasure of possessing things (which alone gives pleasure to sharing) ; they will always possess the desire for individual expression or self-determination, the ambition to improve their circumstances and the motive to excel above others. These qualities are inherent in each generation and cannot be legislated away nor ignored.

Therefore no amount of violence and coercion will ever develop permanent habits of observing the "simple fundamental rules of every-day social life in common" if that social life violates the very nature of man. No matter how man is suppressed he will harbor in his very nature a passionate instinct for freedom to express these desires which are his by inheritance rather than by acquisition. That is why these desires cannot be ignored, and that is why they will not be annihilated even under the ruthless suppressions of a militant Dictatorship of the Proletariat. They will surely rise to assert themselves the very moment the dictatorship shows signs of "withering away."

Sixty centuries of history have demonstrated that society succeeds only when it *tempers* man's natural instincts and inclinations. In fact, these same qualities of human nature which Communism would try to abolish are the very things which, under proper circumstances, men find to be the sources of satisfaction, strength and well-being which lead to progress for both the individual and for society as a whole.

FALLACY 22—Marx and Engels were so anxious to discredit capitalism that they spent most of their time on that particular theme and never got around to revealing the complete pattern for "full communism" which was to replace capitalism; nevertheless, we do have sufficient information to reveal its congenital weaknesses. One of these is the axiom that "Each will produce according to his ability, each will receive according to his need." This perhaps sounds excellent when one is dealing with a handicapped person, because society is willing to make up to an obviously handicapped person that which he cannot do for himself. But what happens when this is applied to the whole society? Recently a teacher asked his students what they thought about this Communist slogan, and they all seemed to think it was fine. The teacher then said he would give them a little demonstration of what would happen in school if "each produced according to his capacity and each received according to his need." Said he:

"To get a passing grade in this class you must receive 75. Therefore, if any of you get 95 I will take off 20 points and give it to a student who only gets 55. If a student gets 90 I will take off 15 points and give it to a student who only makes 60. In this way everyone will get by."

Immediately there was a storm of protest from the brighter, hard-working students in the class, but the lazy or less studious pupils throught it was fine idea. Finally the teacher explained:

"In the long run I don't think any of you would like this system. Here is what would happen. First, the highly productive pupils—and they are always a minority in school as well as in life—would soon lose all incentive for producing. Why strive to make a high grade if part of it is taken from you by 'authority' and given to someone else? Second, the less productive pupils—a majority in school as elsewhere— would, for a time, be relieved of the necessity to study or to produce. This would continue until the high producers had sunk or had been driven down to the level of the low producers and therefore had nothing to contribute to their companions. At that point, in order for anyone to survive, the 'authority'

A Brief Critique

would have no alternative but to begin a system of compulsory labor and punishments against *even the low producers.* They, of course, would then complain bitterly, but without understanding just what had happened."[16]

In terms of Communism this need for "authority" would simply mean returning to the Dictatorship of the Proletariat in order to force all workers to produce more of life's necessities. But the Dictatorship of the Proletariat fails, even with force, to make men produce according to their ability. As in the example cited by the school teacher, this is because Communism has deliberately destroyed the most ordinary work incentives. Let us list four of them:

1. *Increased reward for* increased *production.*
2. *Increased reward for working harder to develop* improved *products.*
3. *Increased reward for working harder to provide* improved *services.*
4. *The right of the worker to* buy *and* develop property *with the accumulation of past rewards (profits) over and beyond the needs of consumption and thereby improve the circumstances of himself and his family.*

The Communist leaders seem to have misunderstood the universal lesson of life that man's greatest enemy is *inertia* and that the mainspring of action to combat inertia is not force but the opportunity for self-improvement. Marx and Engels insisted that such an attitude is selfish and "non-social," but the plain fact is that a worker finds it difficult to work harder in order to fill the stomachs of "society" when the fruits of his labor do not first take care of himself and his family. The Communists thought they could drive out this "non-social" attitude with force, but thirty-five years of Dictatorship in Russia have vividly demonstrated that men will not work according to their ability unless they are compensated according to their ability. Even the Communist leaders know

---

[16] *Related by Thomas J. Shelly, instructor in Economics and History, Yonkers High School, Yonkers, New York.*

force has failed. Under the whip of the Dictatorship the workers have barely produced enough to survive. The Communist leaders therefore say that the Dictatorship must be continued indefinitely. So long as the workers fail to produce according to their ability there certainly can be no talk of "full Communism" where each will receive according to his need.

FALLACY 23—In studying the theories of Marx and Engels the student soon becomes aware that they failed to take into account some of the most elementary facts of life. For example, they assumed that in a stateless society mass-rule (which always turns out to be mob-rule) would be more discriminating and discerning than the executive, legislative and judicial bodies of organized government. To set this up as an expectation under full Communism flies in the face of all past human experience.

FALLACY 24—This theory also assumes that under the suppression imposed by the Dictatorship of the Proletariat men will lose or completely smother their instinct of acquisition. Marx and Engels make it clear that they expected the Dictatorship to get people in the "habit" of not owning property or wanting to own it. But what happens when the stateless society is inaugurated and a whole new generation arrives on the scene which has no memory of the merciless suppression which gave their fathers the habit of observing the "simple, fundamental rules of everyday social life in common"? Suppose large numbers refuse to do the kind of work or the share of work expected of them, so that they are adjudged guilty of not "producing according to their ability"? Or suppose they demand from the classless, stateless society more than is believed to be their share? What will happen if they organize themselves, secretly equip themselves with weapons, and rise up unexpectedly to seize the wealth which the classless, stateless society refuses to give them? Will it not be necessary to immediately set up the Dictatorship of the Proletariat all over again to suppress this opposition? Perhaps the instinct of acquisition is going to be more difficult to suppress than Marx and Engels thought. In fact, with the knowledge which we already have concerning several thousand years of human

A Brief Critique

behavior, is it likely that Communism will ever get past the Dictatorship of the Proletariat?

FALLACY 25—Finally, full Communism promises that even in the absence of ordinary work incentives the classless, stateless society will produce greater quantities of goods than any existing system can produce today. Under this theory it is intended that Communist production will somehow reach a state of absolute saturation where all human needs will be satisfied. Supplies are to be stockpiled and distributed according to the needs of every person. Services are likewise to be made available at central depots and are to be available in such quantity that all elements of competition among consumers will be eliminated. Thus, Communism promises to do away with markets, money and prices.

What happens, then, if the goal of absolute saturation is not reached? Would not the Dictatorship of the Proletariat have to be called into service once more to suppress dissatisfaction? A good example of the problem might be the case of automobiles. How many automobiles would have to be produced to reach absolute saturation for the wants (which must ultimately become synonymous with need if there is to be no state authority) of two billion people? Under capitalism, economic necessity makes a family feel satisfied with one or two cars. What would happen if this economic necessity were removed? Under full Communism a good worker is entitled to all the cars he wants. Unless he gets all he wants the ogre of selfishness will raise its ugly head. Time and again Communist writings promise sufficient production to eliminate the element of selfishness which leads to class struggle.

And what happens when new models come out? Will society automatically scrap all cars every time a new model is developed? Under full Communism who would want an old car? This may seem somewhat preposterous but, as a matter of fact, it would be a most commonplace problem and would arise in connection with all types of production. Someone would have to decide who must keep their old cars for an extra year or two since otherwise every family would most certainly demand a new one. Each family might even demand

several new ones. The problems under such a system obviously
assume mountainous proportions and any hope of eliminating
money, markets and prices fades into oblivion. Such a system
also would require many times more government machinery
than free-enterprise capitalism, and the prospect of producing
goods and services in such quantities that the state might
"wither away" defies both reason and experience.

Communism as a Negative Approach
To Problem-Solving

In concluding this discussion of the basic fallacies in
Communism we should perhaps make a summary comment
on the most significant fallacy of them all. This is the Communist doctrine that problems can be solved by eliminating
the institution from which the problems emanate. Even Marx
and Engels may have been unaware that this was what they
were doing, but the student will note how completely this
approach dominates every problem they undertook to solve.

Take, for example, the problems of government. Marx
and Engels would solve these problems by working for the
day when they could eliminate government. Problems of
morals would be solved by doing away with morals. Problems growing out of religion would be solved by doing away
with religion. Problems of marriage, home and family would
be eliminated by doing away with marriage, home and family.
The problems arising out of property rights would be resolved
by not allowing anyone to have any property rights. The
problem of equalizing wages would be solved by abolishing
wages. Problems connected with money, markets and prices
would be solved by doing away with money, markets and
prices. Problems of competition in production and distribution would be solved by forcibly prohibiting competition.
Finally, they would solve all the problems of modern society
by using revolution to destroy this society. It seems the
phantom of Communist hope can only arise from the bowels

A Brief Critique

of the earth through the ashes of all that now is. Communism must be built for one purpose—to destroy. Only after the great destruction did the Communist leaders dare to hope that they might offer to their disciples the possibility of freedom, equality and justice.

It is this dismal and nebulous promise for the future which Communism offers the world today. Until such a day comes, the Communist leaders ask humanity to endure the conflagration of revolutionary violence, the suppression and liquidation of resistance groups, the expropriation of property, the Dictatorship of the Proletariat which they themselves describe as "based on force and unrestricted by any laws," the suspension of all civil liberties—suppression of free press, free speech and assembly, the existence of slave labor camps, the constant observation of all citizens by secret police, the long periods of service in the military, the poverty of collective farming, the risk of being liquidated if discovered associating with deviationists, and finally, the tolerance of an economic order which promises little more than a life of bare subsistence for generations to come.

More than forty years have come and gone since Communist leaders first seized a nation to demonstrate to a curious world what marvelous wonders might be wrought. From that one nation they have expanded their grip until one-third of the human race now bows to their iron-clad dictates. Those who have escaped their tyranny bear witness that Marxist Man has produced a political monstrosity containing the collected relics of practically every form of human degradation and torture invented by the mind of man since the dawn of history. While pretending to liberate mankind from the alleged oppression of capitalism Marxist Man has defied the warm, white light of Twentieth Century civilization to introduce slavery on a scale unprecedented in the history of the race. While claiming to foster the "rights of the common man" the Marxist has butchered his fellow citizens from Kulaks to aristocrats in numbers that baffle rational comprehension. And while describing himself as the epitome of the best in nature—the creature of science, the supreme intelligence of the universe—*Homo-Marxian* has exploited his cunning to compound crimes which scarcely would be duplicated by the most predatory tribes of pre-historic times.

It is for this reason that discerning men have described Communism as reversing and negating history. It has turned man against himself. Instead of solving the many complex problems of modern life, Marxism's negative approach has simply resurrected primitive problems which past generations of struggling humanity had already succeeding in solving.

To more fully appreciate precisely what has been happening we shall now examine the circumstances which led to the launching of the first Communist controlled nation in the history of the world.

V

The Rise of the
Revolutionary Movement in Russia

The events described in this chapter are intimate facts in the minds of all well-informed Marxists. Communists often base their arguments on their interpretation of these events and therefore the student should find this historical background helpful.

This chapter also includes the biographies of the principal Communist leaders — Nikolai (V. I.) Lenin, Leon Trotsky and Joseph Stalin.

A review of the following questions will indicate some of the answers which this chapter is designed to provide.

Who launched Marxism in Russia in 1868? Why did Marx consider this man his "enemy"? After the assassination of Alexander II what did Marx say about the possibility of a Communist revolution in Russia?

What kind of environment produced Nikolai Lenin? Why was his brother hanged?

Who organized the Bolsheviks? What does the name

mean? What did they call their enemies? Was this an accurate designation or a matter of strategy?

What was the background of Leon Trotsky? How did he get this name? How did he escape from Siberia? Why did he oppose Lenin in 1903?

Was the Russian Revolution of 1905 led by a few radicals or was it a general uprising of the whole people? Why did Lenin and the Bolsheviks oppose the "October Manifesto" which promised the people representative government?

From what kind of home did Joseph Stalin come? Why was he expelled from the seminary where he was being trained as a priest? What did the criminal activities of Joseph Stalin during 1907 reveal about his personality? How extensive were Stalin's activities as a union organizer, propagandist and revolutionary leader during this period? What was his relationship to Lenin?

What brought Russia to the brink of another general uprising during the First World War? What was the Tsar's attitude during this crisis?

Marxism Comes to Russia

In 1885 a U.S. citizen, Andrew D. White, returned from a tour of duty as attache in the American Embassy at St. Petersburg and described the Russian situation as follows: "The whole governmental system is the most atrociously barbarous in the world. There is on earth no parallel example of a polite society so degraded, a people so crushed, an official system so unscrupulous."[1]

When White made this statement, the population of Russia was slightly over 70,000,000. Of these, 46,000,000 were in virtual captivity as serfs.

It will be recalled that Marx and Engels had been aroused to wrathful vehemence when they saw conditions among the

---

[1] *From a letter of Andrew D. White dated at Berlin, November 9, 1885, in the White Collection, Cornell University.*

The Revolution in Russia

industrial workers of England, but the status of life among the English was far above that of the peasants in Russia. The Russian serfs were not only starved, exploited and pauperized, but they were subjected to an iron-clad system of feudal political suppression. Always there was the plague of the secret police, the threat of arrest and sentencing to forced labor camps in Siberia and the cruel indecencies imposed upon them by the Tsar's everpresent military. A Russian serf seemed to enjoy no sacred immunities whatever, neither in his person, his possessions, his children, nor, sometimes, his wife. All were subject to the petty whims of grasping officials in the Tsar's corrupt bureaucracy.

Between 1861 and 1866, Tsar Alexander II sincerely attempted to do away with the institution of serfdom by approving several acts of emancipation. However, for all practical purposes, the impoverished lives of the peasants continued to be insecure, harsh and austere. Circumstances leading to a revolution were in the making.

Marxism came to Russia in 1868 when Bakunin's translation of *Capital* escaped the Tsar's censors and passed among liberals and radicals like a choice morsel of spiritual meat. For Russia it meant the kindling of the bright red flame in the original Communist Manifesto: "Let the ruling classes tremble at a Communist revolution. The proletarians have nothing to lose but their chains. . . . Working men of all countries, unite!"

Russian revolutionary movements soon began to take shape and by 1880 Marxism could be described as definitely taking hold. The first significant violence came in 1881 when Tsar Alexander II fell dying beneath the shattering impact of a bomb which was hurled into the royal carriage by Ignatius Grinevitsky, a member of a revolutionary group called "The People's Will."

The successful murder of the Tsar led many Marxists to feel that the hour for unrestricted revolution might be very near. Over in London, the aging Marx began receiving inquiries from his Russian disciples. They wanted to know whether or not it might be possible to have a revolution in

Russia even though the Russian economy had never passed through the capitalistic development which Marx had always said was a prerequisite. Marx studied the problem diligently. Finally, he gave it as his opinion that Russia had "the rarest and most suitable opportunity ever offered to any country to avoid (skip) the phase of capitalistic development." In other words, Marx was suggesting the possibility of an early revolution in Russia.

This was a complete theoretical switch for Marx. He was also admitting the error of one of his earlier prophecies; namely, that the revolution would come first among highly developed capitalistic nations such as Germany and England. Among his friends he declared: "It is an irony of fate that the Russians, whom I have fought for twenty-five years, and not only in German (publications), but in French and English, have always been my patrons." It was indeed ironical that the Russian Marxists had remained loyal to Marx and his theories in spite of the verbal and editorial abuse he had heaped upon them. This was never more true than in the case of Bakunin, the first Russian Marxist, who promoted the theories of Marx and Engels with such zeal that they both feared he might take over the First International. They, therefore, marked him for political liquidation.

Even at the end, however, Bakunin reaffirmed his faith in Marxism, and after referring to the "furious hatred" of Marx toward himself, he concluded: "This has given me an intense loathing of public life. I have had enough of it, and after devoting all my days to the struggle, I am weary. . . . Let other and younger persons put their hands to the work. For my own part, I no longer feel strong enough. . . . I, therefore, withdraw from the arena, and ask only one thing of my dear contemporaries—oblivion."

In 1876 Bakunin laid down the burden of his life, but the "younger persons" to whom he bequeathed Marxism and the Russian people's revolution were already commencing to make their appearance among men.

In 1870, Nikolai Lenin was born, and in the year 1879, there arrived on earth both Joseph Stalin and Leon Trotsky.

The Revolution in Russia

Others would come, but these three were to be the principal leaders in carrying forward the traditions of Bakunin and at the same time doing for Marx what he was never able to do for himself; these three would convulse a great nation in a revolution and would serve as midwives at the birth of the world's first Communist dictatorship.

The Early Life of Nikolai (V. I.) Lenin

Marx would hardly have guessed that the first Communist dictator would be a man like Lenin, who was born on April 22, 1870, in Simbirsk, on the Volga. His father was a Councilor of State with an hereditary title of nobility while his mother was a German of the Lutheran faith. Lenin had red hair, high cheek bones, and the slanting eyes of his Tartar ancestors from Astrakhan.

Originally, Lenin was named Vladimir Ilich Ulyanov, but "Nikolai Lenin" is the revolutionary pseudonym under which he became famous. As a boy he had strict training under a father who was called a "liberal" even though he was a Councilor of State. His father was a man of humanitarian ideals who worked himself to death setting up four-hundred and fifty primary schools during a period of seventeen years. Lenin was fifteen when his father died, and soon afterwards an even greater tragedy struck the family—his older brother was hanged.

This brother, named Alexander, was nearing twenty-one. He had lost his religious faith some time before and had become deeply impressed with the philosophy of materialism. He had also come to feel the need for direct and decisive action in getting social reforms in Russia.

While attending the University at St. Petersburg (now Leningrad), Alexander agreed with several associates to construct a bomb which could be used to kill Tsar Alexander III. The bomb was built inside a bogus medical dictionary and consisted of dynamite and strychnine-treated bullets. The police discovered the assassination plot just before it was to have been executed and the entire group was summarily arrested. Trials and convictions soon followed, and in May, 1887, the St. Petersburg papers announced that Lenin's older brother had gone to the gallows.

When the excitement subsided, Lenin, who had just turned 17, went back to reading Marx and other revolutionary writers in deadly earnest. Like his brother, Lenin had lost his religious faith two or three years before and was becoming reconciled to the cynicism of the Marxist interpretation of life. Furthermore, the death of his brother accelerated his determination to become an active revolutionist as soon as possible.

To give himself some kind of professional status, Lenin made an intensive study of law. Through the intercession of his mother, he was allowed to take his final examinations at the Univerity in St. Petersburg and came out first among one hundred and twenty-four students. Lenin then attempted to practice law, but for some reason lost nearly all his cases and, therefore, abandoned the law and never returned to it.

In 1891-92 the Russian famine and cholera epidemic broke out. Lenin was living in a region where Tolstoy, the famous Russian writer and philanthropist, was trying to sustain the courage of the people by organizing hundreds of soup-kitchens and distributing seed-grain and horses to the impoverished peasants. But Lenin would have none of it. He would not help set up soup-kitchens nor join a relief committee. Later he was accused of welcoming the famine as a means of accentuating the suffering of the people and firing up their revolutionary will to act. There is no doubt that during these years the Marxist program was ramrodding Lenin's thinking into that of an uncompromising revolutionist.

Shortly after this, Lenin took up residence in St. Petersburg. He was now twenty-three and anxious to begin active revolutionary work. He therefore joined the "Fighting Union for the Liberation of the Working Class." However, in 1895 Lenin learned that he had tuberculosis of the stomach. This made it necessary for him to go to Switzerland and undergo a cure at a special sanitarium. While in Western Europe, he made contact with George Plekhanov, the leader of the exiled

The Revolution in Russia

Russian Marxists. Lenin spent long hours with Plekhanov and felt highly flattered that the big man among the exiled Russian radicals would share with a newcomer his plans for a violent revolution and the overthrow of the Tsar. Plekhanov was equally impressed with Lenin. He felt the heat of Lenin's glowing hatred for everything tainted by the Tsar's regime, and therefore decided that Lenin should return to Russia, rally the Marxists, and organize a national Communist political party patterned after the highly successful Social Democrats in Germany. Lenin was also asked to begin publishing a revolutionary periodical.

This assignment was accepted by Lenin as a heroic mission for which fate had predestined him. Upon returning to Russia, he organized strikes, trained recruits, formulated political strategy and wrote inflammatory articles. But in the midst of this promising campaign, a police agent betrayed the group and Lenin found himself sentenced to exile in faraway Siberia. Lenin accepted this interruption of his revolutionary career with bitter resignation.

Soon after his arrival in Siberia Lenin was joined by a Marxist girl, whom he had met in 1894, named Nadezhda Krupskaya. She was allowed to come, at Lenin's request, on condition that she and Lenin legalize their union with a marriage ceremony. This violated their Marxist principle of "abolition of the family," but they consented in order to remain together. Lenin now had a companion as dedicated to the revolution as himself. They had no children, and close associates stated that they intentionally planned against children because they both felt their missions in life would not permit them to be thus encumbered.

Lenin spent his time in Siberia studying, writing reams of letters in secret ink, solidifying the program of the new Social-Democratic Party of Russia and completing his book called, *Capitalism in Russia.*

When he was released in 1900, Lenin had become a cautious, calculating, full-fledged, conspiratorial revolutionist. He immediately headed for Munich, Germany, where he started printing a paper called *The Spark,* which could be smuggled into Russia. Thus began seventeen years of almost continuous exile in Western Europe for Lenin and his wife. Only on rare occasions did they secretly visit Russia. They lived modestly and traveled light. It was as though they were waiting for the voice of history to assign them to their revolutionary roles.

Origin of the Bolsheviks

By 1903 Lenin and his wife had set up headquarters in London. They had the feeling they were carrying on where Marx had left off. Marx had been dead seventeen years and often they made pilgrimages to the cemetery where the grave of Marx is located.

In July of that year a Russian-Social-Democratic congress convened in London. Forty-three delegates came from Russia as well as from various groups of Russian exiles in Western Europe. As chairman of the congress, Lenin started off with a moderate and impartial attitude, but as the discussions continued he was horrified to discover that the congress was moving toward pacifistic socialism rather than militant revolution. Lenin immediately gathered his friends and followers around him. He split the congress wide open on the issue of whether party membership should be limited to hard-core revolutionists (as advocated by Lenin) or broadened to include anyone who felt a sympathy for the movement.

In this dispute Lenin temporarily rallied around him a majority of the congress and thereafter used this as a basis for calling those who supported him "Bolsheviks" (which comes from a Russian word meaning "majority"), while those who opposed him were called "Mensheviks" (which is taken from the Russian word meaning "minority"). The propaganda value of a party title meaning "majority" will be quickly recognized. It was another illustration of Lenin's absolute determination to exploit every situation so as to make it a tool to further his over-all political strategy.

At this particular congress, however, Lenin's victory was short-lived. Several groups combined their strength against

The Revolution in Russia

him and before long he found himself representing the minority view on most matters. Nevertheless, Lenin continued calling his followers "the Bolsheviks" and any who opposed him "the Mensheviks."

Background of Leon Trotsky

One of those who now opposed Lenin was a young, twenty-three-year-old zealot named Leon Trotsky. At a future day Lenin and Trotsky would join forces, but at this congress of 1903 they stood in opposite camps. Let us pause in our narration to consider briefly the early life of Trotsky.

In many respects the background of Lenin and Trotsky was similar. Both had come from substantial families, both had been well-educated, both had become disillusioned and had engaged in revolutionary activity and both had served sentences in Siberia.

Leon Trotsky had been born to the name of Lev Bronstein. His father was a Kulak or rich peasant. Originally, Trotsky's father had been a fugitive from the Tsar's anti-Jewish campaign and had fled from city life to settle in a farming district near the Black Sea, where there was more religious tolerance. However, as the members of the family prospered, they gradually dropped the local synagogue as well as the observance of the Jewish Sabbath. Finally, the father came out openly in favor of atheism.

When Trotsky went away to school, he carried along with him these sympathies for materialism which he had gained from his father. These attitudes soon began to bear fruit. Toward the completion of his school, Trotsky was not only exhibiting the cynicism of a confirmed materialist, but he was also showing strong signs of becoming a political radical. Although this tendency was most displeasing to Trotsky's father, nothing would dissuade him. Boisterous scenes erupted between the two whenever Trotsky went home for vacations and after a few years Trotsky was completely alienated from his family

The Naked Communist

Under these circumstances it was not at all difficult for Trotsky to find a place in his mind for Marxism when it was finally presented to him. His conversion was further facilitated by the fact that he was taught Marxism by an attractive young woman six years his senior whom he later married. Her name was Alexandra Lvovna.

Trotsky was only nineteen when he and Alexandra decided to help organize the South Russian Workers' Union. Among other things, Trotsky was assigned the task of printing an illegal paper. As might have been expected, this soon led to his arrest. Trotsky spent the next three months in solitary confinement and after a series of assignments to various prisons, he ended up in Siberia where he was joined eventually by Alexandra. They were both sentenced to serve four years in a cold, barren region where there were few settlements. Two children were born to them during this exile.

Trotsky escaped in 1902 by burying himself in a peasant's load of hay. He reached the Siberian railroad and then used a fake identification paper to pass himself off as "Trotsky"— the name of his late jailer! He used this name from then on. With the help of several Marxist comrades, he made his way to London and arrived there in time to participate in the Social-Democratic Congress which we have already mentioned. Sometime later he was joined by his wife and children.

Upon their first meeting Lenin and Trotsky struck it off well. Lenin described Trotsky as a revolutionist of "rare abilities." Trotsky reciprocated by suggesting that Lenin be made the chairman of the congress. During the congress, however, Trotsky saw enough of Lenin to make him apprehensive about the cold, blue-steel razor edge of Lenin's mind. He was shocked by the reckless indifference Lenin exhibited as he lopped off some of the oldest and most respected members of the party when they opposed his views. (Trotsky's gentle concern for the feelings of fellow comrades in 1903 stands in sharp contrast to his position in 1917-1922 when he personally supervised the ruthless liquidation of many hundreds of comrades whom he suspected of deviating from established party policy.)

The Revolution in Russia

As it turned out, Trotsky's temporary opposition to Lenin in 1903 did not hurt his revolutionary career. In the years immediately following, Trotsky developed into a brilliant writer and public speaker and he became a well-known personality in Western Europe long before Lenin. He is described as a handsome, arrogant, anti-social intellectual who sometimes offended his fellow-Marxists because of his flare for elegant clothes. The down-sweep of his nose and moustache won for him the title of "The Young Eagle."

Now let us return to the swift course of events in the history of the Russian revolutionary movement.

The Russian Revolution of 1905

By 1903 the political situation in Russia had become explosive. Tsar Nicholas II did not realize it, but he was to be the last of the Tsars. As an administrator, he had turned out to be amazingly weak. When he was a young man he had been very pleasant and friendly, and Russian liberals had hoped that after he ascended the throne he would adopt the badly needed reforms which his country required in order to take its place among the progressive nations of the world. But in this they were disappointed. Nicholas II perpetuated the imperialistic policies of his father, Alexander III, and enforced the stringent domestic policies of his grandfather who was assassinated. In fact, to satisfy his own expansive ambitions, Nicholas II plunged Russia into a senseless war with Japan in 1903. Almost immediately he found the Russian forces suffering humiliating defeat.

This Russo-Japanese War lasted a little over two years and as it neared its mortifying conclusion, the economic and political pressure on the Russian people split the seams of the Empire asunder. Government officials were assassinated, mass demonstrations were held, and a general strike was called which eventually idled more than 2,500,000 workers. The Tsar used every form of reprisal available to suppress the uprising, but mass arrests, mass imprisonment, and mass executions failed to stem the tide. The entire population was up in arms; bankers, peasants, professors, and illiterates walked side by side in the demonstration parades.

A typical example of the Tsar's clumsy maneuvering which brought on the revolution was the Winter Palace Massacre. This event occurred on Sunday, January 22, 1905, when a priest named Father George Gapon led a parade of several thousand unarmed workers to the front of the Winter Palace to present a peaceful petition for the amelioration of labor conditions. As the marchers drew near they could be seen carrying large portraits of Nicholas II which they waved back and forth while lustily singing "God Save the Tsar." It was a strange scene. The obvious poverty of the workers stood out in vivid contrast to the magnificent splendor of the Tsar's Winter Palace, which was a large and extravagant structure capable of housing more than 6,500 guests in its richly decorated apartments.

But the Tsar did not come out to welcome them. Instead the marchers found the palace completely surrounded by massed troops. At first the workers were apprehensive about the situation, but they felt reassured when there was no command to disperse. Then suddenly they heard the hoarse shout of a staccato military command. Immediately the Tsar's troops opened direct fire on the crowd. The withering volley leveled the front ranks to the ground while the remaining marchers trampled one another as they fled in terror trying to escape. The troops continued firing until the crowd completely dispersed. Approximately 500 were killed outright and 3,000 were wounded. This became notorious in Russian history as "Bloody Sunday."

News of this atrocity spread like a tidal wave across the steppes and plains of Russia. Already the people were bristling with resentment against the burden of the Russo-Japanese War, and this new outrage was sufficient to trigger a universal revolt. At first a few of the people tried to use violence, but generally speaking, the principal method of retaliation was one which paralyzed the Tsar's wartime econ-

The Revolution in Russia

omy—the people stopped working. In a matter of months the entire economic machinery of Russia came to a standstill. Factories were closed, stores were empty, newspapers were not printed, dry-goods and fuel were not moved and newly harvested crops were left rotting on the loading docks. For the first time in his career, Tsar Nicholas II was deeply frightened. He abandoned the Russo-Japanese War and agreed to hear the people's demands.

These consisted of four things:

1. *Protection of the individual, allowing freedom of conscience, freedom of speech, freedom of assembly, and the right to form unions.*
2. *The right of the people of all classes to vote for the Duma (the people's assembly.)*
3. *The automatic repeal of any law enacted by the Tsar without the consent of the people's assembly.*
4. *The right of the people's assembly to pass on the legality of any decrees issued by the Tsar.*

These demands were set in a document called "The October Manifesto." This Manifesto clearly illustrates that the masses of the people had no intention of destroying the Tsar, but merely wanted to set up a limited monarchy similar to England. Such a compromise infuriated the Marxists. They wanted the revolution continued until the Tsar was forced to surrender unconditionally and abdicate. Not until then could they set up a Communist dictatorship.

Leon Trotsky, who had hastened to Russia when the uprising started, stood before a crowd of people who were celebrating the Tsar's acceptance of the Manifesto and tore up a copy of it, declaring that the Manifesto was a betrayal of the revolution. He immediately joined with other Marxists in setting up political machinery to fan the flame of renewed revolutionary activity. This was done primarily by organizing a great many soviets (workers' councils in the various labor unions). Lenin arrived belatedly in November, 1905, and agreed to join with Trotsky for a "a second revolution."

After sixty days, however, the Marxist movement collapsed. Trotsky was caught and arrested while Lenin fled in the night to safer regions.

Thus ended fourteen months of desperate revolt against the Tsar; the first twelve belonged to the whole people, the last two to the Marxists. Altogether, the troops throughout the Empire had been called out more than 2,500 different times. In these battles between the people and the troops, fourteen thousand had been killed, approximately one thousand had been executed, twenty thousand had been wounded or injured, and seventy thousand had been arrested.

Trotsky's leadership in the final stages of the revolution won him a stiff sentence from the Tsar's court. He was convicted of revolutionary violence and exiled to Siberia for an indefinite period. But Trotsky never reached Siberia. He made a daring escape in midwinter and, after traveling four hundred and thirty miles in a deer-sleigh, crossed the Ural Mountains on horseback and then escaped to Finland where he joined Lenin and several other Marxists.

It was while Trotsky was staying in Finland that he carefully worked out his theory of "Perpetual Revolution." This theory advocated a continuous Communist attack on all existing governments until they were overthrown and the dictatorship of the proletariat established. This brought Trotsky into nearly perfect focus with Lenin. Perhaps, without quite realizing it, he had talked himself into becoming a full-fledged Bolshevik.

At this particular time, the Bolshevik movement was at its lowest ebb. The Bolshevik leaders had failed in their promises to force the Tsar to abdicate, and their continuation of the revolution after the October Manifesto had embittered the Tsar to the point where he had practically repudiated the Manifesto. He allowed the people to elect a Duma (people's assembly) but he managed to strip it of all its real powers. The people knew they were being defrauded, but there was no way to enforce the Manifesto without fomenting another revolution, and at the moment this seemed unlikely. Individual groups did continue agitating against the Tsar and his

The Revolution in Russia

ministers, but most of these, like the Bolshevik leaders, were forced to flee to Western Europe for safety.

To rejuvenate the dwindling influence of the Bolshevik Party, Lenin began holding a series of meetings. At one of these conclaves, a new revolutionary figure appeared on the scene. It was Joseph Stalin. Stalin came as an obscure delegate from a small Bolshevik group in Transcaucasia. Lenin immediately recognized him as a true revolutionary member of the peasant class—a rough, unrelenting, two-fisted man of ruthless action. Lenin had a place for such a personality and therefore enlisted Stalin in his service.

This brings us to the third important personality who figured prominently in the revolutionary movement in Russia.

Background of Joseph Stalin

Joseph Stalin was originally named Djugashvili. He was born December 21, 1879, in the little town of Gori near the border of Turkey. Today the humble wooden house which first sheltered him has been made into a national monument with a marble canopy covering it.

Stalin's father was a shoemaker with an addiction for alcohol which eventually cost him his life. Stalin was only eleven years old when his father died. Thereafter, Stalin's mother washed, scrubbed, sewed, and baked to earn enough money to put Stalin through school. Since his mother wanted him to be a priest, he was enrolled in the nearby theological seminary at Tiflis. As he learned his way around, Stalin soon discovered that the seminary was honeycombed with secret societies. Many of them were fostering the atheistic writings of Feuerbach and Bauer and the revolutionary writings of Marx and Engels. Before long Stalin convinced himself that he had a preference for revolution rather than religion and he therefore became vigorously active in the clandestine organizations which existed among the students of the seminary. He continued these activities for nearly three years, but he was finally exposed in May, 1899, and was expelled from the seminary for "lack of religious vocation."

Once he joined the outside world, Stalin spent his full time as a professional Marxist revolutionary. He organized strikes, conducted illegal May Day festivities, and finally fled to Batumi where he became the principal labor agitator for the Social-Democratic party. Eventually he was arrested and after remaining in prison until 1903, he was sentenced to three years of exile in Siberia.

He was still in Siberia when he heard about the split between the Bolsheviks and the Mensheviks. Stalin almost instinctively felt himself to be a hard-core Bolshevik and after successfully escaping from Siberia the following year, he returned to Tiflis and became the leader of the Transcaucasian Bolsheviks. During the Revolution of 1905 he led an abortive revolution in his home province of Georgia and then departed immediately for Finland to attend a Bolshevik conference and make contact with Lenin.

From then on Stalin remained the aide-de-camp to Lenin whom he deeply admired. It was not long before his zeal for the Communist cause began to forcefully manifest itself.

Stalin Engages in Criminal Activities

In the sumer of 1907 Joseph Stalin held a secret meeting with Lenin in Berlin. Afterwards he returned to Tiflis and organized a holdup. It was no mere Robin Hood adventure to steal money from the rich, but a major gangster operation with complete disregard for the lives of men, women, and children in Stalin's own home-town.

A powerful bomb was thrown in front of a convoy carrying money from the post office to the Tiflis Branch of the State Bank. The bomb destroyed the horses pulling the carriage, killed several by-standers, and wounded more than fifty children and adults. In the hysteria which followed, the moneybags containing 341,000 rubles (about $170,000) were

The Revolution in Russia

snatched from the carriage by the bomb-throwers and hurriedly carried away.

The crime reflected such complete disregard for human life that authorities both inside and outside of Russia attempted to run down every possible clue which would disclose the identities of the criminals. Finally, the money was found in the possession of a close associate of Stalin named Maxim Litvinov (the man Stalin later sent to the United States in 1933 to seek U.S. recognition for Soviet Russia). Litvinov and a companion were arrested in Paris by the French authorities when they tried to change the rubles into francs before sending the money on to Lenin. Details of the crime were finally unraveled by the authorities, and the names of original perpetrators were disclosed. Nevertheless, Stalin succeeded in remaining at large for several more years and continued his revolutionary activities.

Stalin as a Union Organizer, Writer and Bolshevik Leader

The years 1907-1913 were pick-and-shovel years for Joseph Stalin. No one could accuse him of being merely an "intellectual Communist" as they sometimes described Lenin. Stalin learned every trick of propaganda, pressure politics, mass communications, strike techniques and labor agitation. Some of his most significant experiences occurred in the highly active industrial district at Baku. There he was assigned to organize tens of thousands of oil well and refinery workers. To do this he set up a triple-system of legal, semi-legal, and totally illegal organizations. He imposed his leadership so completely on the workers in this large industrial center that he was able to organize a powerful industrial soviet (workers' council) dominated from top to bottom by his own loyal Bolshevik colleagues.

Stalin was never very effective as a speaker because of his strong Georgian accent, but between 1907 and 1913, he became proficient as a revolutionary writer. For awhile he edited a Socialist newspaper in Tiflis called *Dio* (Time) in which he aroused astonishment even among Bolsheviks because of his bitterness in attacking the Mensheviks. In 1910 he went to St. Petersburg (now Leningrad) and wrote for the *Social Democrat,* the *Zvezda* (Star), and later for *Pravda* (Truth). It was in these periodicals that Joseph Djugashvili first became known by his pen name, "Man of Steel," or Stalin.

In 1912 Stalin received special recognition when Lenin broke away completely from the Social Democrats and set up an independent Bolshevik Party. In the new organization Lenin appointed Stalin to the Central Committee.

The very next year, however, Stalin's career was interrupted when he was arrested and sent to Siberia. For Stalin it was an old story. Since 1903 he had been arrested eight times, exiled seven times, and escaped six times. But there was to be no escape on this latest arrest. He was sent to one of the most remote regions of Siberia. And with the arrival of World War I, Stalin had no particular desire to escape. He told his friends he would relax and enjoy his "vacation" in Siberia since escape might result in his being drafted into the armed services. He wanted no part of military service.

The Role of Russia in World War I

It will be recalled that the year 1914 found all the major nations of Europe flexing their military muscles. It was inevitable that the slightest miscalculation in diplomatic relations might turn loose a churning volcano of human destruction. The spark in the powder keg was the assassination of the heir to the Austria-Hungarian throne by a member of a Serbian secret society. This occurred June 28, 1914. Austria-Hungary had been looking for an excuse to take over Serbia, and therefore her troops began marching in. This angered the Tsar because Serbia was on his own calendar of conquest so he declared war on Austria-Hungary. Germany came to the

The Revolution in Russia

defense of Austria-Hungary and declared war on Russia. At the time France was an ally of Russia, so Germany used this as an excuse to declare war on France. This brought England into the War as an ally of France. Thus the machine of war began to roll.

From the point of view of the Russian Tsar, the First World War did not come as any particular surprise. For years he had been busily preparing for it by building a powerful military machine. Nevertheless, the Russian people were not psychologically prepared for war. For nearly a decade there had been a growing tension between the people and the Tsar because he had failed to provide them with the constitutional government which he had promised in the October Manifesto of 1905. Of course, when the people were threatened by attack at the outbreak of World War I, they instinctively banded together in the common defense, and Tsar Nicholas promptly took this as an omen that they would support him loyally throughout the conflict.

But within a few months the strain of war began to tell. By 1915 there were widespread complaints, and by 1916 the Tsar's war machine was sputtering and jerking as it bordered on collapse. In three years Russia had mobilized more than 13,000,000 fighting men, but of these approximately 2,000,000 were killed, approximately 4,000,000 were wounded, and 2,500,000 were taken prisoners. For 24 months the news from the front was consistently bad. Russian armies were pushed out of Galicia, Russian Poland, part of Lithuania, Serbia and the Dardanelles. When the Ottoman Empire entered the war it cut Russian foreign trade to a trickle and thereby isolated Russia from the arms and munitions of her allies. Replacement troops sent to the front were often so ill-equipped that some of them had to pick up their rifles from dead soldiers along the way. Lack of ammunition often forced commanding officers to restrict the infantry to a daily ration of no more than four shells per gun.

At this juncture the Tsar was warned by the British Ambassador that the whole Eastern Front might collapse if things did not improve. Desertions from the Russian Army had reached scandalous proportions and the workers and peasants were threatening revolt. Food shortages were growing because the government was buying grain with paper money which was practically worthless. In the cities the cost of living had tripled while wages had risen only slightly.

But the Tsar could not see any reason for alarm. He had ridden out the revolt of 1905; he intended to do the same now. To demonstrate his complete confidence in the situation, he announced that he would go to the front to cheer the troops with his presence.

What he seemed to forget was the fact that conditions among the people were almost identical with those which precipitated the revolution of 1905. It was far too late to cheer the troops with the Tsar's presence. Already the reign of the Tsar was doomed. Though he did not know it, Nicholas II was going to lose the throne in a matter of months, and shortly thereafter, his life.

LENIN   TROTSKY

VI

How Russia
Became a Communist World Power

The history of the Bolshevik Revolution in Russia and the twenty years that followed might well be called the modern New Testament of Marxism. The Communists present it as their historic proof that the theories of Marx can be carried out successfully. Interestingly enough, however, some of the strongest proof against Communism is also revealed in this same epic of history. All of the pertinent facts have been brought together in this chapter so that the student might judge for himself.

A review of the following questions may help to identify some of the problems which frequently arise when this period of history is discussed:

Who forced the Tsar to abdicate? Where were the Communist leaders at the time? In what way was the Russian revolution of March, 1917, identical with the Russian revolution of 1905?

How did Lenin get back into Russia? Why did the German officers want to help him?

The Naked Communist

When the national elections were held on November 25, 1917, what percentage of the people voted against Lenin's regime?

What was Lenin's motive in taking Russia out of World War I? Why was the treaty he signed with the Germans called "a great catastrophe for Russia"?

What happened when Lenin applied the theories of Marx to the Russian economy? Why did Lenin order the execution of the Tsar and his family?

What were the circumstances which forced Lenin to abandon many of Marx's favorite theories?

Why did Lenin write from his deathbed that he hoped Joseph Stalin would never be allowed to seize power?

What was the purpose of Stalin's first Five-Year Plan?

Why did the Communist Party in Russia try to depose Stalin in December 1932? What saved Stalin?

Why did Stalin execute nearly all the leaders of the Communist Party?

By 1938, what did Stalin say he was ready to do?

The Russian Revolution of March, 1917

It was March 8, 1917, when the swelling spirit of revolution in Russia burst its banks and sent a flood of political indignation streaming after the Tsar and his regime. There was comparatively little violence. The feeling of revolt was so universal that as soon as the signal was given, a quarter of a million demonstrators appeared in the streets of the capital. When the masses of demonstrators had taken over the capital, the revolution automatically swept across the Empire.

This revolution was of vast significance to the entire world. It will be recalled that the spring of 1917 was a highly critical stage of World War I. The United States was just getting into the fight, and France, Britain and Italy were almost exhausted. Because the Western Front was barely holding together against the onslaught of Germany and her Central Powers, the collapse of the Eastern Front with its war machine

Russia as a World Power

of several million Russians could have meant unequivocal disaster for the Allies.

The Russian revolution also held great significance for Germany. The Kaiser knew that if Russia withdrew from the war the large German forces in the East could be transferred to the West. This would have given him a vastly superior force capable of smashing all resistance.

But the people behind the Russian revolution never intended to allow the Eastern Front to collapse. Their revolt against the Tsar was to save Russia, not destroy her. As soon as the Provisional Government had been set up, it announced an all-out program to create a democratic, constitutional form of government and to press for vigorous continuation of the war. This restored hope to the western Allies. The United States, England, France and Italy immediately recognized the new regime and the hearts of free people everywhere went out to the new star of freedom which seemed to be rising over the jubilant people of Russia.

As for the Tsar, it was difficult for him to realize just what had happened. At the beginning of the revolution, Nicholas II categorically refused to admit that his government had disintegrated. When the demonstrations first began he dissolved the Duma (the people's assembly) and ordered the troops to disperse the crowds. Within a week, however, his own ministers were urging him to abdicate since his cause was hopeless. Not until his generals also urged abdication did he finally capitulate. He and his family were then placed under house arrest at the imperial palace outside of Petrograd. Although the people had suffered greatly under his rule, it was not the intention of the Provisional Government to kill the Tsar but to send him and his family to England as soon as war conditions would permit.

With the Tsar taken care of, the Provisional Government then launched into the double task of initiating widespread domestic reforms and, at the same time, reassembling Russia's military strength. At the front the troops began responding by exhibiting a new fighting spirit, and within a month remarkable progress was made in providing domestic reforms on the home front. For the first time in their history, the Russian people had the prospect of a liberal democratic regime to govern them. Prince Lvov, who had joined the people's revolt, confidently declared: "We should consider ourselves the happiest of men, for our generation finds itself in the happiest period of Russian History."

The Destruction of Russia's Plans for a Democracy

The most significant thing about the abdication of the Tsar and the setting up of the people's Provisional Government in Russia, is the simple historical fact that the Bolsheviks, or Communists, had practically nothing to do with it! This revolution had been initiated by the same kind of people as those who started the revolt against the Tsar in 1905. They represented Russia's best people—the liberal aristocrats, the intellectuals, the businessmen, the millions of peasants and the millions of workers. But the Bolshevik leaders were nowhere in sight. Lenin was in exile in Switzerland, Trotsky was in exile in New York and Joseph Stalin was in prison in Siberia. Unfortunately for their future propaganda, the Bolsheviks would never be able to take credit for the revolution of March, 1917, which brought about the overthrow of the Tsar.

It was the generosity of the Provisional Government which permitted the Bolshevik leaders to return. All political prisoners were released from Siberia and all political exiles abroad were invited to come home. When the British heard that Lenin was being allowed to return, they warned their Russian ally that this was a serious mistake. As a matter of fact, the only way Lenin was able to get back into Russia was through the assistance of German agents. The reason for this German cooperation is readily apparent.

The Germans had become alarmed at the prospect of a comeback among the Russian people, and they were looking about for some opportunity to create a spirit of con-

Russia as a World Power

fusion and disunity within Russia's Provisional Government. A brief conversation with Lenin in Switzerland convinced them that he was the man to accomplish it. They, therefore, transported Lenin and his wife and a number of Russian exiles across Germany into Sweden. It was simple for Lenin to proceed immediately to the Russian capital.

When Lenin arrived in Petrograd (the new name for St. Petersburg, later changed to Leningrad), he was welcomed by the crowds of people as a sympathetic colleague of the revolution. A military escort helped him to the roof of an armored car where the vast throng waited expectantly for his commendation of their success. But when Lenin's lip-clipped words began to stream forth, they were far from commendatory. His inflammatory declamation literally amounted to a new declaration of war!

He bitterly denounced the efforts of the Provisional Government to set up a republic. He demanded a Communist dictatorship of the proletariat and called for a struggle to take over the landed estates and immediately subject the Russian people to the economic discipline of full socialism. He denounced all further efforts to continue the war and said an immediate peace with Germany should be negotiated. (He was later accused of trying to take Russia out of the war to repay his obligation to the Germans.)

It was only a matter of weeks until all Russia began hearing the propaganda of the Bolshevik leaders as they echoed the program which Lenin had laid down in his Petrograd speech. Stalin, who was back from Siberia, wrote articles in the new Communist paper urging counterrevolution. Trotsky, who had returned from New York, used his brilliant oratory to incite the labor unions and the military forces to overthrow the Provisional Government. "Peace, Land and Bread," was the Bolshevik slogan. Under the circumstances, this propaganda was bound to have some appeal.

The Provisional Government tried to warn the people against the tempting promises of the Bolsheviks, but the government was beginning to lose prestige because the masses had been demanding reforms faster than the new regime could provide them. This tended to discredit the warning voices of government leaders. In fact, during July, 1917, the outbreaks among the peasants, workers and troops were again beginning to crop out and Lenin concluded that the time to strike was ripe. He assumed that since the Russian Army was desperately involved in trying to hold back the German forces at the front it would not be difficult to overcome the home guard of old men and young boys. However, in this he miscalculated. When Lenin struck out with his Bolshevik forces, the Provisional Government not only suppressed the uprising, but forced Lenin to flee to Finland to save his life.

From then on Lenin proceeded more cautiously. He allowed his subordinates to organize fresh revolutionary forces while he directed the work from abroad. One of these subordinates was Trotsky who had now openly identified himself with the Bolsheviks and was rapidly rising to the number two position. He was assigned the task of organizing the "Red Guard" of armed insurrectionists among the labor unions, the Army, the Navy and the peasants.

By early October, Lenin felt it was safe to return to Russia and on November 7, he made the fateful decision to commence an all-out revolution against the Provisional Government. The revolution began when Lenin ordered Trotsky to have the Red Guard open fire on the Winter Palace and try to seize all other strongholds of the government. Under fierce attack, these centers soon surrendered, and nearly all the officials of the Provisional Government were captured. This was the beginning of what Communist writers call "the ten days that shook the world."

Before many weeks the use of force and violence permitted the Bolsheviks to seize power in nearly all important cities. The regular army could not come to the assistance of the Provisional Government and consequently the people found themselves attacked by the Bolshevik anarchists at a time when they had practically no forces whatever with which to resist. By the middle of December the Bolsheviks were putting down the last remnants of stubborn resistance, although long before this the masses of the people knew that their dreams for a democracy were dead.

Russia Repudiates Communism at the Polls

Before the Provisional Government had been overthrown it had set November 25 as the date for a national election in order to create a people's assembly or congress. The Bolsheviks themselves had made the most noise in demanding this election and therefore Lenin did not dare postpone it even though it came while he was still consolidating his power. The election was held as scheduled.

The results were catastrophic insofar as Lenin's dream of popular backing was concerned. Over 75 per cent of the population voted against him. Obviously this meant that the people's elected representatives would be opposed to the Bolshevik regime; therefore when these representatives convened on January 18, 1918, Lenin had already decided what to do.

He demanded that the people's congress turn over all their legislative functions to the Bolshevik-controlled "Congress of the Soviets" and then vote to dissolve themselves. This, of course, was so illegal and ridiculous, that they would not hear of it. Lenin therefore invoked his "means of last resort"—force. Early the next morning, armed guards entered the meeting hall and ordered the delegates to adjourn. As the delegates looked at the bristling rifles, they knew there was no alternative. Reluctantly, they left. This illegal act sounded the death knell for democracy in Russia. Nevertheless, Lenin knew this act of ruthless expediency had given his enemies potent propaganda to discredit him. It was resolved that all future coups by Red forces would provide the illusion of being achieved through normal democratic processes. For the moment, however, the damage was done. The Communists had overthrown the nearest thing to representative government the

Russians had ever known. Now the people would learn something about the Dictatorship of the Proletariat.

Lenin Takes Russia Out of the War

It was one of Lenin's first ambitions to wipe out the Eastern Front and take Russia out of the war. In addition to fulfilling any promises he might have made to the Germans, Lenin had a highly important reason of his own for this action. He believed that the strain of the war would make it possible to set off a series of Communist revolutions in every major capitalist nation. Therefore, he wanted to disentangle Russia from the conflict in order to get her prepared for her role as the "Motherland of Communism." This would give him a chance to consolidate his power in Russia and then to supervise the revolutions in the war-weary capitalist nations so as to bring the whole world under the dictatorship of the proletariat within a very short time.

However, getting Russia out of the war did not prove to be an easy task. For months the Russian armies had been retreating in the face of superior military forces. Consequently, when Lenin finally obtained an armistice with the Central Powers and offered to negotiate a peaceful settlement, they treated him as the defeated leader of a conquered nation. The demands which Germany made upon Russia were outrageous. Lenin hesitated. To further persuade him, the Germans marched even deeper into Russian territory, and were soon threatening the very precincts of Petrograd. Lenin hurriedly moved his government to Moscow and then did something which was deeply humiliating to a Communist revolutionary; he appealed to Russia's old capitalist allies—France, England and the United States—for help.

He was further humiliated when these countries completely ignored him. Lenin had destroyed the balance of the Allied defense when he pulled the Russian armies out of the conflict. Now these nations were so busy preparing to defend

Russia as a World Power

themselves against the all-out German offensive being planned for the spring that they had neither the desire nor the means to help Lenin out of his self-inflicted predicament.

Like the shrewd political gambler that he was, Lenin now weighed his chances for survival in the balance and decided to force his own party to support him in accepting the indecent demands of the Central Powers. Even the iron-disciplined members of the ruling committee of the Bolshevik Party balked at Lenin's proposal, but, nevertheless, he finally forced it through with a vote of seven to four.

As a result, a settlement was signed between Russia and the Central Powers on March 3, 1918, which has become known as the notorious treaty of Brest-Litovsk.

In it, Lenin accepted terms which took from the Russian Empire 62,000,000 people, 1,267,000 square miles of her arable lands, 26 per cent of her railroads, 33 per cent of her factories, 75 per cent of her coal mines and 75 per cent of her iron mines. In addition to this, Lenin promised that Russia would pay the Central Powers 1½ billion dollars in indemnities!

Such was to be the end of a war that had cost the Russian people 8½ million casualties.

The First Attempt to Communize Russia

With Russia out of the war, Lenin now felt sufficient confidence to subordinate the whole Russian economy to the theories of Communism. He confiscated all industry from private owners and set it up under government operation. He seized all land which belonged to the aristocracy, the Tsar and the church. He also seized all the livestock and implements which ordinarily served this land. He then abolished wages and replaced them with direct payment "in kind." This saddled Russia with a sluggish and primitive barter system. He ordered all domestic goods to be rationed among the people according to their class. For example, a worker or soldier was allocated thirty-five pounds of bread, while a nonworker, such as a manager, received only twelve. Lenin also made all labor subject to mobilization. People with technical skills could be compelled to accept any work assigned to them. The selling of retail goods was taken over by the government.

As for the peasants, Lenin distributed the confiscated land to them, but required them to work the land without hiring any help and without selling any of the produce. It was all to go to the government. Furthermore, the land could not be sold, leased nor mortgaged.

In March, 1918, the Bolsheviks changed their name to the "Russian Communist Party."

But from the very beginning the Russian people did not take well to the new order. Without any personal incentive among the workers, production on the farm and in the factory dwindled to a trickle. The factories were soon down to 13 per cent of what they had been producing before the war started, and the farmers cut their production in half. Black markets began to flourish. Workers often stole goods from the factories to exchange for food which the peasants secretly withheld from the government. Before long, the peasants were holding back more than one-third of their crops.

As might have been expected, this decomposition of the Russian economy brought down upon the heads of the people all the wrath and frustration of the Bolshevik leaders. Every terror method known was used to force the people to produce. This led to retaliation.

During the summer of 1918, violent civil war broke out as the "White Guard" vowed they would overthrow the Reds and free the Russian people. The western Allied Nations, though hard-pressed themselves, were sympathetic to this movement and sent supplies, equipment and even what troops they could spare to help release the Russian people from the Bolshevik grip.

Lenin knew this was a crisis of the highest order. He therefore decided to strike back in three different directions simultaneously. To resist organized military groups, he authorized Trotsky to forcibly mobilize a Red Army which ultimately totaled five million. To resist the people's anti-Bolshevik sentiment and refusal to work, he organized the

Russia as a World Power

secret police or Cheka. This body could investigate, arrest, adjudicate and execute suspected persons. Authorities state that during the civil war, literally tens of thousands went down before its firing squads. Finally, Lenin struck out at the Tsar. To prevent any possibility of a new monarchial party being developed, he had the Tsar, the Empress, their children and all their retainers shot to death at Yekaterinburg and their bodies completely destroyed. This mass assassination occurred July 16, 1918.

Six weeks later the scalding vengeance of the White Russians nearly cost Lenin his life. The Bolshevik aristocracy was caught under vulnerable circumstances and a volley of rifle fire assassinated the Cheka chief and seriously wounded Lenin. To avenge itself, the Cheka summarily executed 500 persons.

When the end of World War I came on November 11, 1918, it had little effect on the situation in Russia. The civil war continued with even greater violence, and the Bolsheviks redoubled their efforts to communize Russia. Lenin continued to set up Soviets or workers' councils, in every part of the empire, and these Soviets in turn sent delegates to the supreme Soviet at the capital. Through the channels of this Bolshevik-dominated labor-union empire, Lenin carried out his policies. Behind the Soviets stood the enforcing power of the Red Army, and the terror of the Cheka secret police.

In spite of all these coercive methods, however, Lenin eventually discovered he was fighting a losing battle. For a while he took courage from the fact that United States, England, France and Japan began withdrawing their troops and supplies under the League of Nations policy of "self-determination for all peoples," but the ferocious fighting of the White Russians continued.

The breaking point for Lenin came in 1921-22 when the economic inefficiency of the Bolshevik regime was compounded by a disastrous famine. There was a complete crop failure along the Volga—the bread basket of Russia. Nikolaus Basseches wrote: "No one who was ever in that famine area, no one who saw those starving and brutalized people, will ever forget the spectacle. Cannibalism was common. The despairing people crept about, emaciated, like brown mummies. . . . When those hordes fell upon an unprepared village, they were apt to massacre every living person."

Packs of wild, orphaned children roamed like hungry wolves through cities and country sides. It is estimated that during the year 1922, over 33 million Russians were starving, and 5 million died. The people of the United States were so shocked by this almost inconceivable amount of human suffering that they raised funds for the Hoover Commission to feed over 10 million Russians during 1922.

The End of a Communist Dream

Even before this disaster, however, Lenin had forced himself to admit that he had assigned his country an impossible task. His Bolshevik revolution had not brought peace to Russia, but a terrible civil war in which 28 million Russians had lost their lives. The principles of socialism which Lenin had forced upon the people had not brought increased production as Marx had promised, but had reduced production to a point where even in normal times it would not adequately clothe nor feed half the people.

It was under these circumstances and in the light of these facts that Lenin acknowledged defeat and ordered a retreat. As early as 1921 he announced that there would be a "New Economic Program"—afterwards referred to as the NEP.

This humiliating reversal of policy was adopted by the Communists to keep from being dethroned. Lenin brought back the payment of wages to workers, which immediately generated the circulation of money in place of the old barter system. In place of the government trading centers, he allowed private concerns to begin buying and selling so that in less than a year three-fourths of all retail distribution was back in private hands. He violated the sanctity of Marx's memory by even encouraging the peasants to lease additional land and hire other peasants to work for them. He also tried to encourage private initiative by promising the peasants they could sell most of their grain on the open market instead of having it seized by agents of the government as in the past.

In merely a matter of months, the pauperism and starvation of the old Communist economy began to disappear. The law of supply and demand began to have its effect so that private initiative commenced to provide what the people needed. In the cities an air of relative prosperity rapidly returned to the bleak streets and empty shops.

The Rise of Stalin to Power

Lenin barely lived long enough to see the New Economic Program go into effect. He had his first stroke in 1922, and died January 20, 1924. As Lenin saw the end drawing near, he became alarmed over the possibility of Joseph Stalin becoming his successor. For many years Lenin had been using Stalin to perform tasks requiring the most ruthless methods, but now he became fearful of what might happen if Stalin used these same methods to take over the Communist Party.

On December 25, 1923, while lying speechless and half-paralyzed on his deathbed, Lenin wrote the following dramatic appeal to the members of the Politiburo (the supreme governing council of the Communist Party, and hence, of all Russia):

"Stalin is too rude, and this fault, entirely supportable in relations among us Communists, becomes insupportable in the office of the General Secretary. Therefore, I propose to the comrades to find a way to remove Stalin from that position and appoint to it another man who in all respects differs from Stalin . . . namely, more patient, more loyal, more polite, and more attentive to comrades, less capricious, etc. This circumstance may seem an insignificant trifle, but I think that from the point of view of preventing a split, and from the point of view of the relation between Stalin and Trotsky . . . it is not a trifle, or it is such a trifle as may acquire decisive significance."

Time proved that Lenin knew whereof he spoke. Stalin's whole attitude toward life may be caught in a statement which he later made as he was rising to power: "To choose one's victim, to prepare one's plans minutely, to stake an implacable vengeance, and then go to bed . . . there is nothing sweeter in the world."

By 1927 Stalin had achieved precisely what Lenin feared he might—the outright control of the Russian Empire. He had not only unseated Trotsky, but had driven from the arena every formidable source of opposition. He had attained such complete victory in the battle for the control of world Communism that he now felt strong enough to try and satisfy one of his greatest ambitions. He determined to make a second attempt to communize Russia.

The First Five-Year Plan

The first Five-Year Plan began in 1928. It was aimed at wiping out the prosperous independence of businessmen and the peasant farmers who had been thriving during the New Economic Program. Once again there was widespread confiscation of property, and once again the secret police began executing masses of Russians who resisted. Stalin was determined that the Russian economy should be immediately forced into the confines of theoretical socialism and demonstrate to the world that it could out-produce and out-distribute the capitalistic industrial nations, such as the United States and Great Britain. Within weeks, however, the Five-Year-Plan had wiped out the warm glow of prosperity and comparative abundance which Russia had known under the NEP. Rationing was necessary and the hated revolutionary "starvation bread" made of birch bark had to be reintroduced.

The basic theme of the Five-Year-Plan was collectivized industry and collectivized agriculture. Stalin knew he would get resistance from the prosperous peasants (called Kulaks) and he therefore ordered a complete genocidal liquidation of the Kulaks as a class. Some of the Kulaks destroyed all their

Russia as a World Power

property, burned their homes, slaughtered their cattle and fled toward the Caucasus mountains, but most of them were caught or died on the way. Official reports tell how rebellious villages were leveled to the ground by artillery fire and in one area of the Don region, 50,000 men, women and children were destroyed, leaving a vestige of only 2,000 people who were shipped off to central Asia, while the land which they had cultivated for generations was taken over for collectivized farming.

Stalin also included in the Five-Year-Plan an acceleration of the Communist fight against religion. By 1930 the Union of Militant Atheists had an active membership of two-and-one-half million. Churches and cathedrals were turned into secular buildings. The Christmas festival was prohibited and the buying and selling of Christmas trees was a criminal offense. Sunday was eliminated as a day of worship, and workers were required to rotate their days off so that industry would continue day and night, seven days a week.

Stalin also attempted to follow Engel's suggestion to break up the family. All the theories of Marx and Engels were coming to life under the dictatorship of Joseph Stalin.

By 1930 Stalin was beginning to realize that he may have pressed the long-suffering endurance of the people too far. He therefore came forth with an expression of deep anguish for the suffering masses. He blamed all the troubles on the government officers who, in their zeal, were overshooting the mark and imposing unreasonable demands upon the people, particularly the peasants. He wrote as though he had just heard of the terrible misery which had overtaken the people. But, having cleared himself for the record, Stalin then went firmly ahead with terror tactics which made conditions more frightful than ever.

The Communist Crisis of 1932-33

By 1932 the situation had reached a crisis. The Russian people had suffered starvation, mass executions, ruthless liquidation of the Kulak class, suppression of all private enterprise, deportations to Siberia and long sentences to forced labor camps. The crimes against humanity were on a scale comparable to the Nazi atrocities subsequently committed at Dachau, Buchenwald, and Belsen.

In a recent biography of Stalin, Nikolaus Basseches states that during 1932 the leaders of the Communist Party knew they would have to dethrone Stalin or face revolution. Even the army was about to revolt. The Politburo held a secret meeting in December and Stalin made a number of proposals to further suppress the people, but this time even these men who owed their political existence to Stalin voted him down flatly. It is reported that Stalin was so amazed by this display of opposition that he admitted to Molotov that perhaps he should accept defeat and resign. Molotov, however, is said to have encouraged him to hold on a little longer to see if conditions might not improve.

U.S. Recognition of Communist Russia Comes at a Critical Time

Molotov was right. Future circumstances did offer Stalin a solution to his crisis. The first thing that happened was Hitler's rise to power in January, 1933. Hitler's strong anti-Communist policies led many Russians to believe that there might be a war between Russia and Germany, and they therefore began to forget their resentment against Stalin because of their worry over Hitler. The second factor which helped Stalin was the recognition of his Communist regime by the great leader of world capitalism—the United States. This last factor was a singular development.

For sixteen years the United States had refused to recognize Russia, and the U.S. Secretaries of State during that period were very precise in explaining why. For example, in 1923 Secretary Charles E. Hughes declared: "There can be no question of the sincere friendliness of the American

Russia as a World Power

people toward the Russian people. And there is for this very reason a strong desire that nothing should be done (such as granting recognition) to place the seal of approval on the tyrannical measures that have been adopted in Russia, or to take any action which might retard the gradual reassertion of the Russian people of their right to live in freedom."

Many such statements over a period of years placed Stalin on notice that if the United States were to recognize Russia, it would require many changes in Communist policies and Communist tactics. Therefore, early in 1933, when Stalin sent his old comrade in arms, Maxim Litvinov, to Washington to negotiate for U.S. recognition, he knew what the terms would have to be. In written statements, Litvinov promised that henceforth the U.S.S.R. would not attempt to interfere in the internal affairs of the United States; he said the U.S.S.R. would not allow its officials to use propaganda or agitate for the overthrow of the United States Government, and furthermore, he promised that the U.S.S.R. would not permit any group to organize in Russia for the purpose of agitating for the overthrow of the United States Government. At the moment it looked as though the Communists were going to repudiate the Communist International and world revolution. On the basis of these solemn promises by an official of the Russian government, recognition was extended by the United States to the U.S.S.R. late in 1933. Such were the circumstances which led the U.S. to change its policy toward Communist Russia from one of co-REsistance to co-EXistence.

But within ten months, officials of the United States knew this nation had been defrauded. William C. Bullitt, the first U.S. ambassador, reported from Moscow that world revolution was on the tongue of every Soviet official. Plans were already under way for the Communist International (an organization to promote world revolution) to hold its seventh conference in Russia, even though this violated both the letter and the spirit of the promises made by Litvinov. The U.S. vigorously protested to Litvinov, but he merely shrugged his shoulders and said the U.S.S.R. had absolutely no "obligations of any kind with regard to the Communist International." It was obvious that conditions in Russia had changed. Stalin once more felt secure in his dictatorship. The prestige of U.S. recogniton had served its purpose, and the promises of the U.S.S.R. were now scraps of paper.

When the Seventh World Congress of the Communist International convened, the United States was denounced along with all other capitalistic countries, and plans were openly advocated for the violent overthrow of the U.S. Government. In fact, as we shall see in the next chapter, at the very time Litvinov was promising not to interfere in the domestic affairs of the United States, Soviet intelligence officers were busy in Washington setting up elaborate spy rings in various agencies of the government.

There were political authorities who believe the United States should have broken off diplomatic relations with the Soviets the very moment it was discovered that the Communist leaders were brazenly violating their promises. But this did not happen. Diplomatic strategists at the time advocated that we treat the Bolsheviks like big blustering boys and overlook their delinquencies. They further rationalized that at least we would have a listening post in Russia by maintaining an ambassador there. It was on the basis of this recommendation that the U.S. policy of coexistence fell another notch. Our diplomats decided to eat humble pie made out of apathetic tolerance for broken promises and abject submissiveness to Communist abuse. This boosted Stalin's political stock in Russia tremendously.

Joseph Stalin's Return to Power

When Stalin saw the outward signs of public resentment in Russia disappearing, he felt he could once more assume a bolder front. But a deep-seated hatred continued to fester in the minds of the Communist Party leaders. They secretly admitted among themselves that Stalin must be removed "for the good of the Party." Therefore, the top revolutionaries of

Russia as a World Power

Russia surreptitiously combined their ideas on how best to do away with Stalin. Finally, they decided the best plan was to first destroy those immediately around him and then effect a coup. The initial attempt was against Sergei Kirov—a favorite of the Man of Steel who had been officially designated by the Politburo as Stalin's successor.

Kirov was shot and killed gangster style December 1, 1934. It is said that nothing had ever so deeply affected Stalin as this murder. It was perfectly clear to him what his enemies were up to and he therefore struck back with a viciously effective blow. Lists were published of more than one thousand persons selected from every district in Russia and all these were summarily shot.

Stalin then directed the secret police to plunge into every devious crevice of the party and dig and prod until they had found out who was behind the murder of Kirov. This was not difficult. Even many of the most insignificant members of the Party were aware that some of the biggest names in Russia were involved in the conspiracy. To save their own skins they quickly confessed. Stalin ordered the arrest of every suspect together with their families, associates, friends and even their correspondents.

Tens of thousands went down before firing squads in secret executions while the more prominent officials were exhibited before the world at Stalin's famous purge trials. In these trials Stalin's former comrades of the revolution sought to win mercy for their families by confessing in the most self-degrading language to all the crimes of which they were accused. But it gained them nothing. The list of those publicly condemned with their families and friends is described by Nikolaus Basseches as involving "not only ex-leaders of the party . . . but also fully a dozen members of the Government who were still in office, and the supreme commander of the army, the Chief of Staff, almost all the army commanders, and in addition a considerable number of senior officers; the Minister of Police and the highest police officials; the Deputy People's Commissar for Foreign Affairs, almost all the ambassadors and ministers representing the Soviet Union abroad, almost the whole of the diplomatic staff at the Ministry in Moscow; and also highly placed judges and members of the governments of the federal republics."

Even Whittaker Chambers who was an American Communist spy at the time suspected that a horrible crime against humanity was being enacted in Russia. He later wrote: "The great purge was in the most literal sense a massacre. . . . This great massacre, probably the greatest in history was deliberately planned and executed. . . . Those killed have been estimated from several hundred thousand to several million men and women. The process took about three years, 1935-1938."

Stalin Creates a New Class

At the very end of the process came the execution of the executioners. Since time immemorial it has been a favorite trick of political pirates and brigands to use a hand-picked band of followers to commit murder and then murder the murderers to cover up the original crime. Stalin followed the same procedure. He selected a pathological personality named Yeshov to set up the secret police machinery for the purge and then drew certain judges into the conspiracy. Both police and judges faithfully performed their miserable missions on the assumption that they were basking in the radiant light of Stalin's affection and trust.

Only when they found themselves being flung into dirty dungeons or facing firing squads did they realize that Stalin's supposed affection and trust was nothing but the figment of their own imaginations. By the hundreds, the chiefs of secret police units, the heads of forced labor camps and the examining judges who had conducted the purge in every district of the U.S.S.R. found themselves sharing the fate of their victims.

Even Yeshov, whose unbalanced mind had not only heaped cruelty and violence on Stalin's enemies but upon their wives and children as well, now faced extinction. He was

Russia as a World Power

swept up in the great final dragnet of terror and disappeared into oblivion along with those who had served under him.

Once Stalin had skirted the brink of political disaster he immediately determined to consolidate his power by the innovation of a Communist spoils system. Prior to this time, the Communist leaders had recognized only two classes—the workers and the peasants. Stalin now decided to give recognition to a new class—the Communist bureaucracy or official class. He bestowed special favors on them by allowing them to shop in "closed" distribution centers. These centers had great quantities of items which were never distributed to the workers. And Stalin arranged it so that his party appointees received other favors—dwellings, luxuries, special holidays, special educational opportunities for their children. This was Stalin's way of building a new Communist Party with members who owed absolute allegiance to him.

He likewise protected them in the new constitution which he presented to the Congress of Soviets in 1936. It provided for the protection of "occupational property." Thus the official class could not be deprived of wages, articles of consumption, houses nor savings. It even provided that this "occupational property" could be bequeathed. Substantial estates could, therefore, be accumulated by the official class and passed on to a selected beneficiary. These gifts of inheritance (which Communist propaganda had denounced with vehemence for over a century) could also be given to non-relations and in any amount without restrictions.

To further illustrate the whole change in Stalin's attitude, he adopted a series of "reforms" which were purely capitalistic in nature. These included payment of interest on savings, the issuing of bonds to which premiums were attached and the legalizing of a wider disparity in wages. A laborer, for example, might receive only one hundred rubles a month while a member of the official class could now get as high as six thousand rubles per month!

All of this clearly illustrated one simple fact concerning developments in Russia. The "have nots" of yesterday had taken possession of the realm. Their policy was likewise simple: to stay in power permanently and enjoy the spoils of their conquest.

By 1938 Stalin was supremely confident of his position. He announced that the regime had no enemies left inside of Russia, and there was no longer a need for terrorism or suppression. He made it clear, however, that there must be undeviating prosecution of the Communist program abroad and that the acts of terrorism against the outer world of capitalism should be accepted as necessary and unavoidable.

Russia was now asserting herself as a world power. Stalin was clearly manifesting a determinaton to enter the next phase of his dictatorship—the expansion of world Communism

VII

Communism in the United States

We have now traced the history of Russian Communism up to 1938. In order to appreciate what happened after 1938 it is necessary to understand the historical development of Communism in the United States.

The conquest of the United States by Marxist forces has been an important part of the plan of Communist leaders for many years: "First we will take Eastern Europe; then the masses of Asia. Then we will encircle the United States of America which will be the last bastion of Capitalism. We will not have to attack it; it will fall like an over-ripe fruit into our hands." This clearly reflects the Marxist intent to overthrow the United States by internal subversion.

It is sometimes difficult for us to realize how enthusiastically encouraged the Communist leaders have frequently felt toward the progress of their program in the United States. The answers to the following questions will indicate why:

Have Americans who embraced Communism overlooked a vigorous warning from the Pilgrim Fathers? Why are the Pilgrim Fathers described as having practiced Communism under "the most favorable circumstances"? What were the results?

How soon after the Russian Revolution was Communism launched in the United States? How extensive was the first wave of Communist violence?

What was William Z. Foster's testimony under oath concerning a Communist revolution in the United States?

Why was Whittaker Chambers able to furnish so many details concerning Communism in the United States? In June, 1932, Chambers was asked to pay the full price of being a Communist—what was it? How did Chambers' small daughter influence him to abandon Communism?

What was the background of Elizabeth Bentley? How did she happen to become the Communist "wife" of a man she did not even know?

How did Communists who were employed as Russian spies successfully clear themselves?

How would you expect the Communist leaders in Russia to react as they reviewed the U.S. list of top-level government employees who were risking imprisonment and disgrace to commit espionage and otherwise carry out the orders of the Soviet leaders?

American Founding Fathers Try Communism

One of the forgotten lessons of U.S. history is the fact that the American founding fathers tried Communism before they tried capitalistic free enterprise.

In 1620 when the Pilgrim Fathers landed at Plymouth, they had already determined to establish a Communist colony. In many ways this communal society was set up under the most favorable circumstances. First of all, they were isolated from outside help and were desperately motivated to make the plan work in order to survive. Secondly, they had a select group of religious men and women who enjoyed a cooperative, fraternal feeling toward one another. The Pilgrims

Communism in the United States

launched their Communist community with the most hopeful expectations. Governor William Bradford has left us a remarkable account of what happened. The Governor reports:

"This community . . . was found to breed much confusion and discontent and retard much employment that would have been to their benefit and comfort. For the young men that were most able and fit for labor and service did repine that they should spend their time and strength to work for other men's wives and children without any recompense. The strong . . . had no more in division of victuals and clothes than he that was weak and not able to do a quarter the other could; this was thought an injustice . . . and for men's wives to be commanded[1] to do service for other men, as dressing their meat, washing their clothes, etc., they deemed it a kind of slavery, neither could many husbands well brook it."

But the colonists would have continued to endure Communism if it had only been productive. The thing which worried Governor Bradford was the fact that the total amount of production under this communal arrangement was so low that the colonists were faced with starvation. Therefore, he says:

"At length, after much debate . . . the governor, gave way that they should set corn every man for his own purpose, and in that regard *trust to themselves* . . . and so assigned to every family a parcel of land according to the proportion of their number."

Once a family was given land and corn they had to plant, cultivate and harvest it or suffer the consequences. The Governor wanted the people to continue living together as a society of friends but communal production was to be replaced by private, free enterprise production. After one year the Governor was able to say:

"This had very good success; for it made all hands very industrious, so that *much more corn was planted than otherwise would have been.* . . . The women now went willing into the fields, and took their little ones with them to set corn,

---

[1] *Note that even in a Christian brotherhood, Communism cannot be practiced without setting up a dictatorship.*

which before would allege weakness and inability; whom to have compelled would have been thought great tyranny and oppression."

The Pilgrim fathers had discovered the great human secret that a man will compel himself to go ever so much farther than he will permit anyone else to compel him to go. As Governor Bradford thought about their efforts to live in a Communist society, he wrote down this conclusion:

"The experience that was had in this common cause and condition, tried sundrie years, and that amongst godly and sober men, may well evince the vanity of that conceit of Plato and other ancients—applauded by some in later times—that the taking away of property, and bringing it into a commonwealth, would make them happy and flourishing; as if they were wiser than God."[2]

It becomes apparent that Governor Bradford concluded that Communism is not only inefficient but that it is unnatural and in violation of the laws of God. This may raise a question in the minds of some students who have heard that Communism provides the most ideal means of practicing the basic principles of Christianity. Elsewhere, we have considered the historical background of this problem.[3]

It is interesting that after the Pilgrim Fathers tried Communism they abandoned it in favor of a free enterprise type of capitalism which, over the centuries, has become more highly developed in the United States than in any other nation. In its earliest stages this system was described as a heartless, selfish institution, but economists have pointed out that after a slow and painful evolution it has finally developed into a social-economic tool which has thus far produced more wealth and distributed it more uniformly among the people of this land than any system modern men have tried.[4] The evolutionary process of further improving and further

---

[2] *Bradford, William,* "HISTORY OF PLYMOUTH," *pp. 160-162.*
[3] *For a discussion of this question, see the essay,* "DID THE EARLY CHRISTIANS PRACTICE COMMUNISM?" *page 343.*
[4] *For a discussion of this subject, see the essay,* "WHAT IS FREE-ENTERPRISE CAPITALISM?" *page 327.*

Communism in the United States

adapting capitalism to the needs of a highly industrialized society is still going on.

Marxism Comes to the United States

When the Bolshevik Revolution took place in Russia in 1917, it held a particular interest for a certain group of Americans. This was the left wing faction of the Socialist Party. For years, the Socialists had been trying to get the Federal Government to take over all major industries and socialize the country, but this attempt at peaceful legislative reform had failed. Then suddenly, in November, 1917, these people heard that the Russian Bolsheviks had used revolutionary violence to seize power and had thereafter socialized their country overnight. This was promptly accepted by the left wing Socialists as the formula for America. They immediately determined to form a Communist party and use violent revolutionary activity to sovietize America at the earliest possible date. They were greatly encouraged in this venture by a man named John Reed, a journalist, who had recently returned from Russia with glowing enthusiasm for the revolution and world Communism.

This group made contact with Moscow and was invited to send delegates to Russia in March, 1919, to help form the Third International (copied after Marx's First International to promote world revolution). When they returned home they started their campaign. John Reed used the columns of the "New York Communist" to agitate the workers to revolt. The Communist ranks were swelled by members of the old I.W.W. (International Workers of the World) who gravitated to the new movement with suggestions that the party members learn to use the techniques of sabotage and violence which the I.W.W. had employed during World War I.

Further encouragement came to the movement when the Russian Communist Party sent over an official representative of the Soviet Government to help organize a full-fledged Bolshevik program. His name was C. A. Martens. He brought

The Naked Communist

136 along substantial quantities of money to spend in building cells inside the American labor unions and the U.S. armed forces. It was not enough that the Communists should save the proletariat of Russia; Comrade Martens assured all who heard him that his mission from Moscow was to free the downtrodden workers of capitalistic America. As the movement progressed, American representatives were sent to Russia to get permission to set up the "Communist Labor Party of the United States" as a branch of the Russian-sponsored Communist International (organization for world revolution). Later the word "Labor" was dropped.

The officers of the new Communist Party signed the "Twenty-one Conditions of Admission" which were to embarrass them many years later when the Party was ordered to register in 1952 as an agency under the control of the Soviet Union.

Here are typical commitments from the "Twenty-one Conditions of Admission":

"The Communist Party (of the USA) must carry on a clear-cut program of propaganda for the hindering of the transportation of munitions of war to the enemies of the Soviet Republic."

"The program (of the U.S. Communist Party) must be sanctioned by the regular congress of the Communist International."

"All decisions of the Communist International . . . are binding upon all parties belonging to the Communist International (which would include the U.S. Communist Party)."

"The duty of spreading Communist ideas includes the special obligation to carry on a vigorous and systematic propaganda in the Army. Where this agitation is forbidden by exceptional laws, it is to be carried on illegally."

"Every party wishing to belong to the Communist International must systematically and persistently develop a Communist agitation within the trade-unions."

It was basic commitments such as these which led the U.S. Subversive Activities Control Board to make the following statement in 1953 after extended hearings:

Communism in the United States

"We find upon the whole record that the evidence preponderantly establishes that Respondent's leaders (leaders of the Communist Party, USA) and its members consider the allegiance they owe to the United States as subordinate to their loyalty and obligations to the Soviet Union."[5]

The First Wave of Communist Violence Strikes the United States

Beginning April 28, 1919, a series of 36 bombs were discovered in the mails addressed to such persons as the Attorney General, Justice Holmes of the Supreme Court, J. P. Morgan, John D. Rockefeller and similar persons of prominence. One of the bombs got through to the home of Senator Hardwick who had been trying to shut off the migration of Bolsheviks to the U.S. A servant opened the package and the bomb exploded, blowing off her hands.

On September 16, 1920, a large bomb was carried in a horse-drawn carriage to the corner of Broad and Wall Streets in New York City—the vortex of American capitalism. The vehicle was brought to a halt across the street from the unostentatious three-story limestone building occupied by the firm of J. P. Morgan and Company.

Suddenly a great roar went up from the carriage, and blue-white flame shot into the sky. The bomb exploded with tremendous violence, killing thirty people outright and injuring hundreds more. It wrecked the interior of the Morgan offices, smashed windows for blocks around and shot an iron slug through a window on the thirty-fourth floor of the Equitable Building.

These acts of murder and violence created a blistering resentment against the Bolsheviks in every part of the United States. Occasionally counter-violence was used by aroused citizens in retaliation. Numerous arrests were made by the

---

[5] *Final Report of the Subversive Activities Control Board, April 20, 1953, p. 208.*

The Naked Communist

Attorney General and finally a whole shipload of Bolshevik aliens and Communist leaders were deported to Russia via Finland on the S. S. Buford. Aboard the boat was the notorious Emma Goldman whose anarchist speeches a quarter of a century earlier had induced Leon Czolgosz to assassinate President McKinley. Little did she know that in twenty-four months she would not only repudiate Lenin and his Bolsheviks but that by 1940 her great last hope would be to die in the United States.

William Z. Foster Launches the Communist Labor Union Drive

Few names among Communist leaders today are better known to the American public than the name of William Z. Foster. He was a charter member of the party in the United States and was the person designated by the party to take over the U.S. labor unions. Most of the money for the campaign came from Moscow where the Profintern (Red International of Trade Unions) had received $1,000,000 from the Soviet Government to help spread Communism in the labor unions of other nations.

Foster's drive hit the labor front soon after the armistice, when the workers were already in a state of agitation resulting from wartime conditions. Foster found little difficulty in sparking strikes in several important industries and even where he had nothing to do with a strike he was often given the credit. As a result, many people began to identify their pro-labor sympathies with Communism without completely realizing it. The coal miners were believed to have come under Foster's influence when they voted enthusiastically to have the coal industry nationalized and a similar label seemed to attach itself to the steel strike because Foster was very much in evidence as an agitator and promoter of the strike. Many people knew that both the coal miners and the steel workers had many legitimate reasons for striking and to them

Communism in the United States

the fact that Foster and his Communist associates seized this opportunity to worm their way into the labor movement seemed of little importance.

But William Z. Foster never really concealed his fundamental ambition to overthrow the United States government by violence and subordinate the American laborer (as well as every other American) to the mandates of a Communist dictatorship copied after the Russian pattern. In fact, Mr. Foster visualized himself as the coming dictator. He was the Communist candidate for President on two occasions and wrote a book called *Toward Soviet America*, telling just how the Communists would take over.

When a Congressional committee placed him under oath and asked him about Communism, he was voluble and frank:

THE CHAIRMAN: "Do the Communists in this country advocate world revolution?"

MR. FOSTER: "Yes."

THE CHAIRMAN: "Do they (the Communists) advocate revolution in this country?"

MR. FOSTER: "I have stated that the Communists advocate abolition of the capitalist system in this country and every other country. . . ."

THE CHAIRMAN: "Now, are the Communists in this country opposed to our republican form of government?"

MR. FOSTER: "The capitalist Democracy—most assuredly."

THE CHAIRMAN: "What you advocate is a change of our republican form of government and the substituting of the soviet form of government?"

MR. FOSTER: "I have stated that a number of times."

THE CHAIRMAN: "Now, if I understand you, the workers in this country look upon the Soviet Union as their country; is that right?"

MR. FOSTER: "The more advanced workers do."

THE CHAIRMAN: "They look upon the Soviet flag as their flag?"

MR. FOSTER: "The workers of this country and the workers of every country have only one flag and that is the red flag."

The Naked Communist

THE CHAIRMAN: ". . . If they had to choose between the red flag and the American flag, I take it from you that you would choose the red flag, is that correct?"

MR. FOSTER: "I have stated my answer."

THE CHAIRMAN: "I don't want to force you to answer if it embarrasses you, Mr. Foster."

MR. FOSTER: "It does not embarrass me at all. I stated very clearly the red flag is the flag of the revolutionary class, and we are part of the revolutionary class."[6]

From 1921 to 1924, members of the Communist Party sought to avoid arrest by operating underground, but when the wartime emergency acts were repealed the Communist leaders gradually surfaced again and continued their campaign for a revolution to overthrow the United States government.

However, during the next few years the general psychology of the country was not particularly security conscious. It was an era of fads, frivolity and general post-war frenzy. The national scene was entirely too prosperous and intoxicating to worry about a few fanatic-minded men who wanted to rule the world. Somehow or other the word "Communist" began to have a far-away flavor, and people jokingly spoke of the former years of bomb-throwing, strikes, arrests and deportations as the days of "the great Red scare."

However, a fertile field for future Communist conquests was being developed among the very people who feared it least. The United States was going sophisticated in an atmosphere of half-baked intellectualism. Pedestals of the past crumbled to the cry of scandal and the rattling of closeted skeletons. An age of daring debunking had arrived. At the time few people realized that the economic and spiritual collapse toward which the nation was drifting would produce an intellectual revolt that would permit the agents of Communism to propel themselves into every echelon of American society—including some of the highest offices of the United States Government.

This brings us to the story of Whittaker Chambers. Be-

---

[6] *Excerpts from the report of the House Committee on Un-American Activities to the 76th Congress, January 3, 1939, pp. 18-21.*

Communism in the United States

cause Chambers was converted to Communism during this period and worked himself up to the highest levels of intrigue as a leader of Russian espionage, his disclosures give a sweeping panoramic picture of the growth of Communism in the United States from 1925-1938.

The Growth of U.S. Communism as Seen by Whittaker Chambers

A brief review of Whittaker Chambers' conversion to Communism will perhaps reveal an evolutionary pattern which was followed by a considerable number of young American intellectuals during the Nineteen-Twenties and early Thirties.

Whittaker Chambers was raised on Long Island not far from suburban New York. In the Chambers home was an impersonal and disinterested father (a newspaper illustrator), an over-loving and therefore overbearing mother (who had formerly been an actress), an insane grandmother and a younger brother toward whom Chambers felt no particular fraternal affection.

Both Chambers and his younger brother came to maturity during the hectic post-war period and, like many people of their time, both became moral and spiritual casualties. Chambers' younger brother returned from college cynical and disillusioned. He became an alcoholic and finally committed suicide. The whole family seemed to have degenerated into a pattern of life which was precisely the mess of purposeless pottage that Marx and Engels had declared it to be. Whittaker Chambers describes his own experiences as follows:

"When I entered (college shortly after World War I) I was a conservative in my view of life and politics, and I was undergoing a religious experience. By the time I left, entirely by my own choice, I was no longer a conservative and I had no religion. I had published in a campus literary magazine an atheist playlet. . . . The same year, I went to Europe and saw Germany in the manic throes of defeat. I returned to

The Naked Communist

Columbia, this time paying my own way. In 1925, I voluntarily withdrew for the express purpose of joining the Communist Party. For I had come to believe that the world we live in was dying, that only surgery could now save the wreckage of mankind, and that the Communist Party was history's surgeon."[7]

Chambers went to work for Communism in real earnest. He became co-editor of *The Textile Worker*, wrote for the *Daily Worker*, took a Communist "wife" and learned the strike tactics of trade union violence. He writes that during this period, "I first learned that the Communist Party employed gangsters against the fur bosses in certain strikes. . . . I first learned how Communist union members would lead their own gangs of strikers into scab shops and in a few moments slash to pieces with their sharp-hooked fur knives thousands of dollars worth of mink skins."[8]

It was his intention to make the Communist program the permanent pattern of his life. Before long, however, his Communist "wife" left him to go her own way and Chambers felt it would be more to his liking to make his next union (which took place in 1931) an official "bourgeois marriage" at some city hall. At this stage, Chambers would never have guessed that he also had other sensibilities which would one day take him out of Communism and make him senior editor of *Time* magazine at a salary of around $30,000 per year!

In 1928, Chambers saw the first series of purges in the American Communist Party. For several years, the party had been dominated by Charles E. Ruthenburg, "the American Lenin." When Ruthenburg suddenly died there was a mad scramble for power. Jay Lovestone came out on top with William Z. Foster representing a small, noisy minority. But soon Lovestone made a serious political mistake. He sided with one of Stalin's most powerful Russian opponents. Nikolai Bukharin, who stood for a less violent program than Stalin had in mind. Lovestone and William Z. Foster were sum-

---

[7] *Chambers, Whittaker,* "WITNESS," *p. 164.*
[8] *Chambers, Whittaker,* "WITNESS," *p. 229.*

Communism in the United States

moned to Moscow. When they returned, Lovestone was a broken man. He had been called a traitor by Stalin and thrown out of the party. Stalin had named Foster the heir to the throne. The next step was to force every member of the party in the United States to support Foster's radical program or be expelled. Most Communists picked up the new set of signals from Moscow and immediately swore allegiance to Foster. But not so with Chambers. It looked to him as though Stalin were behaving exactly like a Fascist dictator by forcing the majority of the American Communists to follow leadership they had already voted against. Chambers stopped being active in the party.

For two years, by his own choice, Chambers remained outside the regular ranks. He was never expelled, nor did his loyalty to Communism change, but he deeply resented Stalin. The entire situation was changed, however, by the great depression. Chambers' sympathies for the unemployed once more drew him back toward the party program. He also felt forced to admit that from all appearances the long-predicted collapse of American capitalism had arrived. In the spirit of the times, Chambers wrote a story called, "Can You Hear the Voices?" It was a great success. It was made into a play, published as a pamphlet and hailed by Moscow as splendid revolutionary literature. The next thing Chambers knew he was being feted by the American Communist Party as though he had never left it. Chambers soon went back to work for the revolution.

It was in June, 1932, that Chambers was asked to pay the full price of being a Communist. The Party nominated him to serve as a spy against the United States in the employment of the Soviet Military Intelligence. For the sake of his wife Chambers tried to get out of this assignment, but a member of the Central Committee in New York told him, "You have no choice."

Chambers soon found himself under the iron discipline of the Russian espionage apparatus. Because Communism had become his faith, Chambers blindly followed instructions. He became expert in the conspiratorial techniques of clandestine meetings, writing secret documents, shaking off followers, trusting no one, being available day and night at the beck and call of superiors.

Before long Chambers was assigned to be the key contact man for Russia's most important spy cell in Washington, D.C. Chambers has described his espionage associations with the following persons who were later to become top officials in the United States Government:

1. ALGER HISS whom Chambers says became a close personal friend. Hiss started out in the Department of Agriculture, then served on the Special Senate Committee investigating the munitions industry. For awhile he served in the Department of Justice and then went to the State Department. There he made a meteoric rise, serving as Director of the highly important office of Political Affairs. He served as advisor to President Roosevelt at Yalta and as Secretary-General of the International Assembly which created the United Nations.

2. HARRY DEXTER WHITE who later became Assistant Secretary of the United States Treasury and author of the Morgenthau Plan.

3. JOHN J. ABT who served in the Department of Agriculture, the WPA, the Senate Committee on Education and Labor and was then made a Special Assistant to the Attorney General in charge of the trial section.

4. HENRY H. COLLINS who served in the NRA, the Department of Agriculture, the Department of Labor, and the Department of State. During World War II he became a major in the Army and in 1948 became Executive Director of the American Russian Institute (cited by the Attorney General as a Communist front organization).

5. CHARLES KRAMER who served in the National Labor Relations Board, the Office of Price Administration, and in 1943 joined the staff of the Senate Sub-committee on War Mobilization.

6. NATHAN WITT who served in the Department of Agriculture and then became the Secretary of the National Labor Relations Board.

Communism in the United States

7. HAROLD WARE who served in the Department of Agriculture. **145**

8. VICTOR PERLO who served in the Office of Price Administration, the War Production Board, and the Treasury.

9. HENRY JULIAN WADLEIGH who became a prominent official in the Treasury Department.

Chambers testified that he received so many confidential government documents through his contacts that it took the continuous efforts of two and sometimes three photographers to microfilm the material and keep it flowing to Russia. Chambers says he considered Alger Hiss his number one source of information. He has described how Hiss would bring home a brief case each night filled with material from the State Department. Some of these documents would be microfilmed. Others would be copied by Hiss on his typewriter or he would make summaries in longhand. It was a number of these typed documents and memos in the certified handwriting of Alger Hiss which became famous as the "Pumpkin Papers" and subsequently convicted Hiss of perjury.

In later years when Chambers was asked to give his explanation as to why so many well-educated Americans were duped into committing acts of subversion against their native country, he explained that once a person has been converted to the ideology of Communism he will consider espionage to be a moral act—a duty—committed in the name of humanity for the good of future society.

The unbelievable extent to which Americans participated in Russian-directed espionage against the United States during the depression and during World War II has only recently become generally recognized. Many complete books have now been written which summarize the evidence unearthed by the FBI, the courts and Congress.

Whittaker Chambers Breaks with Communism

In 1938, at the very height of his career as a Russian courier and contact man, Chambers found his philosophy of materialism collapsing. It was one morning while feeding his small daughter that Chambers suddenly realized as he watched her that the delicate yet immense complexity of the human body and human personality could not possibly be explained in terms of accumulated accident. Chambers dated his break with Communism from that moment.

At first he was highly disturbed and tried to thrust the new conviction from his mind, but as he opened his thinking to the evidence around him he finally became completely persuaded that he was living in a universe of amazingly immaculate design which was subject to the creative supervision of a supreme intelligence. Consequently, just as Communist philosophy had brought him into the movement its collapse made him determined to get out. It was many months later before he finally disentangled himself and ran away from the Soviet Intelligence Service.

Chambers says that when he ultimately made his break with Communism he did everything in his power to get his close friend, Alger Hiss, to leave with him. Alger Hiss, however, not only refused but, according to Chambers heatedly denounced him for trying to influence him.

From watching the fate of others, Chambers already had some idea of what it meant to try and leave the conspiratorial apparatus of Communism. Nevertheless, the course he followed brought physical and mental suffering that not even he had suspected.

Today, no more complete account of the agonizing experiences of those who dare to wear the badge of an ex-Communist can be found than that contained in the pages of Chambers' autobiography, *Witness*. At one point he worked with a gun beside him for fear the Russian secret police would take his life just as they were doing to so many others. At another point he tried to take his own life to keep from having to expose those who had formerly been his most intimate friends. Most of these details can only be appreciated in their full text. For our purposes it is sufficient to point out that up until the time Chambers did finally make up his mind to tell the whole story, the American public was almost

Communism in the United States

completely unaware of the vast network of spy activities which Russia had built into every strata of American society. And this unfortunate condition existed even though the FBI had been carefully gathering facts and warning government officials concerning Communist activities for many years.

Finally, a cloud of witnesses confirmed that it was true.

Elizabeth Bentley Takes Over
After Chambers Leaves

Chambers had no way of knowing that after he deserted the Russian espionage system, the Soviets would replace him with a woman. Her name was Elizabeth Bentley.

She came from a long line of New England American ancestors. She had attended Vassar, traveled and studied in Italy for a year and returned to the United States in 1934 to find the country deep in a depression. Having failed to get a job, she decided her only chance was to learn a business course so she enrolled at the School of Business at Columbia University. There she met up with a number of people who were friendly and sympathetic toward her. It was quite some time before she knew they were Communists. As these friends explained Communism to her it seemed rather reasonable—in fact, the way they explained it, Communism would be a great improvement over American Capitalism (which at that moment was bogged down like an iceberg with unemployment and bankruptcy). So Elizabeth Bentley became a Communist. She entered the campaign with all the zeal that could come from a girl in her twenties who suddenly believes that a new era of history is about to open up which will solve all of humanity's problems.

For some time Elizabeth Bentley worked in New York's Welfare Department and while there she was made the financial secretary of the Columbia University Communist unit. She attended the Communist Workers' School and joined so many front organizations under different names that on at

least one occasion she went to a meeting and could not remember who she was supposed to be!

Before long the activities of Elizabeth Bentley had attracted the leaders of the Russian underground apparatus
and before she really knew what had happened to her she
had been carefully shifted from the day-to-day assignments of
the U.S. Communist Party to the underground network of
Soviet espionage.

She worked for three different individuals before she was
finally assigned to an over-worked, old-time revolutionary
called "Timmy." Elizabeth Bentley fell in love with Timmy.

One day he said to her: "You and I have no right to feel
the way we do about each other. . . . There is only one way
out, and that is to stick together and keep our relationship
unknown to everyone. . . . You will have to take me completely on faith, without knowing who I am, where I live, or
what I do for a living."

This was how Elizabeth Bentley became the Communist
wife of a man who turned out to be Jacob Golos, one of the
all-powerful chiefs of the Russian Secret Police in the United
States.

Under his training Elizabeth Bentley became what she
later called a "steeled Bolshevik."

In May, 1940, she read that an attempt had been made
against the life of Leon Trotsky in Mexico. The attempt had
failed but his personal bodyguard had been kidnaped and shot
in the back. For years Stalin had been trying to liquidate his
old enemy and from the way Jacob Golos behaved Elizabeth
Bentley knew her Communist mate was in on the plot. Several
months later a killer actually got through to Trotsky and
smashed his skull with an alpenstock.

Beginning in 1941, Elizabeth Bentley was used by the
Russian espionage apparatus to collect material from contacts in Washington, D.C. She says she first became the
courier for the Silvermaster spy group which was extracting
information from Communist contacts in the Pentagon and
other top-secret governmental agencies. Before she was

through she had picked up nearly all of Whittaker Chambers' former contacts and many more besides.

Occasionally there was near disaster, as was the case just after Gregory Silvermaster got a job with the Board of Economic Warfare through the influence of Lauchlin Currie (an administrative assistant at the White House). She says that after taking the job he was shown a letter addressed to his superior from the head of Army Intelligence indicating that the FBI and Naval Intelligence had proof of his Communist connections. The letter demanded that Silvermaster be discharged. The panicky Silvermaster asked Elizabeth Bentley what to do. She gave him the same instruction that other exposed Communists were being given: "Stand your ground, put on an air of injured innocence; you are not a Communist, just a 'progressive' whose record proves you have always fought for the rights of labor. Rally all your 'liberal' friends around. . . . If necessary, hire a lawyer to fight the case through on the grounds that your reputation has been badly damaged. Meanwhile, pull every string you can to get this business quashed. Use Currie, White (Harry Dexter White, top official of the Treasury Department), anybody else you know and trust."[9]

Anyone familiar with the format of defense followed by suspected Communists who were hailed before Congressional investigating committees will immediately recognize the Party's trade mark on the trite pretension of abused innocence recommended by Elizabeth Bentley. When one considers its relatively naive and childlike simplicity it is almost a cause for national chagrin that it confused and deceived such an amazing number of people for such an inexplicable number of years. As with practically all of the others Elizabeth Bentley's suggestions paid off handsomely for Silvermaster and he soon gained support from many powerful and unexpected sources.

After three months of "fighting back" the Under-Secretary of War became convinced from hearing various pleas that

---

[9] Bentley, Elizabeth, "OUT OF BONDAGE," pp. 173-174.

an injustice had been done to Silvermaster and therefore ordered his dismissal cancelled. Silvermaster was allowed to resign and return to his old job in the Department of Agriculture with a clean slate. Elizabeth Bentley concludes by saying, "After a sigh of relief that must have echoed throughout the entire Russian Secret Police apparatus, we went back to our normal routine."

According to the sworn testimony of Elizabeth Bentley, she worked with three major spy cells. The first was the "Ware Cell"—the same group Chambers had handled. In addition she handled the "Silvermaster Cell" and the "Perlo Cell." She said these three cells were charged with the task of supplying her with an almost endless stream of information for transmittal to Moscow. She testified under oath that the members of the Silvermaster Cell and the Perlo Cell were as follows (the departments in which the members were working during the time she had contact with them are also listed):

THE SILVERMASTER CELL

1. NATHAN GREGORY SILVERMASTER served as Director of the Labor Division of the Farm Security Administration; was detailed for a short period to the Board of Economic Warfare.

2. SOLOMON ADLER served in the Treasury Department as an agent to China.

3. NORMAN BURSLER worked in the Department of Justice as a special assistant.

4. FRANK COE worked as Assistant Director, Division of Monetary Research, Treasury Department; special assistant to the United States Ambassador in London; assistant to the Executive Director, Board of Economic Warfare; Assistant Administrator, Foreign Economic Administration.

5. WILLIAM GOLD, known also as Bela Gold, worked as assistant head of the Division of Program Surveys, Bureau of Agricultural Economics, Department of Agriculture; Senate Subcommittee on War Mobilization; Office of Economic Programs in Foreign Economic Administration.

6. MRS. WILLIAM (SONIA) GOLD worked as research assistant, House Select Committee on Interstate Migration; labor-market analyst, Bureau of Employment Security; Division of Monetary Research, Treasury Department.

7. ABRAHAM GEORGE SILVERMAN served as Director of the Bureau of Research and Information Services, U.S. Railroad Retirement Board; economic adviser and chief of analysis and plans, Assistant Chief of Air Staff, Materials and Services, U.S. Air Force.

8. WILLIAM TAYLOR worked in the Treasury Department.

9. WILLIAM LUDWIG ULLMAN worked in the Division of Monetary Research, Treasury Department; Material and Service Division, Air Corps Headquarters, Pentagon.

PERLO CELL

1. VICTOR PERLO (also connected with the Ware Cell), worked as the head of a branch in the Research Section, Office of Price Administration; served the War Production Board handling problems relating to military aircraft production. (In 1951 he wrote a book on American Imperialism and on page 220 declared: "The USSR, the People's Democracies, and China lead the world struggle for peace.")

2. EDWARD J. FITZGERALD served on the War Production Board.

3. HAROLD GLASSER served in the Treasury Department, loaned to the government of Ecuador; loaned to the War Production Board; worked as adviser on North African Affairs Committee in Algiers, North Africa.

4. CHARLES KRAMER (also connected with the Ware Cell), worked for the National Labor Relations Board; Office of Price Administration; economist with the Senate Subcommittee on War Mobilization.

5. SOLOMON LESHINSKY worked for the United States Relief and Rehabilitation Administration.

6. HARRY MAGDOFF worked for the Statistical Division

of the War Production Board and the Office of Emergency Management; the Bureau of Research and Statistics of the W.P.B., the Tools Division of W.P.B. and the Bureau of Foreign and Domestic Commerce.

7. ALLAN ROSENBERG worked in the Foreign Economic Administration.

8. DONALD NIVEN WHEELER worked in the Office of Strategic Services.

In addition, Elizabeth Bentley named the following individuals who cooperated in obtaining information from government files even though they were not tied in to any particular cell:

1. MICHAEL GREENBURG—Board of Economic Warfare; Foreign Economic Administration, specialist on China.

2. JOSEPH GREGG—Coordinator of Inter-American affairs, assistant in Research Division.

3. MAURICE HALPERIN—Office of Strategic Services; head of Latin American Division in the Research and Analysis Branch; head of Latin American research and analysis, State Department.

4. J. JULIUS JOSEPH—Office of Strategic Services, Japanese Division.

5. DUNCAN CHAPLIN LEE—Office of Strategic Services; legal adviser to General William J. Donovan.

6. ROBERT T. MILLER—Head of political research, Coordinator of Inter-American Affairs; member, Information Service Committee, Near Eastern Affairs, State Department; Assistant Chief, Division of Research and Publications, State Department.

7. WILLIAM Z. PARK—Coordinator of Inter-American Affairs.

8. BERNARD REDMONT—Coordinator of Inter-American Affairs.

9. HELEN TENNEY—Office of Strategic Services, Spanish Division.

These lists of names are set forth to illustrate the remarkable and devastating pipelines of information which Elizabeth

Communism in the United States

Bentley says the Soviet underground tapped in Washington during the time she served as the Russian Secret Police paymaster and courier in the nation's capital.

Elizabeth Bentley worked doggedly for the Soviets until 1944. However, a great shock had come to her in 1943 when Jacob Golos died suddenly of a heart atack on Thanksgiving eve. Just before his death, Golos revealed to her the ruthlessness of his Soviet superiors who were driving him unmercifully and forcing him to engage in activities which were nauseating even to the revolutionary-hardened sense of his own calloused conscience.

And after Golos' death further disillusionment came to Elizabeth Bentley when she learned that Earl Browder had agreed to turn over a group of American Communists in Washington to a most unscrupulous set of Soviet espionage agents. When she challenged Browder, he reportedly told her, "Don't be naive. You know that when the cards are down, I have to take my orders from them. I just hoped I could sidetrack them in this particular matter, but it didn't work out."

"But Greg's an old friend of yours," Elizabeth Bentley said (referring to a member of the group).

"So what?" replied Browder. "He's expendable."

Shortly afterwards Elizabeth Bentley was surprised by a visit from a top Soviet official from Moscow who told her she had been awarded the highest medal of the Soviet Union—the Order of the Red Star. But she was not nearly so impressed by the proffered honor as she was disgusted and revolted by the kind of individual the Soviet official turned out to be. From that moment on she felt that the Communist leaders in Russia were absolutely incapable of building a great new world—no matter how much information she sent them.

The final blow to her idealism came when the Soviets tried to force her to turn over to them a girl-friend who was wanted for the immoral role of an entertainer for high government officials.

One night, alone, Elizabeth Bentley challenged herself, "What has happened to all of us who started out so gallantly to build a new world?" Deep inside herself she was finally able to admit what had happened. "We had been corrupted and smashed by a machine more merciless than anything the world had ever seen."

Many weeks later, Elizabeth Bentley finally walked into the FBI ready to do everything in her power to make amends to her native country.

In some ways it was simultaneously a triumph and a tragedy. For her, personally, it was a triumph. It was the chance she needed to square herself with her conscience and her country. However, in 1948, when she gave her sworn testimony before a congressional committee, it threatened to become a tragedy. The Communist press was joined by many so-called "liberal" factions to accuse her of being everything from a degenerate to a psychopathic liar or a victim of insanity. It took time and corroborative testimony of many witnesses to finally halt the clamor.

Elizabeth Bentley and Whittaker Chambers have testified that they were both typical members of a small but extremely dangerous segment of Americans who, through misguided ideologies, swelled the ranks of Communism during the interval betwen World War I and the close of World War II. The vast majority passed through the same evolution—first, an ideological conversion followed by a desire to take action; secondly, an exposure to the hard-core realities of Communism in actual operation; and finally, an awakening followed by a dynamic determination to desert the delusion and fight it from the outside. Fortunately for America, as well as for its citizens who served the Communist cause, these erstwhile members of the party usually returned to the American way of life more loyal to its principles than when they left. Only a few have still refused to open their eyes and ears to all that has been revealed. This unreclaimed group still labors day and night in a dedicated service to "the cause."

STALIN   MOLOTOV

VIII

Communism and World War II

While Communist espionage channels were being perfected in the United States, similar subversive networks were being built throughout the world. Soon Stalin found the state secrets of all the major powers pouring in so fast that he was able to play the world-wide game of power politics like a professional gambler who sits at the poker table carefully planning his strategy as he reads the marked cards held by each of the other players.

We now know that it was from this supremely satisfying position of political omniscience that Stalin initiated a series of schemes which had their part in precipitating World War II. Defected Russian Intelligence officers have revealed that World War II was fomented and used by the Russian leaders as an important part of the long-range strategy for the expansion of World Communism.

This chapter will answer the following questions:

What is the explanation for Stalin's attempt to reach a secret understanding with Hitler in 1933?

Why did Stalin claim credit for starting World War II?

The Naked Communist

Why did Stalin's pact with Hitler in 1939 surprise Communists throughout the world?

Was Stalin caught off guard when Hitler scrapped the pact and attacked Russia?

What was the U.S. attitude during the early months of the Nazi invasion of Russia? What changed that attitude?

What do you deduct from this statement in 1942 by a Presidential advisor: "Generations unborn will owe a great measure of their freedom to the unconquerable power of the Soviet people"? Did Allied leaders appear to have had a basic understanding of Communist strategy?

How did the Communist leaders use Lend-Lease to get atomic bomb secrets?

When did U.S. coexistence with Communism begin? Name the four steps of degeneration through which it passed. On what presumption was Russia made a full partner with the U.S. in shaping the post-war world?

How do you account for the fact that the United Nations Charter follows the format of the Russian Constitution of 1936 rather than the format of the League of Nations? Would you feel there was any significance in the fact that the general secretary for the organization which drew up the charter was Alger Hiss?

What was the attitude of the Communist leaders when they emerged from World War II as the second greatest political power on earth?

The Rise of Adolf Hitler and Nazism in Germany

It is said that Communism was largely responsible for the rise of Adolf Hitler and the Nazi Party. It will be recalled that when the German Kaiser capitulated in 1918 the Communists tried to take over Germany. Anti-communist political groups immediately sprang up and through a frantic coalition they prevented the Communists from seizing power. It was in this anti-Communist atmosphere that Adolf Hitler began his political career. He joined the National Socialists

Communism and World War II

(Nazi) Party which had a strong anti-Bolshevik platform and by 1921 he had become its leader.

Hitler organized his notorious Nazi Storm Troopers to retaliate against a spreading rash of Communist violence. He had his Brown Shirts trained in street fighting, rioting and the suppression of political opponents by direct physical attack. By 1923 the Storm Troopers numbered 10,000 and Hitler felt strong enough to try and take over the German province of Bavaria. But this uprising failed. Hitler was thrown into prison and while there began expressing his frustrated ambitions in a feverish manuscript on total war called *Mein Kampf*—My Battle. In this book Hitler revealed that he was not only bitterly anti-communistic but that he stood for outright violation of the Treaty of Versailles. He said he would fight for the complete restoration of Germany as a world power. He was planning for the creation of a great Nordic empire embracing all the people of German blood in Europe regardless of their national residence. *Mein Kampf* constituted a threat to every nation bordering on Germany. It also contained a threat against Russia because Hitler declared that the natural course of German expansion would eventually carry the Nazi conquest into the fertile Ukrainian agricultural region and then into the rich Russian oil fields.

Later as Stalin watched Hitler cudgel and jostle his way into power he recognized in the Nazi dictator a formidable opponent of his own breed and kind. He saw that Hitler was shrewd and ruthless. He was completely amoral. He had no compunction whatever against violence, the purging of his own people, the use of deceit in propaganda, nor the sacrifice of millions of lives to achieve personal power. Materialism had produced precisely the same product in Germany that it had produced in Russia. Although called by different names Nazism and Communism were aimed at the same identical mark and were forged in very similar ideological molds.

Perhaps this explains why Stalin secretly tried to negotiate a personal understanding with Hitler shortly after the latter came into power during 1933. One of Stalin's leading secret agents, General W. G. Krivitsky, has furnished the de-

tails of these efforts.[1] When Stalin's gestures of friendship
were rejected by Hitler, Stalin knew the German Fuehrer
could be dealt with only as an outright enemy.

Stalin then hastened to gain the sympathies of the democracies. He attempted to identify Russia's policies with the
political and economic welfare of freedom-loving people in
other nations. He called this campaign the "Popular Front."
At the Seventh World Congress of the International in 1935,
he instructed loyal Communists in every country to combine
with any political groups which opposed Hitler and his allies—
even right wing parties which the Communists had previously
attacked. Judged by its results, the "Popular Front" was the
most successful tactic ever adopted by Communist strategists.
It permitted Communists to associate openly with the most
conservative and highly respected political groups in capitalist
countries.

The Communists Claim Credit for Starting World War II

In 1938 Stalin watched closely as Hitler decided to test
the temper of the Western Allies by occupying all of Austria.
When no serious consequences resulted, the Fuehrer prepared
to assimilate other areas along the German borders. At
Munich he threatened to blitzkrieg Europe unless England and
France let him take over the industrial section of Czechoslovakia. When they agreed, he immediately extended his
occupation to nearly all of that valiant little country.

In 1939 Hitler seized Memelland in Lithuania and then
prepared to march into Poland. However, at this point he
hesitated. Russia wanted Poland, too. As a matter of fact,
Russia held the balance of power in Europe and Hitler did
not dare take steps which would start an all-out war in the
West unless he could be assured that Russia would not inter-

---

[1] *This chapter in Stalin-Hitler relations is discussed by General Krivitsky in his book, "IN STALIN'S SECRET SERVICE."*

Communism and World War II

fere. Hitler, therefore, made overtures to Stalin to sign a nonaggression pact. To the astonishment of the whole world, Stalin accepted! This meant that Hitler could go to war with the assurance that Russia would not interfere.

This caught most of the Communist world completely off guard. For years Red propaganda had portrayed Stalin as the world's leading opponent of Nazism and Fascism. Now Stalin's regime had ratified a pact with the Nazis which gave them a carte blanche to start a war in the West.

In America it took the Communist press several days to get their propaganda in reverse. Whittaker Chambers says it was absolutely incomprehensible to American Communists that Stalin would capitulate to his greatest enemy. It was not until Chambers talked with Stalin's former director of espionage in Western Europe that he heard the official explanation. General W. G. Krivitsky said this pact demonstrated Stalin's genius as a strategist. He explained that Stalin knew this pact would turn Hitler loose on Europe but that he also knew that as the war progressed it was likely that the western nations would fight themselves into exhaustion. At that point Soviet troops could march in. Almost without a blow the Soviet troops would be able to take over all of Europe in the name of the dictatorship of the proletariat!

And just as Stalin had suspected, Hitler was not at all slow to take advantage of the political shove Stalin had given him. The pact was signed August 23, 1939. By September 1, the German Panzers were pouring through the valiant, but helpless ranks of the Polish horse cavalry, and thousands of tons of bombs were falling on Polish cities.

Also, as Stalin had expected, England and France were immediately dragged into the war because of their commitments to Poland. This was a war which these countries were neither physically nor psychologically prepared to wage. Before a year had passed, Poland had been divided between Germany and Russia and France had been occupied. Soon afterwards the British troops were bombed off the European continent at Dunkirk, and the Nazis were then left practically without resistance as they expanded their occupation into Denmark, Norway, Holland and Belgium.

Assuming that the war would now settle down to a struggle between Germany and England, Stalin felt ready to make his next carefully calculated move. Only two major capitalist nations still remained outside of the conflict: Japan and the United States.

On April 13, 1941, Stalin nudged the Japanese war lords into an offensive in the Pacific. This was accomplished by the same simple device as that which had turned Hitler loose on Europe—a pact.

At that moment Russia, even more than the United States, was the greatest single impediment to Japanese expansion in East Asia and the Pacific. By accepting a pact with Russia, the Japanese war lords were left free to launch their pan-Asiatic campaign in the Pacific and the Far East. They made immediate preparations for their attack.

Stalin Suffers a Strategic Defeat

Stalin now intended to sit back and wait for the capitalist nations to endure their baptism of fire. He had assured the Soviet military leaders that World War II would be won by the nation which stayed out the longest. That nation, of course, must be Russia. What he did not know, however, was that Adolf Hitler had been planning a disastrous surprise for the Communist Motherland. In fact, at the very moment Stalin was promoting his neutrality pact with Japan, Adolf Hitler was secretly announcing to his general staff: "The German armed forces must be prepared to crush Soviet Russia in a quick campaign."

The great surprise came on June 22, 1941. Hitler scrapped the pact and attacked Russia on a 2,000 mile front with 121 divisions and 3,000 planes. He had written all about it years before in *Mein Kampf*.

This sudden blitzkrieg attack changed the history of the

world. It shattered Stalin's intention to stay out of the war while the capitalistic nations fought themselves to exhaustion. It meant that Russia would enter the war prematurely and with the most meager preparations.

World War II Moves Closer to the United States

To many observers in the United States, this new development in World War II appeared favorable to the interest of peace-loving countries. Hitler's attack on Russia locked the world's two greatest aggressor nations in deadly combat and even military leaders thought this might relieve future world tensions. But within six months the Germans had occupied 580,000 square miles of the richest land in the U.S.S.R.—land originally occupied by more than one third of Russia's population, and in spite of the "scorched earth" policy of Russia, the Nazi troops successfully extracted their supplies from the people and the land so that they were able to race forward without waiting to have supply lines established. Soon German Panzers had penetrated to a point only sixty miles from Moscow and Hitler announced exuberantly that "Russia is already broken and will never rise again."

All of this shocked the rest of the world into the reprehensible possibility of a Nazi empire which might extend from England to Alaska. Instinctively Americans began cheering for the Russians. It was considered to be a matter of vital self interest, implemented by the traditional American tendency to cheer for the underdog.

Then the fatal dawn of Sunday, December 7, 1941, brought the devastating attack of the Japanese on Pearl Harbor and the United States found herself in the holocaust of World War II before she was even halfway prepared. In desperation American leaders reached out in all directions for friends. It is important to remember that the black boots of Hitler's marching Wehrmacht had pounded a paralyzing fear into the hearts of peoples on every continent. It was Nazism—not

Communism—that was blotting out the light of civilization around the earth. Therefore, since Russia had already been brought within the orbit of American sympathy, it is not difficult to understand how she became an intimate U.S. ally almost over night. Somehow it seemed impossible to remember that this was the very same Russia that had joined a nonaggression pact with Hitler to turn him loose in Europe, and had joined a neutrality pact with the Japanese to turn them loose in the Pacific.

The U.S. Policy of Coexistence Goes into Its Third Stage

By the early spring of 1942 it was not only apparent that the war had caught U.S. military strength at a very low level, but it was also equally obvious that the Axis had practically destroyed all of America's traditional allies. Perhaps, as George F. Kennan suggests, this may partially account for the desperate gamble taken at that time by certain U.S. diplomatic strategists in dealing with Russia.

Already the diplomatic navigators had gone from a policy of plain coexistence with Communism in 1933, to one step lower where they had decided to accept the abuse and the broken promises of the Communist leaders. Now they resolved to go even further. They decided to try to convert the Communist leaders to the American way of thinking by showering them with such overwhelming generosity that there could be no vestige of suspicion concerning the desire of the United States to gain the cooperative support of the Communist leaders in winning the war and later preserving the peace. It was assumed that they would then become permanently and sympathetically allied with the United States and the western democracies in building a "one world" of peace and prosperity.

If this plan had worked, it would have been truly a master stroke of diplomatic genius. Unfortunately, however, it turned

Communism and World War II

out to be just what many military officials and heads of intelligence agencies predicted it would be—the means by which Russia would catapult herself into a world power by capitalizing on the treasure and prestige of the very nation she most desired to destroy.

Nevertheless, the program was inaugurated and America's attitude toward Russia both during and after World War II can only be understood in terms of this policy.

In early June, 1942, Molotov came secretly to Washington and stayed at the White House. After his departure preparations were made to break the new U.S. policy to the American people. On June 22, 1942, (the anniversary of Hitler's attack on the U.S.S.R.) a Russian Aid Rally was held in New York's Madison Square Garden. There a top government official announced: "A second front? Yes, and if necessary, a third and a fourth front. . . . We are determined that nothing shall stop us from sharing with you all that we have and are in this conflict, and we look forward to sharing with you the fruits of victory and peace." Then there followed the pathetic, but blindly hopeful statement: "Generations unborn will owe a great measure of their freedom to the unconquerable power of the Soviet people."[2]

The Story of American Lend-Lease to Russia

This American policy of generosity immediately began to manifest itself. Billions of dollars of Russian Lend-Lease were authorized. Even the deliberate sacrifice of American self-interest was evident in some of the orders received by U.S. military services. An order to the Air Service Command dated January 1, 1943, carried this astounding mandate: "The modification, equipment, and movement of Russian planes have been given first priority, *even over planes for the U.S. Army Air Forces.*"

---

[2] *Speech of Harry Hopkins quoted in* "ROOSEVELT AND HOPKINS," *by Robert E. Sherwood, p. 588.*

The Naked Communist

The U.S. Congress was not quite as enthusiastic toward Russia as the diplomatic strategists. Congress specifically restricted Russian Lend-Lease to materials to be used for military action against the Axis enemy. It forbade the shipment of materials which would be used for civilian personnel or the rehabilitation of Russia after the war. This was in no way designed to show unfriendliness toward the Russian people. It was simply an expression of belief that U.S. resources should not be used to promote Communist Russia into a world power. Some day the Russian people would perhaps regain their freedom, and that would be the time to share resources. Meanwhile, non-military generosity would only strengthen the post-war position of the Communist dictatorship.

In spite of these legal restrictions, however, the uninhibited generosity of the diplomats dominated Lend-Lease rather than Congress or the leaders of the Military.

General John R. Deane, for example, who was in Moscow as Chief of the U.S. Military Mission, turned down a Russian request for 25 large 200-horsepower Diesel marine engines because the engines already sent to Russia were rusting in open storage and from all appearances were simply being stockpiled for post-war use. Furthermore, the engines were badly needed by General MacArthur in the South Pacific. After hearing General Deane's decision, the Russians appealed to Harry Hopkins (head of the Lend-Lease program) who overruled General Deane. During the following two years a total of 1,305 of these engines were sent to Russia at a cost to the American people of $30,745,947.

After Pearl Harbor, when Navy officials were given the highest possible priority for copper wire to be used in the repair of U. S. battleships, they found the Russians had an even higher priority for an order of copper wire which was apparently to be used for post-war rehabilitation of Russian cities. The wire was turned over to the Russians in such quantities that it had to be stored on a 20-acre lot in Westchester County, New York, where it remained until the war was nearly over. A few months before the Armistice, it was

Communism and World War II

shipped to Russia for the rehabilitation of their communications systems.

Since the close of World War II, the American people have gradually learned the details concerning the flood of goods and treasure which went to Russia under Lend-Lease. The lists which have been published are from Russian records. They were secured by an American officer, Major George Racey Jordan, who was the official U. S. expediter for Russian Lend-Lease at the Great Falls Air Base in Montana. An analysis of these lists showed that according to Russian records, the Communists received over eleven billion dollars worth of Lend-Lease and that in spite of the legal restrictions against it, the diplomatic strategists included $3,040,423,000 worth of American goods, paid for by American taxpayers, which definitely does not appear to be authorized by the Lend-Lease act. These lists show shipments of vast stockpiles of "non-munition" chemicals together with voluminous shipments of cigarette cases, phonograph records, ladies' compacts, sheet music, pianos, *antique* furniture, $388,844 worth of "notions and cheap novelties," women's jewelry, household furnishings, fishing tackle, lipstick, perfumes, dolls, bank vaults, playground equipment, and quantities of many other types of illegal, non-military merchandise.

Students of Russian wartime history point out that American Lend-Lease began feeding into Russia at a time when she was almost prostrate. She had lost most of her crops as a result of the scorched earth campaign designed to slow Nazi advances. Even with Lend-Lease food the troops had to be rationed at a bare subsistence level so it is likely that without Lend-Lease the Russian resistance might well have collapsed. Furthermore, the Germany occupation cut the Russians off from many of their major industrial centers. In addition to U.S. planes, munitions, chemicals, tools, heavy machinery, and so forth, the amazing American "Arsenal of Democracy" provided Russia with 478,899 motor vehicles. This was nearly half of all the motor vehicles used on the Soviet front.

It is an interesting commentary on the Communist psychology to note that the United States never received an official "thank you" from Russia for the eleven billion dollars worth of Lend-Lease goods which were paid for and literally "donated" to the Communist Motherland by the American people. Stalin's excuse was that his government felt the United States made an error when it stopped Lend-Lease at the close of the war. He made it icy clear that under the circumstances his people did not feel an expression of gratitude would be either appropriate or justifiable.

Russian Attempts to Secure the Secrets of the Atomic Bomb

Throughout World War II Russian espionage vigorously concentrated on the most important thing to come out of the War—the harnessing of atomic energy. A two-pronged thrust was employed to get the information as it was developed: one by espionage and the other by diplomatic channels. For a time the diplomatic channels were particularly productive, not only for atomic energy secrets, but for all military and industrial information.

Major Jordan first became aware of this at the Great Falls Lend-Lease Air Base when the Russians began bringing large quantities of cheap, black suitcases along with them whenever they left the United States. They refused to let Jordan see the contents on the grounds that the suitcases were pieces of "diplomatic luggage" and therefore immune to inspection.

One night the Russian commander at the base almost demanded that Jordan go into Great Falls as his dinner guest. Jordan was suspicious but accepted. About midnight he received an excited call that a plane had just landed and the Soviets were going to take off for Russia without waiting for Jordan's clearance. Jordan raced back to the airfield. Sure enough, the plane was a joker. In it were fifty black suitcases protected by armed Russian guards. Jordan ordered a GI to

Communism and World War II

hold the guards at bay and shoot to kill if they forcibly interfered with his inspection.

Jordan later testified under oath before a congressional committee that he found each suitcase to contain a file of information about U.S. industry, harbors, troops, railroads, communications, and so forth. In one suitcase Jordan said he found a letter on White House stationery signed by Harry Hopkins and addressed to the number three man in the Russian hierarchy. Attached to the letter was a map of the top-secret Manhattan (atomic energy) Project, together with descriptive data dealing with atomic energy experiments! One folder in this suitcase had written on it, "From Hiss." At the time Jordan did not know who Hiss was. Inside the folder were numerous military documents. Another folder contained Department of State documents. Some of them were letters from the U.S. embassy in Moscow giving confidential evaluations of the Russian situation and detailed analytical impressions of Russian officials. Now they were being secretly shipped back for the Russians to read.

When Major Jordan reported the facts to Washington he was *severely criticized for holding up the plane!*

In April, 1943, the Russian liaison officer told Jordan that a very special shipment of experimental chemicals was coming through. The Russian officer called Harry Hopkins in Washington and then turned the phone over to Jordan. Major Jordan reports that Harry Hopkins told him: "I don't want you to discuss this with anyone, and it is not to go on the records. Don't make a big production of it, but just send it through quietly, in a hurry."

The Russian officer later told Jordan the shipment was "bomb powder" and Jordan saw an entry in the officer's folder which said "Uranium." The shipment came through June 10, 1943. It was the first of several. At least 1,465 pounds of uranium salts are said to have been sent through to the Soviet Union. Metallurgists estimate that this could be reduced to 6.25 pounds of fissionable U-235. This is two pounds more than would be necessary to produce an atomic explosion.

On July 24, 1945, at Potsdam, President Truman announced to Winston Churchill and Joseph Stalin that the United States had finally developed a highly secret bomb. He told them this bomb possessed almost unbelievable explosive power. Secretary of State James F. Byrnes was watching Stalin and noted that he did not seem particularly surprised, nor even interested in the announcement. Four years later (September 23, 1949), President Truman announced to the world that Russia had successfully exploded an atomic bomb— years ahead of U.S. expectations! Some officials wondered why, with all the help they received, the Russians had not exploded one long before.

Closing Months of World War II

Historically, Russia has always been stronger in defense than in attack. During World War II the Russian people displayed an incredible will to resist during the days when even Hitler thought they were completely beaten. They suffered astronomical losses: 7 million dead (including 2.5 million Russian Jews exterminated by the Nazis and 1.5 million other Soviet civilians killed by the Germans), while approximately 3 million died in combat. From 3 to 4 million were taken prisoners but the number of wounded and maimed is not given. As a result of the war there was a destruction of 1,700 Russian towns, 70,000 villages and hamlets, 31,000 factories, 84,000 schools, 40,000 miles of track, in addition to the destruction of 7 million horses, 17 million head of cattle, and 20 million hogs. This represented about one-fourth of all Soviet property.

There is no way of knowing whether or not Stalin ever forced himself to acknowledge it, but this almost incomprehensible toll of monstrous destruction might very well have been avoided if Stalin had not made the insidious mistake of deliberately signing the pact with Hitler in 1939 which triggered the opening campaign of World War II. There are leading political authorities who now state that if Hitler had been forced to delay his campaign into Poland because of a threat from Russia, it would have given the Western Nations sufficient time to build up their forces, and by restoring a balance of power in Europe the entire saga of World War II might never have occurred.

U.S. Policy of Coexistence Enters the Fourth Stage

During World War II the President of the United States received two different interpretations of Communist policy and two different recommendations as how best to deal with the Communist leaders. One group of advisers took the historical approach, accepted the Communists as the world revolutionists which they described themselves to be, and assumed that their past conduct was the safest criterion of how they might be expected to act in the future. A second group of advisers presented a much more idealistic view of the Communist leaders. They wanted people to forget the past; to look upon Communist boorishness as nothing more than political immaturity, something which could be changed by patient endurance and expansive generosity.

To this second group, there rapidly gravitated not only theoretical idealists, but men and women who were later found to be deeply involved in outright subversion against the United States government.[3] Historians now find it difficult to define just where idealism left off and subversion took over. In any event this was the group which dominated the Lend-Lease program and set the stage for policies which controlled U.S. relations with Russia for approximately fifteen years.

This was also the group of presidential advisers who acclaimed with the greatest enthusiasm the slightest suggestion that the Communists were "changing." For example, when the Communist International was disbanded May 22, 1943,

---

[3] *A rather complete summary of Communist infiltration of the United States Government is contained in the book of James Burnham,* "THE WEB OF SUBVERSION," *John Day Company, New York, 1954.*

this group hailed the announcement as incontrovertible evidence that the Communist leaders had renounced world conquest. Others suspected that this was merely a propaganda device. The latter proved to be the case, as Igor Gouzenko, the former Russian code clerk, testified: "The announcement of the dissolution of the Comintern (Communist International) was probably the greatest farce of the Communists in recent years. Only the name was liquidated, with the object of reassuring public opinion in the democratic countries. Actually the Comintern exists and continues its work, because the Soviet leaders have never relinquished the idea of establishing a Communist dictatorship."[4]

When many high officials of the President's own party saw the dangerous direction in which U.S. policy was moving, they hastened to warn him. One interesting conversation took place during the war between the President and his good friend, William C. Bullitt, whom the President had sent to Russia as the first U.S. ambassador in 1933. Mr. Bullitt had just finished outlining to the President many of his personal experiences with Joseph Stalin, and had warned the President to keep up his guard when dealing with the Communist leaders.

"Bill," replied the President, "I don't dispute your facts; they are accurate. I don't dispute the logic of your reasoning. I just have a hunch that Stalin is not that kind of a man. Harry (Hopkins) says he's not, and that he doesn't want anything but security for his country. And I think that if I give him everything that I can, and ask nothing from him in return . . . he won't try to annex anything, and will work with me for a world peace and democracy."[5]

The philosophy reflected in this statement is the keynote to an understanding of the conferences held by the "Big Three" toward the close of the war. By that time the diplomatic strategy of the United States (which began with simple coexistence in 1933) had passed into its fourth phase—the com-

---

[4] "THE REPORT OF THE ROYAL CANADIAN COMMISSION," *p. 663.*
[5] LIFE MAGAZINE, *August 30, 1948, p. 94.*

Communism and World War II

plete acceptance of the Russian Communists as full partners in the plans for preserving future world peace.

Creation of the United Nations

During August and September 1944, the representatives of Britain, China, Russia and the United States, met at Dumbarton Oaks in Washington, D. C. At this conference the constitutional foundation for the United Nations was laid. In it Russia was not only made a full partner, but a dominant stockholder. A most significant development was the fact that, while other nations objected, Russia insisted on the right to exercise the veto power even if she were a party to the dispute. This violated the very foundation of international jurisprudence but the democracies consented. They were ready to pay almost any price to get Russia to participate.

By December 28, 1944, the American Ambassador to Russia began to express misgivings about U.S.-Soviet relations and the part Russia would play in the post-war period: "The Soviets have definite objectives in their future foreign policy, all of which we do not as yet fully understand. . . . From Soviet actions so far, the terms 'friendly' and 'independent' appear to mean something quite different from our own interpretation."[6]

Once the tide of war had turned, there was an increased arrogance in Soviet treatment of U.S. officials. General Deane wrote to Washington about Lend-Lease and said: "Even our giving is viewed with suspicion. . . . The party of the second part (the U. S.) is either a shrewd trader to be admired or a sucker to be despised. . . . I have yet to see the inside of a Russian home. Officials dare not become too friendly with us, and others are persecuted for this offense."[7]

By the following April the Prime Minister of England was becoming fed up with the whole Russian picture. He

---

[6] "U. S. NEWS AND WORLD REPORT," *April 1, 1955, p. 41, in an article entitled: "U. S. Was Warned of Soviet Double Cross."*
[7] "U. S. NEWS AND WORLD REPORT," *April 1, 1955, p. 40.*

appealed to President Roosevelt: "I deem it of the highest importance that a firm and blunt stand should be made at this juncture by our two countries in order that the air may be cleared and they (the Russians) realize that there is a point beyond which we will not tolerate insult."[8]

There is some evidence that the President of the United States was also beginning to awaken to the realities of the situation, but one week after this message was written, President Roosevelt died. The monumental task of finishing the war and building the United Nations fell into the hands of those who still insisted that the Russians were being misunderstood and that a successful partnership could be definitely achieved.

On April 25, 1945, 1,400 representatives from 46 nations met in San Francisco, and after due deliberation agreed upon a United Nations Charter.

Anyone familiar with the Communist Constitution of Russia will recognize in the United Nations Charter a similar format. It is characterized by a fervent declaration of democratic principles which are sound and desirable; this is then followed by a constitutional restriction or procedural limitation which completely nullifies the principles just announced. For example, the Russian Constitution provides for universal suffrage and voting by secret ballot. Then, in Article 126, it provides for a single political party (the Communist Party) which will furnish the voters with a single roster of candidates. This, of course renders completely meaningless all the high-flown phrases dealing with universal suffrage and secret ballots. Freedom of the press is likewise guaranteed, and then wiped out by the provision that all writings must be "in the interest of the workers."

In precisely this same way the United Nations Charter provides for "the sovereign equality of all its members" (Article 1) and then sets up a Security Council which is dominated by five permanent members (Britain, Russia, China, France and the United States) any one of which can nullify

---

[8] "U. S. NEWS AND WORLD REPORT," *December 10, 1954, p. 29, in an article entitled: "Six Weeks That Shaped History."*

Communism and World War II

the expressed desires of all other member nations by the simple device of exercising the veto power.

The Charter allows each member nation to have one vote in the General Assembly. This sounds like democracy, but then it provides that the General Assembly can do nothing more than make recommendations, and must refer all of its suggestions to the Security Council for action! (Articles 11-14). This makes the Security Council the *only* legally binding legislative body in the UN. To make this absolutely crystal clear the Charter provides in Article 24 that any nation which joins the UN must "agree to accept and carry out the decisions of the Security Council."

This means that in spite of the bold declaration that the UN is "based on respect for the principle of equal rights and self-determination of peoples" the cold fact is that the members are all committed to obey the will of a handful of nations in the Security Council. As the next ten years dramatically demonstrated, all members of the UN — particularly the little nations—could be subjected to the choke-hold which the U.S.S.R. had provided for herself by holding membership in the Security Council and dominating that body through the frequent use of the veto power.

The Charter further provides that membership in the UN shall be restricted to "peace-loving" states (Article 4). This was thoroughly discussed at San Francisco, and Secretary John Foster Dulles has emphasized that the UN was designed to be a collective organization of friendly nations to preserve peace rather than an assemblage of all the nations in the world. In other words, the United Nations was built on the premise that its members would only include those nations which had had a demonstrated history of being "peace-loving." Eight years after the adoption of the UN Charter, Secretary Dulles explained to the American Bar Association why the United Nations had failed to preserve the peace: "Now we see the inadequacy of an organization whose effective functioning depends upon cooperation with a nation which is dominated by an international party seeking world dominion."[9]

---

[9] "THE U.N. TODAY," *H. W. Wilson Company, New York, 1954, p. 198.*

The Naked Communist

As some authorities have since pointed out, the UN provided for a world-wide police commission and then made the top international gangster a member of that commission. It was like setting up a fire department to put out the conflagration of war and then putting the world-community's foremost firebug on the department. From the point of view of the little nations, it was like promising to provide a good shepherd to protect the small, weak countries, and then appointing the wolf and all her pups to protect the flock.

All this became apparent during the "decade of disillusionment" which immediately followed. In 1945, however, a war-weary, hopeful free world felt the United Nations was all it purported to be—an organization for collective security designed to stand like a bastion against aggressor nations.

Communist Attitudes
at the Close of World War II

A clear indication of what the United States could expect from post-war Communism came on May 24, 1945, when the leading French Communist, Jacques Duclos, wrote a letter on behalf of his Russian superiors demanding that the Communists in the United States be required to immediately abandon their policy of friendly collaboration with capitalism and return to their historic mission of world revolution. Back in 1940 the Communist Party of America had formally withdrawn from the Third International to avoid having to register as a foreign agent under the Voorhis Act. Later the Communist Party of America was dissolved in an attempt to attach the Communist membership to one of the major U.S. political parties. For this purpose they called themselves the Communist Political Association.

All of this twisting and turning was in complete harmony with Soviet policy until 1945. After World War II, the announced policy reverted to traditional Marxism. To justify the complete switch in policy, Earl Browder, the American

Communism and World War II

Communist leader, was accused of being personally responsible for the "errors" of the former policy. He was expelled from the party.

The party leadership was immediately taken over by William Z. Foster. Foster, it will be recalled, had written an inflammatory book in 1932 called *Toward Soviet America.* Just before World War II he had testified before a Congressional Committee: "When a Communist heads a government of the United States, and that day will come just as surely as the sun rises, that government will not be a capitalistic government, but a Soviet government, and behind this government will stand the Red Army to enforce the dictatorship of the proletariat."[10]

It is no longer difficult to understand why Moscow wanted men like Foster at the head of its Communist parties throughout the world. We now know that the Russian leaders approached the conclusion of the world's greatest war with the conviction that World War III might be in the near offing. In their secret circles they hopefully speculated that this next war might be Communism's final death struggle with capitalism.

Igor Gouzenko states that after the armistice, he and the other employees in the Russian Embassy at Ottawa, Canada, were warned against an attitude of complacency. Colonel Zabotin gathered the employees together and then referred to the free-world democracies as follows: "Yesterday they were our allies, today they are our neighbors, tomorrow they will be our enemies!"[11]

Remarkable insight into the Communist mind during this period can also be obtained from a speech delivered to an intimate circle of Communist leaders by Marshal Tito, head of the party in Yugoslavia:

"The second capitalist war, in which Russia was attacked by her most dangerous and strongest fascist enemy, has ended

---

[10] *See the Report of the Special Committee on Un-American Activities, January 3, 1939, pp. 18-21.*
[11] *Report of the Royal Commission of Canada, p. 655.*

The Naked Communist

in a decisive victory for the Soviet Union. But this does not mean that Marxism has won a final victory over capitalism. . . . Our collaboration with capitalism during the war which has recently ended, by no means signifies that we shall prolong our alliance with it in the future. On the contrary, the capitalist forces constitute our natural enemy despite the fact that they helped us to defeat their most dangerous representative. It may happen that we shall again decide to make use of their aid, but always with the sole aim of accelerating their final ruin. . . .

"The atomic bomb is a new factor by means of which the capitalist forces wish to destroy the Soviet Union and the victorious prospects of the working class. It is their only remaining hope. . . . Our aims have not been realized in the desired form because the construction of the Atomic bomb was speeded up and perfected as early as 1945. But we are not far from the realization of our aims. We must gain a little more time for the reorganization of our ranks and the perfecting of our preparations in arms and munitions.

"Our present policy should, therefore, be to follow a moderate line, in order to gain time for the economic and industrial reconstruction of the Soviet Union and of the other states under our control. Then the moment will come *when we can hurl ourselves into the battle for the final annihilation of reaction.*"[12]

Such were the reflections of Communist leaders as they emerged from World War II as the second greatest political power on earth. They felt Communism might have unprecedented possibilities as the "brave new world" entered the postwar period.

---

[12] *Report by the Continental News Service, November 8, 1946, and quoted in* "THE COMMUNIST THREAT TO CANADA," *Ottawa, 1947, pp. 10-11.*

MALENKOV KHRUSHCHEV BULGANIN

IX

Communist Attacks on the Free World During the Post-War Period

Stalin's plan for the expansion of Communism after the war involved three techniques: the creation of pro-Communist puppet governments in occupied territory, the military conquest of new territory by satellite armies, the further infiltration of free countries by Soviet espionage and propaganda organizations. In this chapter we shall try to account for the phenomenal success of these three programs. It should provide the answers to these questions:

Toward the last part of World War II did Allied leaders begin to suspect a Russian double cross? Why did Harry Hopkins make a special trip to Moscow a few months before he died?

How did the free world lose 100,000,000 people to the Iron Curtain through Soviet strategy?

How did the free world lose 450,000,000 more people through the conquest of China? What did the Wedemeyer Report reveal?

Do you think diplomatic blunders may have encouraged

the attack on South Korea? What significance do you attach to Owen Lattimore's amazing statement in 1949: "The thing to do is let South Korea fall, but not to let it look as if we pushed her"?

What was the turning point in the Korean war which gave the UN forces their first military advantage?

After the Korean cease-fire in 1953, what did the U.S. Secretary of State say to indicate that the U.S. was abandoning a twenty-year policy of appeasement?

What was the role of the FBI in the "Battle of the Underground?"

Why did the U.S. not do more to prevent the loss of French Indo-China?

In the dispute over Formosa, why did the Red Chinese call the U.S. a paper tiger?

What did Dimitry Z. Manuilsky say about the strategy of "peaceful coexistence"?

The Decay in U.S.—Soviet Relations at the End of World War II

The evidence of Communist subversion and aggression became so apparent toward the close of World War II that even some of those who had staked their professional careers on the friendship of the Soviet leaders began to sense a feeling of alarm. This included Harry Hopkins. Within a month after the death of President Roosevelt, Hopkins became so concerned with developments that he hurriedly made arrangements to see Stalin in person. At the time Hopkins was critically ill, with only a short time to live, but he forced himself to make this final pilgrimage to Moscow to try and salvage some of the remnants from the wreckage of what was to have been a master plan for post-war peace.

When he arrived in Moscow, however, Hopkins was confronted by a blunt and angry Stalin. We are indebted to

Post-War Communist Attacks

former Secretary of State, James F. Byrnes, for an account of what happened.[1] Stalin made an amazingly antagonistic verbal assault on the handling of the program Hopkins had sponsored for Russia—the program of Lend-Lease. The shock of this attack may be better appreciated when it is remembered that Hopkins considered himself to be the best friend the Soviets had in America. He and his associates had just spent billions of dollars and risked an atomic war to try and create a Russo-American partnership for peace. Probably Hopkins would not have been more startled by the treatment he received if Stalin had physically slapped him in the face. In reply, Hopkins vigorously pointed out "how liberally the United States (through him) had construed the law in sending foodstuffs and *other non-military items to their aid.*" Stalin admitted all of this but roughly crossed it off by saying the Soviets still could not forgive the United States for terminating Lend-Lease after V-Day in Europe.

At the moment it seemed that nothing would pacify Stalin but a brand new round of wide-open American Lend-Lease generosity; otherwise he apparently could think of no particular reason for even pretending to want the friendship of the United States any longer. He even threatened to boycott the United Nations Conference which was soon to be held in San Francisco.

For reasons which now seem quite incongruous, Hopkins continued to plead with Stalin to stay on the team and reiterated the many concessions which he was sure the Communists could gain by taking part in the United Nations organization. Like a pouting and spunky child, Stalin assumed an air of studied reluctance, but gradually gave in. By agreeing to join the United Nations Conference at San Francisco he wanted Hopkins to know he was doing the United States a tremendous favor.

Finally, Hopkins returned home. By the time of his death in January, 1946, there was already ample evidence

---

[1] *Byrnes, James F.,* "SPEAKING FRANKLY," *Harpers, New York, 1947.*

that peace-loving nations were in for a violent and stormy era as a result of the strategy of writing in the Soviets as full-fledged partners of the free world.

The Free World Loses 100 Million People

Obviously, a primary object of World War II was to liberate all of the countries occupied by the Axis powers. Russia was well aware that if she were to expand her influence into these liberated nations—particularly the ones which bordered the U.S.S.R.—she would have to do it in such a way as to create the illusion that these nations had gone Communistic through their own political self-determination. It became established Soviet policy to take secret but highly active interest in the affairs of these countries—to make them "voluntary" satellites through infiltration and subversion.

In some nations this plan brought immediate results. For example, it made satellites of Yugoslavia and Albania almost overnight because the Communists had captured the leadership of the anti-Nazi, anti-Fascist resistance movements during the war and as soon as these countries were liberated the Communists demanded the right to set up the new governments. Later, Stalin tried to purge Tito's regime but found it would not purge. Tito temporarily pulled Yugoslavia away from the Russian orbit but remained openly devoted to Marxism in spite of generous U.S. economic aid.

Russia also found a highly favorable condition for her schemes in the Eastern European countries. As a result of the military campaigns carried out by Soviet troops during the final phase of World War II, Red forces occupied all of Poland, Rumania, Bulgaria, Hungary, Czechoslovakia and most of what is now East Germany. The Soviet strategy for the "peaceful" conquest of these countries prior to withdrawing the Red troops was to encourage the creation of coalition governments including only left-wing parties. This gave the impression that these nations had some semblance of repre-

Post-War Communist Attacks

sentative government. The next step was to maneuver Communists into all key governmental positions. The third and final step was to force all parties to join in a "monolithic bloc" with the Communist leaders assuming complete dictatorial power.

Through this carefully executed maneuver the complete subjugation of all these countries was completed by 1949. The Communist Iron Curtain came clanking down on all their western borders and the free world found itself completely cut off from any contact with these former allies who represented approximately 100 million people.

The Free World Loses China with Her 450 Million People

At this same time there also came to the free world powers one of the most bitter lessons they had to learn in dealing with World Communism—the loss of China.

After fighting the Japanese militarists for fourteen years, China had approached the end of World War II with high hopes. The war had been fought under a dictatorship led by Chiang Kai-shek but his Nationalist Government had promised to set up a democratic constitution as soon as national unity would permit. As the war ended Chiang Kai-shek ordered the restoration of civil rights and inaugurated freedom of the press.

The Chinese leaders knew their greatest threat to peace was the small but well-trained army of Chinese Communists in the northwest; nevertheless, they went right ahead with their plans for a constitution which would allow the Communists full representation but would require them to disband their armed forces. There was confidence that a representative government could be worked out for all parties in China if armed insurrection were eliminated. In fact, Chiang Kai-shek invited the Communist leader, Mao Tse-tung, to come to the capital and see if they could reach a peaceful settlement of their difference. Mao came. He promised to cooperate in setting up a democracy but Chiang Kai-shek and his aides were not at all impressed with his superficial display of professed sincerity. Chiang later promised his nervous associates that he would never relinquish his dictatorial powers until he was completely satisfied that the government was safely in the hands of a substantial majority of the people—not just some noisy militant minority.

Effect of the Yalta Agreement on Post-War China

An early blow to China's hopes for a post-war peace came when it was learned that back in February, 1945, British and American diplomatic leaders at Yalta had agreed to give Russia extensive property rights in Manchuria if the Soviets would join in the war against Japan. Chiang Kai-shek was outraged by this unilateral arrangement (China was never consulted) and he never ceased to blame much of the subsequent disaster on this initial blunder.

The Yalta agreement allowed Russia to come racing into Manchuria (and North Korea) just six days before the Japanese capitulated. After a typically brutal Russian occupation, the Soviet troops fixed the Communist grip on this territory which the Japanese had extensively industrialized and which was one of the richest agricultural regions in all China. In fact, it was Manchuria that the Nationalists were expecting to use as the working base in bolstering China's battered economy.

However, after taking Manchuria, Stalin suddenly and unexpectedly agreed to withdraw his troops and recognize the Nationalist Government of China as the legal sovereign of that territory providing China would acknowledge Russia's property rights in Manchuria which Stalin had previously demanded at Yalta. This consisted of half ownership in the Manchurian railroads and the right to lease Port Arthur as a Russian naval base. Under strong pressure from the United

Post-War Communist Attacks

States and Great Britain, China signed this agreement with Russia on August 14, 1945.

Almost immediately Chiang Kai-shek knew this was a serious mistake. The treaty was nothing but a Russian tool of strategy which legally codified the mistakes at Yalta. As Chiang Kai-shek had feared, the Russians operated the Manchurian railroads as though they owned them outright. They not only set up a naval base at Port Arthur, but arrogantly refused to allow the Chinese to use their own port of Dairen. Instead of evacuating Manchuria, the Soviets began looting the entire region of all its heavy industry and shipping it to Russia as "war booty." This represented a stunning blow to China's future economic recovery.

But even more important than this was the Russians' strategy of delaying the removal of their troops by various pretexts until the Chinese Communists could come in from the northwest and occupy Manchuria. As the Communists came in, the Russians turned over to them the vast quantities of ammunition and war materiel which they had seized from the Japanese.

Consequently, when the Nationalists arrived to take over Manchuria, they were outraged to find that the Chinese Communists were already dug in. Immediately civil war loomed up as an inescapable consequence.

Chiang Kai-shek Attempts to Create A Democracy in China

All of this was happening right at the time the Nationalists were trying to prepare China for a constitutional form of government. On his own initiative Chiang had set May 5, 1946, as the first meeting of the Chinese National Assembly in which all parties were to take part. But, of course, this entire program to unify and democratize China was seriously jeopardized by the outbreak of war in Manchuria.

At this point the U.S. diplomats decided to take a hand.

The Naked Communist

They had planned the United Nations to preserve world peace and had insisted from the beginning that the Red leaders were potentially peaceful and had no territorial ambitions. Assuming this to be true they denounced Chiang for resisting the Chinese Reds. They accused him of creating new world tensions. General George C. Marshall was therefore sent over to China to stop the civil war.

General Marshall arrived in January, 1946. What happened after that is a long series of incidents, each one tragically demonstrating the error of trying to incorporate the ideas of world revolutionists within the framework of representative government. The Communists demanded a coalition government but insisted on keeping their own private army. They wanted a voice in the government of all China, but would not allow the central government to have a voice in the affairs of Communist-occupied areas of China. They agreed to a cease-fire and then launched aggressive attacks as soon as it served their own advantage to do so. They agreed to help set up a State Council representing all parties and then advised at the last moment that they would not participate. When the date for the first National Assembly was postponed so the Communists could participate, they used it as an excuse to accuse Chiang Kai-shek of setting the new date without proper authorization. After a second postponement, with the Communists still refusing to participate, the National Assembly finally convened on November 15, 1946, and a democratic constitution was approved and adopted on Christmas Day. But the Communists would have no part of it.

Chiang Kai-shek became completely convinced that the Communists would never negotiate a peaceful settlement but were out to win the whole domain of China by military conquest. He also believed the Communists could never represent the interests of China because their policies were created and imposed upon them by Moscow.

Time was to prove this analysis correct, but U.S. diplomatic strategists were the last to be convinced—and then only after the Chinese mainland had been lost. Furthermore, Chiang could not convince the U.S. diplomatic corps that he was justified in striking back when the Communists attacked him. When he tried to regain the territory recently seized by the Communists, it was described in Washington as "inexcusable aggression."

Disaster Strikes Down an Old U.S. Ally

Finally, in the summer of 1946, when the Communists had repeatedly violated the truce agreement, the Nationalists decided to vigorously counterattack and penetrate deep into Manchuria. The diplomats frantically ordered Chiang to stop, but he refused to do so. He said another truce would only allow the Communists time to re-group and come back even more fiercely than before. He also said it was his intention to continue the campaign to forcibly disarm the Communists and restore them to civilian status so that China could get on with her program of constitutional government without fear of constant insurrection.

This line of reasoning did not appeal to the State Department. Three different times Chiang was ordered to issue an unconditional cease-fire. To make it stick a U.S. embargo was finally placed on all aid to China. Only after United States aid abruptly halted did Chiang reluctantly agree to a cease-fire. General Marshall stated: "As Chief of Staff I armed 39 anti-Communist divisions (in China), now with a stroke of the pen I disarm them."

This proved a great boon to the Communists. While the Nationalists were being held down by U.S. diplomatic pressure, the Communists re-grouped their forces and prepared for the all-out campaign which later proved fatal to China. It is strange that even after Chiang had surrendered his own best judgment and issued a cease-fire, the U.S. embargo was not lifted. The Nationalist forces sat idly by, consuming many of their supplies which they feared would never be replaced. Later, when the Red tide had begun to roll in on Chiang, Congress did finally force through an "Aid to China" bill, but actual delivery of goods was not processed in time to be of any significant assistance.

From 1947 on, the morale of the Nationalist army disintegrated. It seemed apparent to Chinese military leaders that they were the victims of Communist aggression on the one hand and the victims of a total lack of insight by U.S. and British diplomats on the other.

After Chiang issued his unconditional cease-fire, General Marshall appealed to the Communist leaders to reopen negotiations for settlement. The Communists replied, but talked as though they were victors and made demands which even General Marshall labeled as completely unreasonable. They wanted all the rich areas of Manchuria from which they had just been driven. They wanted the National Assembly dissolved and demanded a predominant place in the proposed coalition government. It was obvious that any hope of settlement under such circumstances was impossible. General Marshall accepted this as a Communist pronouncement that the Communists were no longer interested in mediation and he therefore ended his mission by having President Truman call him home. He returned to America in January, 1947, and immediately became the new U.S. Secretary of State.

The Wedemeyer Report

There were many leaders in the United States Government who were completely dissatisfied with the way the Chinese Civil War had been handled. Therefore, in the summer of 1947, General Albert C. Wedemeyer was sent to Asia under Presidential orders to find out what was wrong in China. Upon his return he submitted a report which was extremely critical of the entire formula for peace which had been followed by General Marshall and the diplomatic corps. He indicated that not only had the interests of free China been violated, but the self-interests of the United States and all her Allies had been subordinated to the whims of the Communists. He recommended prompt and voluminous aid to the Nationalist Government and predicted that the situation could still be salvaged if help were provided in time.

Unfortunately, this report fell into the hands of the very people whom General Wedemeyer had criticized. Consequently, it was buried in department files for nearly two years and was not brought to light until long after it was too late to take the action it recommended.

Meanwhile, the forces of collapse were rapidly moving toward their inexorable climax. During 1947 and the early part of 1948 the armies of Chiang Kai-shek held up remarkably well, but toward the latter part of 1948, the lack of supplies and the internal disintegration of the Chinese economy took its toll. The fall of the Nationalist forces was not gradual—it was sudden and complete. Many thousands abandoned their positions and raced southward in disorganized confusion but other thousands threw down their arms and surrendered to the Chinese Communists on the spot.

By September, 1949, the Communist leaders were already wildly celebrating their victory as they set up the "People's Republic of China." Shortly afterwards Chiang acknowledged he was temporarily beaten and abandoned the entire mainland of China in order to flee with the straggling remnants of his army to Formosa.

The State Department White Paper of 1949

The fall of free China produced a wave of boiling indignation throughout the United States. Both political leaders and lay citizens felt that somehow an old ally had been subverted or betrayed. At the time few Americans were really aware of what was involved in the Chinese debacle, but they knew Chiang Kai-shek and America's interests had suffered a catastrophic defeat. There was widespread demand for the facts.

The men who had engineered the fatal Chinese policy

quickly collaborated on a report designed to justify their handling of America's interests in the Far East. It was called "United States Relations With China" and was published as a "White Paper" in 1949. To many people the arguments in this paper were highly persuasive, but not to all; in fact, the loss of China brought a startling awakening to some of those who had been with General Marshall and had trusted the Communists almost to the very last. One of these was America's ambassador to China during that critical period, Dr. John Leighton Stuart.[2] As a former missionary to China and president of Yenching University, he could not help but evaluate the fall of China as a vast human disaster. He criticized himself for having a part in it and censured his colleagues for trying to cover up their mistakes in the *White Paper*. Dr. Stuart frankly declared: "We Americans (who were carrying out the China policy) mainly saw the good things about the Chinese Communists, while not noticing carefully the intolerance, bigotry, deception, disregard for human life, and other evils which seem to be inherent in any totalitarian system. We kept Communist meanings for such adjectives as progressive, democratic, liberal, also bourgeois, reactionary, imperialist, as they intended we should do. We failed to realize fully the achievements to date and the potentialities of Chinese democracy. Therefore, we cannot escape a part of the responsibility of the great catastrophe—not only for China, but also for America and the free world—the loss of the Chinese mainland."

Concerning the *White Paper* he said: "I was, in fact, merely one of many persons who were perplexed and filled with apprehension by what they found in this extraordinary book. . . . It is clear that the purpose was not to produce a 'historian's history' but to select materials which had been used in making the policy in effect at the moment. What had

------

[2] *For a rather full report by this official who saw the fall of China see "FIFTY YEARS IN CHINA," by John Leighton Stuart, Random House, N.Y., 1955.*

been omitted were materials rejected in the making of policy, materials which had *not* been relied upon."

This had been General Wedemeyer's complaint. The diplomatic strategists were not willing to recognize the realities of the situation nor reverse their evaluation of Communist leaders even though the evidence of duplicity was everywhere.

An Amazing Development

By 1949 there was little excuse for any alert American to be further deceived by Communist strategy. Dozens of American-Communist spies had been exposed, the leading American Communists had been arrested by the FBI and convicted of conspiring to overthrow the U.S. Government by violence, Whittaker Chambers, Elizabeth Bentley and a swarm of ex-Communist agents had laid bare their souls, the Western Allies had gone through the vicious squeeze play of the Berlin blockade and the United States had spent billions in foreign aid to keep Russia from consuming all of Europe the same way she had taken over China. But in spite of all this, a meeting was sponsored by the State Department in October, 1949, which almost defies explanation.

It was held for the announced purpose of deciding what the "experts" believed should be done in the Far East. The meeting was presided over by Philip Jessup of the State Department, and those in attendance included not only State Department officials, but many select guests who were interested in Asia. Dr. John Leighton Stuart was present and afterwards expressed deep apprehension concerning the slant of the entire discussion. Harold Stassen was also present and later testified that the majority present favored the following policies:

1. European aid should be given priority over Asia.
2. Aid to Asia should not be started until after a "long and careful study."
3. Russian Communists should be considered "not as

aggressive as Hitler" and "not as apt to take direct military action to expand their empire."

4. *Communist China should be recognized by the U. S.*
5. Britain and India should be urged to follow suit in recognizing the Chinese Communists.
6. *The Chinese Communists should be allowed to take over Formosa.*
7. The Communists should be allowed to take over Hong Kong from Britain if the Communists insisted.
8. Nehru should not be given aid because of his "reactionary and arbitrary tendencies."
9. The Nationalist blockade of China should be broken and *economic aid sent to the Communist mainland.*
10. *No aid should be sent to Chiang* or to the anti-Communist guerillas in South China.

Two of the men at the conference who were foremost in promoting these policies were Owen Lattimore and Lawrence Rosinger. Both were eventually identified by Louis Budenz (former editor of the Daily Worker testifying under oath) as members of the Communist Party.*

Even if there had been no such identification, the glaring truth which every man at the conference should have known was the fact that this entire list of policies was a carbon copy of the prevailing "party line" coming out of Moscow. For months these very policies had been hammered out in every edition of the Communist press. It was a singular commentary on the judgment and professional discernment of those officials who fell in with these fantastic recommendations —particularly in the light of the provocative and inflammatory policies which Russia was using at that very moment to threaten nations in nearly every region of the free world.

Three months after this conference, the new Secretary of State, Dean Acheson, announced several policies portending the loss of Formosa and the liquidation of the Chinese Nation-

---

* See "REPORT OF THE MCCARREN COMMITTEE TO THE SENATE," *p. 1049 and also* "REPORT OF THE HEARINGS ON PHILIP JESSUP'S NOMI-NATION," *pp. 714-721. For Budenz's testimony, see* "REPORT OF THE MCCARREN COMMITTEE TO THE SENATE," *p. 148.*

Post-War Communist Attacks

alists by the Communists. First, he overruled the recommendation of the Joint Chiefs of Staff (to give strong military aid to Chiang) by announcing on January 12, 1950, that the principles itemized above as point No. 6 and point No. 10 were to be official U.S. policy. He also stated that the U.S. defense perimeter in the Pacific did not include either Formosa or South Korea. He stated that if an attack should occur outside the U.S. defense perimeter "the initial reliance must be on the people attacked to resist it." Then he suggested that they could appeal to the United Nations. This was simply a blunt statement that the U.S. diplomats were abandoning Formosa and Korea. This announcement was shocking to many students of the Far East, not only because the policy violated U.S. self-interest, but because it literally *invited* Communist attack on these free-world allies by giving advance notice that these areas could be invaded without interference from the United States.

It took just six months for the Communists to select and prepare their point of attack. They chose the practically defenseless territory of South Korea as the first theater of war.

The Communist Attack on South Korea

It will be recalled that the Yalta agreement allowed Russia to take over North Korea at the same time the Soviets occupied Manchuria. As elsewhere, the Russians did not withdraw their troops until a strong Communist puppet government was firmly entrenched. As for South Korea, U.S. forces occupied the territory up to the 38th parallel.

During 1949 a United Nations mandate required both Russia and the U.S. to withdraw their troops. The Russians left behind them a powerful North Korean Red Army consisting of 187,000 well-trained and well-equipped troops, 173 Russian tanks, quantities of Russian-built artillery and 200 Russian planes. On the other hand, South Korea was a new-born Republic with an army of 96,000 men who were poorly equipped, with practically no tanks, anti-tank weapons, heavy artillery or fighter planes. This meant that by the end of 1949 South Korea was even more vulnerable to attack from North Korea than Formosa was from Communist China. And the Washington diplomats had assured both Formosa and Korea that in case of attack they definitely could not expect any military help from the United States. As spokesman for the diplomatic left-wing contingent, Owen Lattimore explained the situation: "The thing to do is let South Korea fall, but not to let it look as if we pushed it!"[3]

In the early dawn of Sunday, June 25, 1950, 8 divisions of the North Korean Red Army spilled across the 38th parallel and plunged southward toward the city of Seoul. Frantic calls went out from President Sigmund Rhee to the Security Council of the United Nations, to President Truman in Washington and to General Douglas MacArthur in Japan. All three responded. The Security Council pronounced North Korea guilty of a breach of the peace and ordered her troops back to the 38th parallel. (If Russia had been represented, she no doubt would have vetoed this action, but the Soviet delegates were boycotting the Security Council because China continued to be represented by the Nationalists rather than by the Chinese Communists.) General MacArthur responded by flying to Korea and reporting the desperate situation to Washington. President Truman responded by completely reversing the policy of his diplomatic advisers and ordering General MacArthur to pour U.S. ground troops in from Japan to stop the red tide. Thus the war began.

For several weeks the situation looked very black. General MacArthur was made supreme commander of all United Nations forces, but at first these were so limited that the shallow beachhead at Pusan was about all they could hold. Then General MacArthur formulated a desperate plan. It was so difficult and illogical that he felt certain it would come to the Communists as a complete surprise. It did. On September 15, half way up the Korean Peninsula, the U.S. Navy (with two

---

[3] *A full article on this theme appeared in the New York "*DAILY COMPASS*," under date of July 17, 1949.*

Post-War Communist Attacks

British carriers), the Air Force, Army and Marine Corps combined to launch an ingenious invasion at Inchon—a point where the 29-foot tide made a landing seem fantastic. Split-second timing permitted landings and the next thing the North Koreans knew they were trapped in the jaws of a mighty military pincer movement which cut across their supply lines and then rapidly closed in to wipe out the flower of the whole North Korean Army which, of course, was concentrated in the South. It was a magnificent victory.

MacArthur then turned his armies toward the north. The ROK's (South Koreans) went up the East Coast while other UN troops went up the West Coast. In doing this, General MacArthur was required to act on obscure hints rather than specific directions from Washington and the UN. For a while it appeared that he might be forbidden to pursue the enemy forces retreating to the North.

By the middle of October the coastal spearheads of the UN offensive were nearing the northernmost parts of Korea and the war appeared practically over. There was the immediate prospect of unifying the entire Korean Peninsula and setting up a democratic republic. Then, in November, unexpectedly disaster struck.

From across the northern Korean boundary of the Yalu River came the first flood tide of what turned out to be a Chinese Communist army of one million men. As these troops came pouring into North Korea, the UN forces found themselves smothered by a great wave of fanatical, screaming, suicidal humanity. MacArthur radioed to Washington: "We face an entirely new war!"

The UN lines were cut to ribbons as their wall of defense was pushed back below the 38th parallel. General MacArthur could scarcely believe that the Chinese Communists would dare to risk the massive retaliation of the United States atomic bombing Air Force by this inexcusable assault on UN forces. However, what he did not know, but soon discovered, was the appalling fact that the Chinese had already been assured by their intelligence agents that the diplomats in Washington, London and New York were not going to allow Mac-

Arthur to retaliate with the U.S. Air Force. MacArthur was going to be restricted to "limited" warfare.

It was in this hour that General MacArthur found that pro-Communist forces in the UN and left-wing sympathizers in the State Department were swamping the policies of the White House, the Joint Chiefs of Staff and those who had charge of the Korean War. He found that vast supplies which he badly needed were being diverted to Europe in accordance with point No. 1 of the State Department Conference. He was specifically restricted from following Chinese jets to their bases or bombing the Manchurian Railroad which was dumping mountains of supplies on the north banks of the Yalu River. He was forbidden to bomb the Yalu bridge over which troops and supplies were funneled, and his own supplies and replacements were cut back to the point where a counter-offensive became strategically difficult, if not impossible. The final blow came when the diplomats flatly turned down Chiang Kai-shek's enthusiastic offer to send thousands of trained Nationalist troops from Formosa to fight in Korea.

Over a period of four months General MacArthur watched the slaughter resulting from these stalemate policies. Finally, he could contain himself no longer. He violated a presidential gag order dated December 6, 1950, and answered a written inquiry from Congressman Joseph W. Martin concerning the inexplicable reverses which UN forces were suffering in Korea. The General's letter giving recommendations for the winning of the war was read in Congress April 5, 1951, and five days later, President Truman ordered MacArthur summarily withdrawn from all commands.

General MacArthur was relieved by General Matthew B. Ridgeway and he returned to the United States completely perplexed by the sudden termination of his military career. It was not until he landed in San Francisco and met the first wave of shouting, cheering, admiring fellow citizens that he realized that the sickness in the American body politic was not in all its members but only in one corner of its head.

It will be recalled that two more years of military stagnation followed the recall of General MacArthur. Subsequently,

Post-War Communist Attacks

hearings before Congressional committees permitted General Mark Clark, General George E. Stratemeyer, General James A. Van Fleet, Admiral Charles Joy and others to explain what happened to their commands in Korea. Each one verified the fact that the military was never permitted to fight a winning war. The diplomats had imposed upon them a theory called "Communist Containment," which in actual operation resulted in the containment of the UN fighting forces instead of the Communists. It soon became apparent that the Korean War had been run by the same team and according to the same policies as those which resulted in the fall of China.

It was also to be revealed at a later date that not only had the machinations of confused diplomats contributed to the semi-defeat in Korea but that fulltime under-cover agents of Soviet Russia had often stood at the elbows of officials in London, Washington and at the UN in New York to argue the Moscow line. Among the high-level spies for Russia during this critical period were two top British diplomats, Donald MacLean and Guy Burgess. MacLean was head of the American desk in Britain's diplomatic headquarters at London, Burgess was the second secretary of the British Embassy in Washington. Both fled behind the Iron Curtain when they were about to be arrested by British Intelligence.

The Korean Armistice

By the time President Eisenhower took office in January, 1953, there was a general feeling of gloom and despair concerning Korea. The people desperately desired to somehow stop the bloodshed. The hopes for peace were suddenly accelerated by a news flash of March 5 which swept round the world. Joseph Stalin was dead!

The next day a new government took over in Russia and the leader turned out to be Stalin's former secretary and the keeper of the secret Communist files—Georgi Malenkov. He had seized power by joining forces with Lavrenti P. Beria, head of the secret police who had an army of agents and troops numbering two million. Beria also had charge of the forced labor camps and supervised the atomic energy plants.

However, when Malenkov and Beria took over as heirs of Stalin they immediately found themselves confronted by an explosive economic crisis. Pressure was building up inside Russia (and her satellites) just as it did in 1922 and again in 1932. Malenkov therefore offered respite to his people: "Let us now lay heavy industry aside for awhile. The people cannot eat heavy industry. . . . We should care for the needs of our people." This was the beginning of a radical new policy for the U.S.S.R. At home the slogan was "More Food"; abroad Malenkov's slogan was a campaign for "Peaceful Coexistence" with all the democracies.

It was just twenty-three days after Stalin died that the Communist Chinese acted on their new signals and opened negotiations with the UN commanders for an armistice. This finally led to the signing of a truce on July 27, 1953. It became effective twelve days later.

Thus ended the Korean War. It had cost the United States 20 billion dollars and more than 135,000 casualties. It had cost South Korea 1 million dead, another million maimed and wounded, 9 million left homeless and saddled South Korea with 4 million refugees from North Korea.

The U.S. Summarily Abandons Its Twenty-Year Policy of Appeasement

The people of the United States came out of the Korean War sadder and wiser than when they went in. Authorities have stated that two things happened in the Korean War which may yet brand it as the greatest blunder the Communist strategists ever made. First, it awakened the United States to the necessity of vigorously rearming and staying armed so long as the Communist threat exists. Second, it demonstrated to the people of the United States the inherent weaknesses of the United Nations. As Senator Robert A. Taft

Post-War Communist Attacks

summed it up: "The United Nations serves a very useful purpose as a town meeting of the world . . . but it is an impossible weapon against forcible aggression."

Back in 1950 when the UN called upon all its members to furnish the means to resist the Communists, only 16 countries responded with the highly essential ingredient of armed troops. Altogether, these 16 nations furnished an army of 35,000 fighting men. Little South Korea maintained a fighting force of 400,000 men while the United States made up the difference by furnishing a force of 350,000. More than one million American GI's had to be rotated through Korea to maintain the U.S. quota of military strength. In the mind of the average American the UN had therefore ceased to represent "collective security." It was difficult to forget that while Americans and South Koreans were taking the brunt of the war, Russia and Britain had both violated the UN embargo by shipping strategic materials to Red China. On the floor of the UN, Andrei Vishinsky had thrown down the Russian challenge: "The Soviet Union has never concealed the fact that it sold and continues to sell armaments to its ally, China!"

The end of the Korean War marked the end of an era. During the summer of 1953 the United States served notice on Britain and France that if the Communists broke the cease-fire agreement in Korea we would immediately launch a major war against China. Both Britain and France agreed to support this stand. Many did not realize it at the time, but by this action the United States was passing the death sentence on a twenty-year-old policy of Communist appeasement.

The Role of the FBI
in the Battle of the Underground

No one could have welcomed the end of appeasement with greater relief than John Edgar Hoover, head of the FBI and the number-one law enforcement personality in the United

States. Since 1919 he had struggled to illuminate the minds of government leaders as well as the public generally concerning the conspiratorial nature of Communism. As an assistant to the Attorney General in 1919 he had prepared one of the first legal briefs reflecting the subversive aspects of the world-wide Communist movement.

During the twenty years of appeasement, when many Americans had been lulled into a sense of security by the "sweet talk of Communist United Front propaganda," John Edgar Hoover had struck out with two-fisted blows at the Red menace which was gnawing at the vitals of American life:

"The American Communist . . . must be placed in the same category as the Ku Klux Klan, the now defunct German-American Bund, and other totalitarian groups. . . . As common criminals seek the cover of darkness, Communists, behind the protection of false fronts, carry on their sinister and vicious program, intent on swindling and robbing Americans of their heritage of freedom."

John Edgar Hoover was a great disappointment to the Communists. In most countries the Red leaders had been able to completely discredit the agencies handling the police powers of government by blasting them with charges of corruption and violation of civil liberties. However, the Director of the FBI had spent his adult lifetime building the FBI so that the public would know that any such charges would be false and fraudulent. Over the years the public had learned that FBI agents spent as much time checking out innocent suspects as they spent in ferreting out the guilty. In fact, by careful investigation and humane treatment of the guilty, the FBI had secured confessions in 85 per cent of its cases.[4]

Therefore, the Communists were deeply disappointed with the results of their campaign to portray the FBI as an American Gestapo. The Communists leaders were further embittered by the knowledge that the FBI had trained its personnel to be just what governmental officers in a free nation

---

[4] *The role of the FBI is well presented in* "THE FBI STORY," *by Don Whitehead, Random House, 1956.*

Post-War Communist Attacks

should be—alert, intelligent, scientific and hard working. And what particularly frightened the Reds was the quiet methodical way in which Bureau agents went after subversives—all of which foreshadowed a day of reckoning for Communist strategists. It came July 20, 1948, when all the top leaders of the Communist Party of America were indicted. The "Big Eleven" who stood trial were all convicted. Six of their attorneys were also fined or imprisoned for contemptuous conduct during the trial. Four of the eleven Communists jumped their $20,000 bail bond and the FBI had to launch an international investigation to have them returned.

Shortly afterwards the Government became convinced that Soviet espionage agents had been stealing atomic information and the FBI was given jurisdiction. Within weeks the FBI had gristed through tons of records, interviewed hundreds of "restricted" employees at various atomic energy plants and emerged from the slow elimination process to point the finger of justice at a physicist, Klaus Fuchs, who had spent considerable time at Los Alamos. However, at that moment the German-born, naturalized Britisher was the dignified director of England's atomic energy establishment at Harwell.

Acting on the FBI tip that Klaus Fuchs was the principal suspect in the subversion of the free world's monopoly of the atomic bomb, British Intelligence went to work. Within one month they saw some evidence that the FBI might be right. After another month they had no doubt about it. On February 3, 1949, the British announced that Fuchs had been arrested and had made a full confession.

Fuch's confession sent the FBI on another hunt. Fuchs said he gave packets of information dealing with the atomic bomb to a person known to him only as "Raymond." This person had to be identified and located since he was apparently the courier who delivered the bomb secrets to the Soviet Consulate in New York. Although the FBI had nothing to start with but a physical description, a phony name and the possibility that the courier might be a chemist, agents finally came up with the right man. It was Harry Gold.

Harry Gold confessed and this enabled the FBI to finally

unravel the answer to a question which had puzzled the whole nation: "How did the Russians get hold of information on the ingenious trigger mechanism of the atomic bomb which should have taken the Russians many years to discover?" Harry Gold said they stole it. The FBI once more took up the trail and this time it led to the doorstep of two U.S. citizens, Julius and Ethel Rosenberg.

The investigation revealed that Julius Rosenberg had pressured his young brother-in-law, David Greenglass, to turn over to Harry Gold and himself all the basic information about the trigger device without which the bomb could not be exploded. David Greenglass worked at the atomic energy laboratory at Los Alamos and had a rather intimate knowledge of the construction of the bomb and the lens apparatus by which it was detonated. Greenglass was finally induced to draw up sketches of the bomb dropped on Hiroshima and to provide detailed drawings of the detonator lens. The Rosenbergs then channeled this information into the regular Russian espionage apparatus.

As soon as the Communist scientists received this data they quickly closed the gap in the atomic race and exploded a Russian bomb. It will be recalled that this came as a great shock to the startled West. The Red leaders capitalized on this temporary advantage by rattling their atomic sabers and telling the Communist leaders in China and North Korea to start casting about for some early military conquest. Eagerly they went to work preparing for the Korean War. In fact, by the time Julius and Ethel Rosenberg had been convicted and were ready for sentence the United States was in the midst of the Korean conflict. Thousands of American lives were being sacrificed to hold back the tide of desolation which the Rosenbergs had helped to turn loose.

Judge Irving Robert Kaufman looked down at this man and woman and said:

"Plain, deliberate contemplated murder is dwarfed in magnitude by comparison with the crime you have committed. . . . I believe your conduct in putting into the hands of the Russians the A-bomb, years before our best scientists pre-

Post-War Communist Attacks

dicted Russia would perfect the bomb has already caused in **201**
my opinion, the Communist aggression in Korea, with the re-
sultant casualties exceeding 50,000 and who knows but that
millions more of innocent people may pay the price of your
treason. Indeed, by your betrayal you undoubtedly have
altered the course of history . . . What I am about to say is not
easy for me. I have deliberated for hours, days and nights . . . .
I have searched the records—I have searched my conscience
—to find some reason for mercy—for it is only human to be
merciful and it is natural to try and spare lives. I am convinced, however, that I would violate the solemn and sacred
trust that the people of this land have placed in my hands were
I to show leniency to the defendants Rosenberg. It is not in
my power, Julius and Ethel Rosenberg, to forgive you. Only
the Lord can find mercy for what you have done . . . you are
hereby sentenced to the punishment of death."

David Greenglass was sentenced to fifteen years.

It was a tragic chapter in American history, but it verified Mr. Hoover's original assertion that the Red leaders "carry
on their sinister and vicious program, intent on swindling and
robbing Americans of their heritage of freedom."

But John Edgar Hoover knew that the communist revolutionists would never try to strike their final, deadly blow at
the United States as long as they were losing the battle of
the underground. He also felt that carefully selected and
carefully trained young Americans could match strategems
with the Red leaders and win. The history of the FBI during Mr. Hoover's remarkable administration gives ample
justification for his feelings of enthusiasm and complete confidence in the ultimate victory of America's underground
soldiers of freedom.

The Crack in the Iron Curtain

By 1953 the Kremlin was not only suffering embarrassment abroad but a wide crack in the Iron Curtain revealed that

The Naked Communist

202 the Communist empire was in desperate straits at home. The myth of Communist strength and unity was uncovered. In East Germany riots broke out as the people faced tanks with bricks and bare hands. To make matters worse, insubordinate Russian officers and soldiers had to be executed for refusing to fire into the German crowds. A rash of uprisings also broke out in Czechoslovakia and threatened to break out in Poland, Bulgaria and the Ukraine.

Economists discovered from admissions of Malenkov in his speeches and official releases that Russians were working 38 hours a week for food that took only 26 hours to earn in 1928. Furthermore, Russia—with a substantial increase in population—was producing less food under State Socialism than she had produced under the NEP in 1928. The riots in the satellite countries were the result of the realization that Russia would probably never fulfill her propaganda promise to furnish them food, clothing and machinery. On the contrary, the bankrupt U.S.S.R. had been feeding like a great parasite on the satellite countries.

In contrast to the Iron Curtain countries the Western European nations were enjoying the greatest period of prosperity in forty years. The American people had donated 50 billion dollars to the post-war recovery of these countries and they were rapidly reaching the point where they could begin to stand alone. There was a healthy resurgence of faith in free enterprise capitalism as the United States reached the zenith of its prosperity and demonstrated its capacity to not only produce more wealth than any other nation but to distribute it more equitably among its people.

A leading Socialist in Britain, Professor W. Arthur Lewis, openly acknowledged that Socialism had been a great disappointment in England: "What has been done . . . is to transfer property not to the workers but to the Government. Workers continue to be employees, subject to all the frustrations of working under orders in large undertakings. . . . Those who expected nationalization to raise wages have . . . been disappointed. . . . It does not solve the problem of labor relations; it reduces private wealth . . . it raises unsolved problems of

Post-War Communist Attacks

control; and it raises the issue of how much power we want our Government to have."[5]

The Communist Conquest in Indo-China

After the Korean Armistice the Chinese Communists did not allow Russia's domestic problems to dull their appetite for further aggression. They marched off to complete the Red conquest of Indo-China. Originally the war in Indo-China had been an attempt by the native population to **free** itself from French colonialism. However, Red infiltration by the Communist Chinese had finally changed the conflict from a war for freedom to a war between France and the Chinese Reds. The compromising influence of the French Communist Party (the largest single party in France) made the fatal outcome of the war dependent only on the passing of time. Defeat to the French came on July 21, 1954. At Geneva the Red Chinese jubilantly agreed to stop fighting in exchange for 12,000,000 people and 61,000 square miles of Indo-China.

Mao Tse-tung was now intoxicated with double success. Even Russia felt it necessary to make concessions to Mao and his Chinese Communists in order to insure their continued loyalty to the Communist Motherland. In October, 1954, Russian officials trekked to Peiping and flattered Mao with the following promises:

1. *To evacuate Port Arthur which Russia was authorized to lease at Yalta.*
2. *To sell to China (on easy terms) the railroads and other industries which Russia had been operating since the war as a "Partner."*
3. *To loan China 130,000,000 dollars.*
4. *To help build two railroads across China.*
5. *To help China build 15 new heavy industrial projects.*
6. *To campaign for the seizure of Formosa.*

---

[5] "U. S. NEWS AND WORLD REPORT," *"Socialists Sour on Socialism," July 8, 1955, p. 48.*

7. *To campaign for the inclusion of Japan in the Communist orbit.*

It was apparent that even though Russia was talking "peaceful coexistence" the free world would have little relief from the war-making plans of Red China.

The Task of Isolating a World Aggressor

From the point of view of the United States, the Indo-China fiasco was a dismal political tragedy. The 100 Communists in the French Parliament (who even refused to stand in tribute to the French war dead) engineered the collapse of the seven-year war. As the U.S. Secretary of State addressed the armistice meeting at Geneva he lashed out at the cowardice and subversion which had sacrificed 12,000,000 more human beings to Red aggression: "Peace," he said, "is always easy to achieve—by surrender. Unity is also easy to achieve—by surrender. The hard task, the task that confronts us, is to combine peace and unity with Freedom!"

Secretary Dulles left Geneva to carry out a feverish, round-the-world campaign to get all free nations to make an "agonizing reappraisal" of the ridiculous concessions which were being made to Communist imperialism. In 20 months he covered over 152,000 miles and when he was through the United States had become a party to (or strengthened its position in) a chain of regional compacts specifically designed to reinforce Communist containment. To the dismay of the Soviet strategists, Article 52 of the UN Charter contained a loophole which permitted this procedure. Therefore, the United States openly began to use NATO, SEATO and similar regional organizations as collective agencies for mutual security. To a large extent this nullified the paralyzing choke-hold which the Soviets had previously held on the West through its abusive use of the veto power in the UN Security Council.

The United States also announced that she did not intend to sit back and watch Russia construct its armada of long-

Post-War Communist Attacks

range bombers which Communist press releases described as capable of dropping H-bombs on American cities. The U.S. answer to this was the rapid construction of a ring of U.S. defense bases on the fringe of the Iron Curtain. Immediately the roar of an injured bear came thundering out of Russia: "We are being threatened with annihilation!"

Secretary Dulles soberly reaffirmed a truth which he was well aware the Communists already knew—namely, that no nation need fear these bases except an aggressor. Then he expounded in clear-cut, hard-hitting terminology the new U.S. doctrine of "massive retaliation" which he warned would be triggered instantly in case the Soviet Empire dared fulfill its oft repeated threat of a surprise attack on the free world.

For awhile there was an ominous silence in Moscow.

Russia Tests the New U.S. "Get Tough" Policy

Toward the latter part of 1954 it became apparent that serious political adjustments were going on inside Russia. A bellicose, bullet-headed personality named Nikita S. Khrushchev and a punctilious party politician named Nikolai Bulganin began to appear more frequently in the news. An ex-Soviet official (Nikolai E. Khokhlov) declared this to be a bad sign. He described Khrushchev and Bulganin as promoters of world Communism, in contrast to Malenkov and Beria who wanted first to improve living conditions for Russians.

In the fall of 1954, Khrushchev and Bulganin led a delegation to Peiping. There the Chinese were given instructions to prepare for an assault on Formosa. From this, it became apparent that completely new lines of power had been drawn in Russia. Eventually it came out that Malenkov had deserted his partner, Beria, and joined forces with the new Khrushchev-Bulganin forces. In the latter part of December, Beria and three of his aides were shot. Malenkov was summarily demoted but he had switched sides in time to save his life. Bulganin took his place and Khrushchev hovered in the backround setting policy and announcing the new slogans, "return to heavy industry—armaments" and "the growing of food by decree."

Meanwhile the Chinese Communists had also caught the spirit of the new leadership and began fronting for Moscow by tantalizing the democracies with the shocking announcement that they had deliberately held back U.S. officers and men in violation of the prisoner-exchange agreement at the close of the Korean War.

The armistice agreement at Panmunjom had specifically provided that all UN prisoners who desired repatriation would be returned even though some of them might be charged with some crime. Now, however, the Chinese Communists were defiantly announcing that they had secretly held back a number of American prisoners because they were charged with espionage or some other type of crime. U.S. indignation reached a white heat as many Americans began to realize for the first time how completely impossible it is to depend on a Communist pledge.

In spite of public indignation, however, American feelings were somewhat compromised at this particular moment by a rapidly growing desire on the part of many citizens to forget the whole foreign "mess" and get on with home-front developments which promised to provide an all-time record of American free enterprise prosperity.

Mao Tse-tung accurately diagnosed this national feeling as an anti-war sentiment, and he therefore accelerated his campaign of propaganda throughout Asia by representing the United States as a "paper tiger." He taunted the United States with additional disclosures of illegally-held American prisoners of war and by open implication boastfully defied the United States Government to try and do something about it.

He became so enthusiastic in his campaign that he finally decided to prove the impotency of American influence to all the world by acting on Khrushchev's fighting orders and strike at Formosa. In a matter of weeks the offshore islands in the hands of the Nationalists began to be bombed from the Chinese mainland. It was the preliminary phase of an all-out attack on Chiang Kai-shek's last outpost.

This was a highly critical hour for the United States since

Post-War Communist Attacks

she had committed herself to defend Formosa. If she wavered, the light of freedom could very easily go out in Southeast Asia. One-half billion "neutral" Asians also watched keenly as U.S. leaders measured the risk and fathomed the depths of their own moral convictions.

Early in February, 1955, the Chinese Reds and the other World Communists got their answer. It was a U.S. Congressional resolution supported by both parties which confirmed the authority of the President of the United States to throw the Seventh Fleet into the Formosa Straits and give orders to wage an all-out war if attacked. This would obviously include the use of nuclear weapons.

The "little nations" of South East Asia stood up and cheered. It was apparent that the U.S. not only had the will to talk "massive retaliation" but the will to wage it. At the Afro-Asian conference at Bandung several of the little nations boldly showed their colors. They badgered the Chinese Communist delegates with cries of "Communist colonialism" and "Communist aggression." It was a severe blow to the prestige and propaganda of Mao Tse-tung and his Communist backers in Moscow.

Within a matter of weeks the "stand firm" policy of the U.S. and her Pacific Allies began bearing miraculous fruit. Orders went out from Moscow that coexistence was once more the sweet theme of the hour. The Chinese began releasing U.S. prisoners they had held illegally. The issue of Formosa was allowed to slip quietly into the background. Khrushchev extended an invitation to the United States to exchange visitors —editors, congressmen, farmers—he even said he might come himself, sometime. All over the world the hard-knuckled tension of the ten post-war years began to subside. There seemed to be general satisfaction with the new and unexpected turn of events throughout the world and the democracies settled back once more to the pursuit of their own normal domestic affairs.

But in the midst of it all came a sinister warning from military intelligence. Reports indicated that while the emphasis of "soft" policies toward the democracies was being promoted abroad, a tough, imperialistic policy was being fed to the troops at home. Soviet troops were being taught that "the importance of the surprise factor in contemporary war has increased enormously," and "the Communist Party demands that the whole personnel of our Army and Navy should be imbued with the spirit of maximum vigilance and constant and high military preparedness, so as to be able to wrest the initiative from the hands of the enemy, and, having delivered smashing blows against him, finally defeat him completely."[6]

All this had a familiar spirit. It reminded alert Americans of a significant statement made by Dimitry Z. Manuilsky who represented the U.S.S.R. in presiding over the Security Council of the United Nations in 1949. At the Lenin School of Political Warfare in Moscow he had taught: "War to the hilt between communism and capitalism is inevitable. Today, of course, we are not strong enough to attack. . . . To win we shall need the element of surprise. The bourgeoisie will have to be put to sleep. So we shall begin by launching the most spectacular peace movements on record. There will be electrifying overtures and unheard of concessions. The capitalist countries, stupid and decadent, will rejoice to cooperate in their own destruction. They will leap at another chance to be friends. As soon as their guard is down, we shall smash them with our clenched fist!"[7]

---

[6] *Article in* "PRAVDA," *May 5, 1955, by Major General D. Korniyenko.*

[7] *Quoted by Joseph Z. Kornfeder who was a student at the school. In a letter to Dr. J. D. Bales of Harding College dated March 7, 1961, Mr. Kornfeder said: "Enclosed is a copy of the quote you asked for. It is part of what he (Manuilsky) said to a group of senior Lenin School students at a conference held in Moscow, March, 1930, at which I, as one of the students, was present."*

KHRUSHCHEV

X

Communism Under Khrushchev

By 1955 it was vividly apparent that the most vicious kind of political in-fighting was being waged in Moscow by the Communist contestants for Stalin's throne. Already Beria and his aides had been shot. There were signs of vast power shifts behind the scenes and out of the rancor and roar of the secret battle in the Kremlin the personality which seemed to be emerging on top of the conspiratorial heap was Nikita Khrushchev.

Of all the contenders for power in Russia, Khrushchev was probably the least well known in the West. Therefore, a U.S. Congressional committee decided to get the Khrushchev story. They invited anyone who had known Khrushchev to come in and testify. A stream of witnesses responded, but the story they told was gruesome and ugly. The hopes of many Western diplomats for improved Russian relations collapsed as they heard the record of the Red leader with whom free men would now have to deal. Here was no ordinary Communist politician or party hack. Khrushchev was revealed to be a creature of criminal cunning with an all-consuming passion for power.

Khrushchev as the Dictator of the Ukraine

Many of the witnesses told of the early days when Khrushchev was first grasping for power and recognition. They revealed that his loyalty to Communism was the blind, senseless kind. Having been raised almost an illiterate, Khrushchev did not get his elementary education until after he had become a full-grown adult. As a boy he had been a shepherd, later learning the trade of blacksmith and locksmith. At 17 he ran away from the obscure Ukrainian village of Kalinovka where he had been born April 17, 1894. For several years Khrushchev was a roaming itinerant worker but in 1918 he joined the Communist Party and fought with the Red Army during the Russian civil war. In 1922 he commenced his first formal education which lasted three years. By 1929 his dogged party loyalty had won him a berth in the Joseph Stalin Industrial Academy, and by 1931 he had become a local party official in Moscow.

Khrushchev soon won favor with Stalin by joining in a drive to purge Stalin's enemies from the local party machinery. More than 500 men and women were turned over to the secret police for execution. Later Stalin said that while Khrushchev was repulsive to him, he was impressed with the Ukrainian's capacity to kill or turn on old friends when party policy demanded it. Stalin therefore assigned Khrushchev the task of going back to the Ukraine and forcing his own people to live under the lash of total Communist suppression. The Red leaders had been using wholesale executions to stifle resistance. Khrushchev said he had a better way. He would use mass *starvation!* Witnesses to this man-made famine told of the suffering and death:

NICHOLAS PRYCHODOKO: I observed covered wagons moving along the street on which I lived and also on other streets in Kiev. They were hauling corpses for disposal. . . . These

Communism Under Khrushchev

were peasants who flocked to the cities for some crust of bread. . . . My personal friend . . . was a surgeon at a hospital in the Ukraine. . . . He put a white frock on me, just as he was in a white frock, and we went outside to a very large garage in the hospital area. He and I entered it. When he switched on the light, I saw 2,000 to 3,000 corpses laid along the walls.

MR. ARENS: What caused the death of these people?

MR. PRYCHODOKO: Starvation.

MR. ARENS: What caused the starvation?

MR. PRYCHODOKO: . . . We found some statistics in hiding places in the cellar of the Academy of Sciences. They revealed that the food in 1932 was sufficient to feed all Ukrainians for 2 years and 4 months. But except for about 10 per cent, the crop was immediately dispatched from the threshing machines for export to parts outside of Ukraine. That was the cause of the hunger.

MR. ARENS: Why did the Communist regime seize the crops in Ukraine during this period?

MR. PRYCHODOKO: Because at all times there was . . . various kinds of resistance to the Communist government in Ukraine and the collectivization drive in Moscow. . . .

MR. ARENS: How many people were starved to death by this man-made famine in Ukraine in the thirties?

MR. PRYCHODOKO: It is estimated to be 6 to 7 million, most of them peasants.[1]

Witnesses testified that after millions of lives had been destroyed under Khrushchev's administration, the collectivized farms were finally set up. Khrushchev was rewarded in 1934 when Stalin appointed him to the powerful Central Committee of the Communist hierarchy in Moscow.

However, because of continued unrest and resistance to Communism, Khrushchev was sent back to the Ukraine as its political dictator in 1938. Once again the people were subjected to a vast purge. So violently did they react to this new barbarity that when World War II broke out and the

---

[1] "THE CRIMES OF KHRUSHCHEV," *House Committee on Un-American Activities, September, 1959, Part 2, pp. 1-2.*

Nazis moved in the Germans were welcomed by the Ukrainians as liberators. Nikita Khrushchev never forgave them for that. Before fleeing toward Moscow, he poured out his vengeance against them. Official reports show that when the Nazis arrived, they found numerous mass graves. In one area alone there were over 90 mammoth burial plots containing approximately 10,000 bodies of "peasants, workers and priests," each with hands tied behind the back and a bullet in the head.

After the Germans were driven out in 1944, Khrushchev once more returned to the Ukraine grimly determined to annihilate "all collaborationists." Whole segments of the population were deported, a complete liquidation of the principal Christian churches was launched, "people's leaders" were arrested and executed, and the NKVD was turned loose on the populace with a terrible ferocity intended to terrorize the people and eliminate all resistance to the Communist reoccupation. "Hangman of the Ukraine" became the people's title for Nikita Khrushchev.

By 1949 Khrushchev had so completely demonstrated his total dedication to Stalin that he was returned to Moscow as the secretary of the powerful Central Committee. He was then given the assignment of trying to make the sluggish centralized farms produce more food. Khrushchev used terror tactics to get more work and more produce, but he failed. Khrushchev could raise only enough food to keep the people at a bare-subsistence level.

This was the status of Khrushchev at the time of Stalin's death.

How Khrushchev Seized Power

When Stalin died March 5, 1953, he left a bristling nest of problems for his quarreling Communist comrades. Each Red leader carefully eyed his competitors, weighing the possibility of seizing power. Khrushchev immediately went to work maneuvering for a position of strategic strength. Com-

Communism Under Khrushchev

pared to the other Red leaders, Khrushchev was described both inside and outside of Russia as "low man on the totem pole."

The first in terms of strength was Malenkov, secretary of Stalin, who had charge of all secret Communist files. It was said he had collected so much damning evidence on the others that they tried to curry his favor by pushing him forward as the temporary head of the government.

The second in line was Beria, hated leader of the secret police and an administrator of the nuclear development program, all of which gave him a hard core force of 2,000,000 armed men.

The third in line was Molotov, intimate Bolshevik associate of Stalin himself and the most shrewd, deceptive diplomat Soviet Russia had ever produced.

The fourth in line was Bulganin, official representative of the Communist Party in the Red Army and therefore the Red Army's principal politician.

The fifth in line was Khrushchev, head of the State collectivized farms.

Many people did not take Khrushchev seriously. They thought of him merely as the paunchy, bullet-headed hatchet man of Stalin. But Khrushchev took himself seriously. Doggedly and desperately he pushed for every possible personal advantage. His method was to use an old Communist trick which is the very opposite of "divide and conquer." His technique was to "unite and conquer."

First he united with Premier Malenkov. He convinced Malenkov that Beria was his greatest threat, his greatest enemy. In December, 1954, Beria and his associates were arrested and shot.

Now Khrushchev united with Bulganin to get rid of Malenkov. Khrushchev told the bearded political army leader that he (Bulganin) should be premier instead of Malenkov. Bulganin heartily agreed. Immediately there was a shift of power behind the scenes which permitted Bulganin to replace Malenkov by the spring of 1955.

Molotov was the next to fall. He had no machine in back

of him but had depended upon his prestige as Stalin's partner. Suddenly he found himself exiled to the Mongolian border.

Now the partnership of Bulganin and Khrushchev began running the entire Communist complex. But Khrushchev was not through. His next step was to persuade Bulganin to force Marshal Zhukov of World War II fame into retirement and to demote other key officials in the government. Some of these officials were the very ones who had originally sponsored Khrushchev's promotions in previous years. Suddenly they found themselves politically emasculated. By destroying his friends as well as his enemies, Khrushchev felt he was preventing them from regrouping and ousting him the way he was ousting them.

Finally Khrushchev was prepared for the big step—to oust Bulganin. By forcing Bulganin to get rid of Marshal Zhukov, Khrushchev created a rift between Bulganin and his main source of support, the Red Army. This allowed Khrushchev to move into the breach and fill powerful key positions with his own followers. By 1956 Bulganin found himself the captive puppet of Khrushchev. For two more years Khrushchev ran the government through Bulganin, but there was no question whatever as to who was in line for Stalin's throne.

Such was Nikita Khrushchev's slippery and dangerous ascent to the summit.

But all of these battles in the Kremlin and the resulting shift of power had not solved the terrifying economic problems which continued to plague Soviet socialism. Nowhere—in China, Russia or the satellites—was Communism proving successful. Uprisings had been occurring for over three years in the Communist-controlled countries. Heavy Soviet armament had to be maintained in all of them.

Just as Khrushchev was consolidating his power in 1956, a major satellite cut loose and struck for freedom.

The Hungarian Revolution—1956

While bargaining for American lend-lease during World War II, Stalin had promised that any nation coming under

Communism Under Khrushchev

the domination of the Red Army during the war would be allowed free elections and self-determination after the war. Hungary was the first nation to demand self-government and the overthrow of the Communist regime.

Perhaps no better historical example exists to illustrate the extreme treachery to which Khrushchev would extend himself than the Hungarian Revolution.

On the 23rd of October, 1956, a massive but peaceful demonstration took place in Budapest with thousands of people participating. The people said they wanted to end Soviet colonial rule and set up a democratic government with free elections. When the crowds refused to disband, the Russian secret police were ordered to fire on them. Thus the revolution began. The first major action of the revolution was toppling down the hugh statue of Stalin, the symbol of Soviet domination. The freedom fighters then hoisted the Hungarian flag on the stump. Soviet occupation troops were immediately ordered in to smash the revolution, but they were resisted by Communist trained Hungarian troops who defected and joined the Freedom Fighters. Many of the Soviet occupation troops also defected. As a result, the remaining Soviet troops were beaten in five days. Then General Bela Kiraly describes what happened:

> "To avoid annihilation of the Soviet units, Khrushchev himself carried out one of his most sinister actions. He sent to Budapest his first deputy, Mikoyan; and he sent Mr. Suslov from the party leadership. These two Soviet men sat down with the revolutionary government. They found out they were defeated. After talking with Khrushchev by means of the telephone—and by the approval of Khrushchev they concluded an armistice. . . . Diplomatic actions were further developed. . . . It was positively declared that the aim of further diplomatic negotiations (would be) how to withdraw the Soviet troops from

Hungary and how to allow Hungary to regain her national independence."[2]

The Soviet representatives proposed that final details be drawn up at the Soviet headquarters in Tokol, a village south of Budapest. The entire Hungarian delegation was therefore invited to come and discuss the precise date when Soviet troops would leave Hungary. In response to this invitation, the elated and victorious Hungarians went to the Soviet headquarters. To their amazement they were suddenly surrounded, siezed and imprisoned. Simultaneously a new all-out attack was ordered by Khrushchev against the whole Hungarian population.

The new Soviet attack was in the form of a massive invasion. It involved 5,000 tanks and a quarter of a million soldiers. They poured in from Czechoslovakia, Russia and Rumania. On Sunday, November 4, 1956, the radio station in Budapest pleaded:

"People of the world, listen to our call! Help us. . . . Please do not forget that this wild attack of Bolshevism will not stop. You may be the next victim. Save us! SOS. SOS"[3]

A little later the voice said:

"People of the civilized world, in the name of liberty and solidarity, we are asking you to help. Our ship is sinking. The light vanishes. The shadows grow darker from hour to hour. Listen to our cry. . . . God be with you—and with us."

That was all. The station went off the air.

As the student of history contemplates those tragic days, he cannot help but wonder: Where was the conscience of the Free West? Where was the UN? Where were the forces of NATO? What had happened to the whole fabric of gilded promises of the UN made at San Francisco in 1945:

---

[2] "THE CRIMES OF KHRUSHCHEV," *House Committee on Un-American Activities, 1959, Part 3, p. 12.*
[3] "HOW A FREE NATION WAS KILLED," *U.S. News and World Report, November 16, 1956, p. 94.*

". . . to save succeeding generations from the scourge of war.
". . . to reaffirm faith in fundamental rights, in the dignity and worth of the human person, in the equal rights of men and women and of nations large and small.
". . . to establish . . . respect for the obligations arising from treaties.
" . . . to ensure that armed force shall not be used."

(PREAMBLE UN CHARTER)

As it turned out, the massacre of tens of thousands of Hungarians finally smothered into oblivion the heroic Hungarian fight for freedom. Prime Minister Imre Nagy was executed. Most of the other leaders of the revolution were deported to Russia and never heard of again. In the UN Security Council America's Ambassador Lodge introduced a resolution proposing that Russia be censured for this atrocious Hungarian attack. *Russia vetoed it!*

This amazing and treacherous series of events was personally supervised by Nikita Khrushchev. Without any serious challenge whatever, he was allowed to carry them out in direct violation of the Yalta agreement, the Warsaw Pact and the first two articles of the UN Charter. It was the greatest opportunity the Western Bloc had ever had to show whether or not the mighty and strong had the courage to expel Russia and then put the high-sounding phrases of the UN to work.

Instead, the UN appointed a committee to gather the facts, prepare a report, and then submit it to the General Assembly.

This gave pro-Soviet forces an additional chance to pull sensitive strings in the UN and further obscure the vicious conquest of Hungary.

The UN Investigation of the Hungarian Revolution

The average American has no conception of the deep penetration of the Communist conspiracy inside the United Nations.

The Naked Communist

A Danish diplomat, Povl Bang-Jensen, said he began feeling strong Communist pressures soon after he started serving as the deputy secretary of the UN committee which was investigating the Russian attack on Hungary.[4] He claimed pro-Soviet influence came sweeping down upon him from the Secretary General's office and even from many of the committee members. Bang-Jensen did not know where to turn for help. Finally he started writing protests both to the committee and the Secretary General. He pointed out errors in the report which would allow the Russians to discredit it. He said the Committee Chairman had refused to correct these errors. He stated that important facts were being eliminated which established the official responsibility of the Russian government for what had happened. He also noted that the committee was going soft in its treatment of Janos Kadar who headed up the new Communist puppet government in Hungary.

But most of all, Povl Bang-Jensen was outraged when the Secretary General demanded that he reveal the secret list of Hungarian witnesses. He had been authorized in writing to tell the witnesses that their names would never be disclosed since this would bring cruel and immediate reprisal on their families in Hungary. Bang-Jensen stood by this commitment. He declared that turning over the names to the UN Secretariat would permit possible leaks to the Russians. The word was already getting around the UN that Russian agents were offering extravagant bribes to anyone who would get them the list.

Suddenly Bang-Jensen found the UN Secretariat and the investigating committee attacking him personally. Instead of dealing with the issues, high UN officials began describing Povl Bang-Jensen as "mentally ill."

Three leading American employees in the UN participated in the attack on Bang-Jensen. They were Andrew Wellington Cordier, a former associate of Alger Hiss, who had become No. 2 man in the UN; Ernest A. Gross who had tried to get

---

[4] *The Bang-Jensen case is treated fully in a recent book, "*BETRAYAL AT THE UN," *by DeWitt Copp and Marshall Peck, Devin-Adair, 1961.*

the United States to allow recognition of Red China; and Dr. Ralph Bunche, UN Under Secretary, who was one of the first to put the "mentally ill" label on Bang-Jensen in an official memorandum.

Gradually Povl Bang-Jensen felt himself going down under the avalanche of opposition. When the UN officials could not force him to disclose the secret list of Hungarian witnesses, he was ordered to burn them in the presence of a UN representative. This he did. Then they fired him. Povl Bang-Jensen was discharged by Dag Hammarskjold on December 4, 1957. Nevertheless the UN pressure against Bang-Jensen as a mentally-ill person continued. Derogatory reports from the UN prevented him from securing several highly important positions.

For some time Bang-Jensen had also feared the possibility of physical harm. He had been a Danish underground fighter against the Nazis and Communists in World War II and was familiar with the technique of doing away with an enemy by making it look like a suicide. Therefore he wrote the following note to his wife on November 30, 1957:

> "Under no circumstances whatsoever would I ever commit suicide. This would be contrary to my whole nature and to my religious convictions. If any note was found to the opposite effect in my handwriting, it would be a fake."

It was Thanksgiving Day, 1959, that the body of Povl Bang-Jensen was found in a secluded area two miles from his home with a bullet hole in his head. A pistol and scribbled note were by his side.

He had left home 72 hours earlier to catch a bus. The coroner found he had been dead only a few hours. What had happened during that tragic interval of two days or more while Bang-Jensen was still alive?

Professional investigators suspected murder. If so, it was carefully executed to look like suicide. And suicide was the final, official verdict. Many remained unconvinced.

But by this time the UN investigation of the Hungarian Revolution had long since been completed. The expurgated,

distorted and watered down report had been turned over to
the UN and officially accepted by the General Assembly.

Inside Khrushchev's Russia

Communism has only one fragile excuse for all the un-
paralleled brutality, cruelty and crimes against humanity
which it commits. This is the Marx-Engels-Lenin promise
that it is the historical shortcut to a better life for all mankind. But even Communists are men with minds that seek
tangible evidence for the faith they live by. The most bitter
reality in the Communist hierarchy is the fact that after 40
years of all-out effort, numerous five-year plans, the purging,
executing, torturing and liquidation of millions of human
beings, the Communist Motherland has still produced little
more than a dull and monotonous existence.

A five-year analysis of Russian economics revealed the
humiliating fact that less economic progress had been made
under 40 years of Communism than under the last 40 years
of the Tsars![5]

Although stealing technical knowledge from the West and
kidnaping the scientists of vanquished foes has made it possible for the Communist leaders to make several spectacular
crash exhibitions in the technical field, nevertheless the plain
irrefutable fact remains that Russia just cannot compete with
capitalism in massive production. This continues to be a nest
of cockleburs in the craw of Communist leadership.

After 1955, when Americans were finally allowed to visit
the Soviet Union, it was observed that the whole socialist production system sloppily squandered vast quantities of man-
power. Often, for each man working, another stood idly
looking on. Capitalistic work incentives had been introduced
to create work motivation, but even so, monolithic socialized
planning continued to hold back production schedules and production speed.

[5] *"Russia's Growth Under Communism Less Rapid," by Dr. Warren
Nutter,* U. S. NEWS AND WORLD REPORT, *November 2, 1959, p. 75.*

Communism Under Khrushchev

American tourists with eyes alert to such problems observed that Khrushchev was resorting to child labor to try to make up the difference. In fact, the Russian government admitted it was recruiting students from the schools to work for the farms and factories. Khrushchev announced his plan to limit most Russian youth to seven or eight years of schooling and said much of this would be at night. Only very select students would be allowed to go to college.[6]

As for the collectivized farms, even with half of the entire Russian population working on socialized farms the USSR had not been able to do more than feed the people at a bare-subsistence level. The fact that the American system permits a mere 12% of the people to produce more than Americans can either eat or sell stuns the comprehension of Red farm experts like Khrushchev. And he has made no secret of his resentment. Every so often he lashes out at the sluggish Russian farm program. These are direct quotes from his 1955 speech denouncing Russian agriculture:

"Lag in production"
"Intolerable mismanagement"
"State farms fail to fulfill their plan for an increase"
"Hay fields remain unharvested"
"No silo buildings are being erected"
"Unfortunate situation has arisen with regard to seed"
"For six years work has been in progress on the design of a tractor . . . and the tractor has not been designed"
"Machinery is not being used on many collectivized farms"
"There is considerable disorder on our state farms"
"Cases of damage (labor sabotage) to trucks and tractors"
"Absenteeism"
"Undernourished cattle delivered to the State"
"Serious shortcomings in pig breeding"
"Production of milk decreased 10 per cent"
"Cows bearing calves amount to only 34 per cent"

---

[9] *"Russian Plan Cuts Down Schooling,"* U. S. NEWS AND WORLD REPORT, *October 3, 1959.*

"Weight of fattened pigs and wool clippings decreased"
"Americans succeeded in achieving a high level of stock breeding"
"In the United States this crop (corn) gives the highest harvest yield."[7]

This was the reason Khrushchev abandoned the last Five-Year-Plan and substituted a Seven-Year-Plan. The latest plan is supposed to equal U. S. production by 1965, but in 1961 Khrushchev roared out his anger at the Russian farmers. There had been a continuous slump in farm production for five years![8]

The Hazardous Life of a Communist Dictator

By 1958 Nikita Khrushchev had officially declared himself head of the Communist Party and the supreme dictator of all Russia. Nevertheless he had some cold, hard facts to face.

By that time the Red timetable of conquest was at a virtual standstill; the Iron Curtain was surrounded by NATO and SEATO defense bases with atomic warheads zeroed in to discourage Communist aggression.

Mao and Chou, the Red Chinese leaders, were becoming increasingly defiant, critical and independent.

It was taking more than six million soldiers and secret police to maintain the "state of siege" behind the Iron Curtain so as to give the appearance of "domestic tranquility."

Russia had worn out her good offices in the UN and was beginning to feel the united pressure of the Western Bloc.

There was continued unrest in the satellites and large Red Army garrisons had to be stationed in each of them since the local armies were likely to join any uprising just as they did in Hungary.

---

[7] *"Why Russia Is in Trouble,"* U. S. NEWS AND WORLD REPORT, *February 25, 1955, p. 58.*
[8] *"Russ Admit 50 Per Cent Drop in Farm Output,"* LOS ANGELES EXAMINER, *January 11, 1961.*

Communism Under Khrushchev

There was also serious unrest in the Red Army where deep resentment against Khrushchev's ruthless political decapitation of Marshal Zhukov still existed.

Khrushchev had been only partially successful in opening up the world market so that the Sino-Soviet Bloc could buy the things which its collectivized economy could not produce. He also faced the unpleasant fact that the Red economy was not in a position to pay for foreign trade because it was continually operating on the brink of bankruptcy.

Finally, and most important of all, Khrushchev lived under the constant threat of possible "regrouping" by disgruntled Red leaders to oust him from power the same way he had ousted Malenkov and Bulganin. Khrushchev felt a desperate need to boost his personal political status. He determined to achieve this by forcing the United States to honor him with an invitation to visit America.

Khrushchev's Scheme to Force the U.S. to Invite Him to America

Ever since 1955 Khrushchev had tried to get the United States to invite him to America, but failed. Finally he decided to accomplish it by creating a crisis over Berlin. In 1958 he issued an ultimatum that America and her allies must get out of West Berlin by a certain date or he would turn the Communist East Germans loose on them. This demand was a flagrant violation of all existing treaties. When President Eisenhower announced that any efforts to force us out of Berlin would be met with military resistance, Khrushchev immediately said he didn't really want war and that he thought the whole thing could be worked out amicably if he just came to the United States and talked it over with the President. He also mentioned on several occasions that President Eisenhower would be welcome to visit Russia.

At first President Eisenhower demurred. Bringing the Communist dictator to the United States was precisely what Secretary Dulles had warned against right up to the time of his death. However, President Eisenhower felt that such a visit might impress Khrushchev with the power of the United States and deter him from hasty military action. Furthermore, the President felt much good might arise from a visit to Russia by the President of the United States. It would be in furtherance of his own program of "people to people" relations. Therefore an official invitation was extended to the Communist dictator—making him the first Russian ruler ever to visit the United States.

Was Khrushchev's Visit a Mistake?

American strategists on Communist problems immediately warned that a serious tactical error was being made. Several of them testified before Congressional Committees. Eugene Lyons, a senior editor of The Readers Digest, a biographer of Khrushchev and a former press correspondent in Russia, called the invitation to Khrushchev "a terrific victory for Communism." Then he continued:

> *"It amounts to a body blow to the morale of the resistance in the Communist world. It's a betrayal of the hopes of the enemies of Communism within that world, and their numbers can be counted by the hundred million.*
> *"The announcement of the invitation was a day of gloom and despair for nearly the whole population of every satellite country and for tens of millions inside Russia itself."*[9]

When asked if Khrushchev's visit to the United States might cause him to slow down or abandon his plans for world conquest, Mr. Lyons replied:

> *"It's a childish fairy tale. The Communists in high places are perfectly well informed about our material prosperity and political freedom. Khrushchev is not coming here to confirm his knowledge of our strengths, but*

[9] "THE CRIMES OF KHRUSHCHEV," *House Committee on Un-American Activities, 1959, Part 1, p. 3.*

Communism Under Khrushchev

to feel out our weaknesses. The notion that he will be impressed by our wealth and liberty to the point of curbing Communist ambitions is political innocence carried to extremes. . . .

"In the first place, the new Soviet boss, despite his homespun exterior, is one of the bloodiest tyrants extant. He has come to power over mountains of corpses. Those of us who roll out red carpets for him will soon have red faces."[10]

Even while Khrushchev was on his tour of the United States, Americans felt the icy thrust of numerous snarling threats which crept out between his propaganda boasts, his quaint platitudes and his offering to swear on the Bible. The press observed that he was supersensitive and hot tempered about questions on any of the following matters:

The ruthless and illegal suppression of the Hungarian revolt after all of Khrushchev's recent preachments about "self determination."

Questions about his role as the "Hangman of the Ukraine."

Questions about Soviet jamming of Voice of America broadcasts.

Questions about the continuous flight of thousands of refugees from satellite states.

Aftermath of the Khrushchev Visit

The whole world-wide program of Communist aggression was swiftly accelerated as a result of Khrushchev's visit. The Communist Party in the United States came boldly out into the open. It began a new recruiting program. It openly attacked the House Committee on Un-American activities and marked the FBI for early dismantling if it succeeded in destroying the Congressional Committees. Convicted Communists from the Hollywood cells moved back into the cinema capital and boldly began writing, producing and

---

[10] "THE CRIMES OF KHRUSHCHEV," *House Committee on Un-American Activities, 1959, Part 1, p. 3.*

propagandizing through multi-million dollar productions. The president of the Communist Party announced the launching of a nationwide Communist youth movement.

The same thrust became apparent all over the world—in Japan, Southeast Asia, India, Africa, Cuba, Central and South America. Everywhere the Red tide ran stronger. The dire prediction of strategists like John Foster Dulles and Eugene Lyons had been literally fulfilled.

Nevertheless, the visit of the Russian Dictator to the United States also carried a certain penalty for Khrushchev. This was the devastating effect which could result from President Eisenhower's reciprocal visit to Russia. Khrushchev was deeply impressed with the acclaim which Vice President Nixon received when he visited Russia and the satellites. He knew that if President Eisenhower were granted the same freedom of expression on radio, TV, in public meetings and in press interviews that Khrushchev had enjoyed in the United States, the pro-Communist tide could be reversed. Desperately, Khrushchev looked around for some semblance of an excuse to cancel the Eisenhower visit. Almost as though the Communists had planned it, a monumental excuse dropped into Khrushchev's lap right out of the sky.

The U-2 Incident

On May 1, 1960, Francis G. Powers, piloting an unarmed U-2 jet reconnaissance plane, was captured 1200 miles inside Russia. The Communist leaders triumphantly announced that they had shot down the U-2 spy plane with a marvelous new rocket. This story was discredited when the Russians displayed Power's undamaged equipment and the U. S. monitors reported hearing the Russian pilots as they followed the plane in a forced landing. Government officials revealed that the U-2 plane came down because of a flameout.

In Washington the incident created consternation. Since Americans were not accustomed to spying, they hardly knew what to do when this plane was caught spying. At first it was

Communism Under Khrushchev

simply claimed that the U-2 was a weather plane which must have "drifted." Finally, it was rather clumsily admitted that the plane was in fact flying on an espionage mission with the highly important assignment of photographing Russian missile bases.

Khrushchev professed outraged indignation, criticized the "morals" of the American leaders for spying, and denounced the U-2 incident as an act of aggression. He also immediately announced that he was canceling President Eisenhower's visit to Russia. A few days later he used the U-2 incident to scuttle the Paris Summit Conference.

Meanwhile, in America, citizens were peppering Washington with a multitude of questions:

Was this an isolated mission or one of many espionage
    flights?
Was it in violation of international law?
What did such flights accomplish?
Why hadn't the Russians objected to such flights earlier?
Should the flights be continued or terminated?

Since Russia had now captured one of the U-2 planes and all of its equipment, the U. S. Government felt justified in telling the inside facts on this rather ingenious American defense device which had been operating over Russia and China for more than 4 years. The May 1 flight was one of more than 200 which had been mapping offensive war preparations of the USSR. It was revealed that the U-2's had been ordered aloft in 1956 when the U.S. had first learned that the Communist leaders had officially adopted a mammoth "sneak attack" plan as part of their over-all strategy. The planes had been flying over Russia at an altitude of between 12 and 14 miles—far out of reach of any jets or rockets which the Russians possessed.

Was this illegal? Since Russia had refused to negotiate any international law on air space, these flights were not illegal. Ernest K. Lindley summarized the views of Secretary of State Christian Herter: "The altitude above the earth to which a nation's sovereignty extends has never been determined by international agreement. The traditional rule is said to be that a nation s sovereignty extends as high as it can exert effective control. By that rule, the U-2 flights were not illegal so long as the planes flew above the reach of Soviet air defenses."[11]

Then how effective had the U-2's been? The Defense Secretary told the Senate Foreign Relations Committee:

"From these flights, we got information on airfields, aircraft, missile testing and training, special-weapon storage, submarine production, atomic production and aircraft deployment."[12]

How was this achieved? The Air Force revealed that it was done with high precision photographic equipment which performed miracles. This equipment could photograph a golf ball from 9 miles up. In fact a published photograph of a golf course taken from that altitude showed the greens, cars, club house and players. The picture caption read: "Even golf balls are clearly identifiable to photo-interpreters."[13]

But Russia and China cover such vast territories. How could precision photography be effective over so wide a terrain? The Air Force answered this question by revealing that this photographic equipment not only had high precision qualities but was also extremely comprehensive. Officials pointed out that 2 jets carrying these special cameras could photograph one third of the United States in 4 hours!

During Khrushchev's verbal blast against the U-2 flights, he let it slip that he had known about these planes for over three years. Some people wondered why he had not protested long before. Experts pointed out that if Khrushchev had complained, it would have exploded his propaganda boasts about the invincible strength of Soviets defenses. He had been claiming that Soviet radar, jets and rockets could prevent any nation from successfully attacking Russia. U-2 photographs

---

[11] "*U-2 Making the Points,*" NEWSWEEK *June 12, 1960, p. 38.*
[12] "*Arms Chief Weighs U-2 Future,*" U. S. NEWS AND WORLD REPORT, *June 27, 1960, p. 45.*
[13] "*The World's Big Spy Game,*" U. S. NEWS AND WORLD REPORT, *May 23, 1960, p. 47.*

Communism Under Khrushchev

had revealed that Russian defenses were wide open to massive retaliatory attack. It was for this reason that Khrushchev had waited until he finally got hold of a U-2 plane so that he could claim the Russians had shot it down. The Communists even succeeded in getting Francis Powers to testify at his Moscow trial that he had been shot down at 68,000 feet. But when his father came from America to visit him, the U-2 pilot said he was *not shot down.* This seemed to confirm Washington military statements that the Russians had neither jets nor rockets that could reach 68,000 feet.

The question of future U-2 flights was finally settled when President Eisenhower agreed that there would be no more. He made it clear that this was not because the flights were illegal or unjustified but simply that the United States would soon have other means of staying informed about Russian bases. The U.S. successfully launched its first Midas satellite into orbit on May 23, 1960. This one carried a 3,000 pound payload of technical equipment designed to detect a missile launching anywhere in the world. A few months later the U.S. launched its Samos satellite. The Samos was specifically designed to photograph Russia and China from 300 miles out as it made an orbital journey around the earth every $94\frac{1}{2}$ minutes. Of course, from 300 miles distance, additional photographic miracles were necessary. The Air Force revealed that the cameras on the Samos would photograph and identify any object larger than one square foot.

The RB-47 Incident

An American RB-47 reconnaissance plane disappeared over the Berents Sea on July 1, 1960. For several days Russia pretended to be helping in the search for the missing plane and then bluntly admitted that it had been shot down. All of the crew were killed except two. The Russians said they were holding the two survivors as prisoners.

The United States was shocked. President Eisenhower sent Russia one of the most indignant protests of his entire career as President. Russia claimed that the plane was shot down because it had violated Russian territory just like the U-2. The United States Ambassador said this charge was an absolute falsehood. He pointed out that the plane had been under British electronic surveillance and that the United States was prepared to prove the RB-47 had never been closer than thirty miles to the Soviet border.

On July 26, 1960, the United States demanded an impartial investigation by the United Nations to fix responsibility for this inexcusable and illegal attack which had resulted in the killing of four Americans and the kidnaping of two others. The request was referred to the Security Council. It was generally agreed that a UN investigation should be held. How else could the UN Charter be enforced unless investigations of alleged violations were conducted? But there was no investigation by the UN. *Russia vetoed it!*

The Italian representative then moved that the International Red Cross be allowed to interview the two American survivors. Russia vetoed that, too.

Most Americans missed the ugly significance of this entire UN fiasco. Once more Russia had violated the first two articles of the UN charter and gotten away with it. There were no particular protests from the press or the public. There was no sweeping demand that Russia be expelled. There was no stirring demand that the whole UN structure be completely re-examined. Across the country, school children continued to be told that the UN was the only hope for peace and justice among men.

The Space Race

In October, 1957, Russia electrified the world with her first Sputnik. Built on plans stolen from the United States after World War II, Sputnik I, with a payload weighing 184 pounds, was successfully launched into orbit October 4th.

Immediately the United States went into "panic production" to catch up. However, U.S. missile experts insisted on a

Communism Under Khrushchev

broad range of experimental effort rather than single-focus crash programs such as the Russians seemed to be following. Long range, the American approach soon began to pay off. Russia continued to put up bigger payloads but America started getting far better scientific data. Gradually the U.S. satellite and missile teams began forging ahead.

By April 1, 1960, the U.S. had the highly successful Tiros I in orbit which circled the earth every 99 minutes at a height of 450 miles. This space vehicle had solar batteries which operated earth-controlled television cameras to transmit pictures of weather formations. This was the most successful picture-taking vehicle ever put into space.

On August 11, 1960, the U.S. was the first to de-orbit a satellite capsule from space. This one weighed 300 pounds. On August 12 the U.S. put an inflated balloon into space. It was as high as a 10-story building and was described as the "first radio mirror" for a huge satellite communications network. 1960 also marked the launching of America's first inter-continental ballistic missiles from submerged submarines. This meant that never again could Russia plan a sneak attack on the West because massive retaliation could be launched from America's moving missile bases at sea.

Officials revealed that future satellites would carry infra-red sensors capable of detecting atomic explosions and ballistic missile launchings by the Communists. These also would be able to follow the trail of missiles in flight. America's long-anticipated Midas and Samos satellites ranged into orbit during 1960 and early 1961.

Payload size also gradually became important to the U.S. as it neared the time when a man would be put into space. A 15-ton satellite was promised for about 1963. However, experts promised that there would be an American in space even before that.

Prodded by the unknown proportions of the Russian effort, American wealth and technology poured its strength into the space race. The score by 1961 seemed significant:

Space launching to date:	......U.S. 32	......RUSSIA 7
Still in earth orbit:	..............U.S. 16	......RUSSIA 1
In solar orbit:	..................U.S. 2	......RUSSIA 1
Still transmitting:	..............U.S. 9	......RUSSIA 0
Successful moon shots:	..........U.S. 0	......RUSSIA 1
Recovery from orbit:	...........U.S. 4	......RUSSIA 1

The March of Communism in Africa

The year 1960 saw a clear manifestation that the Communist time table of conquest for Africa was right on schedule. In 1953, the Communist leaders had promised themselves that during the 1960's "a wave of revolution will sweep over the whole continent of Africa and the imperialists and colonizationists will be quickly driven into the sea."[14] They also made it clear that the agitating and provoking of the "wave of revolution" was the Communist program for the capture of Africa.

However, by 1960, the European nations with colonies in Africa were already busily trying to prepare the people for independence and self-government by *peaceful* means. From a Communist standpoint this would have been a defeat. Red leaders knew that any well-ordered government of natives would undoubtedly resist Russian-Chinese domination. It was therefore decided to urge the natives to demand freedom immediately, before they had actually been prepared for self-government. The Communists figured that in the resulting chaos, they could probably take over. This is exactly what began to take place.

The Tragedy in the Congo

The 1960 chain of events in the Belgian Congo illustrated the devastating effect of turning self-government over to primitive people prematurely. The tragedy was compounded by the fact that the natives had already been promised independ-

---

[14] CONGRESSIONAL RECORD, *April 29, 1954, p. 5708.*

Communism Under Khrushchev

ence by 1964. Consequently, their uprising was not so much for independence as for "freedom now."

To see the big picture it is necessary to realize that 75 years before when the Belgians first settled the Congo, it consisted of around 120 cannibalistic tribes living on the lowest levels of human existence.

By 1960 the Belgians had created vast resources of wealth in the geographical heart of Africa. Most of it was concentrated in the province of Katanga which produced 7.5% of the world's copper, 60% of its cobalt, most of the world's supply of radium and large supplies of uranium and zinc.

As with the French and British, the Belgians had hoped self-government could be developed among the Africans by having the natives learn technical skills and gradually assume responsibility for a stable government. Business leaders and investors were also willing to take the risk of a political transition providing the new government was well managed. In this rather cordial setting it was agreed that Congolese independence could be granted by 1964. The Belgians promised liberal loans to the newly planned government and also promised to keep their civil service staff working alongside the natives for several years until they could safely take over.

Then Patrice Lumumba came storming back from the Pan-African conference chanting the current Communist theme: "Independence now, now, now!" Lumumba, a former postal clerk from Stanleyville, had been trained in the special Communist schools in Prague and had a brother living in Moscow. He had managed to become the head of the most left-wing political contingent in the Congo and, at the moment, enjoyed a popular following. The Belgian officials began to sense a threatening tone in his demands and saw the possibility of an Algerian type of civil war. Therefore the Government suddenly agreed to go ahead with the independence of the Congo by June 30, 1960, instead of waiting until 1964.

The Belgians thought this would satisfy Lumumba and therefore the government was turned over to him on the prescribed date. But no sooner had Lumumba become Premier than he began a volcanic tirade against "the whites" in general

234 and "the Belgians" in particular. The whole structure of "peaceful transition" went out the political window overnight.

The Congolese troops caught the spirit which Lumumba had exhibited and promptly mutinied against their white officers. Soon they became a roaring mob. They swept through the white sections of the principal cities beating, robbing and raping. As violence spread, the whites fled the Congo in terror. Some congregated temporarily in embassies, some rushed to the airports. At Leopoldville, doctors estimated that at least one out of every four women escaping to the airport had been raped, some of them a dozen times.

The evacuation of the whites left the Congo almost devoid of government, schools, hospitals, or business services. The native literacy rate was one of the highest in Africa, but in all of the Congo there was not one native engineer or doctor and only a few college graduates.

To avoid total collapse and to protect the fleeing whites, the Belgian government brought in paratroopers. Lumumba, however, treated them as enemies and demanded that UN troops be flown in. No sooner had the UN forces begun to arrive than Lumumba turned against them and invited Khrushchev to send strong Communist forces to take over the entire Congo. Soon Communist planes, trucks, equipment, technicians and propagandists were arriving. Lumumba began collectivizing the land and assembling an army to drive out both the UN and the Belgian troops. He also began acting like a fully disciplined Communist dictator by committing genocide against his own people. In the Kasai province, Lumumba's troops wiped out the Balubas tribe while Lumumba's cousin, Surete Chief Omonombe, personally directed the massacre of the Bakwanga tribe. Rescuers were prevented from bringing out women, children or the wounded.[15]

In spite of all this, the UN Secretariat continued to support Lumumba as the legitimate head of the government.

But this was too much for the Congolese. They felt they had been betrayed. On September 5th, President Joseph

---

[15] PARIS REPORT OF HILAIRE DU BERRIER, *Sept., 1960, p. 1.*

Communism Under Khrushchev

Kasavubu told the world he was ousting Lumumba as Premier. The very same day Lumumba's own troops turned bitterly against him. The Army Chief, Joseph Mobutu, clapped the blustering Lumumba in jail and told his Communist followers to get out of the Congo immediately.

All of this looked like a healthy improvement to most people, but to the amazement of both Congolese and outside observers, Dag Hammarskjold continued to use his office as UN Secretary General to intercede for Lumumba. Responsible Congolese like Premier Moise Tshombe of Katanga began asking whose side Dag Hammarskjold was on!

In the beginning Dag Hammarskjolds' personal representative in the Congo had been Dr. Ralph Bunche, an American Negro serving as Under Secretary of the UN. But when Bunche failed in his attempt to get the Congolese to accept the Communist-dominated regime of Patrice Lumumba, he was replaced. The replacement turned out to be a UN official named Rajeshwar Dayal of India. Dayal had functioned for only a short time when President Kasavubu became equally alarmed with his policies. By January, 1961, Kasavubu had written two letters to Dag Hammarskjold begging the UN to remove Dayal because of his strong "partiality."

During the latter part of 1960 and the early part of 1961, the violence of Lumumba's forces continued to spread havoc in the central and northern sections of the Congo. Press dispatches told of the raping of nuns and other atrocities against whites. Then in early February, 1961, it was suddenly announced that Lumumba had escaped from Katanga and was believed to be heading back toward the central Congo to join his forces. Because Lumumba was the principal voice for both Communism and violence the Premier of the Katanga Province put a high price on Lumumba's head. A few days later it was announced that Lumumba had been caught and killed by Congolese natives.

Immediately a cry of outrage came rumbling forth from Moscow and a storm of protest emanated from the UN. President Kasavubu and Moise Tshombe could not understand why

The Naked Communist

UN Secretary, Dag Hammarskjold, insisted on being so sentimentally concerned over Lumumba after the terrible blood bath he had inflicted on the Congo.

The Congolese were also amazed when Hammarskjold tried to force President Kasavubu to set up a Communist coalition government. This was exactly the way each of the East European nations had been trapped into becoming Soviet satellites. Tshombe was further outraged when UN officials tried to force him to terminate all relations with the Belgians and discharge his Belgian advisors. Tshombe accused Dag Hammarskjold of trying to drive out the Belgians so a UN power grab could be achieved. This actually took place in September, 1961. Dag Hammarskjold engineered an attack on Katanga with UN troops which temporarily forced Tshombe from the government. Tshombe was replaced by the right hand man of Communist leader, Antoine Gizenga.

However, Tshombe rallied the people under the battle cry of "Liberty or Death!" and the resistance to the UN conquest began. It was then that Dag Hammarskjold flew to Africa to negotiate a cease-fire before the UN-sponsored regime was overthrown. Enroute to Katanga, the UN plane crashed and Dag Hammarskjold was killed. In Washington, D. C., Senator Thomas A. Dodd told the U. S. Senate that Hammarskjold's campaign had been turning the whole Congo into a Communist camp. He charged that the State Department had made a monumental blunder in using American money to back the UN conquest of the Congo.[16]

During all of this excitement many Americans thought the UN was actually trying to protect the Congo from a Communist take-over. They drew this conclusion from the fact that Khrushchev had been violently criticizing Hammarskjold's program in the Congo. Now it appeared that the fight between Khrushchev and Hammarskjold was not on the issue of a Communist take-over since they had both been pushing for one. Their dispute was to determine who would control the Communist regime once it was in power.

---

[16] *The four speeches of Senator Thomas A. Dodd have been published in a pamphlet by the Government Printing Office. It is called* THE CRISIS IN THE CONGO (1961).

CASTRO

XI

The Communist Conquest of Cuba

Now we turn our attention to Cuba.

During 1960, while the world was focusing attention on events in the Congo, a far more serious development was taking place just 90 miles from the shores of the United States. For many months shocked Americans had been watching Fidel Castro completely destroy his pretended image as the "George Washington of Cuba" and triumphantly portray himself in his true role as a hard-core Communist conspirator.

Everything Lumumba would have done in the Congo, Castro actually accomplished in Cuba: drumhead justice, mass executions, confiscation of industry, collectivization of the land, suspension of civil rights, suspension of democratic processes, alliances with the Iron Curtain. All these became the trade marks of the Castro regime.

To millions of Americans this was bitterly disappointing. They had read Herbert Matthews' pro-Castro articles in the New York Times and watched prominent TV personalities portray Castro as the savior of Cuba.

The Naked Communist

As a matter of research, however, there was no real excuse for missing Fidel Castro's Communist connections. For years he had been clearly identified with their leaders, their insurrections, their ideology and their plans. And even if all of this evidence had been absent, the official records of the Havana and Bogota police departments should have told the most casual observer that Fidel Castro was certainly no pillar of hope for Cuba. Even before he graduated from law school his checkerboard career included such crimes as assault with a deadly weapon, arson, insurrection and murder.

Who Is Fidel Castro?

Fidel Castro is one of five illegitimate children born to a servant woman on the sugar plantation of Fidel's wealthy father, Angel Castro.[1] Biographers point out that his early upbringing was not particularly conducive to promoting the best qualities in a human personality. When Fidel was sent to secondary school he turned out to be a mediocre student with an aggressive, ambitious and rebellious nature. He was not well liked at the school and to overcome his lack of popularity he decided to impress the students by mounting a bicycle and riding it full tilt into a high stone wall. This accident left him unconscious for days. Some authorities have wondered if he really ever recovered. At 16 he obtained a gun and tried to kill a teacher because of an argument over poor grades.

By the time Castro was 19, he had determined to become a lawyer. To achieve this his father sent him to the University of Havana. Almost immediately, however, he identified himself with the most radical element on campus and joined a group of beatniks who prided themselves in being unshaven and unclean. Castro is still remembered at the University of Havana by his nickname of "Bola de Churre"—Ball of Dirty Grease.

---

[1] *Thus far the best political history on Fidel Castro is* "RED STAR OVER CUBA," *by ex-Communist Nathaniel Weyl, Devin-Adair, 1960.*

The Communist Conquest of Cuba

Castro told Diaz Balart (who later became his brother-in-law) that he intended to become studentbody president and then use his prestige to agitate the students into a revolutionary force which would ultimately make him the political leader of Cuba. But his jealous ambition did not make him studentbody president. Instead, it led him to engineer his first attempt at murder in 1947.

The victim was Leonel Gomez, the popular studentbody president of Havana High School #1. For "political reasons" Castro shot him through the chest with intent to kill. Fortunately the boy recovered. Castro, however, expected him to die and fled from the city to join a Communist-directed expedition which was training to invade the Dominican Republic and overthrow Trujillo. Before the expedition was launched Castro heard that Gomez had recovered and therefore felt it was safe to return to the University.

Castro's Second Attempt at Murder Is Successful

By 1948 Castro had gained considerable confidence in his own political prospects and was determined that nothing should stand in the way. He had made himself the head of a University terrorist organization and on February 22, 1948, he used machineguns to kill the ex-President of the University Student Federation and a friend named Carlos Pucho Samper. Two others were wounded. Castro was arrested for this murder but the investigation had not been thorough and he was able to get released. It is also suspected that the judge was influenced by the fact that one of Castro's confederates was the nephew of the Cuban President.

A short time after this he left for Bogota, Columbia. Castro's student activities had brought him to the attention of Soviet agents who were looking for young firebrands to lead out in the subversion of Latin American countries. Castro was ordered to go to Bogota and take Rafael del Piño with him. In view of his recent brush with the law it seemed an excellent time to be taking a trip.

Castro as a Soviet Agent in the Bogota Riots

In April, 1948, the eyes of the world were watching Bogota, Colombia, where the Ninth Inter-American Conference was to be held. It was under the direction of U. S. Secretary of State, George C. Marshall. This occasion was chosen by the Soviet strategists to stage a Communist-directed insurrection. It was to unseat the conservative government of Colombia and break up the Inter-American Conference.

Alberto Niño, Security Chief of Colombia, published a book in 1949 on the insurrection. He has much to say about Fidel Castro. Niño describes how Castro and Rafael del Piño were put under surveillance the moment they arrived at the airport: "These two men came as replacements for two Russian agents stationed in Cuba, whose plans were known and who were expected by the Colombian police. Instead these two came. . . . Before the 9th of April, a telegram was taken from them announcing the arrival of one of the Russians."[2]

Niño and his men found that the planned insurrection was not being led by the Communist Party of Colombia but by a group of "international Communists" who worked out of the Soviet legation in Bogota. There were nine of these international Communists who fronted for the Soviet apparatus. Fidel Castro and Rafael del Piño were two of the nine.

When the insurrection struck it was triggered by having Communist agents kill Dr. Jorge Gaitán, the most popular political leader in Colombia. Communist handbills, printed in advance, blamed the murder on the Government and urged the people to avenge themselves by sacking the city. Within an hour Bogota was converted into a holocaust of violence and flaming devastation.

Niño found that the Soviet apparatus had arranged to

---

[2] *Niño, Alberto*, "ANTECENTES Y SECRETOS DEL 9 DE ABRIL," *Editorial Pax, Bogota, 1949, p. 77.*

have a crew move through the city ahead of the mob smashing off locks and opening stores and warehouses. After the mob had looted the buildings, another crew went through spraying gasoline on floors and walls. The last stage was to have trained arsonists methodically burn these structures which ultimately gutted the center of the city.

When it was all over the "destruction of the civic center was complete." The Palace of Justice which contained most of the civil and criminal records was demolished to its foundations. Colleges, churches, stores and other public buildings were burned. Altogether 136 major buildings were destroyed representing a loss of more than $21,000,000. After the battles between the police and the mobs had subsided more than 1,000 corpses were left lying in the streets.

Some of Castro's biographers have tried to gloss over Castro's complicity in this terrible destruction but the files of the Bogota police state that detectives secured a "carnet, which the office of Detectives now has in its possession, with a photograph of the two Cubans, identifying them as first-grade agents of the Third Front of the USSR in South America."[3]

It was further discovered that Castro and del Piño were apparently the ones assigned to arrange the murder of Jorge Gaitán. Their activities became so completely exposed that President Perez went on a nationwide broadcast to denounce the two Cubans as "Communist leaders in the insurrection."

When it became obvious that the insurrection had failed, Castro and del Piño left quickly for Cuba.

Castro Commits His Third Murder

Castro had barely returned, however, when he learned that Sgt. Fernandez Caral of the Havana Police had been carefully investigating the machinegun murders which occurred earlier in the year and now had positive evidence that Castro was responsible. Castro immediately rounded up his associ-

---

[3] *Weyl, Nathaniel*, "RED STAR OVER CUBA," *p. 33.*

ates and when they saw an opportunity, they killed Caral on July 4, 1948. A police net was thrown out over the city. That same day Fidel Castro was arrested and charged with the murder. But now the police had a chance to see what kind of influence Castro possessed. They soon discovered that the witnesses to the murder were so intimidated by fear of reprisal from Castro's terrorist organization that none of them would testify. Once again the authorities were forced to release Castro and he promptly scurried away into hiding.

From this point on, Castro moved through the seething revolutionary underground of Cuba as a force to be reckoned with.

By 1948 the sensational disclosures of Whittaker Chambers, Elizabeth Bentley and a host of defected American Communists had exposed Russia's world-wide conspiracy to Sovietize all humanity. As a result, a strong wave of anti-Communist sentiment was rising everywhere. Up and down the Western hemisphere Communists were being instructed to run for cover and do their work through "fronts." In Cuba, Fidel Castro decided to ally himself with the Orthodox Party which was a reform movement led by Eddie Chibas. Eddie Chibas soon detected something wrong with Castro and warned his associates that Castro was not only Communistic but had propensities for violent revolution of the gangster variety. This warning blocked Castro from gaining further power in the leadership of the party but he still was allowed to remain a member.

The Batista Regime in Cuba

By 1952 it was time for another general election, and, as usual, revolutionary activity was threatening on every hand. Candidates were being physically attacked and some blood had been spilled. In the Cuban Army it was beginning to get around that some of the political factions were thinking of using the Army to seize power and restore order. General Fulgencio Batista suddenly decided to seize Cuba's political reigns and restore order himself.

The Communist Conquest of Cuba

In order to evaluate the Batista coup it is necessary to appreciate that never for any appreciable time since Cuba won her independence has she enjoyed genuine democracy or stable self-government. Her political history has been a tragic composite of illegal elections, assassinations, inefficiency in government, graft, nepotism, intimidation and dictatorships. Although popular elections have been held, these have nearly always been so corruptly and fraudulently conducted that it was never certain whether the "elected" officials were actually the people's choice. Defeated candidates often became the leaders of revolutionary parties seeking to seize control. This would lead to dictatorial reprisal by the party in power, and thus the political pendulum would swing between the "ins" and the "outs" with popular uprisings and military suppressions following each other in quick succession.

As far as General Batista was concerned, 1952 was not the first time he had used the Army to seize power and establish order in Cuba. Back in 1933-34 he had quelled civil strife long enough to have a new president put in office; but when the people were not satisfied with this or any other candidate for president, he finally had himself elected in 1940. A new constitution was adopted in 1940, but when the general election was held in 1944, Batista's candidate was defeated. The Batista regime was followed by two extremely corrupt, graft-ridden administrations which once more destroyed confidence in the democratic processes. By 1952 these politicians were also destroying the stability of Cuba's economy. Batista was a candidate for president himself but felt the elections would be a fraud and civil war would result; therefore he considered the circumstances sufficiently critical to justify his taking over again and re-establishing a temporary military government.

There was a cry of outrage both in the United States and Cuba as Batista suspended the elections and dissolved the congress. Nevertheless, he forged ahead with a four-pronged program: 1—stabilizing Cuba's economy through diversified agriculture and accelerated industrial development; 2—strengthening economic and political ties with the United

States; 3—resisting Communism, and 4—raising the Cuban standard of living. He also promised the U. S. Ambassador that free elections would be held no later than 1958.

By 1957 the International Monetary Fund ranked Cuba fourth among the 20 Latin American Republics in per capita income. Although it was only one sixth as high as the United States, it was 90% as high as Italy, far higher than Japan, and six times higher than India. The U. S. Department of Commerce reported: "The Cuban national income has reached levels which give the Cuban people one of the highest standards of living in Latin America."[4]

Batista's biographers agree that the General was not the usual Latin American "army strong man," but was actually very pro-labor and tried to persuade the people that he wanted to carry out policies which would be popular rather than dictatorial. It soon became apparent that Batista's policies were making a highly profitable tourist mecca out of Cuba and attracting vast quantities of American capital for industrial development. It also became apparent that Cuba was gradually changing from a strait-jacket, sugar-cane culture to a better balanced industrial-agriculture-tourist economy. Wages went up from 10 to 30% and many Cuban workers were covered with health, accident and medical insurance for the first time. Between 1950 and 1958 the overall national income jumped 22%. This is after deducting 10% for rising living costs.

This, then, was the promising development of Cuba which was taking place at the time Batista was overthrown.

Politically, Batista's administration was typical of Cuba's past. The Batista regime indulged itself in certain quantities of graft; when there were armed insurrections, Batista met violence with violence; when there were minority uprisings he suspended civil rights and established full military control. Nevertheless he insisted that once conditions were stabilized, he would submit himself to the people in a popular election and would be willing to stand by the results just as he had done in 1944. His opponents, particularly Fidel Castro, jeered

---

[4] *U. S. Department of Commerce Report*, "INVESTMENTS IN CUBA," *p. 184.*

The Communist Conquest of Cuba

at such promises and accused Batista of being opposed to con- stitutional government. The record shows that several times when Batista tried to slacken the reigns of control there were immediate outbursts of violence and he would therefore tighten them again.

But it was during the Castro Revolution that Batista's political sincerity was actually demonstrated. He announced that in accordance with his previous commitment there would be a general election June 1, 1958. He invited Castro to restore peace so that the will of the people could be determined.

Castro responded with a bloodthirsty manifesto in which he declared that as of April 5, 1958, any person who remained in an office of trust in the executive branch of the government would be "considered guilty of treason." He said candidates for the elections must withdraw immediately or suffer "ten years imprisonment to the death sentence." He authorized his revolutionary militia in the towns and cities to shoot down candidates summarily.

Responsible Cubans such as Dr. Marquez Sterling made contact with Castro in his mountain retreat and pleaded with the revolutionary leader to stop the bloodshed and allow the elections. Castro arrogantly turned him down. There would be no elections.

During the emotional white heat of the revolution many Americans missed the highly significant overtures which Batista was making. As it turned out, these might have made the difference in saving Cuba from the Communist conquest which Castro was planning.

Earlier, U. S. Ambassador Arthur Gardner had been removed because he urged support of Batista until Cuba's problems could be settled at the polls. He was replaced by Ambassador Earl Smith who soon received a horrified State Department stare when he tried to put over the point that Castro was obviously leading Cuba and the United States into a Soviet-built Communist trap.

These shocked State Department "experts" reflected their complete disdain for their Ambassador's advice by deliberately engineering a tight arms embargo against Batista. Then they went further. To completely assure Batista's defeat they promoted an agreement among the Central and South American republics that they would not sell arms to Batista either. The results were inevitable.

In desperation, Batista tried to buy 15 *unarmed* training planes from the United States. It was finally agreed that this would be satisfactory. Batista paid for them in advance. Then Castro ordered Raul to launch a project specifically designed to intimidate and humiliate the United States. Raul kidnapped 30 U. S. Marines and sailors, 17 American civilians and 3 Canadians. Threats against the lives of these hostages were used to force the United States to cancel the shipment of training planes to Batista. The experts in the State Department meekly capitulated!

Some American citizens were bold enough to suggest that if Teddy Roosevelt had been alive he would have taken the U. S. Marine Corps and landed in the middle of Castro's mountain retreat with such an earthshaking velocity that the Cuban tyrant would have gladly released the Americans—and without any price.

The Castro Coup D'Etat

When Batista first took over in 1952, Fidel Castro had immediately projected himself into the front lines of opposition. As indicated previously, Castro had been working behind the facade of the Orthodox Party, but after the Batista Coup he insisted that this organization include the Communist Party and set up a "popular front" against Batista. The Orthodox Party leaders refused to do this. Castro promptly bolted the party and said he would form his own movement.

It was only a short time after this—July 26, 1953—that he made his disastrous attack on the Army barracks at Santiago. This turned into a real tragedy for the men in the barracks hospital (who were cut to pieces by Castro's raiders)

The Communist Conquest of Cuba

and also for Castro's men. They were met with overwhelming odds and captured or killed. Survivors were subjected to torture and eventual death in retaliation for their attack on the wards in the hospital. Thus the "26th of July Movement" was born.

Castro had managed to assign himself to a less dangerous post in the 26th of July attack and when he saw the assault was failing he fled, shouting, "Every man for himself!" His brother Raul also escaped. Later both of the Castro brothers were captured and sentenced to prison. Fidel was sentenced to 15 years and Raul to 13. However, both of them served only 22 months because after Batista had put down the attempted insurrection he commuted their sentences.

For this gesture of political generosity by Batista, the Castro brothers displayed only contempt. During July, 1955, they left Cuba declaring that they would organize an invasion force and soon return to pull down Batista and "liberate" Cuba.

The headquarters for this invasion movement was established near Mexico City. All kinds of people flocked there to support Castro's so-called liberation of Cuba. Some were political enemies of Batista, some were opportunists, many were sincere liberals. But just as with Lumumba in Africa, sinister hard-core Communist personalities immediately moved in close to provide the "guiding hand." Castro's chief of staff turned out to be Dr. Ernesto "Che" Guevara, an Argentinian Communist assigned to work with Castro by the Soviet apparatus called "Asistencia Tecnica." Raul Castro had received considerable training during a recent trip to Prague, Moscow and Red China. He was therefore made commander of Castro's army. Other trained Communists moved deftly into every phase of the program.

But in spite of all the training, intrigue and planning, the famous "Invasion of Cuba" by Castro's forces turned out to be a real fiasco. Castro's total strength was a mere handful of only 82 men who clambored aboard a leaky yacht on November 25, 1956, and set out to sea. The Captain of the yacht was Hipolito Castillo, well known strategist of the Soviet organization

The Naked Communist

248

for the subversion of Latin America. The sluggish yacht was slow in reaching Cuba and when the men waded ashore to make their heroic invasion they were cut to pieces with gunfire. Most of them were captured or killed. Castro managed to escape into the hills and eventually work his way up into the 8,000 foot heights of the Sierra Maestra. He arrived there with only a handful of his original force. "Che" Guevara took over and began using propaganda and tactical strategy to dominate the immediate area and gradually rally others to the cause—especially young Cubans "full of life, ideals and faith." Thus the strange forces of revolutionary fire began to be built and soon civil war was reaching out across Cuba.

Two major factors led to the final success of Castro's revolution. One was centered in the Soviet Union and the other was centered in the United States.

Raul Castro who had previously been behind the Iron Curtain made several trips to Russia and Czechoslovakia to negotiate for arms and finances. The arms arrived by submarine, the money came through by couriers. During the last months of the revolution, observers were amazed at the quantities of Czech and Russian equipment being used by the Castro forces. They were equally surprised at the vast supplies of money which Castro had available—money for wages, food, equipment, liquor, bribery and favors.

Batista, on the other hand, suddenly found himself at the other end of the horn. Because of his pro-U. S. policies he had assumed that when the struggle for Cuba became critical he would be able to rely on the United States to sell him arms and supplies. To his amazement he discovered that his request for permission to buy arms in the U. S. fell on deaf ears. What he had not realized was that Herbert Matthews, Edward Murrow, Ed Sullivan, Ruby Phillips, Jules Dubois and a multitude of other writers and opinion makers had been eulogizing Castro and castigating Batista. In Congress, Senator Wayne Morse, Representative Charles O. Porter and Representative Adam Clayton Powell had thrown their combined weight behind the Castro cause. All this "Robin Hood" propaganda definitely had its effect.

The Communist Conquest of Cuba

At the same time Assistant Secretary of State Roy Ru-
bottom and Caribbean Director William Wieland—the two
persons who were supposed to know what was going on—
blandly assured all inquirers that Fidel Castro was the hope
of Cuba and had no Communist taint whatever. As late as
June, 1959 (and that was extremely late), Congressman Porter was assuring his colleagues: "No one in the State Department believes Castro is a Communist, or a Communist
sympathizer, nor does any other responsible person who wants
to get his facts straight."[5]

Of course, as time marched on toward Cuba's inexorable
doom, the course of history embarrassed the Congressman
and also the State Department. In the closing months of the
conflict American policies followed blind alleys which authorities have since attributed to either "stupidity, incompetence,
or worse."

The Communist Take-Over

It was January 1, 1959, that Fidel Castro became the
political steward of a dazed, war-weary Cuba. Batista had
fled. All opposition was crushed. In many circles of American liberals and confused newspaper readers there was a great
huzza as though liberty and constitutional government had
come to Cuba at last.

But many students of international problems saw ominous signs that the suffering and blood-letting for Cuba had
barely begun. The first warnings were exultant boasts from
the Communist press that "they" had won. In Moscow,
Pravda pointed out that from the very beginning of the Castro movement "our party considered it its first duty to aid the
rebels, giving them the correct orientation and the support
of the popular masses. The party headed the battles of the
peasants for land and thereby increased its authority among
the peasantry. Our party . . . appealed to the popular masses
to support Fidel Castro in every way. . . ."[6]

---

[5] *Weyl, Nathaniel,* "RED STAR OVER CUBA," *p. 157.*
[6] PRAVDA, *Moscow, Feb. 29, 1960.*

The Naked Communist

The Communist Party of Cuba also came out in the open to boast that they had provided an important part of the revolutionary action "to overthrow the bloody tyranny of Batista which served as the instrument of imperialistic interests and was supported by imperialism."[7]

If General Batista read this statement he may have wondered where this "imperialistic" support was supposed to have come from. He knew that if the Communists were accusing him of enjoying U. S. support they were really confused.

As soon as Castro took over he used his revolutionary courts of mob justice to send over 600 persons to the firing squads. American liberals described the punishment as "harsh, but deserved." Then he reached out and began a "reform" movement of typical Communist dimensions:

> *Confiscation of land and settling Cuban workers on what turned out to be large, Soviet-type collectivized farms.*
>
> *Confiscation of more than a billion dollars worth of American industry which Castro had neither the technicians nor finances to operate.*
>
> *Breaking up of Cuban family life and placing medium-aged children in special farm communes so "the children will be under the influence of teachers and not their families."*
>
> *Reorganization of the schools to serve as propaganda transmission belts to dispense Communist doctrine and the "Hate Yankee" line.*
>
> *Suspension of civil liberties and other constitutional guarantees.*
>
> *Elimination of free elections.*
>
> *Capture of all press, TV and radio for government propaganda purposes.*
>
> *Termination of all cultural, political and economic ties with the United States.*
>
> *Alliances with Russia.*

---

[7] NEW YORK TIMES, *April 22, 1959 "Fear of Red's Role in Castro Regime Alarming Havana."*

The Communist Conquest of Cuba

While all of this Communist machinery was being put into operation during 1959 and early 1960, many American apologists for Castro continued to insist that he was neither Communist nor dictatorial, just "misunderstood." They snatched at every hopeful atom of news from Cuba indicating that Castro might be "getting more reasonable now," or "Castro is changing."

But all of these dreams of hopeful illusion were smashed by Castro himself when he dutifully answered the call of Nikita Khrushchev in the summer of 1960 and went to the United Nations as part of the Red Bloc "show of strength." At Castro's Harlem headquarters the two dictators warmly embraced each other. They were brothers and comrades.

Now that the Iron Curtain has come rumbling down on little Cuba perhaps some Americans occasionally reflect on the glowing description of Castro which Herbert Matthews wrote for the New York Times in 1957: "Castro," he said, "has strong ideas of liberty, democracy, social justice, the need to restore the constitution, to hold elections."

Other Americans who chose the wrong side have since said, "It is all so unfortunate. Perhaps it was inevitable."

This last statement has a familiar ring. This is precisely the theme which Dean Acheson put in his White Paper when he tried to explain why we lost China. He excused it as "inevitable." But the Wedemeyer Report revealed that China was also lost because of stupidity, incompetence or worse. China was lost when the State Department promoted an arms embargo against this long-standing U.S. ally at a time when she was fighting for her very existence. The same kind of thinking put the arms embargo on Batista. Both were lost. Both were casualties of Communism.

All of this led former Ambassador Gardner to remark sadly:

"We could have prevented it all and we didn't. If we'd

carried out normal relations with Batista, just carried out our contracts, he (Batista) would have got out as scheduled, come to live in Florida, and been replaced by an ideal candidate."

"A pro-Batista man?" Gardner was asked.

"No, Marquez Sterling, a doctor, whom everybody loved, was Batista's opponent. Ironically, although against Batista, he had to flee Cuba because of Castro."[8]

Events during 1961 demonstrated that the United States was still not giving the Cuban situation sufficient attention. None of the tragic errors of the past were any worse than the fatal blunder which occurred on April 17, 1961, when an abortive invasion of Cuba was attempted at the Bay of Pigs under circumstances which doomed it to failure before the attack was even launched.

Badly organized, poorly equipped, and carrying the sagging prestige of the United States with it, a little band of less than 1400 Cubans landed from antiquated ships to spark an "uprising against Castro." Castro was waiting for them with Soviet tanks, jet planes and Soviet guns. When the shooting was over the "invaders" were captured in a body. Communist propaganda machinery all over the world went into a hysteria of screaming headlines against American imperialism. "A first-class disaster for U. S. prestige" wailed the free world press.

In the panic atmosphere which followed, Castro facetiously said he might trade tractors for the prisoners. Immediately misguided U. S. liberals began collecting money for tractors to pay off Castro's blackmail demand. Castro was so pleased to see citizens from the most powerful nation in the world cowering at his feet that he gleefully tantalized the negotiators by boosting his demands. As should have been expected, the negotiations came to nothing.

Responsible Americans began to demand a halt to all this ridiculous pampering of a Soviet puppet. Serious political leaders began to set down the plans for a long-range strategy which would eventually liberate the beleaguered people of Cuba.

---

[8] *Weyl, Nathaniel*, "RED STAR OVER CUBA," *p. 180.*

XII

The Future Task

In this study we have made no attempt to cover up the blunders of the past which free men have made in dealing with Communism. In fact, all of these mistakes may be counted a benefit if we have learned a lesson from each of them. Nevertheless, we certainly would be guilty of the "decadent stupidity" which the Communists attribute to us if we allowed ourselves to repeat these mistakes in the future.

In this chapter we shall deal with the task at hand. To appreciate the problem we shall first discuss the progress which the Communists have made under their Timetable of Conquest. Then we shall deal with the current line of Communist strategy. Finally we shall describe some of the most important things which must be done to win.

The Communist Timetable of Conquest

To head off an enemy it is first necessary to know where the enemy wants to go. The Communists have made no secret about this. Their plan first of all is to take Asia, then Africa, next Europe and finally America. Although this plan of conquest has been in Communist literature for several decades, it was vigorously restated in 1953 when Red leaders decided to set up a timetable of conquest for the entire world and then take it continent by continent. Total conquest is to be completed by around 1973. Fortunately American military intelligence captured this timetable at the close of the Korean War and Senator William Knowland placed it in the Congressional Record under date of April 29, 1954, page 5708.

Although the timetable is too lengthy to quote in its entirety, selected statements are being presented with comments so the student may know what progress the Communists have made in their plans to take over the world.

"We have to, until we are certain of victory, take a course which will not lead to war."

Official Communist strategy is to press for advantages on all fronts but to back down in the face of major military resistance. This will continue to be their policy unless they could be certain of sudden victory by a sneak attack which would wipe out all U.S. capacity to retaliate. U.S. success during 1960 in launching a Polaris missile from a submerged submarine made Soviet sneak attack plans obsolete. A Red attack would bring devastating retaliation from these constantly moving missile bases which now will be roaming the seas. For the present, Red policy will therefore have to be "a course which will not lead to war."

"Britain must be placated by being convinced that . . . the Communists and the capitalist countries can live in peace."

Peaceful coexistence was not only sold to the people of Britain but to Americans as well. Coexistence means to accept Communism as a permanent fixture in the earth; to write off as past history the conquest of the satellite nations; to placate Communist demands so as to avoid crises and international tensions.

The Future Task

"Opportunities for trade will have a great influence on the British mind."

This worked even better than the Red leaders planned. Today not only Britain but the U.S. and 37 other members of the Western bloc have succumbed to the lure of trade with the Sino-Soviet bloc.

"In the case of France . . . she must be made to feel a sense of greater security in cooperating with us."

After World War II, Red forces in France made the Communist party the largest in the country. Before De-Gaulle's seizure of power in 1958, Red influence had helped to carry France to the brink of bankruptcy, anarchy and civil war.

"Japan must be convinced that rearmament endangers her national security and that . . . the American forces distributed all over the world cannot spare sufficient strength for the defense of Japan."

This was the kind of Communist agitation which produced the 1960 Japanese riots and prevented President Eisenhower from visiting Japan.

"Her (Japan's) desire for trade will offer great possibilities for steering Japan away from the United States."

By 1960 Japan had regained her position as fifth in world trade. The U.S. steered Japan away from the Sino-Soviet bloc by buying 23% of her exports and providing 34.8% of her imports.

"By 1960 China's military, economic and industrial power will be so developed that with a mere show of force by the Soviet Union and China, the ruling clique of Japan will capitulate."

This did not occur. Japan, with U.S. help, became strong while China floundered under Communist disci-

*pline and headed for widespread famine and economic
collapse.*

"The United States must be isolated by all possible
means."

> *This Communist project was making alarming prog-
> ress by 1960. Anti-U. S. propaganda all over the world
> had created the image of the "ugly American." And this
> in spite of 50 billions in foreign aid. Red expansion in
> Asia, Africa, Cuba, Central America and South America
> has begun to awaken Americans to the real threat of pos-
> sible isolation.*

"Whether we can prevent the United States from starting the war (to defend her rights and liberties) depends upon
how much success we have in isolating her and how effective
is our peace offensive."

> *This clearly reflects the perfidy of Red propaganda
> to use "peace" as a means of paralyzing U. S. resistance
> as the Communists gradually take over. Here we see the
> Red definition of "peaceful coexistence." It means
> "peaceful surrender."*

"In the case of India, only peaceful means should be
adopted. Any employment of force will alienate ourselves
from the Arabic countries and Africa, because India is considered to be our friend."

> *This plan to betray India through peaceful conquest
> is definitely on the march. Nehru claims neutrality but
> is a trained Marxist-socialist who has consistently lined
> up with the Red leaders on most major issues. In the
> hour of his downfall, he will no doubt ask the Western
> nations to save him.*

"After India has been won over, the problems of the
Philippines and Arabic countries can be easily solved by economic cooperation . . . and coalitions. This task may be completed by 1965."

The Future Task

Already the forces of Red subversion are clearly apparent in both the Philippines and in Nasser's Pan-Arabic Republic.

"Then a wave of revolution will sweep the whole continent of Africa and the imperialists and the colonizationists will be quickly driven into the sea."

Even by 1960 the Communists had built the fires of revolutionary violence all over Africa. The colonial powers were trying to get the natives to follow a policy of "peaceful transition to independence" but many of them were following the Red formula: "From colonialism to chaos to Communism."

"With Asia and Africa disconnected with the capitalist countries in Europe, there will be a total economic collapse in Western Europe. Their capitulation will be a matter of course."

In 1960 when the Belgians relinquished the Congo, it created havoc in the Belgium economy. Each of the colonial powers is being affected as the trade relations with Africa are being disrupted. Eventually the Reds hope to get an African-Asian strangle hold on the economy of Europe. Every year this noose is drawing tighter.

As for the United States, "crushing economic collapse and industrial breakdown will follow the European crisis."

The plunging of the U. S. into a paralyzing depression is part of the last-stage Soviet plan of conquest for America.

"Canada and South America will find themselves in the same hopeless and defenseless condition."

It is true that if the U. S. were totally isolated, intimidated and subverted, the whole Western hemisphere would fall.

258   "Twenty years from now (which would be 1973) world
revolution will be an accomplished fact!"

*Some phases of this plan of conquest have been frus-
trated, but other phases are far ahead of expectations.
Considered overall, the Communist Timetable of Conquest is alarmingly close to being right on schedule.*

Experts on Communist strategy point out that this entire
plan of conquest would collapse if the West awakened and
took the initiative to start pushing Communism back on all
fronts.   They say the tragic blunder of the West has been
its continuous willingness to coexist, to accept Communism
as a permanent fixture in the earth, to assume that Communist conquests were unalterable, to ignore the fact that
the Red leaders have admitted in the timetable that they
have more reason to be frightened of military action than
the West, and to allow free nations to be intimidated and
bluffed into appeasing a weak enemy.

How was this achieved?

Importance of the Psychological War

The biggest mistake of the West has been allowing itself to drift into a state of mental stagnation, apathy and in-
action.   In some circles, motivations of patriotism, loyalty
and the traditional dream of "freedom for all men" have been
lying dormant or have been paralyzed by a new kind of
strange thinking.   Authorities say there is an urgent need
for a revolutionary change in our state of mind.

What is wrong with our "state of mind?"

First and foremost, we have been thinking the way the
Communists want us to think.   Our founding fathers would
be alarmed to learn how confused many of our people have
become over such fundamental problems as coexistence, disarmament, free trade, the United Nations, recognition of
Red China, and a host of related problems.   Instead of main-

The Future Task

taining a state of intellectual vigilance, we have taken Communist slogans as the major premises for too many of our conclusions. Let us go down a list of current strategy goals which the Communists and their fellow travelers are seeking to achieve. These are all part of the campaign to soften America for the final takeover. It should be kept in mind that many loyal Americans are working for these same objectives because they are not aware that these objectives are designed to destroy us.

Current Communist Goals

1. *U. S. acceptance of coexistence as the only alternative to atomic war.*
2. *U. S. willingness to capitulate in preference to engaging in atomic war.*
3. *Develop the illusion that total disarmament by the United States would be a demonstration of moral strength.*
4. *Permit free trade between all nations regardless of Communist affiliation and regardless of whether or not items could be used for war.*
5. *Extension of long-term loans to Russia and Soviet Satellites.*
6. *Provide American aid to all nations regardless of Communist domination.*
7. *Grant recognition of Red China. Admission of Red China to the UN.*
8. *Set up East and West Germany as separate states in spite of Khrushchev's promise in 1955 to settle the Germany question by free elections under supervision of the UN.*
9. *Prolong the conferences to ban atomic tests because the U.S. has agreed to suspend tests as long as negotiations are in progress.*
10. *Allow all Soviet satellites individual representation in the UN.*

11. *Promote the UN as the only hope for mankind. If its charter is rewritten, demand that it be set up as a one-world government with its own independent armed forces. (Some Communist leaders believe the world can be taken over as easily by the UN as by Moscow. Sometimes these two centers compete with each other as they are now doing in the Congo.)*

12. *Resist any attempt to outlaw the Communist Party.*

13. *Do away with all loyalty oaths.*

14. *Continue giving Russia access to the U.S. Patent Office.*

15. *Capture one or both of the political parties in the United States.*

16. *Use technical decisions of the courts to weaken basic American institutions by claiming their activities violate civil rights.*

17. *Get control of the schools. Use them as transmission belts for socialism and current Communist propaganda. Soften the curriculum. Get control of teachers' associations. Put the party line in textbooks.*

18. *Gain control of all student newspapers.*

19. *Use student riots to foment public protests against programs or organizations which are under Communist attack.*

20. *Infiltrate the press. Get control of book-review assignments, editorial writing, policy-making positions.*

21. *Gain control of key positions in radio, TV and motion pictures.*

22. *Continue discrediting American culture by degrading all forms of artistic expression. An American Communist cell was told to "eliminate all good sculpture from parks and buildings, substitute shapeless, awkward and meaningless forms."*

23. *Control art critics and directors of art museums. "Our plan is to promote ugliness, repulsive, meaningless art."*

24. *Eliminate all laws governing obscenity by calling*

The Future Task

them "censorship" and a violation of free speech and free press.

25. *Break down cultural standards of morality by promoting pornography and obscenity in books, magazines, motion pictures, radio and TV.*

26. *Present homo-sexuality, degeneracy and promiscuity as "normal, natural, healthy."*

27. *Infiltrate the churches and replace revealed religion with "social" religion. Discredit the Bible and emphasize the need for intellectual maturity which does not need a "religious crutch."*

28. *Eliminate prayer or any phase of religious expression in the schools on the ground that it violates the principle of "separation of church and state."*

29. *Discredit the American Constitution by calling it inadequate, old-fashioned, out of step with modern needs, a hindrance to cooperation between nations on a world-wide basis.*

30. *Discredit the American founding fathers. Present them as selfish aristocrats who had no concern for the "common man."*

31. *Belittle all forms of American culture and discourage the teaching of American history on the ground that it was only a minor part of "the big picture." Give more emphasis to Russian history since the Communists took over.*

32. *Support any socialist movement to give centralized control over any part of the culture—education, social agencies, welfare programs, mental health clinics, etc.*

33. *Eliminate all laws or procedures which interfere with the operation of the Communist apparatus.*

34. *Eliminate the House Committee on Un-American Activities.*

35. *Discredit and eventually dismantle the FBI.*

36. *Infiltrate and gain control of more unions.*

37. *Infiltrate and gain control of big business.*

38. *Transfer some of the powers of arrest from the police*

to social agencies. Treat all behavioral problems as psychiatric disorders which no one but psychiatrists can understand or treat.

39. *Dominate the psychiatric profession and use mental health laws as a means of gaining coercive control over those who oppose Communist goals.*
40. *Discredit the family as an institution. Encourage promiscuity and easy divorce.*
41. *Emphasize the need to raise children away from the negative influence of parents. Attribute prejudices, mental blocks and retarding of children to suppressive influence of parents.*
42. *Create the impression that violence and insurrection are legitimate aspects of the American tradition; that students and special-interest groups should rise up and use "united force" to solve economic, political or social problems.*
43. *Overthrow all colonial governments before native populations are ready for self-government.*
44. *Internationalize the Panama Canal.*
45. *Repeal the Connally Reservation so the U.S. cannot prevent the World Court from seizing jurisdiction over domestic problems. Give the World Court jurisdiction over nations and individuals alike.*

If the student will read the reports of Congressional hearings together with available books by ex-Communists, he will find all of these Communist objectives described in detail. Furthermore, he will come to understand how many well-meaning citizens have become involved in pushing forward the Communist program without realizing it. They became converted to Communist *objectives* because they accepted superficial Communist *slogans*. Soon they were thinking precisely the way the Communists wanted them to think.

Let us examine some of these problems at closer range.

The Future Task

What About Disarmament?   **263**

The Communists have created the illusion in free men's minds that "the way to peace is through disarmament." We must not forget that this originated as a *Communist* slogan. Now free men have adopted it as their own and are even setting up special commissions to explore ways and means to carry it out. In this action we are deliberately closing our eyes to everything we promised ourselves at the close of World War II and again at the end of the Korean War. Experts tell us that to disarm in the face of an obvious and present danger is an *immoral* act. It is an act of self-destruction.

Here are just a few fundamental facts on disarmament which the experts who know Communism are pleading with us to consider:

Disarmament means to depend upon *agreements* instead of strength.

Agreements are absolutely useless unless they can be enforced.

The fallacy of a disarmament agreement with Russia (a nation which has violated 51 out of 53 agreements already) is this: if Russia chose to secretly rearm we would have lost our capacity to enforce the agreement. Such an agreement gives a dishonest party a devastating advantage because of his capacity to "arm secretly." In a vacuum of disarmament, a government with criminal intentions requires very few secret arms to overcome all opposition. This is what Hitler and Mussolini taught us.

On February 3, 1961, Dr. Arnold Wolfers told the Senate Committee on Foreign Relations: "A few easily concealed or clandestinely manufactured weapons would, in a totally disarmed world, give one nation decisive military power over others. . . . A totally disarmed world is also one in which Communists' characteristics of secrecy and of a society organized along military lines would give them maximum advantage."

But in all this talk about disarmament the thing to remember is that Khrushchev would not dare disarm. His armed forces of six million—including two million secret police—are not to fight the West but to maintain "domestic tranquility" behind the Iron Curtain. They are to suppress uprisings which have occurred in the satellites and in Russia. Furthermore, Khrushchev is continually haunted by the spectre of the Red Chinese who would like nothing better than to see the Russians disarm. So we repeat, Khrushchev would not dare disarm.

Finally, in answer to those who claim that an arms race will lead to war, let us point out the rather obvious fact that *an arms race is not an underlying cause of war, but a symptom of political conflict.* To disarm in the face of political conflict invites war. The United States was well on the way to disarming and demobilizing when the Korean War jolted us into the realization that vicious forces of conquest were still stalking up and down the earth. Because that predatory force has not relented, we have had to stay armed.

In view of all these facts, it should be clear to anyone that the cry for disarmament is not the message of peace and freedom. It is the message of the enemy.

What About Peaceful Coexistence?

The Communists have created another illusion with reference to peaceful coexistence. This is the idea that the West must be willing to coexist with Communism since the only alternative would be annihilation through atomic war.

The real alternative to co-EXistence is co-REsistance. Experts in the field have been saying for years that Communism does not have to be tolerated. It has no moral, economic or political excuse for existing. Furthermore, it is extremely vulnerable to many types of peaceful pressures which free men have not yet used. We will discuss these in a later section. At this point it is important simply to emphasize that Communism can be beaten—and it can be done without atomic war. Therefore the whole basis for arguing coexistence collapses. Coexistence is a contradiction of terms because it means trying to coexist with world conquest, which is impossible. One must resist or be conquered. It also means accepting the status quo of one-third of the human race in bondage as a permanent working arrangement. It means accepting Communism in spite of its deceit, subversion and broken covenants. It means tolerating Communism without resistance.

The United States Congress was right when it proclaimed in its Captive Nations Resolution of July, 1959:

"The enslavement of a substantial part of the world's population by Communist imperialism makes a mockery of the idea of peaceful coexistence."[1]

And the President sounded a note of awakening resistance when he said:

"It is appropriate and proper to manifest to the peoples of the captive nations the support of the Government and the people of the United States of America for their just aspirations for freedom and national independence."[2]

What About the United Nations?

All over the world people demand that some type of international arena be created where disputes between nations can be arbitrated or settled without resorting to war. Two attempts have been made to create such an arena—the League of Nations and the United Nations. Both ran into difficulty and for the same reason. Both organizations started out as exclusive federations of "peace-loving" nations and then turned right around and tried to convert themselves into world parliaments where all nations could be represented *including* warlike or predatory nations. In both cases the predatory nations successfully seized power and almost completely nullified all the high-sounding phrases contained in their original statements of purpose.

---

[1] *The full text of the Captive Nations Proclamation is contained in* U. S. NEWS AND WORLD REPORT, *August 3, 1959, p. 87.*
[2] *The above issue of* U. S. NEWS AND WORLD REPORT *also contains the Presidential Proclamation, p. 87.*

The Naked Communist

As far as the United Nations is concerned, this weakness was emphasized by John Foster Dulles when he addressed the American Bar Association. He said the failures of the UN are due primarily to the fact that its "effective functioning depends upon cooperation with a nation which is dominated by an international party seeking world domination."[3]

Henry Cabot Lodge pointed out the same thing: "In 1945 and 1946 . . . the United States assumed that Russia was a peace-loving nation, and the whole United Nations was based on the assumption that the alliance between the United States and the Soviet Union would continue, which of course, was a very false, tragically false, assumption."[4]

There are numerous provisions in the UN Charter which permit predatory powers such as the USSR or her satellites to bring the orderly processes of the UN to a dead halt. In the UN's 15 years of existence, the USSR has used this organization for subversion behind the scenes and legal sabotage in her open councils. This has not only frustrated the peace-preserving powers of the UN but has almost completely paralyzed individual action by the other members because they have committed themselves to rely on the UN to settle disputes.

When one reflects upon the Soviet veto of the UN attempt to censure Russia following her invasion of Hungary and her veto of the UN attempt to have an investigation of the killing of four Americans on the RB-47 in 1960, it emphasizes the long list of atrocities which Soviet leaders have committed without punishment or censure even though every one of them violated Article 2 of the UN Charter. Consider these provisions:

1. *The Organization is based on the principle of the sovereign equality of all members.*

---

[3] *Wade, William W.*, THE UN TODAY, *H. W. Wilson Company, New York, p. 134.*
[4] *"The Case for Severing Relations with Soviet Rulers,"* U. S. NEWS & WORLD REPORT, *Dec. 17, 1954, p. 139.*

The Future Task

2. *All Members . . . shall fulfill in good faith the obliga-*
tions assumed by them in accordance with the present
Charter.
3. *All Members shall settle their international disputes*
by peaceful means. . . .
4. *All Members shall refrain . . . from the threat or use*
of force against the territorial integrity or political
independence of any state. . . .
5. *All members shall . . . refrain from giving assistance*
to any state against which the United Nations is tak-
ing preventive or enforcement action.

In Hungary, China, Southeast Asia, Cuba, Africa, Central and South America, Korea—one might say in every sector of the world—the USSR has violated these principles *continually.*

As a result of this vast contradiction between promise and performance, the whole UN complex is gradually reaching an impasse or stalemate. What then can be done with Red aggression, with its worldwide program of insurrection, riots, civil war and conquest? And what should be done with the UN?

Because the United States is the most wealthy and powerful nation in the world, she is expected to provide an answer. And because practically every other imaginable suggestion has been presented, it is time to come up with the simple, direct answer which we should have adopted long ago: "Turn back to the original intent of the Charter. *Restrict UN membership to peace-loving nations!*"

This is precisely what Article 4 provides, and it has been the violation of this article which has produced most of the trouble. Because we have waited so long to eliminate the warlike nations, this change will involve some difficulties. But this would be nothing compared to the difficulties which lie ahead if free men pursue their present course. Due to the veto technicalities and numerous violations of American constitutional law in the existing Charter, it would be necessary to reconstruct the entire framework of the UN. Nevertheless it could be done.

No doubt some would object to the elimination of Russia and her satellites from the UN on the ground that it would prevent the UN from serving as a world parliament.

The answer to that objection is the proven fact that the UN can never serve peace-loving peoples as long as the UN tries to accommodate its forum to the harassment and bedevilment of nations who make no pretense at fulfilling their obligations either under the Charter or under international law.

What if the founding fathers of the United States had tried to include King George in the Constitutional Convention? The results would have been as frustrating and aggravating as they have turned out to be with a predatory nation and her satellites sitting in the UN Assembly of peace-loving nations. The founding fathers would no doubt look at our present UN operation and say: "It is illogical. It is illegal. It is impossible." Fifteen years of UN history painfully prove it.

But would not such action drive Russia and her satellites into a second association of Red nations and create a contest of power blocs?

This already exists. The only difference would be that the Red bloc would not be in the UN to sabotage the united desires of the peace-loving nations as it does today.

Would not such action provoke war?

Not as long as the West remains strong. It would not weaken the West's military position at all. If anything, such action would strengthen it. It would also create the necessary federation of strength to start putting economic and political pressures on Communism and thereby allow her enslaved peoples to strike from within and eventually destroy this spectre of human tyranny. This new arrangement would give us the ideal vehicle to begin implementing all the fine promises we made in the "Captive Nations' Proclamation" on July, 1959.

Is there no other way? Apparently not. All other approaches turn out to be diversionary. They merely postpone the day of honest decision. If free men united to bring about this needed change, the new federation of peace-loving nations could perform a political miracle—one which would give new assurance for both peace and prosperity.

We have a task to perform and time is running out.

Is the Communist Movement a Legitimate Political Party?

This question grows out of another illusion which the Communists created in our minds. They induced us to accept the idea that Communism is a legitimate expression of political action. The truth is that Communism is a criminal conspiracy. It is a mistake to treat it as a political party.

Political groups solve their problems by entering into negotiations, attending conferences, and working out their differences with bona fide compromises which all parties are expected to perform. This has never worked with the Communists because they use deceit, disregard of laws, violation of treaties, intimidation, subversion and open insurrection as basic tools of conquest. This makes it a criminal conspiracy.

Once we realize that Communism is a criminal operation, many new avenues of action open before us. For example, a criminal problem is not handled by negotiation and compromise but by following four steps:

1. IMMOBILIZE THE CRIMINAL.
2. RENDER HIM HARMLESS.
3. GAIN HIS CONFIDENCE.
4. REHABILITATE HIM.

It may be recalled that these are the four steps which were used in dealing with both Germany and Japan when their leaders pursued the criminal course of action which precipitated World War II. The Western allies followed these steps and Germany and Japan were not only immobilized and rendered harmless but they were successfully rehabilitated. After the war West Germany and Japan became two of America's closest supporters.

Does this mean a preventive war should be waged against the criminal Communists? Not at all. It means that while there is still time and before a major shooting war is necessary, free men should utilize available peaceful pressures to immobilize the Soviet empire and work for the day when her own people can overthrow the tyrannical rule of Red leaders from within.

What peaceful pressures are available?

We have already mentioned the importance of taking away the illegal membership which the USSR and her satellites hold in the UN. Another highly potent weapon is available which would cut off Communist and espionage machinery. This is the peaceful weapon of severing diplomatic relations. It is the action Thomas Jefferson recommended for nations which treat us "atrociously." He said:

"I am anxious that we should give the world still another lesson by showing to them other modes of punishing injuries than by war. . . . I love, therefore . . .(the) proposition of cutting off all communications with the nation which has conducted itself so atrociously."[5]

Recently Senator Barry Goldwater and other students of the problem have advocated this very type of action against the Soviet empire. There are plenty of reasons to justify it. Russia is guilty of:

Continuous violations of treaties and covenants.

Repeated violations of international law.

Vicious subversion and interference in the domestic affairs of other nations.

---

[5] WRITINGS OF THOMAS JEFFERSON (*Thomas Jefferson Memorial Association, 1904-1905) Vol. IX, p. 285.*

The Future Task

Open warfare against peace-loving peoples.

Provocative acts with the leveling of insults and false charges against the United States.

Illegal killing of American servicemen.

Illegal shooting down of American planes.

Illegal imprisonment of American citizens.

The lack of political courage to sever diplomatic relations with Russia is often covered up with the plea that we might lose some important advantages by isolating Russia in this manner.

What advantages? Senator Goldwater has pointed out that there are none. Since the United States recognized the USSR in 1933, not one single advantage has accrued to the United States which could not have been achieved equally well—and often far more easily—without recognition. Recognition turned out to be a tool of conquest for the Communists.

In addition to isolating Communism internationally, it also needs to be outlawed domestically. This is so important that Lenin said the Communists must do everything possible to avoid it. Whittaker Chambers summarized this point when he said: "Lenin had tirelessly taught that when a whole Communist Party is outlawed, it is almost wholly paralyzed because it can no longer send into the surrounding community the filaments whereby it spreads its toxins and from which it draws its strength of life."[6]

But would not a statute outlawing the Communist party threaten legitimate political parties? Not if the statute were aimed at any organization "advocating the overthrow of the government by force and violence." Criminal law strikes at illegal acts or any conspiracy to commit illegal acts. A conspiracy to overthrow the government by force and violence is therefore criminal in nature. Any organization which promotes such illegal activities should be outlawed.

As a number of authorities have already pointed out, it

---

[6] *Chambers, Whittaker, "WITNESS," page 210.*

is foolish to treat the Communists as a legitimate political party as it would be to give bank robbers business licenses.

Is the Soviet Empire Vulnerable to Economic Pressure?

Probably the greatest single weakness of the Sino-Soviet bloc is her shaky economy. Here is a soft spot where peaceful pressures could be devastating. No amount of Soviet propaganda can cover up the obvious collapse of the Chinese communes and the sluggish inefficiency of the Soviet collectivized farms. Every single Soviet satellite is languishing in a depression. Even *Pravda* has openly criticized the lack of bare essentials and the shoddy quality of Russian-made goods.

These factors of austerity and deprivation add to the hatred and misery of the people which constantly feed the flames of potential revolt. Terrorist tactics have been used by the Red leaders to suppress uprisings. In spite of the virtual "state of siege" which exists throughout the Soviet empire, there are many outbreaks of violent protest.

All of this explains why the Soviet leaders are constantly pleading for "free trade," "long-term loans," "increased availability of material goods from the West." Economically, Communism is collapsing but the West has not had the good sense to exploit it. Instead, the United States, Great Britain and 37 other Western powers are shipping vast quantities of goods to the Sino-Soviet bloc.

Some business leaders have had the temerity to suggest that trade with the Reds helps the cause of peace. They suggest that "you never fight the people you trade with." Apparently they cannot even remember as far back as the late Thirties when this exact type of thinking resulted in the sale of scrap iron and oil to the Japanese just before World War II. After the attack on Pearl Harbor it became tragically clear that while trade with friends may promote peace, trade with a threatening enemy is an act of self-destruction. Have we forgotten that fatal lesson so soon?

Could Peaceful Pressures Cause the Communist Empire to Explode Internally?

The Communist leaders have always been extremely sensitive to their own internal weaknesses. They frequently resort to capital punishment to suppress the bitter criticism of their own enslaved people. They use propaganda to boast of pretended success in the very areas where they suffer the greatest failures. A close scrutiny of recent history will demonstrate that time and again free men could have tied the Communist conspiracy in knots if only they had been watching for opportunities to exploit fuming internal pressures which were ready to explode.

Many of these pressures are building today. Each one of them represents a golden opportunity for direct action by the free West. But free men must first make up their minds whether they really *want* freedom for the Iron Curtain captives. Is it worth giving up a little trade? Is it worth the temporary political heat of a showdown in the UN? Is it worth the momentary clamor which Red agents would foment if we withdrew diplomatic recognition?

It is extremely confusing to freedom fighters—especially in the satellites—when they watch the failing Communist economy being bolstered and fed by 39 Western nations. In the UN the distortion of justice and common sense bewilders them. In diplomatic circles the constant capitulation and compromise outrages them. A refugee from a Russian slave labor camp wrote to me: "There must be a noose of ignorance around the necks of the West. Don't they know we would eventually overthrow the Communist leaders if the West would just stop feeding, fondling and coddling them?"

In the minds of these people, it borders on criminal neglect when we withhold the impact of powerful peaceful pressures which are available to us. During World War II we promised freedom to all of these satellite peoples. And we should never let the Communists forget that *Stalin promised them freedom.* In his order of the day, No. 130, dated May 1, 1942, Joseph Stalin declared:

"It is not our aim to seize foreign lands or to subjugate foreign people. . . . We have not and cannot have such war aims as the imposition of our will and regime on the Slavs and other enslaved peoples of Europe who are waiting our aid. Our aim consists in assisting these people in their struggle for liberation from Hitler's tyranny and then setting them free to rule in their own lands as they desire."[7]

Neither should the West allow Nikita Khrushchev to forget what he has said: "The Soviet Union deeply sympathizes with all the nations striving to win and uphold their independence. And these nations can rest assured that the Soviet Union, without any meddling in their internal affairs, without stipulating any conditions, will help them to strengthen their independence for which they fought so hard."[8]

The unbelievable bald-faced deception of such statements should motivate free nations in their firm resolve to strike back at Communism on every front. Too often the western apologists for coexistence and "peace at any price" are panicked when it is suggested that economic and political pressures be applied in order to squeeze the Soviet empire into an internal explosion. They wail that such action will disturb the peace behind the Iron Curtain. And indeed it would. In fact, it should be a standard object of strategy to disturb the peace of the Red leaders. This was precisely what President Woodrow Wilson was talking about when he said:

"I will not take any part in composing difficulties that

---

[7] "ON THE GREAT PATRIOTIC WAR OF THE SOVIET UNION," *Foreign Language Publishing House, Moscow, 1946, p. 59.*
[8] *From Nikita Khrushchev's letter to the Mexican Newspaper,* EXCELSIOR, *February 28, 1958.*

ought not to be composed, and a difficulty between an enslaved people and its autocratic rulers ought not to be composed. We in America have stood from the day of our birth for the emancipation of people *throughout the World* who are living unwillingly under governments which were not of their choice. . . . So long as wrongs like that exist in the world, you cannot bring permanent peace to the world. I go further than that. So long as wrongs of that sort exist, you ought not to bring permanent peace to the world, because those wrongs ought to be righted, and enslaved peoples ought to be free to right them."[9]

Just the moment the Western powers develop the courage to clamp a total trade embargo on the Communist empire and then combine it with a policy of "go home and take your spies with you," the hearts of Iron Curtain freedom fighters can once more surge with hope.

Not until then will America's eloquent Captive Nations Proclamation mean anything.

What Can the Ordinary Individual Do?

The war between freedom and slavery is not just a fight to be waged by Congressmen, the President, soldiers and diplomats. Fighting Communism, Socialism and the subversion of constitutional government is everybody's job. And working for the *expansion* of freedom is everybody's job. It is a basic American principle that each individual knows better than anyone else what he can do to help once he has become informed. No citizen will have to go far from his own home to find a faltering battle line which needs his aid. Communist influences are gnawing away everywhere and thousands of confused citizens often aid and abet them by operating in a vacuum of their own ignorance. The task is therefore to become informed and then move out for action!

---

[9] *Quoted in "Uncompromising Idealism," by David Lawrence,* U. S. NEWS AND WORLD REPORT, *Aug. 31, 1959, p. 104.*

Just to stimulate a little positive thinking, here are a few elementary suggestions for different types of individuals:

Suggestions for Parents

1. Stay close to your children to make sure they are being trained to think like Washington and Lincoln, not like Marx and Lenin.

2. In providing physical needs for your family, don't forget their spiritual needs. We are in an ideological war. From a Marxist viewpoint an atheistic mind is already three-fourths conquered.

3. Take your children to church, don't send them. Be sure they are getting true religious values, not modernistic debunking.

4. Help your children grow up. Don't fall for the current Socialist-Communist line that parents are a detriment to their children. They are only a detriment when they don't do their job.

5. Children require a formula of 90% love and 10% discipline.

6. Do not fall for the "permissive" school of psychology which says discipline will harm human development. Such thinking produces hoodlums with maladjusted personalities who are likely to fall for every "ism." that comes along. A child needs to know that he lives in an orderly world. Discipline is part of it—not extreme harshness but a reasonable and consistent enforcement of the rules.

7. Because "youth problems" happened to be one of my own areas of professional study, I wrote a book designed to answer the Communist and Socialist charge that modern parents cannot do a good job of raising children.[10]

8. Be active in PTA. If you are not, Communists and centralized planners will take over.

---

[10] SO YOU WANT TO RAISE A BOY, *Doubleday, New York, release date, January 1, 1962.*

The Future Task

9. Have a "freedom library" in your home. Include good biographies of the founding fathers.

10. Take a little time each day to keep up with political problems at home and abroad.

11. Subscribe to a good news magazine such as U.S. News and World Report.

12. Where you have older children, make current events part of the dinner table talk. Be quick to point out left-wing slanting of news, TV or radio broadcasts. There is far more of this slanting than most people realize.

13. Organize a family, a neighborhood or church study group. Help your family realize that there is a great struggle going on in the world which they can help to win.

14. Let your children see that you are interested in civic affairs, that you participate in political affairs, that you are concerned with what is going on. They borrow many of their own attitudes from you.

Suggestions for Teachers

1. The most important single force in winning against Communism is in the field of education. Therefore you are in the front-line trenches.

2. Be certain you have taken time to get a good background on Communistic thought so you can detect it quickly wherever it appears.

3. Define for students the difference between the factors which made Americans the first free people in modern times and the principles which have destroyed freedom wherever the Socialists and Communists have taken over.

4. Help the students understand that free enterprise has produced and distributed more material wealth than any other system man has yet discovered. Point out that it also permits most of our citizens to make a living doing the things they enjoy. At least they can change jobs if they don't like what they are doing. It is also vital for students to appreciate that the remaining weaknesses in our system are

important, but they are minute compared to the monumental problems of the bare-subsistence economies under Socialism and Communism.

5. Beware of those who come pretending to help education when they are trying to seize control of education. Socialist and Communist planners have ambitions to eliminate all local control—which means the teachers themselves would lose control.

6. Be alert to the fact that education was infiltrated by the Socialist-Communist contingent over thirty-five years ago. Many of them were top-echelon personalities who worked their way into leading educational organizations. Because they were hard workers they gained sweeping control of some of our most respected institutions.

7. Read "Education for One Socialist World," which is Chapter 8 in *The UN Record*, by Chesly Manly (Henry Regnery Co., Chicago, 1955). On page 175 Mr. Manly lists a number of books which every teacher should read in order to be aware of the attack against American education during the past four decades.

8. In addition, you will find the following books helpful:

CONQUEST OF THE AMERICAN MIND, *by Dr. Felix Wittmer, (Meador Publishing Co., Boston)*

WHAT'S HAPPENED TO OUR SCHOOLS? *by Rosalie M. Gordon, a pamphlet published by America's Future, Inc., New Rochelle, N.Y.*

THE TURNING OF THE TIDES, *by Paul W. Shafer and John Howland Snow. (Long House Publishers.)*

PROGRESSIVE EDUCATION IS REDUCATION *by Jones and Olivier. (Meador Publishing Co., Boston.)*

BRAINWASHING IN THE HIGH SCHOOLS *by Dr. E. Merrill Root. (Devin-Adair, New York)*

The Future Task

COMMUNIST-SOCIALIST PROPAGANDA IN AMERICAN SCHOOLS, *by Verne P. Kaub (Published by Lakeshore Press, Madison, Wisconsin.)*

9. If any of the educational organizations to which you belong are Socialist-oriented, try to recapture them. Do not try to do it alone. Gather a group of alerted teachers around you and move forward as an organized group.

10. Encourage the teaching of "Communist Problems" in the school. Such a course can become an excellent vehicle to teach American students how to appreciate their own way of life. The name of the course is important. "Communist Problems" is likely to be more acceptable than teaching "Communism."

11. Watch for slanted passages in text books. Socialist authors have invaded the textbook field. So have some with even more radical views. "Brainwashing in the High Schools," by E. Merrill Root, is an analysis of 11 American history books which reflect the destructive left-wing line.

12. Don't be misled by the current atheistic drive to take God out of the classroom. "Separation of church and state" was to keep creeds out of the curriculum, but not God. It would be as unconstitutional to teach *irreligion* in the classroom as it would be to emphasize some particular religion. As teachers we are not to teach a particular faith, but parents are within their rights when they insist that the classroom is not be used by those few teachers who seek to destroy faith. Teachers who believe that teaching atheism is a necessary part of a good education are not really qualified to teach in a Judaic-Christian culture. They are entitled to be atheists but, as public employees, they are not entitled to teach it. If they do, they are violating an important constitutional principle.

13. Encourage patriotic speakers at school assemblies. Excellent films are also available. Many organizations now have well-informed speakers who can give impressive talks on subjects which arouse excellent student response.

14. When a Freedom Forum is held in your area, try to attend.

Suggestions for Students

1. The mind of the student is considered a major battle-field by Communist strategists. The Communist conquest of a country is always preceded by the extensive activities of "converted intellectuals." However, the most vigorous antagonists of Communism are some of these same intellectuals who have been disillusioned and returned to the side of freedom.

2. You will never have more time to study Communism than while you are in school. Try to get a genuine understanding of it. Learn its philosophy, its history and its fallacies.

3. When you run across dedicated Socialists, remember that the only difference between a Socialist and a Communist is in the method of takeover. The desire to seize monolithic control of society is the same in both. Sometimes people forget that USSR stands for the Union of Soviet *Socialist* Republics. Some people count Socialism "good" and Communism "bad." In reality the two are twins.

4. Be quick to detect left-wing slanting in textbooks and lectures.

5. Become acquainted with the latest Communist "line." Work up answers to their charges and proposals.

6. Be sure to remain fair and forthright. Never stoop to Communist tactics to win a point.

7. You can enjoy school far more when your education becomes purposeful. Get acquainted with the Communist problems and it will suddenly make economics, history, philosophy, political science, sociology and psychology come alive. These are all related to the war for survival in which we are now engaged.

8. Be conscious of the fact that people look at world events through one of two windows. Out of one window

The Future Task

the students (and sometimes the professor) see only blue skies. Out of the other window the student can see storm clouds. This is the window to watch. This is where history is being made, and the person who doesn't keep his eye on this window is caught unawares when the storm breaks. On the day of the Pearl Harbor attack, most Americans had to move from window No. 1 to window No. 2 with great speed. They came close to being too late. Damage from the world's threatening political storms can be avoided only by anticipating them—by being vigilant and alert.

9. If you have difficulty in philosophy and your mind is plagued with doubts, read the experience of a student described in the last chapter of this book.

10. Resist the radical element on campus who advocate "mass action" and violent demonstrations. These are usually the tools of Communist agitators. They get students to demonstrate, and this usually provokes a fight. When the police try to restore order, the Communists slip away in an effort to let the students take the blame. When Communist agitators got the students to wreck the Congressional hearings at San Francisco during May of 1960, the judge decided to release them because he felt the students could already see how they had been duped into fronting for professional anti-Americans.

11. Organize a student group to study Communism and Americanism. Challenge Socialists and pro-Communists on the campus. Publish a paper. Set up a speaker's bureau. Write letters to your school paper. Get experience in making *peaceful* democratic processes work.

12. A rapidly growing student organization with a patriotic purpose is "The Torchbearers." Suggestions on how to set up a school chapter may be obtained by writing to The Torchbearers, 5354 W. 126th Street, Hawthorne, California.

Suggestions for Businessmen

1. Remember that Jefferson, Washington, Franklin, Madison, Adams, and the rest of the founding fathers were

not "colonial aristocrats" as some textbooks proclaim, but were just successful businessmen. Because they were willing to sit down and think through the problems of their day, we inherited a free nation.

2. Take time from the pressures of business to stay informed. Subscribe to a good news magazine such as U.S. News and World Report.

3. Become a member of an organization which will send you frequent intelligence reports on current problems. One of the most effective private agencies in this field is the American Security Council, 205 West Monroe Street, Chicago, Illinois.

4. Take an active part in the political party of your choice. Watch for the strong Socialist influence which is trying to take over both parties. Do not hesitate to throw your financial strength and your time behind the fight for freedom. It cost Washington $65,000 to leave his business and serve in the Revolutionary Army. In current inflated money values this would represent nearly half a million dollars.

5. If you belong to a service club, get it in the fight for freedom. Most civic clubs have a special committee to inspire patriotic interests. Invite speakers to keep the business community alert.

6. Sponsor essay and speech contests in the schools to promote American ideals and resistance to deceptive Communist propaganda.

7. Openly resist the sale of goods to the Soviet empire and call for a total embargo against the USSR and her satellites.

8. Work for a more equitable tax structure which is not arbitrary and confiscatory. Economic freedom is part of political freedom.

9. If your employees are in a union, seek the cooperation of union officials in conducting a study course on Communism for your personnel. If no union is involved, ask your employees whether they would like such a course. The American Security Council can provide a complete program

The Future Task

with speakers, films, tapes and literature. Many other organizations are also available to help.

10. Get your local Chamber of Commerce behind regular Freedom Forums which will help keep the entire community alert.

11. Be careful not to contribute to an organization until you know it is a bona fide patriotic group. Unknowingly, some businessmen have been financing cited Communist-front organizations. If you are a member of the American Security Council, you can check on any organization or any individual through their files.

12. Constantly keep in mind that American business is a major target for Communist propaganda. Be alert to any activities which could feed ammunition to the enemy.

13. Furnish views and suggestions to your State and Federal legislators. A letter to a congressman has more impact than many people realize.

Suggestions for Legislators

1. The war between freedom and slavery can be lost in the legislative halls of free men. The wave of Socialism which is sweeping many free western nations toward a kind of suppressive feudalism is gaining ground. In this battle our legislators are on the first line of defense.

2. The entire fabric of American security has been badly weakened by technical decisions of the Supreme Court in recent years. The only remedy is legislative action to restore these security laws.

3. Federal legislators should continue to support the Congressional Committees which are under attack by the Communist Party and their fellow travelers. This attack is a top priority project of the Communist Party at the present time.

4. Restore to Congressional committees the right to determine whether the questions asked of pro-Communist witnesses are pertinent.

5. Restore to Congressional committees the same freedom to investigate Communists and pro-Communists that these committees have always had when investigating business and labor problems.

6. Restore to the states the right to enforce their own anti-subversive laws.

7. Restore to the Smith Act the provision which makes it a crime to teach or advocate the violent overthrow of the Government.

8. Restore to the Smith Act the meaning of "organize" which includes organizational work done after 1945 so that Communist agents cannot hide behind the statute of limitations.

9. Restore to the executive branch of the government the right to determine "reasonable grounds" and to dismiss security risks in both sensitive and non-sensitive positions of the Government.

10. Restore to the states the right to exclude from public employment and education those who refuse to testify about their Communist activities and associates.

11. Restore to the executive branch the right to question aliens awaiting deportation about subversive associates and contacts, and the right to deport aliens who are found to be Communists after entering the United States.

12. Restore to the executive branch the right to deny passports to those who refuse to sign a non-Communist affidavit.

13. Restore to the states the right to exclude from the practice of law those who have been members of the Communist conspiracy or who refuse to testify about Communist activities.

14. Be alert to any attempt by left-wing forces to dismantle or emasculate the FBI.

15. Put into force the excellent recommendations of the Commission on Government Security which were published in June, 1957, but have never been acted upon.

The Future Task

16. Become familiar with the advantages of using powerful peaceful pressures against the USSR, especially in the economic and political fields.

285

Suggestions for the Press

1. Keep in mind the constant effort of the Communist apparatus to plant its agents in all mass communications media.

2. Familiarize yourself with the current Communist line which appears earlier in this chapter. Watch for individuals who shift with that line—often contradicting themselves to accommodate the latest zig or zag of party strategy.

3. In fulfilling the task of exposing crime, corruption and inefficiency in the American culture, be careful not to destroy confidence in American institutions. Because the negative forces in our society are more likely to be "news" than the positive accomplishments, it is easy to over-emphasize the negative side and provide extremely damaging propaganda to the enemy.

4. Run features on current issues which reflect a solid American interpretation of the problem. The Communist avalanche of literature is often compounded by a left-wing slant to the news on a syndicated wire which leaves the American point of view practically unexpressed. More and more newspaper editors are recognizing this problem and are doing something about it.

5. Use quotations from American patriots for box stories and fillers.

6. Develop a program of liaison with public officials so they will have an assurance of your ability to keep a confidence. It is desirable to have the press briefed on developments even though they may be confidential. Most officials start out with a desire to cooperate closely with the press, but they become secretive when distortions and premature releases weaken or destroy their capacity to get their job done properly.

7. Some members of the press have the knack of detecting Communist influences in public life and have made excellent contributions by pointing these out. Temporarily, this action may not be popular, but it gives a newsman stature as events sustain his analysis. We need more analysts who are informed and sensitive to the techniques of the Communist apparatus.

Suggestions for Ministers

1. The churches became a major target for Communist-Socialist infiltration many years ago. These people were successful in capturing many key positions in a number of important religious organizations. Some religious leaders openly advocate and defend Communist principles. They are apologists for the Soviet Union and even advocate capitulation under threat of atomic war.

2. Study Judaism, Christianity and Communism to a point where you can quickly detect the fallacies which some persons in high places disseminate from their pulpits.

3. Develop a Bible-reading congregation.

4. Make religion a practical, dynamic force in the lives of the people.

5. Resist the erosion of the Modernists who seek to discredit the Bible and to define God as an imaginary nonreality. As we pointed out in the first chapter of this book, many of those who started out a century ago to attack the Bible and to destroy our religious culture were close associates of Karl Marx.

6. Be alert to detect those who use "Social Christianity" to cover up the fact that they are not Christians at all.

7. Watch for those who would use the principles of peace, brotherhood, tolerance, and Christian charity to obscure the conspiratorial aspects of Communist "peace." The peace of Communism partakes of the prison and the grave. Remind professional pacifists who have accepted the paralyzing peace propaganda of the Communists that the same Jesus

The Future Task

who taught "love thy enemy" never advocated surrendering to him. The same Jesus who said, "Turn the other cheek" to avoid quarreling and bickering in the ordinary course of life, also said to take a sword to preserve life (Luke 22:36). The Jesus of Nazareth who cleansed the temple was demonstrating that Right deserves to be defended.

8. If you come across those who labor under the misconception that Communism and Christianity have a common denominator, ask them to read the chapter in this book entitled, "Did the Early Christians Practice Communism?"

9. Because of the counseling which ministers do, there are strenuous efforts to make inroads into the ministry. Be alert to the drive by certain analytical psychiatrists to have ministers accept their amoral philosophy. They opine that feelings of guilt and a sense of right and wrong cause mental illnesses. This entire concept is being discredited. There is far more mental health in the Judaic-Christian concept of resisting temptation and overcoming mistakes than ever emanated from the Freudian couch. I have prepared a rather comprehensive article on this subject, entitled, "Law Enforcement Looks at Mental Health," which appears in the professional police magazine, Law and Order, for March, 1961.

10. In counseling students who are having difficulty reconciling the many conflicting views which they hear in school, you might refer them to the last chapter in this book which is designed to help the student recognize the ideological conflict now in progress. It is hoped that this material will help them find their way through the confusion of many voices so as to maintain both moral and intellectual integrity.

11. Be careful to read books before you recommend them. Recently some church groups have been induced to recommend books which turned out to be filled with obscenity. This is an important part of the Socialist-Communist campaign to discredit religious culture. What technique could better serve their purpose than to have the churches themselves sponsor degenerate literature!

12. Set up study groups on both youth and adult levels to study Communism. Have qualified and well informed persons serve as discussion leaders.

The West Can Win

With every citizen watching for an opportunity to strike a blow for freedom, the force of Communism can be halted, smothered, and then eliminated. This is our task. Without our tolerance and help the Communist empire would never have become the second strongest power in the earth. Now we have the job of dismantling it. Nikita Khrushchev knows the pressures we could bring pouring down upon him if our people ever make up their minds to move.

Any who may lack the courage for positive action might well recall the threat of Manuilsky which we have already quoted. He described Communist strategy for the period we are now passing through:

"We shall begin by launching the most spectacular peace movement on record. . . . The capitalist countries, stupid and decadent, will rejoice to cooperate in their own destruction. They will leap at another chance to be friends. As soon as their guard is down, we shall smash them with our clenched fist!"[1]

Today Communism is advancing on all fronts. Authorities say that if we let her feed on the West just a few more years it may be too late. How much better to send forth the message: "There IS a way to stop Communism and do it without a major war!"

If free men are willing to study the problem and move across the world in one vast united front, it is entirely possible for the human race to celebrate the close of the Twentieth Century with this monumental achievement:

"FREEDOM IN OUR TIME FOR ALL MEN!"

---

[1] See footnote No. 7, page 208.

Historical Photographs

KARL MARX: *"If we can but weld our souls together, then with contempt shall I fling my glove in the world's face, than shall I stride through the wreckage a creator."* |Sovfoto|

FRIEDRICH ENGELS, *Marx's collaborator in development of Communist theory: "We say: 'A la guerre comme a la guerre'; we do not promise any freedom, nor any democracy."* |Sovfoto|

NICKOLAI LENIN, *first Communist dictator: "Marxists have never forgotten that violence will be an inevitable accompaniment of the collapse of capitalism . . . and of the birth of socialist society."* |Sovfoto|

JOSEPH STALIN, *as a young Bolshevik: "To choose one's victim, to prepare one's plans minutely, to stake an implacable vengeance, and then go to bed . . . there is nothing sweeter in the world."* |Underwood & Underwood|

Tsar Nicholas II and his family in their days of power. At the feet of the Empress is the Tsarevitch. Back row: Grand Duchesses, Anastasia, Titiana and Olga; Marie is at her Father's left. [Triangle Photo]

A successful attempt by the Russian Provisional Government to put down a Communist uprising in Petrograd during July, 1917. As a result of this Communist defeat, Lenin fled to save his life. [Sovfoto]

First Russian photo of the Bolshevik revolution to reach the United States. This shows victorious Communist leaders addressing a large crowd in Moscow after seizure of power. [Underwood & Underwood]

Bolshevik atrocities. Fifty bodies of community leaders of Wesenberg are exhumed from a lake after being shot and mutilated in reprisal for the death of two Communists. [Underwood & Underwood]

White Russians retaliate by hanging suspected Bolsheviks. During the Civil War several million lost their lives. |*Triangle Photo*|

Bolsheviks use a confiscated church for a wheat granary. This was part of the Red campaign to discourage religious worship. |*Triangle Photo*|

Trotsky addresses a contingent of the Red Army which he ultimately built up to a force of five million men. |*Underwood & Underwood*|

Trotsky was purged from the Russian Government by Stalin and fled to Mexico to escape assassination. Although Trotsky lived under constant guard, a killer finally got through to him in August, 1940, and smashed his skull with an alpenstock. |*Underwood & Underwood*|

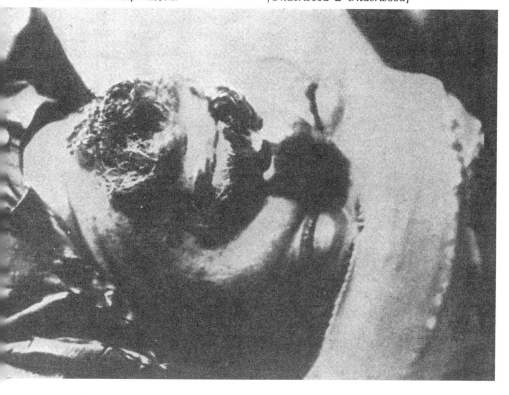

A common sight in New York during the Nineteen Thirties when American Communists paraded through the streets with their familiar slogan: "Defend the Soviet Union." *[Underwood & Underwood]*

One of the meetings of President Roosevelt. Premier Stalin and Prime Minister Churchill. This one was held at Teheran during one of the most critical periods of World War II. *[Underwood & Underwood]*

For over forty years the collectivized farms have continually failed to fulfill the dream of overwhelming abundance expected by Communist leaders. In 1954 official reports showed that Russia was producing even less food than it did in 1928 under the NEP.   [Sovfoto]

In 1923 the Secretary of State, Charles Evans Hughes, explained why the United States should not grant formal diplomatic recognition to the Communist Government of the U.S.S.R.: "There can be no question of the sincere friendliness of the American people toward the Russian people . . . for this very reason . . . nothing should be done to place the seal of approval on the tyrannical measures that have been adopted in Russia, or take any action which might retard the gradual reassertion of the Russian people to their right to live in freedom."   [Sovfoto]

Moscow University where education is often used as a political tool and professors are among the best paid people in the U.S.S.R. [Sovfoto]

The following is a typical official statement on the purpose of education in Russia: "It is important that pupils should clearly realize the doom of the capitalistic world, its inevitable downfall . . . and actively get prepared when they leave school to be ready to take their place in life, in the struggle for a new world, for Communism." [Sovfoto]

FIVE VITAL QUESTIONS

1

What Do Defenders of Communism Say?

The voluminous literature of Communism contains bold and sometimes harsh answers to almost any question a student may care to ask. However, few students have an opportunity to meet anyone who will admit he is a well indoctrinated Communist, and few people have the time or inclination to read the technical, cumbersome documents of Communist lore. Therefore, the following symposium is designed to bring some of these answers together under a number of general headings. It will be observed that Communist propaganda sometimes contradicts these answers when a true statement of doctrine would prove embarrassing. However, the answers presented here are taken in most instances from the foremost exponents of Marxism and in all such cases represent unembellished, non-propaganda answers which teachers of Marxism pass along to their own followers.

PEACEFUL CO-EXISTENCE

STUDENT: *"Do you think there is a possibility that the democracies and the Soviet can somehow co-exist?"*

The Naked Communist

LENIN: "The existence of the Soviet Republic side by side with imperialist states for a long time is unthinkable. One or the other must triumph in the end. And before that end supervenes, a series of frightful collisions between the Soviet Republic and the bourgeois states will be inevitable."

V. I. Lenin, "REPORT OF THE CENTRAL COMMITTEE AT THE 8TH PARTY CONGRESS" (1919).

OFFICIAL STATEMENT: "The proletariat in the Soviet Union harbours no illusions as to the possibility of a durable peace with the imperialists. The proletariat knows that the imperialist attack against the Soviet Union is inevitable; that in the process of a proletarian world revolution wars between proletarian and bourgeois states, wars for the emancipation of the world from capitalism, will necessarily and inevitably arise. Therefore, the primary duty of the proletariat, as the fighter for socialism, is to make all the necessary political, economic and military preparations for these wars, to strengthen its Red Army—that mighty weapon of the proletariat—and to train the masses of the toilers in the art of war."

"THESIS OF THE SIXTH WORLD CONGRESS OF THE COMMUNIST INTERNATIONAL." International Press Correspondence, November 28, 1926, p. 1590.

STUDENT: "Why do you not go ahead and prove that Communism will work in your own country before trying to force it upon other nations?"

LENIN: "Final victory can be achieved only on an international scale, and only by the combined efforts of the workers of all countries."

Quoted by Joseph Stalin in, "LENINISM," Volume I, p. 170.

STALIN: "This means that the serious assistance of the international proletariat is a force without which the problem of the final victory of socialism in one country cannot be solved." Joseph Stalin's letter to Ivanov, p. 9. See also "RESOLUTION OF THE FOURTEENTH PARTY CONFERENCE OF THE COMMUNIST PARTY OF THE SOVIET UNION."

STUDENT: "I am in favor of cordial relations between nations. Would you call me an Internationalist?"

Defenders of Communism

P. E. VYSHINSKY: "At present the only determining criterion . . .is: Are you for or against the U.S.S.R., the motherland of the world proletariat? An internationalist is not one who verbally recognizes international solidarity or sympathizes with it. A real internationalist is one who brings his sympathy and recognition up to the point of practical and maximum help to the U.S.S.R. in support and defense of the U.S.S.R. by every means and in every possible form."

> *P. E. Vyshinsky, "*COMMUNISM AND THE MOTHERLAND,*" Voprosi Filosofi (Problems of Philosophy), No. 2, 1948.*

STUDENT: *"I thought that during World War II, the Communist leaders said they wanted to be friends with the United States. I hoped we could continue to be friends."*

VARGA: "The fact that the Soviet Union and the greatly shaken capitalist countries showed themselves to be in one powerful camp, ranged against the Fascist aggressors (during World War II), showed that the struggle of the two systems within the democratic camp was temporarily alleviated, suspended, but this of course does not mean the end of the struggle." *Varga, "*WORLD ECONOMY AND WORLD POLITICS,*" June, 1949, p. 11.*

MARSHALL TITO: "Our collaboration with capitalism during the war which has recently ended, by no means signifies that we shall prolong our alliance with it in the future. On the contrary, the capitalistic forces constitute our natural enemy despite the fact that they helped us to defeat their most dangerous representative. It may happen that we shall again decide to make use of their aid, but always with the sole aim of accelerating their final ruin."

> *Reported by the Continental News Service, November 8, 1946, and quoted in the "*COMMUNIST THREAT TO CANADA,*" Ottawa, 1947, pp. 10-11.*

STUDENT: *"In other words, you pretended to be our friends merely as a matter of expediency? Why would it not be to our mutual advantage to continue being friends?"*

The Naked Communist

DIMITRY Z. MANUILSKY: "War to the hilt between communism and capitalism is inevitable."

> Stated in a lecture to the Lenin School on Political Warfare in Moscow, 1931.

STUDENT: *"Then why do you even try to maintain peaceful relations with the West?"*

STALIN: "We cannot forget the saying of Lenin to the effect that a great deal ... depends on whether we succeed in delaying war with the capitalist countries ... until proletarian revolution ripens in Europe or until colonial revolutions come to a head, or, finally, until the capitalists fight among themselves over the division of the colonies. Therefore, the maintenance of peaceful relations with capitalist countries is an obligatory task for us."

> Joseph Stalin, "SPEECH TO THE 15TH CONGRESS OF THE SOVIET," Selected Works, Vol. X, pp. 95-96; also see pp. 100-101.

STUDENT: *"Do you think we should expect this "inevitable" conflict soon or far in the distant future?"*

LENIN: "To tie one's hands beforehand, openly to tell the enemy, who is at present better armed than we are, whether and when we will fight him, is stupidity and not revolutionariness. To accept battle at a time when it is obviously advantageous to the enemy and not to us is a crime; and those political leaders of the revolutionary class who are unable to 'tack, to maneuver, to compromise' in order to avoid an obviously disadvantageous battle, are good for nothing."

> V. I. Lenin, "LEFT-WING COMMUNISM, AN INFANTILE DISORDER," Selected Works, Vol. X, pp. 95-96; also see pp. 100-101.

STUDENT: *"Perhaps this explains why you Communists continue building up a tremendous war machine while proclaiming that you want peace. Don't you think the West sincerely wants peace and would like to disarm?"*

OFFICIAL STATEMENT: "There is a glaring contradiction between the imperialists' policy of piling up armaments and

Defenders of Communism

their hypocritical talk about peace. There is no such contradiction, however, between the Soviet Government's preparation for defense and for revolutionary war and a consistent peace policy. Revolutionary war of the proletarian dictatorship is but a continuation of a revolutionary peace policy by other means."

"THESIS OF THE SIXTH WORLD CONGRESS OF THE COMMUNIST INTERNATIONAL." *International Press Correspondence, November 28, 1928, p. 1590.*

STUDENT: *"But would not a so-called revolutionary peace policy by 'other means' simply be a demand for unconditional surrender under threat of extermination? Why do you perpetuate the myth of peaceful coexistence when you openly consider the West your enemy?"*

DIMITRY Z. MANUILSKY: "Today, of course, we are not strong enough to attack.... To win we shall need the element of surprise. The bourgeoisie will have to be put to sleep. So we shall begin by launching the most spectacular peace movement on record. There will be electrifying overtures and unheard of concessions. The capitalist countries, stupid and decadent, will rejoice to cooperate in their own destruction. They will jump at another chance to be friends. As soon as their guard is down, we shall smash them with our clenched fist." *Stated in a lecture at the Lenin School on Political Warfare in Moscow, 1931.*

ILLEGAL OPERATIONS

STUDENT: *"Perhaps this helps to explain why the Communist strategists have never been able to take over a single country by persuasion or by the popular election of legal candidates. Must you Communists always resort to subversion and illegal political operations?"*

LENIN: "The absolute necessity in principal of combining illegal with legal work is determined not only by the sum

total of the specific features of the present period ... but also
by the necessity of proving to the bourgeoisie that there is
not, nor can there be, a sphere or field of work that cannot be
won by the Communists. ... It is necessary, immediately, for
all legal Communist Parties to form illegal organizations for
the purpose of systematically carrying on illegal work, and
of fully preparing for the moment when the bourgeoisie re-
sorts to persecution. Illegal work is particularly necessary in
the army, the navy and police."

V. I. Lenin, "SELECTED WORKS," Vol. X, pp. 172-173.

STUDENT: *"What happens to a person who is selected for
illegal operations?"*

LENIN: "A working class agitator who in any way
shows talent and promise should not work eleven hours a day
in a factory. We should see to it that he lives on the funds of
the Party, that he is able in good time to adopt an illegal manner of existence, that he has the opportunity of changing his
sphere of activities; otherwise he will not gain experience, he
will not broaden his outlook, and will not be able to hold out
for at most several years in the struggle against the police."

V. I. Lenin, "LENIN ON ORGANIZATION," p. 95.

REVOLUTIONARY VIOLENCE

STUDENT: *"Could an American who might be converted to
Communism belong to the Party but still hold out for peaceful
reform instead of revolutionary violence?"*

LENIN: "It is not enough to take sides in the question
of political slogans; we must take sides also in the question of
an armed uprising. Those who are opposed to armed uprising,
those who do not prepare for it, must be ruthlessly cast out of
the ranks of the supporters of the revolution and sent back to
the ranks of its enemies, of the traitors or cowards; for the
day is approaching when the force of events and conditions of

the struggle will compel us to separate enemies from friends according to this principle."

*V. I. Lenin, "*SELECTED WORKS,*" Vol. III, p. 351.*

STUDENT: *"Then apparently you believe social progress is possible only by revolutionary violence rather than by legislative reform?"*

LENIN: "Marxists have never forgotten that violence will be an inevitable accompaniment of the collapse of capitalism on its full scale and of the birth of a socialist society. And this violence will cover a historical period; a whole era of wars of the most varied kinds—imperialist wars, civil wars within the country, the interweaving of the former with the latter, national wars, the emancipation of the nationalities crushed by the imperialist powers which will inevitably form various alliances with each other in the era of vast state-capitalist and military trusts and syndicates. This is an era of tremendous collapses, of wholesale military decisions of a violent nature, of crises. It has already begun, we see it clearly—it is only the beginning."

*V. I. Lenin, "*SELECTED WORKS,*" Vol. VIII, pp. 315-316.*

STUDENT: *"Do you mean it is impossible for an American to be a true Communist without betraying his own country?"*

LENIN: "Hatred for one's own government and one's own bourgeoisie—the sentiment of all class conscious workers . . . is a banal phrase if it does not mean revolution against their own governments. It is impossible to rouse hatred against one's own government and one's own bourgeoisie without desiring their defeat."

*V. I. Lenin, "*SELECTED WORKS,*" Vol. V, p. 147.*

STUDENT: *"Would an American Communist be expected to engage in subversive and disloyal activities even if the United States were at war?"*

The Naked Communist

LENIN: "A revolutionary class in a reactionary war cannot but desire the defeat of its government. . . . And revolutionary action in wartime against one's own government undoubtedly and incontrovertibly means not only desiring its defeat, but really facilitating such defeat."

V. I. Lenin, "SELECTED WORKS," Vol. V, p. 142.

STUDENT: *"But if you are so anxious to break down loyalty to individual governments why do you insist on American Communists maintaining a loyalty toward the U.S.S.R.?"*

OFFICIAL STATEMENT: "In view of the fact that the USSR is the only fatherland of the international proletariat, the principle bulwark of its achievements and the most important factor for its international emancipation, the international proletariat must on its part facilitate the success of the work of socialist construction in the U.S.S.R. and defend it against the attacks of the capitalist powers by all the means in its power." "PROGRAM OF THE COMMUNIST INTERNATIONAL," *p. 66.*

STUDENT: *"In other words—and to be more specific—you are against nationalism except when applied to the U.S.S.R.?"*

P. E. VYSHINSKY: "The defense of the U.S.S.R., as of the socialist motherland of the world proletariat, is the holy duty of every honest man everywhere and not only of the citizens of the U.S.S.R."

P. E. Vyshinsky, "COMMUNISM AND THE MOTHERLAND," (Problems in Philosophy) No. 2, 1948.

STUDENT: *"If American Communists are expected to overthrow their own Government and serve the interests of the U.S.S.R., would that not make them anarchists and insurrectionists?"*

LENIN: "Only insurrection can guarantee the victory of the revolution."

V. I. Lenin, "SELECTED WORKS," Vol. III, p. 327.

Defenders of Communism

LENIN: "The revolution confronts us directly with the problem of armed insurrection. And to speak of this without proper technical preparations, is merely to mouth empty phrases. He who wants the revolution must systematically prepare for it the broad masses, who will, in the process of preparation, create the necessary organs of the struggle."

"LENIN, THE GREAT STRATEGIST OF THE CLASS WAR," *p. 17.*

STUDENT: *"And all this for the violent overthrow of the Government?"*

LENIN: "The purpose of insurrection must be, not only the complete destruction, or removal of all local authorities and their replacement by new . . . but also the expulsion of the landlords and the seizure of their lands."

V. I. Lenin, "SELECTED WORKS," *Vol. III, p. 377.*

WAR AND PEACE

STUDENT: *"Does not such an inflammatory policy completely contradict your widely publicized program for a peace offensive?"*

OFFICIAL STATEMENT: "Complete Communism will know no more war. A real, assured people's peace is possible only under Communism. But the goal cannot be reached by peaceful, 'pacifist' means; on the contrary, it can be reached only by civil war against the bourgeoisie."

"FUNDAMENTALS OF COMMUNISM," *published by the Communist Party of America, p. 31.*

STUDENT: *"In other words, Communists in all countries constitute a war party rather than a political party designed to promote peace?"*

OFFICIAL STATEMENT: "In the capitalist world today, the revolutionary proletariat supports the war of defense of the proletarian state (the U.S.S.R.) against the imperialist states." "FUNDAMENTALS OF COMMUNISM," *published by the Communist Party of America, p. 31.*

The Naked Communist

STUDENT: *"But the Soviet Union has consistently waged or encouraged wars of aggression. How can you conscientiously support these?"*

OFFICIAL STATEMENT: **"Every war of the Soviet Union is a war of defense, even if it is conducted with offensive means."** "FUNDAMENTALS OF COMMUNISM," *published by the Communist Party of America, p. 31.*

STUDENT: *"If you are going to call all Soviet wars 'defensive' even when you admit she is using 'offensive means' what will be your attitude toward other nations which maintain heavy armaments simply as a defense against Communist aggression?"*

OFFICIAL STATEMENT: **(We stand for the)** **"systematic exposure and stigmatizing of all capitalist armaments, war pacts and war preparations and especially of the defense of the Soviet Union against the league of the imperialists."** "FUNDAMENTALS OF COMMUNISM," *published by the Communist Party of America, p. 31.*

STUDENT: *"Are the Communist leaders expecting a spontaneous uprising in various countries or will they order their followers to engineer an uprising?"*

LENIN: **"If the situation is ripe for a popular uprising, in view of the fact that the revolution in social relationships has already taken place, and if we have prepared for it, we can order an uprising."** *V. I. Lenin, "SELECTED WORKS," Vol. III, p. 298.*

STUDENT: *"What methods would you use to overthrow the Government?"*

LENIN: **"Riots — demonstrations — street battles — detachments of a revolutionary army — such are the stages in the development of the popular uprising."** *V. I. Lenin, "SELECTED WORKS," Vol. III, p. 312.*

Defenders of Communism

STUDENT: *"Based on experience, what are the most ideal circumstances for a successful insurrection?"*

LENIN: **"Combining of a mass political strike with an armed uprising."**
V. I. Lenin, "SELECTED WORKS," Vol. III, p. 374.

THE COMMUNIST INTERNATIONAL

STUDENT: *"Originally, what did you say about the organization which was supposed to run the world revolution?"*

OFFICIAL STATEMENT: **"The Communist International is the concentrated will of the world revolutionary proletariat. Its mission is to organize the working class of the world for the overthrow of the capitalist system and the establishment of Communism. The Communist International is a fighting body and assumes the task of combining the revolutionary forces of every country."**
"THE COMMUNIST," Vol. 1, No. 1, July 1921, p. 11.

STUDENT: *"Was the purpose of the Communist International to spread dissension and build the Red Army?"*

OFFICIAL STATEMENT: **"In order to overthrow the international bourgeoisie and to create an International Soviet Republic as a transition stage to the Communist Society, the Communist International will use all means at its disposal, including force of arms."**
"THE COMMUNIST," Vol. 1, No. 1, July 1921, p. 11.

STALIN: **"The tasks of the Party in foreign policy are: 1—to utilize each and every contradiction and conflict among the surrounding capitalist groups and governments for the purpose of disintegrating imperialism; 2—to spare no pains or means to render assistance to the proletarian revolution in**

The Naked Communist

300 the West; 3—to take all necessary measures to strengthen the Red Army."

Joseph Stalin, "PARTY AFTER SEIZURE OF POWER," Pravda, August 28, 1921.

STUDENT: *"What was the program of the Communist International?"*

OFFICIAL STATEMENT: "The Communist International must devote itself especially to . . . everyday organization work . . . in the course of which work legal methods must unfailingly be combined with illegal methods; organized work in the army and navy—such must be the activity of the Communist Parties in this connection. The fundamental slogans of the Communist International in this connection must be the following:

> Convert imperialist war into civil war;
> Defeat 'your own' imperialist government;
> Defend the U.S.S.R. and the colonies by
> every means in the event of imperialist war
> against them."

"PROGRAM OF THE COMMUNIST INTERNATIONAL," *p. 84.*

STUDENT: *"Did the Communist International depend upon Communist parties in various countries or did it operate independently?"*

OFFICIAL STATEMENT: "The successful struggle of the Communist International for the dictatorship of the proletariat presupposes the existence in every country of a compact Communist Party hardened in the struggle, disciplined, centralized, closely linked to the masses."

"PROGRAM OF THE COMMUNIST INTERNATIONAL," *p. 76.*

STUDENT: *"What was the obligation of an organization such as the Communist Party of America when it affiliated with the Communist International?"*

Defenders of Communism

OFFICIAL STATEMENT: "Each party desirous of affiliating to the Communist International should be obliged to render every possible assistance to the Soviet Republics in their struggle against all counter-revolutionary forces. The Communist parties should carry on a precise and definite propaganda to induce the workers to refuse to transport any kind of military equipment intended for fighting against the Soviet Republics, and should also by legal or illegal means carry on a propaganda amongst the troops sent against the workers' republics, etc."

"THE THESIS AND STATUTES OF THE COMMUNIST INTERNATIONAL," *as adopted at the Second World Congress, July 17 to August 7, 1920, p. 28.*

STUDENT: *"Was it intended from the beginning that Communist leaders in Russia would dictate the policies of the Communist Party of America?"*

EARL BROWDER: "The Communist Parties of the various countries are the direct representatives of the Communist International, and thus, indirectly of the aims and policies of Soviet Russia."

"COMMUNISM IN THE UNITED STATES," *p. 8.*

OFFICIAL STATEMENT: "Representatives of Soviet Russia in various countries, engaging in political activities, should co-ordinate these activities in some form or other with the activities and policies of the respective Communist Parties."

"RESOLUTION ON THE RELATION OF COMMUNIST PARTIES TO SOVIET GOVERNMENT REPRESENTATIVES," *adopted by the second convention of the Communist Party of America,* "THE COMMUNIST," *Volume II, No. 8, p. 8, August 1, 1920.*

ALEXANDER TRACHTENBERG: "Consistently supporting the Soviet Union since its inception, American Communists were acting as internationalists and as Americans."

Alexander Trachtenberg, "THE SOVIET UNION AND THE AMERICAN PEOPLE," *appearing in* "THE COMMUNIST," *Vol. XVIII, No. 9, p. 885, September, 1939.*

STUDENT: *"In 1943 the Communist International was*

The Naked Communist

302 *suddenly dissolved. Was this designed to pacify a rising wave of anti-Communist sentiments during World War II?"*

HANS BERGER: "Since correct strategy consists in uniting and concentrating all forces against the common enemy, necessitating the elimination of everything which makes such unification and concentration difficult, therefore, the dissolution of the Communist International, decided upon unanimously by the Communist Parties, was doubtless an act in the interests of facilitating victory over the fascist enemy."

"REMARKS ON THE DISCUSSION CONCERNING THE DISSOLUTION OF THE COMMUNIST INTERNATIONAL," *appearing in* "THE COMMUNIST," *Vol. XXII, No. 11, p. 1020, November, 1943.*

STUDENTS: *"Did the dissolution of the Communist International result in a weakening of the solidarity between Communist Parties throughout the world?"*

HANS BERGER: "Among the reasons which the leaders of the Communist Parties considered in supporting the dissolution of the Communist International was doubtless the question of strengthening the Communist Parties."

"REMARKS ON THE DISCUSSION CONCERNING THE DISSOLUTION OF THE COMMUNIST INTERNATIONAL," *appearing in* "THE COMMUNIST," *Vol. XXII, No. 11, p. 1028, November, 1943.*

STUDENT: *"Did it weaken the plans for world revolution?"*

HANS BERGER: "The Communist Parties have thus never sacrificed their Marxist-Leninist principles, which know no boundaries, and which can never be given up by them, but guided by their principles fight on with the utmost consistency." "REMARKS ON THE DISCUSSION CONCERNING THE DISSOLUTION OF THE COMMUNIST INTERNATIONAL," *appearing in* "THE COMMUNIST," *Vol. XXII, No. 11, p. 1021.*

STUDENT: *"Would this represent the official view of the Communist Party of America?"*

Defenders of Communism

GIL GREEN: "Since November, 1940, our Party has not been an affiliate of the Communist International and has had no organizational ties with it. But who can deny that our Party has nonetheless fulfilled its obligation to the American Working class and people and in this way to the working class and people of the world?"

Gil Green, "THE DISSOLUTION OF THE COMMUNIST INTERNA-TIONAL," *a speech delivered on May 26, 1943, p. 3.*

"Nor is the further existence of the Communist International necessary as the living embodiment of the principle of internationalism and international working class solidarity. The fight for internationalism has not disappeared. It has been raised to new and more glorious heights."

Gil Green, "THE DISSOLUTION OF THE COMMUNIST INTERNA-TIONAL," *p. 8.*

"The dissolution of the Communist International does not, therefore, mark a step backward. . . . Millions all over the world live, work and fight under the bright banner of Marxism."

Gil Green, "THE DISSOLUTION OF THE COMMUNIST INTERNA-TIONAL," *p. 9.*

DIPLOMATIC INTRIGUE

STUDENT: *"During World War II what did Stalin say the Russian policy was toward nations which were then under Nazi domination?"*

STALIN: "We are waging a just war for our country and our freedom. It is not our aim to seize foreign lands or to subjugate foreign people. Our aim is clear and noble. We want to free our Soviet land of the German-Fascist scoundrels. We want to free our Ukrainian, Moldavian, Byelorussian, Lithuanian, Latvian, Estonian and Karelian brothers from the outrage and violence to which they are being subjected by the German-Fascist scoundrels. . . .

"We have not and cannot have such war aims as the im-

position of our will and regime on the slavs and other enslaved peoples of Europe who are awaiting our aid. Our aim
consists in assisting these people in their struggle for liberation from Hitler's tyranny and then setting them free to rule
in their own lands as they desire."

> *Stalin's Order of the Day, No. 130, May 1, 1942, quoted in,*
> "ON THE GREAT PATRIOTIC WAR OF THE SOVIET UNION," *Foreign*
> *Language Publishing House, Moscow, 1946, p. 59.*

STUDENT: *"What excuse could Stalin and the Communist
leaders have for doing the very opposite of what they had
promised?"*

LENIN: "The strictest loyalty to the ideas of Communism must be combined with the ability to make all necessary
practical compromises, to maneuver, to make agreements, zig-
zags, retreats and so on, so as to accelerate the coming to
power." *V. I. Lenin,* "LEFT-WING COMMUNISM—AN INFANTILE DISORDER,"
International Publishers, New York, 1940, pp. 75-76.

STALIN: "Sincere diplomacy is no more possible than
dry water or iron wood."

> *Quoted in Department of State Publication No. 4264, p. 30.*

ETHICS AND MORALS

STUDENT: *"Doesn't this approach to international relations sound more like a criminal code of conduct rather than
sincere diplomacy? Does Communist Morality permit this?"*

LENIN: "We say: Morality is that which serves to
destroy the old exploiting society and to unite all the toilers
around the proletariat, which is creating a new Communist
society. Communist morality is the morality which serves
this struggle. . . ."

> *V. I. Lenin,* "SELECTED WORKS," *Vol. IX, p. 477.*

OFFICIAL STATEMENT: "Morals or ethics is the body of
norms and rules on the conduct of Soviet peoples. At the root

Defenders of Communism

of Communist morality, said Lenin, lies the struggle for the consolidation and the completion of Communism. Therefore, from the point of view of Communist morality, only those acts are moral which contribute to the building up of a new Communist society."

Radio Moscow, August 20, 1950.

STUDENT: *"But this sounds like an excuse for doing whatever one may find expedient rather than following a system of rules for right living. Assuming Communism were right, would that justify a communist in lying, stealing or killing to put Communism into effect?"*

WILLIAM Z. FOSTER: "With him the end justifies the means. Whether his tactics be 'legal' and 'moral,' or not, does not concern him, so long as they are effective. He knows that the laws as well as the current code of morals, are made by his mortal enemies. . . . Consequently, he ignores them in so far as he is able and it suits his purposes. He proposes to develop, regardless of capitalist conceptions of 'legality,' 'fairness,' 'right,' etc., a greater power than his capitalist enemies have."

William Z. Foster, "SYNDICALISM," p. 9.

STUDENT: *"Would you then deny the possibility of there being an eternal, God-given code for moral or ethical conduct?"*

LENIN: "We do not believe in eternal morality, and we expose all the fables about morality."

V. I. Lenin, "SELECTED WORKS," Vol. IX, p. 478.

MARX: "Law, morality, religion are . . . so many bourgeois prejudices, behind which lurk in ambush just as many bourgeois interests."

Karl Marx, "COMMUNIST MANIFESTO," and quoted in the "COMMUNIST HANDBOOK," p. 35.

ENGELS: "We therefore reject every attempt to impose on us any moral dogma whatsoever as an eternal, ultimate and forever immutable moral law on the pretext that the moral world too has its permanent principles which transcend history and the difference between nations. We maintain on the contrary that all former moral theories are the product, in the last analysis, of the economic stage which society had reached at that particular epoch. And as society has hitherto moved in class antagonisms, morality was always a class morality; it has either justified the domination and the interests of the ruling class, or, as soon as the oppressed class has become powerful enough, it has represented the revolt against this domination and the future interests of the oppressed."

Friedrich Engels, quoted in "HANDBOOK OF MARXISM," *p. 249.*

THE BIBLE

STUDENT: *"Then what is the Communist attitude toward the Bible which contains many moral teachings?"*

OFFICIAL STATEMENT: **"A collection of fantastic legends without any scientific support. It is full of dark hints, historical mistakes and contradictions. It serves as a factor for gaining power and subjugating the unknowing nations."**

Quoted from the Russian Dictionary under "CHRISTIAN ECONOMICS," *Vol. III, No. 7, March 27, 1951.*

ENGELS: **"It is now perfectly clear to me that the so-called sacred writings of the Jews are nothing more than the record of the old Arabian religious and tribal tradition, modified by the early separation of the Jews from their tribally related but nomadic neighbours."**

Friedrich Engels, "SELECTED CORRESPONDENCE," *p. 64.*

RELIGION

STUDENT: *"If you reject the Bible, do you also reject all religion and all of the institutionalized morality which it represents?"*

Defenders of Communism

OFFICIAL STATEMENT: "The philosophy of Marxism-Leninism—the theoretical foundation of the Communist Party—is incompatible with religion."

"YOUNG BOLSHEVIK," *No. 5-6, 1946, p. 58.*

LENIN: "Religion is a kind of spiritual gin in which the slaves of capital drown their human shape and their claims to any decent human life."

V. I. Lenin, "SELECTED WORKS," *International Publishers, N.Y. 1943, Vol. XI.*

STUDENT: *"Could not a Communist enjoy religious activity as a matter of conscience and as a private right?"*

LENIN: "To the party of the Socialist proletariat . . . religion is not a private matter."

V. I. Lenin, "RELIGION," *p. 9.*

YAROSLAVSKY: "Every Leninist, every Communist, every class-conscious worker and peasant must be able to explain why a Communist cannot support religion; why Communists fight against religion."

E. Yaroslavsky, "RELIGION IN THE U.S.S.R.," *p. 20.*

STUDENT: *"But supposing I were a Communist and still wanted to go to Church?"*

OFFICIAL STATEMENT: "If a Communist youth believes in God and goes to Church, he fails to fulfil his duties. This means that he has not yet rid himself of religious superstitions and has not become a fully conscious person (i.e., a Communist)." "YOUNG BOLSHEVIK," *No. 5-6, 1946, p. 56.*

LENIN: "A young man or woman cannot be a Communist youth unless he or she is free of religious convictions."

"YOUNG COMMUNIST TRUTH," *October 18, 1947.*

LENIN: "We must combat religion—this is the ABC of all materialism, and consequently Marxism."

V. I. Lenin, "RELIGION," *p. 14.*

STUDENT: *"What is your attitude toward individual churches? Take the Catholic Church, for example."*

YAROSLAVSKY: "The Catholic Church, with the pope in its van, is now an important bulwark of all counter-revolutionary organizations and forces."

E. Yaroslavsky, "RELIGION IN THE U.S.S.R.," pp. 36-37.

STUDENT: *"Are you against all Christianity?"*

LUNARCHARSKY: (Russian Commissioner of Education): "We hate Christians and Christianity. Even the best of them must be considered our worst enemies. Christian love is an obstacle to the development of the revolution. Down with love of one's neighbor! What we want is hate. . . . Only then can we conquer the universe."

Quoted in U. S. Congressional Record, Vol. 77, pp. 1539-1540.

STUDENT: *"How do you justify Communist 'hate' propaganda of this kind?"*

OFFICIAL STATEMENT: "Hatred fosters vigilance and an uncompromising attitude toward the enemy and leads to the destruction of everything that prevents Soviet peoples from building a happy life. The teachings of hatred for the enemies of the toilers enriches the conception of Socialist humanism by distinguishing it from sugary and hypocritical 'philanthropy.' "

Quoted from the "SMALL SOVIET ENCYCLOPEDIA," Moscow, 1947, Vol. XI, p. 1045.

STALIN: "It is impossible to conquer an enemy without having learned to hate him with all the might of one's soul."

Joseph Stalin, "THE GREAT PATRIOTIC WAR OF THE SOVIET UNION," Moscow, 1946, p. 55.

STUDENT: *"And what is your attitude toward the Jewish people and their religion?"*

MARX: "What was the foundation of the Jewish reli-

Defenders of Communism

gion? Practical needs, egoism. Consequently the monotheism of the Jew is in reality the Polytheism of many needs. . . . The God of practical needs and egoism is money. . . . Money is the jealous God of Israel, by the side of which no other God may exist. . . . The God of the Jews has secularized himself and become the universal God. . . . As soon as society succeeds in abolishing the empirical essence of Judaism, the huckster and the conditions which produce him, the Jew will become impossible. . . . The social emancipation of the Jew is the emancipation of society from Judaism."

KARL MARX, "SELECTED ESSAYS," pp. 92-97.

STUDENT: *"In view of all this, why is it that Communist propaganda sometimes pretends a tolerance for religion?"*

YAROSLAVSKY: **"In our work among religious people we must bear in mind Lenin's advice to utilize every method available to us, or, as he said, we must 'approach them this way and that way' in order to stimulate them to criticize religion themselves."**

E. Yaroslavsky, "RELIGION IN THE U.S.S.R.," p. 61.

STUDENT: *"If religion is so bad, do you think it will gradually die out?"*

YAROSLAVSKY: **"It would be a great mistake to believe that religion will die out of itself. We have repeatedly emphasized Lenin's opinion that the Communist Party cannot depend upon the spontaneous development of anti-religious ideas—that these ideas are molded by organized action."**

E. Yaroslavsky, "RELIGION IN THE U.S.S.R.," p. 61.

STUDENT: *"Do you think a person's attitude toward religion should be changed by friendly persuasion?"*

LENIN: **"The fight against religion must not be limited nor reduced to abstract, ideological preaching. This struggle**

must be linked up with the concrete practical class movement;
its aim must be to eliminate the social roots of religion."
*V. I. Lenin, "*RELIGION*," p. 14.*

OFFICIAL STATEMENT: "The struggle against the Gospel
and Christian legend must be conducted ruthlessly and with
all the means at the disposal of Communism."
RADIO LENINGRAD, *August 27, 1950.*

STUDENT: *"Is it true that you have already suppressed
the clergy in Russia?"*

STALIN: "Have we suppressed the reactionary clergy?
Yes, we have. The unfortunate thing is that it has not been
completely liquidated. Anti-religious propaganda is a means
by which the complete liquidation of the reactionary clergy
must be brought about. Cases occur when certain members
of the Party hamper the complete development of anti-religious propaganda. If such members are expelled it is a good
thing because there is no room for such 'Communists' in the
ranks of the Party."
*Joseph Stalin, "*LENINISM*," Vol. I, p. 387.*

STUDENT: *"What do you propose to substitute for religion?"*

LENIN: "We said at the beginning . . . Marxism cannot
be conceived without atheism. We would add here that atheism
without Marxism is incomplete and inconsistent."
*V. I. Lenin, "*RELIGION*," Introduction, p. 3-6.*

STUDENT: *"If you are going to take away the concept of
God, what spiritual substitute do you propose to offer your
people?"*

OFFICIAL STATEMENT: "What better means of influenc-
ing pupils than, for example, the characteristic of the spiritual
figure of Stalin given in the Short Biography: 'Everyone
knows the irresistible, shattering power of Stalin's logic, the
crystal clearness of his intellect, his iron will, devotion to the

Defenders of Communism

party, his modesty, artlessness, his solicitude for people and mercilessness to enemies of the people.' "

"TEACHER'S GAZETTE," *March 17, 1947.*

STUDENT: *"I understand Soviet leaders missed no opportunity when Stalin was alive to indoctrinate the children with the idea of Stalin as a spiritual figure. What was the slogan stamped on children's toys?"*

OFFICIAL STATEMENT: **"Thank you, Comrade Stalin, for my joyous childhood."**

Quoted in the U. S. Dept of State Publication, No. 4264, p. 25.

INDIVIDUAL FREEDOM AND
CIVIL LIBERTIES

STUDENT: *"Is there any opportunity for freedom and democracy under Communism?"*

ENGELS: **"We say: 'A la guerre comme a la guerre'; we do not promise freedom nor any democracy."**

V. I. Lenin, "SELECTED WORKS," *Vol. IX, p. 242.*

STUDENT: *"Then you do not believe that men should be free and equal in the enjoyment of life, liberty and the pursuit of happiness?"*

ENGELS: **"As long as classes exist, all arguments about freedom and equality should be accompanied by the question: Freedom for which class? And for what purpose? The equality of which class with which? And in what relation?"**

V. I. Lenin, "SELECTED WORKS," *Vol. X, p. 266.*

STUDENT: *"But is it not your desire to have freedom and equality for all classes?"*

ENGELS: **"We do not want freedom for the bourgeoisie."**

V. I. Lenin, "SELECTED WORKS," *Vol. X, p. 266.*

The Naked Communist

STUDENT: *"Do not the people in Communist satellites want freedom and equality for their citizens?"*

ENGELS: **"Anyone who talks about freedom and equality within the limits of toiler democracy, i.e., conditions under which the capitalists are overthrown while property and free trade remain—is a defender of the exploiters."**
*V. I. Lenin in "*SELECTED WORKS,*" Vol. X, p. 266.*

STUDENT: *"Do you believe in freedom at all?"*

LENIN: **"While the state exists there is no freedom. When freedom exists, there will be no state."**
*V. I. Lenin, "*SELECTED WORKS,*" Vol. VIII, p. 87.*

STUDENT: *"But the U.S.S.R. still preserves the State. Does this mean the government of Russia is not intended to promote the freedom of the Russian people?"*

ENGELS: **"So long as the proletariat still uses the state it does not use it in the interest of freedom but in order to hold down its adversaries."**
*Quoted by Lenin in his "*SELECTED WORKS,*" Vol. VII, p. 81.*

STUDENT: *"Then do I conclude from this that in Russia you do not even pretend to have the civil liberties which we enjoy over here?"*

VYSHINSKY: **"In our state, naturally there is and can be no place for freedom of speech, press, and so on for the foes of socialism. Every sort of attempt on their part to utilize to the detriment of the state—that is to say, to the detriment of all the toilers—these freedoms granted to the toilers, must be classified as a counter-revolutionary crime."**
*Vyshinsky, "*LAW OF THE SOVIET STATE,*" (MacMillan Co., New York, 1948), p. 617.*

STUDENT: *"Supposing I were living in Russia and wanted to publish a newspaper which criticized the government.*

Defenders of Communism

Would I be granted the same freedom of press which I enjoy in America?"

STALIN: "What freedom of the press have you in mind? Freedom of the press for which class—the bourgeoisie or the proletariat? If it is a question of freedom of the press for the bourgeoisie, then it does not and will not exist here as long as the proletarian dictatorship exists."

Joseph Stalin, "LENINISM," Vol. I, p. 403.

STUDENT: *"Then you mean freedom of the press is only for the privileged proletariat? It would not include a person like myself?"*

STALIN: "We have no freedom of the press for the bourgeoisie. We have no freedom of the press for the Mensheviks and Socialist-Revolutionaries, who represent the interests of the beaten and overthrown bourgeoisie. But what is there surprising in that? We have never pledged ourselves to grant freedom of the press to all classes, and to make all classes happy." *Joseph Stalin, "LENINISM," Vol. I, p. 404.*

STUDENT: *"But how can a government fairly administer its laws unless they apply equally to all the people?"*

LENIN: "Dictatorship is power based upon force and unrestricted by any laws. The revolutionary dictatorship of the proletariat is power won and maintained by the violence of the proletariat against the bourgeoisie—power that is unrestricted by any laws."

V. I. Lenin, "SELECTED WORKS," Vol. VII, p. 123.

STUDENT: *"But if laws are against classes rather than violators, how can there be any justice?"*

VYSHINSKY: "The task of justice in the U.S.S.R. is to assure the precise and unswerving fulfillment of Soviet laws by all the institutions, organizations, officials and citizens of the U.S.S.R. This the court accomplishes by destroying without

314   pity all the foes of the people in whatever form they manifest
their criminal encroachments upon socialism."

Andrei Y. Vyshinsky, "THE LAW OF THE SOVIET STATE," *p. 498.*

EDUCATION

STUDENT: *"Let me ask a few questions about Soviet
schools and the Communist theory of education. How would
you describe the objectives of education in Russia?"*

OFFICIAL STATEMENT: "It is in the schools, at the desk,
in the first class, that the foundations for a Communist outlook are laid in future Soviet citizens. The country entrusts the
school with its most treasured possessions—its children—and
no one should be allowed to indulge in the slightest deviation
from the principles of the Communist materialistic upbringing
of the new generation."

"LITERARY GAZETTE," *September 3, 1949.*

STUDENT: *"Would it not be better to give students a broad
view of all governments and different economies so they could
draw their own conclusions?"*

OFFICIAL STATEMENT: "The Soviet school cannot be satisfied to rear merely educated persons. Basing itself on the
facts and deductions of progressive science, it should instill
the ideology of Communism in the minds of the young generation, shape a Marxist-Leninist world outlook and inculcate the
spirit of Soviet patriotism and Bolshevik ideas in them."

"FOR FURTHER PROGRESS IN SOVIET SCHOOLS," *taken from* "CUL-
TURE AND LIFE," *August 31, 1947.*

STUDENT: *"Is it fair to force the minds of the rising generation to accept only the values which a current political
regime wishes to impose upon them?"*

OFFICIAL STATEMENT: "It is important that pupils should

Defenders of Communism

clearly realize the doom of the capitalistic world, its inevitable downfall, that they should see on the other hand the great prospects of our socialist system, and actively get prepared when they leave school to be ready to take their place in life, in the struggle for a new world, for Communism."

"TEACHER'S GAZETTE," *September 13, 1947.*

LABOR

STUDENT: *"Since Communism claims to represent the interests of the laboring class, what is the official Communist attitude toward the labor movement?"*

LENIN: "It will be necessary . . . to agree to any and every sacrifice, and even—if need be—to resort to all sorts of devices, maneuvers and illegal methods, to evasion and subterfuge, in order to penetrate into the trade unions, to remain in them, and to carry on Communist work in them at all costs." *V. I. Lenin,* "LEFT-WING COMMUNISM," *p. 38.*

STUDENT: *"I think the average American working man would be interested in knowing what the Communists do when they control a labor union. How do the Communists treat labor unions in Russia where they have complete control?"*

VICTOR KRAVCHENKO (Former Government Official now defected): "The local (Communist) party organization elects one of its suitable members to become president of the trade union. Generally speaking, the Soviet trade unions have to see that the workers execute the program."

Quoted in House Un-American Activities Committee publication, "100 THINGS YOU SHOULD KNOW ABOUT COMMUNISM," *U. S. Government Printing Office, 1949, p. 78.*

STUDENT: *"But does that not make the union a subservient arm of government rather than an organization of workers? What if a nation wanted to strike?"*

The Naked Communist

KRAVCHENKO: "The union's job is to see that strict discipline is maintained, that there will be no strikes, that the workers work for wages established by the central government, that the workers carry out all the decisions, resolutions, et cetera, of the party."

House Un-American Activities Committee publication, "100 THINGS YOU SHOULD KNOW ABOUT COMMUNISM," *p. 78.*

STUDENT: *"But what would happen if I were a worker in Russia and wanted to quit my job?"*

KRAVCHENKO: "Every citizen in the Soviet Union has a passport. On the passport is his photograph. There is also a special page on which a stamp is put which indicates the place, date and type of employment. If you leave your job in one factory and go to another without the permission of your director you will be prosecuted under the law for violation of the law prohibiting unauthorized change of employment. This refers not only to laborers but to any kind of employee."

"100 THINGS YOU SHOULD KNOW ABOUT COMMUNISM," *p. 78-79.*

STUDENT: *"In view of these statements I would like to conclude with one more question: Is this the hope for humanity which the Soviet offers the world?"*

OFFICIAL STATEMENT: "The Soviet is an inspiring example for the proletarian revolution in the rest of the world . . . . (It) shows the powerful achievements of the victorious proletariat and the vast superiority of Socialist to Capitalist economy. The Soviet Union is an inspiring example for the national self-determination of the oppressed peoples."

"FUNDAMENTALS OF COMMUNISM," *Published by the Communist Party of America, p. 19.*

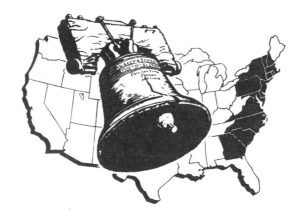

2

How Does a People Build a Free Nation?

During the latter part of the eighteenth century a phe-nomenal political development occurred which created the framework for a new civilization. This was the establishment of the first free people in modern times. In the panoramic history of the human race it was an epic achievement.

At the time this important political leap took place the whole pattern of human existence was bogged down by three man-made systems which had enslaved mankind. The first was the political system throughout the world which consisted of monarchial dictatorships where life, liberty and property were subject to the more or less fickle whims of individual potentates. The second oppressive system was the economic pattern of the world which was rooted in a variety of feudal contracts where the majority of the people wore out their lives as serfs on vast estates carved from the spoils of military conquest. The third system which dominated the lives of mankind was the overexpansion of institutionalized religion. The professional guardians of man's spiritual welfare had practically choked off all channels of free spiritual expression so that matters of opinion and conscience were often scrutinized and controlled by oppressive surveillance.

Rise of the Liberals

For several hundred years prior to the eighteenth century a few liberal rebels had struck out fiercely against the Frankenstein systems which enmeshed mankind, and many of these liberals had left their mark. They were called "liberals" because they desired to liberate the race from these man-made systems. They wanted man controlling the systems instead of the systems enslaving man. Today "liberals" are often those who would like to restore those systems and once more make man their minions, but here we shall speak of liberals in the original sense—"liberators from man-made systems."

The first group of liberals to gravitate together in sufficient quantities to take decisive action was a contingent of visionary men scattered among the American colonies. Historians say it is surprising how few voices in that day were prepared to speak up for complete liberation, but these few were sufficiently strong to chart a blueprint for the first free nation in modern times.

Of course, in many ways it was a most reckless venture. These American political pioneers risked life, property and the rights of citizenship by participating in this liberation movement. Nevertheless, they were successful to a degree never exceeded by political leaders in any other time or generation. Perhaps the following outline will illustrate why.

Political Philosophy of American Founding Fathers

The American founding fathers were very *un*common men. They were neither anarchists nor revolutionists but were among the most successful political and business leaders from each of the colonies. In this sense, they were both phys-

Building a Free Nation

ically and mentally equipped to be empire builders, and before the king had made his imperialism completely intolerable they had, in many cases, been among the most active subjects of the king carrying out the crown's business among the colonies. Therefore, by their own contemporary standards, they could scarcely be called "proletariat." As a group they were students of economics and political science, and when they set their hands to the task of creating a new nation they drained off the best thinking of men like John Locke, Baron de Montesquieu and Adam Smith besides adding many ingenious contributions from the inspiration of their own minds.

All of this evolved into a unique political philosophy worthy of the most careful study. The documents these men produced reflect the ingredients of this philosophy. They reveal that those who subscribed to it had the following fundamental convictions:

They believed that certain inalienable rights of man are derived from God and not from any human agency; therefore, no human agency can rightfully disturb them.

They believed class distinctions must be eliminated, that there is no place among free men for classes or castes. The public officer, the merchant, the banker, the farmer, the mechanic, the teacher—all are honorable and necessary, worthy of being treated as equals. They believed the progress of the human race will not be the result of pitting one class against another but will come by uniting all groups or classes in one concentrated offensive against man's common enemies: poverty, ignorance, disease and war.

They believed that in pursuing happiness, men must be free to work at any livelihood which their experience, training and native qualifications will permit them to secure and hold.

They believed men must be free to enjoy the fruits of their labor—which means the protection of property rights.

They believed men must be secure in their homes and the privacy of their lives.

They believed there must be good will, generosity and

tolerance between those of difference professions, those of different religions and those of different races.

A Philosophy Becomes a Reality

The translating of these principles from theory to practice has been a long and painfully slow process. Nevertheless, the historic steps which were followed constitute the straight and narrow way through which any and every people must pass if they are to gain and retain their freedom. These historic steps were as follows:

FIRST: *The redemption of the people's freedom by an official Declaration of Independence in 1776.*

SECOND: *The enforcement of that Declaration by resort to arms from 1776 to 1783.*

THIRD: *For the first time in the history of the world a government was established with its powers strictly defined in a written document—the United States Constitution.*

FOURTH: *The Constitution provided for a republican form of government. This is government by elected representatives rather than government by emotional mass participation as in a pure democracy.*

FIFTH: *For the first time in history a government was set up under a sovereign trinity—three equal branches of governmental authority—the executive, the legislative and the judicial. The separation of powers among three equal branches of government came from the brilliant mind of Baron de Montesquieu (1689-1755). James Madison was a particularly warm admirer of Montesquieu and was responsible for the introduction of this principle into the framework of the Constitution.*

SIXTH: *Each branch of government was to be subject to a system of checks and balances from the other two branches so as to maintain a healthy balance of power. Government has been defined as society's power of "organized coercion." The genius of Montesquieu's principle of separation of powers is*

Building a Free Nation

the fact that when one branch of government exceeds its authority, one or both of the other branches combine against it to use their powers of coercion to put down the oppression of the offending branch. This makes it unnecessary to have the people rise up in revolutionary force to put down oppression.

SEVENTH: *All powers not specifically delegated to the Federal Government were retained by the states and the people. The doctrine of the contractual basis of government with the reservation of political sovereignty in the people was described by John Locke in his "Second Treatise of Civil Government," published in 1690.*

EIGHTH: *The following freedoms were guaranteed to the sovereign citizen:*

1. Freedom of religion (First Amendment)
2. Freedom of speech (First Amendment)
3. Freedom of press (First Amendment)
4. Freedom of assembly (First Amendment)
5. Freedom to petition the government for grievances (First Amendment)
6. Freedom to bear arms (Second Amendment)
7. Freedom from illegal search of persons, houses, papers or effects (Fourth Amendment)
8. Freedom from prosecution without due process of law (Fifth and Fourteenth Amendments)
9. Freedom from multiple prosecutions for the same offense (Fifth Amendment)
10. Freedom from the necessity of testifying against one's self (Fifth Amendment)
11. Freedom from imprisonment without a speedy and public trial (Sixth Amendment)
12. Freedom from excessive bail, excessive fines or cruel and unusual punishments (Eighth Amendment)
13. Freedom from slavery or involuntary servitude (Thirteenth Amendment added in 1865)
14. Freedom to vote regardless of race or sex (Fifteenth Amendment added in 1870 and the Nineteenth Amendment added in 1920)

NINTH: *Social and political reform along liberal lines was encouraged within the various states. While serving as governor of Virginia, Thomas Jefferson led the way by encouraging public education, dividing church and state, breaking down the medieval laws of inheritance to prevent monopoly of land and wealth, advocating the emancipation of slaves, prohibiting the importation of slaves, revising the criminal laws, suggesting representation according to population; declaring the right to vote should be extended to all men who might be subject to military duty and not merely to landowners; encouraging self-government in the counties and towns of the state.*

TENTH: *The Civil War established the sovereignty of the Federal Government as the dominant authority of the Union (from which individual states could not secede and against which individual states could not pass conflicting laws.) This gave solidarity to the United States and a uniformity among the states which had been previously disputed. The Civil War also opened the way for the emancipation of all men living within its boundaries.*

ELEVENTH: *Down through the years "promotional" legislation was passed to promote the general welfare of all citizens by encouraging interstate transportation, transcontinental communications, colonization of public lands, cheap postal service, development of waterways and resources.*

TWELFTH: *"Restrictive" legislation was passed for the purpose of protecting the individual citizen against various systems which began to encroach upon his welfare. Anti-trust legislation was passed to restrict the activities of monopolies in business and preserve free enterprise. Labor legislation was passed to fix responsibility for union leadership. Anti-crime legislation was passed to protect the citizens against organized underworld forces.*

Thus, a whole new pattern of human government has been born among men. It is a political framework designed to keep the ultimate control of the government in the hands of the people who live under that government. It is an expres-

Building a Free Nation

sion of political philosophy which makes it possible for men to protect themselves against the expanding power of man-made systems. It is a government of the people, by the people, for the people. It is the gradual unfolding of six centuries of true liberalism.

Results of 175 Years of American Liberalism

The encouragement of private initiative and self-determination and the protection of the individual citizen from the encroachment of man-made systems have now had 175 years to prove themselves. Did the liberation of the citizen from the systems of the past prove beneficial?

The United States, like all new countries, started poor in capital and badly in debt. Although other nations have often had equal access to natural resources, the United States slowly but consistently forged ahead. Today, with only 7 per cent of the world's population and 6 per cent of the earth's territory, the United States has acquired through peaceful industry nearly 50 per cent of the world's developed wealth. Each year its citizens grow, build, sell, buy and use more goods and services than any other country in existence. With a population of 180 million it has succeeded in approaching the economists' dream of total employment by providing jobs for 63 million people while approximately 37 million of its youth have been enrolled in school. Each year the people of the United States spend more than 200 billion dollars on personal goods and services. This means a per capita income of $1,453 which is twice the per capita income in Britain, five times the per capita income in Russia, and seven times the per capita income in Italy.

According to the American Automobile Association, the people of the United States spend more than 9 billion dollars on vacations each year. Individual savings amount to 17 billion dollars annually, and 3 out of 4 families are covered by life insurance. Of the 50 million dwelling units in the

MINUTES OF WORK REQUIRED IN VARIOUS COUNTRIES TO EARN ONE POUND OF FOOD

	USA	FRANCE	GERMANY	IRELAND	ITALY	NORWAY	SWEDEN	RUSSIA
1 lb. Wheat Flour	4	20	15	6	15	6	18	27
1 lb. Macaroni	8				20	17		45
1 lb. Rice	6	33			17	17	16	91
1 lb. Bread	6	9	12	8	13	7	7	14
1 lb. Beef	31	126	87	72	128	58		132
1 lb. Pork Chops	32	91	94	68	124	59	97	220
1 lb. Veal	48	120				48	100	
1 lb. Leg of Lamb	31	133		76		61	85	140
1 lb. Fish	18	33	31	42	55	18		135
1 lb. Butter	30	135	150	83	162	63	115	270
1 lb. Cheese	22	140		60	109	38	35	
1 lb. Fresh Milk	8	16	15	16	20	9	12	42
1 lb. Eggs	32	118	125	109	126	82	97	187
1 lb. Fresh Apples	4	19	16				9	89
1 lb. Cabbage	2	7	8			5	6	37
1 lb. Carrots	5	9	3	5		12	7	9
1 lb. Potatoes	2	3	3	5	5	3	4	9
1 lb. Oleomargarine	13	64	39	55		19		152
1 lb. Sugar	4	21	21	9	37	7	14	110

Building a Free Nation

nation, 60 per cent are occupied by their owners. The millions of acres of developed farm land produce more food than its citizens can eat. The productive capacity of the United States is the largest in the world. It owns 30 per cent of the world's railroad mileage, 76 per cent of its automobiles, 51 per cent of its trucks, 47 per cent of its radios, 42 per cent of the electric power output, 47 per cent of its steel.

Each year the United States produces 51 per cent of the world's output of petroleum and about 30 per cent of its coal. The U.S. merchant fleets have replaced Britain's as the rulers of the seas with the greatest volume of foreign trade.[1]

The Pattern for Abundant Living

World travelers or people who have lived abroad can appreciate the abundant living of the United States better than the average American. The table on the opposite page illustrates how little time it takes an American citizen to earn the necessities of life and why he is able to spend so much of his income on travel and items of commerce which foreign citizens would call luxuries. This table shows how many minutes the average citizen of leading countries must work to pay for one pound of the various items listed.[2]

In this list the statistics for potatoes may be used as an illustration of what has been happening in the world. Russia, for example, produces more potatoes than any other country in the world, but a Russian must work four times as long as an American to buy one pound of potatoes. And observe that a Russian must work twenty-seven times as long as an American to buy one pound of sugar; twelve times as long as an American to buy one pound of oleomargarine.

In the United States by 1951 there were 105 million radios.

---

[1] *Statistics taken from the "1954* INFORMATION ALMANAC" *published by the MacMillan Co., New York, p. 80.*
[2] *Statistics taken from U.S. Bureau of Labor and quoted in the "1954* INFORMATION ALMANAC," *p. 130.*

It took the average citizen 1 day and 2 hours to earn enough money to buy an average radio. In France it requires 7½ days of toil to pay for an average radio, in Italy 15 days, in Russia 27 days.[3]

In the United States there are 201,277 physicians, 87,000 dentists and 1,439,030 hospital beds. The life expectancy in the United States is 65.9 years for males and 71.5 years for females. In Russia the last life expectancy tables show the average to be 41.9 years for males and 46.8 years for females.[4]

Certain foreign propaganda agents have tried to depict U.S. wealth as a fortuitous gift of nature. Economists have pointed out that many foreign nations have equal access to resources and could duplicate the wealth of the United States if they were willing to accept the principles of government and economics which make the development of such wealth possible. Propaganda agents have insisted that since the United States has become remarkably wealthy it should divide that wealth with the rest of the poverty-stricken world. Economists have answered this by pointing out that what America has to share with the world is not so much her wealth as her time-tested system of government and economics.

If America's wealth were spread around the world it would soon be dissipated, but if her system of free government and free enterprise were spread around the world, nations would soon find them to be perpetual producers of wealth. What foreign nations envy in America is the fruition of 175 years of true liberalism.

---

[3] "1954 INFORMATION ALMANAC," *p. 80.*
[4] "STATISTICAL ABSTRACT OF THE USA—1952," *published by the U. S. Dept. of Commerce, pp. 946-960.*

3

What is Free Enterprise Capitalism?

Marx made his most damaging mistake while drawing up the blueprints for a Communist society by designing them for a creature which never existed. He misinterpreted the nature of man. Since then, the Communists have expended vast quantities of strategy and energy trying to change the instinctive desires of man, but this has proven impossible.

Marx likewise miscalculated while attempting to analyze free enterprise capitalism. His prophecies concerning its unavoidable collapse failed to materialize. In fact, the very opposite occurred. While nations which toyed with Socialism and Communism progressed slowly, stood still or slid backwards, Capitalism rolled steadily on.

Two things in particular have made modern Capitalism increasingly successful. First, its capacity to satisfy the inherent needs and desires of man, and second, its capacity to function efficiently with very little guidance or supervision. It is sometimes called a *natural* system of economics because it tends to adjust automatically to human requirements. Nevertheless, being a child of nature, Capitalism contains a certain spirit of the jungle when observed in its wild, uncultivated state where men have used it for selfish, *individual* survival. However, under domestication and tempered with the ingredient of good will toward men, Capitalism has proven to be man's most efficient device for the developing of material wealth and for general social advancement; in other words, for *community* survival.

In order to appreciate the natural qualities of Capitalism which have proven beneficial to mankind, we should first ask ourselves, "What is the nature of man? What are his desires and needs?"

The Nature of Man

Under careful scrutiny, man turns out to be a physical-spiritual being. To ignore either facet of his nature would be as fatal for us at it was for Marx.

On the physical side, we observe that man is an elaborate and complex organism with a capacity to register and react to sensations ranging from excruciating pain to ecstatic pleasure. Bradford B. Smith calls this man's pain-pleasure scale. A vast array of human needs grow out of man's desire to avoid pain or discomfort and achieve physical satisfaction and pleasure from life. Some of these would be:

Satisfying hunger
Quenching thirst
Satisfying tastes
Being warm in cold weather, cool in warm weather
Avoiding illness
Being relieved of pain
Having comfortable and attractive clothes
Having a comfortable home and surroundings
Enjoying perfumes and pleasant odors
Hearing pleasant sounds
Enjoying relaxation and recreation
Participating in marital associations
Enjoying the sensation of movement and travel
Seeing colorful objects or colorful scenery

Free Enterprise Capitalism

Now let us take a moment to consider the other half of man's nature—the spiritual side. This is sometimes called man's fear-hope scale. Man, as an intelligent, self-knowing, self-determining being, is capable of having strong feelings ranging all the way from sublime hope to deep fear and despair. Sometimes these are closely related to physical needs and frustrations; sometimes they are purely intellectual. But regardless of their origin, they are very real and result in a wide pattern of intellectual or spiritual needs:

To be of individual importance so as to count for something as a person.

To be a party in interest—to be identified with the system.

To enjoy owning "things."

To be appreciated for some unique and important contribution.

To have a satisfactory degree of economic security.

To feel the satisfaction of sacrificing or risking something to achieve progress. (This is sometimes erroneously called the "gambling" instinct.)

To have the opportunity for creativity.

To feel family solidarity.

To enjoy the right of privacy.

To have freedom of expression in matters of opinion.

To be protected in convictions of religion and conscience.

To feel significant in determining matters of political importance.

Man's Mainspring of Action

In studying the nature of man it soon becomes apparent that his "mainspring of action" is the driving necessity to satisfy both physical and spiritual needs. Many economic systems which men have invented tend to smother or ignore these needs. To that same extent these systems are bound to smother man's greatest source of motivating power—the anxiety to satisfy these deep, throbbing human desires.

The Naked Communist

Forty years of Communism in the U.S.S.R. have eloquently confirmed this. The Communist leaders have suppressed the natural desires of their people and have tried to motivate them to action through fear. But this has not worked because fear is primarily a depressant instead of a stimulant. On the long pull it becomes a dull, paralyzing drug affecting both brain and muscle, and leaves a smouldering ash of combustible hostility. "Work through fear" can never compete successfully with the tantalizing opportunity provided by Capitalism to constantly satisfy natural human needs. Satisfying these needs is almost the entire source of power for Capitalism's productive momentum.

Of course, if human beings made an attempt to rush around in breathless haste trying to satisfy all of these desires to their utmost, they would probably die in their early youth. Therefore Providence has endowed each human being with a built-in reactor against speed which serves to prevent or discourage over-indulgence. It is called "inertia." As each person feels an inward desire to satisfy some physical need, he simultaneously feels the strong gravitational pull of laziness or inertia. Thereby hangs an important principle of economics: "Man ever tends to satisfy his wants with the least possible exertion."

Perhaps we should mention in passing that capitalism gives full vent to this principle by encouraging men to continually seek cheaper sources of power and try to develop more efficient machines to do the world's work instead of using human and animal muscle. Even as late as 1900 over 50 per cent of U.S. power was provided by animals and men, but under a half century of capitalistic development they now supply only 2 per cent of the power. The rest comes from machines. Other political and economic systems claim to be in favor of mechanization, but no other system is able to promote technological development as rapidly as capitalism because competitive survival becomes so important that it makes it worthwhile to throw away machines as soon as they become obsolete, also to discard outmoded sources of power. Mechanization on American farms came about through economic necessity while mechanization on socialized farms is looked upon as desirable but not particularly necessary.

The Law of Variation

The genius of Capitalism is not merely that it satisfies the desires and needs of mankind generally, but it responds to the factor of variation as between individuals. It allows each man to do anything he wishes so long as he can survive at it. Therefore each man continually surveys the field of economic opportunity and gradually tries to push himself into that phase of work which best satisfies him.

This is one of the greatest blessings of free enterprise Capitalism. To a remarkable extent it allows a man to do just about whatever he wants to do. Laborers are not conscripted nor told they cannot strike; nor are they ordered to remain in certain occupations as tends to be the case in socialized and communized countries.

Under Capitalism Everyone Can Gain

A study of human nature reveals that "value" is psychological rather than real. Whether a thing is "worth" a certain amount depends entirely on the mental value attached to it. Capitalism has proven to be a dynamic economy in which everyone participating in a transaction can increase the value of what he has, or, in other words, make a profit. This can be true of both the buyer and the seller. For example, take a man who wants to buy a used car. He has a certain amount of money or credit. When he offers this money to the dealer it means that he would rather have the car than that amount of money—the "value" of the car is greater to him than the "value" of the money. If the dealer agrees it means that the dealer would rather have the money than the car. In fact, he won't sell the car unless the price he gets is of greater value to him than the value of the car. As the car is driven away, both men have made a profit. Both men feel they have improved their position as a result of the transaction.

This is a strong contributing factor to the success of Capitalistic free enterprise. It allows everyone to win, either by making a profit or by improving his position as the result of an honest transaction.

The Meaning of a Free Economy

Capitalism thrives best in a free economy but freedom is a much misunderstood subject. For example, there is no such thing as total, unrestricted freedom. Freedom means simply the chance to choose. Therefore freedom can only relate itself to specific choices such as the freedom to speak or not to speak, the freedom to believe or not believe, the freedom to buy or not to buy, and so forth. Furthermore, freedom can move in only one direction at a time. If a man has ten dollars and chooses to spend it on a night of celebration he has thereby lost the freedom to spend that same ten dollars on some new clothes. Once the choice is made, a person is not free to avoid the consequences of that choice. That is why we say there is no such thing as unrestricted freedom, or freedom in general. Freedom is always restricted to some specific choice and freedom is always restricted to choosing one direction at a time.

It is for this reason that a free economy requires a continuous education of its people so that they will exercise their "freedom to choose" in such a way that it will sustain sound moral principles and build a dynamic economy with a strong social structure to preserve it. In making such choices, the people must sense what is best for both the individual and the community. They must be well informed. They must know enough about each problem so they can anticipate what the result will be when they have made their choice.

There are many notable examples in both modern and ancient history to illustrate what happens when people are only casually concerned with their right to make a choice or

Free Enterprise Capitalism

exercise their freedom. Free peoples require alert, aggressive leadership and a socially and politically conscious citizenry. This is not easily maintained, but it is the price of freedom. Sometimes the streak of natural laziness in people makes them wish that a commission, a dictator or a king would make all the decisions and force the people to do what is good for them. But this is the road to ruin for a free economy. The people must retain the sovereign right to choose, for that is all freedom is.

Now we come to the four great freedoms which must always exist in a truly free economy.

1. FREEDOM TO TRY

One of the most essential ingredients in a healthy economy is the freedom to try. This is really the freedom to achieve and it is based on the principle that "the genius of one or a few men cannot begin to compare in the aggregate to the genius of *all* the people."

Therefore, in a free country a man can develop a new kind of shorthand, a different kind of screwdriver, a new breed of cattle, or an improved type of mousetrap. When he is through, no one may wish to buy the new product or service, but at least he is free to invent it and try to sell it if he can. This is an in indispensable characteristic of Capitalism — the freedom to try.

One of the reasons atomic energy was shared with the people for peacetime development was because Americans have been educated to believe that this is the best way to harness atomic power for a vast multitude of domestic services. With many thousands of scientists working on ways and means to exploit atomic power—instead of using just a few hundred—the results should be correspondingly greater. This is particularly true where each of the scientists is free to try anything his inventive genius may dictate.

This was precisely the way we developed radio, television, the prevention of polio, the wonders of the modern automobile and the sound-barrier-breaking speed of the propellerless jets. By way of contrast, it is interesting to note that the providing of an adequate road system was reserved to the State and Federal Governments. Notice that this monopolized program has never come up to the public needs at any time in our history. It is interesting to consider what might have happened if highways had been left in the open market where businessmen could compete for the opportunity of serving the public with adequate systems of highway facilities. In fact, during recent years there have been several places where toll roads have been built by private capital with the permission of state legislatures because the people were so dissatisfied with the inefficiency of government supervised thoroughfares.

2. FREEDOM TO SELL

If men are to be left free to try their skill and inventive genius they must also be protected in their freedom to sell their product for a profit. Of course, some new product might make a whole industry obsolete, temporarily throw thousands out of work and require numerous economic, social and political readjustments. But this is one of the keys to success in a free enterprise economy. It must not be curbed except in the case of products or procedures which involve an immoral or criminal aspect, such as narcotics, pornographic literature, quack medicines, fake stocks, and so forth.

Freedom to sell also implies the freedom to make a profit even if the price of a product is set at a level which wipes out the profit of a competitor. At first glance this may seem to be a cold, heartless system of economics, but if an American travels abroad through Communist or Socialist countries he begins to appreciate that "Freedom to Sell" is really the opportunity to survive. This means that a competitor must exert his faculties to produce more efficiently and reduce his price, or improve the quality of his product, so that the public will pay the difference to get it. In either case, the public benefits, and newly improved forms of material wealth are created for the use of the public simply because two or more companies are competing briskly in order to survive.

3. FREEDOM TO BUY

Now, of course, if the inventor of some new product is to enjoy the freedom to sell, then the public must certainly enjoy the freedom to buy. One of the most fatal restrictions on a dynamic capitalistic economy is rationing or governmental control of commerce so that the people are told what they can buy, in what quantity, where and at what price. These artificial devices so completely sabotage capitalism that prices get out of phase, black markets develop and many human needs are neglected. This is why the United States moved so quickly after World War II to eliminate price controls and rationing. Both are inimical to a healthy capitalist economy. France and England failed to follow suit but Western Germany did. As a result, the recovery of Western Germany was one of the sensations of the post-war period, while the recovery of France and England was extremely slow and painful.

4. FREEDOM TO FAIL

Last of all, we come to the freedom which harbors in its bosom the golden secret of all successful capitalist economies. This is the freedom to fail. Under free enterprise Capitalism every businessman who wishes to survive must do a lot of long term research as well as make a continuous study of his current operation. Services must be continually improved, waste must be eliminated, efficiency in operations must be constantly pushed. And all of this is simply to keep the individual or company from failing. Occasionally we find a businessman, whose neck may be new to the yoke, refusing to extend himself in order to meet the competition of others who are more alert, more aggressive, more anxious to serve and more accommodating. This newcomer has a lesson to learn. Perhaps, without quite realizing it, he is exercising his freedom to fail.

In some *planned* economies a well-established business is not allowed to fail because it is described as "essential" to the economy. Therefore, if the product of that company will not sell at a profit, it is subsidized from taxes to make up the difference. The company thereby receives a bonus for its inefficiency. No lesson is learned. The expressed choice to fail is not allowed to result in failure. Other companions soon follow. Almost immediately inertia replaces energy. Progress is slowed to a snail's pace and human needs are no longer adequately satisfied.

In a dynamic capitalist economy the fact that a person or company will be allowed to fail is the very thing which spurs the individual or company to succeed. Of course, those who do fail are cushioned in their fall so that they do not starve nor do they lose their opportunity to try again. Nevertheless, the cushion is not a dole nor a stipend which would be so comfortable that the person would want to relax and stay down. Capitalist cushions are thin—by design.

How Capitalism
Makes Things Plentiful and Cheap

It was Marx's dream to produce everything in such overwhelming abundance and distribute goods so freely that no one would need to buy and therefore no one would be able to sell. Unfortunately for Marx, his economic dream was doomed from the start because instead of producing goods in overwhelming abundance, Socialism and Communism were found to stymie production and smother invention. Therefore, it has remained the task of free enterprise Capitalism to push mankind toward the economic millennium of a fully abundant material life.

An excellent example of how this is being accomplished is taken from a personal observation of Dr. George S. Benson

Free Enterprise Capitalism

of Harding College. He says: "In China I burned kerosene carried a hundred miles on the shoulders of a coolie. He owned his means of transportation, he owned a bamboo pole and a scrap of rope on each end of it, and he'd tie a five gallon tin of kerosene to either end of the pole and trot along back into the interior. He traveled over a little, single-file trail that nobody kept up, that wound its way between the rice fields in the valleys and then over the hills. He could make about ten miles a day with that burden.

"How much was he paid? Suppose he had been paid $5.00 a day. In ten days he'd have earned $50.00. But what would he have accomplished? He'd have transported ten gallons of kerosene a hundred miles, he'd have increased the price of kerosene $5.00 per gallon. Of course in China nobody could afford to pay such a price so he was paid what the traffic would bear; he was paid ten cents a day and then he added ten cents a gallon to the price of kerosene when carried a hundred miles—he doubled the price of it.

"A miserable wage, wasn't it? But he could do no better with what he had to work with.

"Now observe how we move kerosene in America where there is an investment of $25,000 in cash for every job created —the roadbed, the steel rails, the great locomotives, the tank cars, the terminals, the loading facilities and so on. We move kerosene at less than one cent per gallon per hundred miles, less than a tenth of the cost in China. What do we pay our workmen? Seventy times what the Chinese coolie gets—and still give to the purchaser a freight rate of less than a tenth of that of a coolie. What's the difference? Simply the investment and management—nothing else—the result of our American way of life."

Here Dr. Benson has pinpointed another of the great secrets of Capitalism's success: to put expensive tools and vast quantities of power at the disposal of the worker. But since the worker cannot afford to provide these tools for himself, who does? The answer is simple: frugal fellow citizens.

These frugal fellow citizens are called capitalists. They are often ordinary people who are willing to scrimp and save and store up goods and money instead of consuming or spending them. Therefore, anyone who has savings, stocks, bonds, investments, insurance or property is a capitalist. In America this includes a remarkably high percentage of all the people. No doubt it would come as a great surprise to Marx if he knew that instead of developing a capitalist class as Marx expected, America is becoming a *nation* of capitalists.

Each capitalist decides what venture he will sponsor with his money. He often risks his money in places where a government agency would never risk a cent. As a result, new oil is found, new inventions are promoted, new industries are started, "impossible things" are made possible and fantastic benefits constantly accrue to humanity.

Of course, investing money which people have been painstakingly saving through a lifetime requires that the project be successful so people will continue backing it with their savings. This puts management under a great deal of pressure to cut expenses and get the product out at a price that will make it sell "in quantity." Management therefore constantly demands more efficient machines which in turn permit the worker to spend fewer hours on the job. The little book called *The Miracle of America* points out that this free enterprise system has:

1. *Increased the real wages of American workers (wages in relation to prices) to three and one-half times what they were in 1850.*
2. *Reduced hours of work from an average of about 70 hours a week in 1850 to around 40 today.*
3. *Increased the worker's share of the national income paid out in wages and salaries from 38 per cent in 1850 to about 70 per cent today.*
4. *Increased the number of jobs faster than the growth of population, so that America has come closer to "full employment" than any nation in the world.*

All of this is made possible because the American worker is furnished expensive equipment to do the job faster and cheaper, and this equipment is purchased with the savings of the worker's business partner. He is the frugal fellow citizen called "the Capitalist."

The Law of Supply and Demand Sets the Price

Capitalism works best in a free market where the "value" of goods is fixed at that point where the graph line of "supply" intersects with the graph line of "demand." For example, if there is an abundant supply of potatoes people lose their anxiety to secure potatoes and the "demand" sinks to a low level. Even so, however, there is a level at which demand will establish itself and that is what "fixes" the price.

Several years ago, unexpected circumstances resulted in a threatened potato famine. The government made the mistake of interfering on the assumption that if it did not interfere the price of potatoes would shoot sky high and people of modest means could not buy them. It was considered "socially desirable" to peg the price of potatoes at a low level. But what happened? With a short supply and an unnatural, low price it was only a matter of a few weeks until the entire stock was exhausted and nobody could buy potatoes at any price. Here is why Socialism or human control of the economy stifles Capitalism and destroys the "natural" laws by which it has so successfully blessed mankind.

If the Government had left the market alone the price of potatoes would have gone up to that point where demand would have carried it. The higher price would have provided an "automatic" control of consumption and would have made the supply of potatoes last much longer because people would have considered it economically necessary to use fewer potatoes. They would have gradually begun to buy substitutes which were in surplus and therefore cheaper. By this means the price factor would have helped people limit their consumption of stocks which were scarce while increasing the consumption of stocks which were plentiful.

All this was turned topsy-turvy when the Government thought it would be "socially desirable" to peg potato prices.

It not only turned out to be unnatural but also impractical. This brings us to our final comment on free enterprise.

Failure of an American Experiment
with Socialism

One of the most impressive modern documents on American free enterprise in action is a dynamic little book by Ezra Taft Benson, former U.S. Secretary of Agriculture, entitled, *Farmers at the Cross Roads.* It verifies with facts and figures the lesson our generation has learned from an experiment with Socialism through Government control of agriculture.

The Government attempted to control farm prices by direct control of farm practices. The so-called "basic crops" which were put under controls were wheat, cotton, corn, rice, tobacco and peanuts. The idea was to protect the farmer by guaranteeing him a certain minimum price. To do this it was necessary to control production. Farmers were therefore restricted as to the amount of acreage they could plant.

The results were amazing. Take wheat for example. More than 30 million acres were taken out of wheat production in an attempt to reduce the supply and thereby maintain a good price for wheat. Each wheat farmer received a Government check which paid him for *not* planting wheat on a certain percentage of his land. This is what happened:

The farmer used the money to buy better machinery, more fertilizer and additional help so that frequently he harvested as much or more wheat from his limited acreage than he had previously raised on his entire farm. In other words, curtailed acreage did not curtail production.

Furthermore, land taken out of wheat production could be used to raise other crops which resulted in an over-supply of feed grains. Feed grain prices went so low that farmers and ranchers were able to greatly increase their cattle and hog production. This pulled the rug out from under meat prices.

The government tried to save the situation by purchasing

Free Enterprise Capitalism

large quantities of each product which was being overpro-
duced. This, coupled with price supports, encouraged even
more people to invest in farming with the result that vast
areas of sub-marginal land were opened up for production.
Many of these investors were not farmers at all, and these
made a loud noise in favor of higher supports when they could
not make their inefficiently operated farms pay off.

The Government's support of artificial high prices also
had another destructive influence. It encouraged customers
to look around for substitute products or foreign imports. As
a result, American farmers not only lost some of their domestic
markets, but found they were unable to compete abroad.

What happened to wheat also happened to cotton and the
other "basic crops." They lost markets everywhere. In the
case of cotton the government reduced acreage from 43 million acres to 17.4 million. Still the surplus quantities continued to climb. Before controls, U.S. cotton farmers exported
7 million bales of cotton per year. During 1955 they sold
only 2 million bales abroad. Foreign cotton growers saw what
was happening and doubled their sales because U.S. cotton
brokers could not compete. So it was with all controlled areas
of U.S. agriculture.

In contrast to this, we find that those areas of agriculture
which resisted rigid price guarantees did better. Take soybean
farming as an example. These producers used the Department of Agriculture to advise and counsel them but not to
control. The Department of Agriculture conducted numerous experiments to reveal new uses for soybeans and
encouraged producers to use cooperative associations for the
exploring of new markets. Today, soybean farmers supply
half the tonnage for high protein feeds—twice as much as that
which comes from cottonseed meal. Soybeans have risen to
fifth place as the farmer's greatest source of farm income. Secretary Benson closes with this significant comment: "A major
difference between cotton and soybeans is the fact that cotton
decided to fight its battles in the legislative halls, while soybeans decided to fight in the market place."

These are merely a few highlights from the lessons which

342 America should have learned during the past twenty-five years of experimentation with socialized agriculture. There are many things which the Government can do to encourage the "general welfare" of all agriculture as it did with soybeans, but to try to control prices by Washington edicts rather than by supply and demand in the market place proves to be the kiss of death for the handsome goose that lays the golden eggs of American free enterprise prosperity.

It is time to sell ourselves on our own economic program so we can more effectively share it with the rest of the world. We have a great system which is operating with demonstrable efficiency. Here is a summary of what it is doing:

1. *Capitalism is by far the best known system to provide for the physical needs of man.*
2. *Capitalism permits man to satisfy his spiritual needs.*
3. *Capitalism allows for variation as between individuals.*
4. *Capitalism is naturally self-expanding which tends to create strong economic ties between communities, states and nations.*
5. *Capitalism can permit everyone to participate in making a profit, thereby eliminating classes or castes which are inherent in so many other types of economies.*
6. *Capitalism promotes the "freedom to try."*
7. *Capitalism allows the "freedom to sell."*
8. *Capitalism allows the "freedom to buy."*
9. *Capitalism preserves the greatest single force of human motivation—the risk of failing.*
10. *Capitalism tends to increase the wages of workers in relation to prices.*
11. *Capitalism tends to reduce the hours of work necessary to make a living.*
12. *Capitalism increases the workers' share of the national income.*
13. *Capitalism increases the number of jobs faster than the growth of population.*
14. *Capitalism promotes rapid technological advances.*
15. *Capitalism is proving to be the most effective means mankind has yet discovered for "sharing the wealth."*

4

Did the Early Christians Practice Communism?

A few students have secretly or even openly defended Communism because they considered it to be an important set of principles practiced by the early Christians. Such persons often say that they definitely do not condone the ruthlessness of Communism as presently practiced in Russia, but that they do consider it to be of Christian origin and morally sound when practiced on a "brotherhood basis."

This was exactly the attitude of the Pilgrim Fathers when they undertook to practice Communism immediately after their arrival in the New World. But as we have seen earlier, not only did the project fail miserably, but it was typical of hundreds of other attempts to make Communism work on a "brotherhood basis." Without exception all of them failed. One cannot help wondering why.

Certain scholars feel they have verified what Governor Bradford has said concerning "brotherhood Communism," namely, that it is un-Christian and immoral because it strikes at the very roots of human liberty. Communism—even on a brotherhood basis—can only be set up under a dictatorship administered within the framework of force or fear. Governor Bradford found this to be true. Leaders in literally hundreds of similar experiments concur. Students are therefore returning to ancient texts with this question: "Did the early Christians really practice Communism?"

The belief that the early Christians may have practiced Communism is based on two passages. Here is the first one:

> *"And all that believed were together, and had all things common; and sold their possessions and goods, and parted them to all men as every man had need."* (Acts 2:44-45)

Two things might be noted here. First, the people formed a community effort by coming together; second, they sold their possessions and goods as they appeared to need cash proceeds for the assistance of their fellow members. It does not say that they sold all their possessions and goods although it is granted that at first reading this may be inferred. Neither does it say that they pooled their resources in a common fund although this has been assumed from the statement that they "had all things common."

What they actually did is more clearly stated in the second passage which is often quoted:

> *"And the multitude of them that believed were of one heart and of one soul; neither* said *any of them that ought of the things which he possessed was his own; but they had all things common."* (Acts 4:32)

Here we have a declaration indicating that the common effort was not a legal pooling of resources in a communal fund but rather a feeling of unity in dealing with common problems so that no man "said" his possessions were his own but developed and used them in such a way that they would fill the needs of the group as well as himself.

That this is a correct reading of this passage may be verified by events which are described in the next chapter of Acts.

There we read of Ananias and Sapphira. They had a

piece of property which they decided to sell. They intended to give the proceeds to the Apostle Peter. But the author of Acts says that when they had sold the property they decided to hold back some of the proceeds even though they represented to Peter that their contribution was the entire value of the property received at the sale. For this deceit Peter severely criticized them and then, in the process, he explained the legal relationship existing between these two people and their property. Said he, "While it (the property) remained, *was it not thine own?* and after it was sold, *was it (the money) not in thine power?*" (Acts 5:4)

In other words, this property had never been required for any communal fund. It belonged to Ananias and Sapphira. It was completely in their power. After the property was sold the money they received from the sale was also in their power. They could spend it or contribute it. If contributed, the money was a freewill, voluntary offering. It will be seen immediately that this is altogether different from a Communist's relationship to property where there is a confiscation or expropriation of each member's possessions, and the proceeds are distributed by a single person or a small committee. The member thereby loses his independence and becomes subservient to the whims and capriciousness of those who rule over him.

It would appear, therefore, that the early Christians did keep legal title to their property but "said" it was for the benefit of the whole community.

This is precisely the conclusion reached in Dummelow's *Bible Commentary.* It discusses the two passages we have just quoted and then says: "The Church of Jerusalem recognized the principle of private property. A disciple's property really was his own, but he did not say it was his own; he treated it as if it were common property."

Dr. Adam Clarke's commentary also makes this significant observation concerning the Apostolic collections for the poor: "If there has been a *community of goods* in the Church, there could have been no ground for such (collections) . . . as there could have been no such distinction as *rich* and *poor,* if every one, on entering the Church, gave up his goods to a common stock."

This, then, brings us to our final comment on this subject, namely, that the Master Teacher made it very clear in one of his parables (Matthew 25:14-30) that property was not to be owned in common nor in equal quantities.

In this parable he said the members of the Kingdom of God were as servants who had been given various stewardships "every man according to his several ability." One man was given a stewardship of five talents of silver and when he "traded with the same and made them other five talents," his Lord said, "Well done!" However, another servant who had been given only one talent of silver feared he might somehow lose it, so he buried it in the earth. To this man his Lord said, "Thou wicked and slothful servant!" He then took this man's one talent and gave it to the first servant where it could be developed profitably.

Two things appear very clear in this Parable of the Talents: first, that every man was to enjoy his own private property as a stewardship from God. Second, that he was responsible to the earth's Creator for the profitable use of his property.

All of the evidence before us seems to clearly show that the early Christians did not practice Communism. They did not have their *property* in common. Instead, they had their *problems* in common. To solve their problems, each man was asked to voluntarily contribute according to his ability "as God had prospered him." (1 Corinthians 16:2)

When carefully analyzed, this was simply free enterprise capitalism *with a heart!*

The student will also probably recognize that whenever modern capitalism is practiced "with a heart" it showers blessings of wealth, generosity, good will and happy living on every community it touches.

The ancient Christian order was a great idea.

5

What is the Secret Weapon of Communism?

(This is the text of a speech delivered May 6, 1953, to 1150 guests at the annual banquet of the Washington State Parent Teachers Association. At the time this speech was given the author was serving on the faculty of the Brigham Young University.)

One hundred years ago there was a little school of philosophers in Europe who called themselves "pure materialists." They had their headquarters in Germany. Two of those materialists carved a place for themselves in history. Through their speeches and books they lighted a flame which, in a century, has created more distrust, insecurity, bloodshed, war-mongering and destruction of property than all the criminal and gangster elements in the world combined.

One of these men was Frederick Wilhelm Nietzsche. It was Nietzsche who rose up out of the school of pure materialism to advance the idea of a superman. His ideas could be summarized as follows: "Since there is not any God and since human beings are only graduate beasts without any souls and without immortality, men should not therefore follow a system of ethics and morals. The natural law of force should prevail in the universe. The weak deserve to serve, the strong deserve to rule. Somewhere on the earth there is a nation which is just naturally superior and which should ruthlessly subdue the rest of mankind. Within that nation a single individual should rise up as the natural leader and dictator to rule over humanity because he is a superman." It was Nietzsche who made up Superman, not the comics.

Who Inspired Hitler?

Now it was Nietzsche's thinking which inspired Adolf Hitler with his apocalyptic nightmare of total war. Hitler envisioned himself as the man of destiny—the superman—who would one day rule the world. When Hitler wrote *Mein Kampf* it was as though Nietzsche were speaking from the dead. Said Hitler, "Look at these young men and boys! What material! I shall eradicate the thousands of years of human domestication. Brutal youth—that is what I am after . . . I want to see once more in its eyes the gleam . . . of the beast of prey. With these I can make a new world . . . and create a new order!"

Mankind felt the crushing, brutal impact of Hitler's mammoth war machine during World War II as he forced millions to join his ranks of imperialistic conquest which was designed to make him dictator of the world. In this country we watched in amazement as he rose to power. Finally, after several years of seeing the black boots of National Socialism stomp out the light of civilization wherever they marched, we rose up in our wrath and joined forces with other nations of the world to smash Nietzsche-inspired Nazism.

However, the spirit of total war which was spawned by the materialists was not confined to the National Socialists in Germany. It had been projected into the ambitions and philosophies of the leaders of several nations. It was codifled into the political aims of the military leaders of Japan and Italy who also collapsed under the mighty blow which struck down National Socialism.

However, with the ending of World War II, many people felt that the conflict with materialism was at an end. Almost immediately the spirit of sacrifice seemed to wither within us. Virtually overnight our armies were demobilized, the world's largest air force was practically scrapped, and the world's largest navy was put into mothballs. All this was on the presumption that the war with materialism was finished. Time, of course, proved this presumption to be a mistake.

In putting down National Socialism and the Axis we had only conquered one form of materialism. Another form, equally strong, immediately rose to take its place. This new form of materialism came from Nietzsche's comrade-in-arms —Karl Marx—a man out of the same school of philosophy, with the same motivations as Nietzsche. Karl Marx thought of himself as the father of dialectical materialism, more commonly known as Communism. Today, the great force of conquest and imperialism which he envisioned stands arrayed against the people of the free world and marches under the banner of the hammer and sickle.

What Was the Mission of Karl Marx?

Some people have mistaken the mission of Karl Marx and his followers as purely economic in nature, but like all other materialists their mission was to gain power through ideological warfare. Note how they denounced any competitive ideology, even religion: "We must combat religion—this is the ABC of materialism, and consequently of Marxism."[1] And another disciple declared that when they took over, "God will be banished from the laboratories as well as from the schools."[2]

Now since we are dealing with the field of ideological warfare, one might well ask, What is the objective of these militant

---

[1] *Lenin, V. I.,* "RELIGION," *p. 14.*
[2] *Foster, William Z.,* "TOWARDS SOVIET AMERICA," *p. 316.*

atheists? What are they trying to set up as the new ideal for human relations? Listen to the words of Lenin:

"We must hate—hatred is the basis of Communism. Children must be taught to hate their parents if they are not Communists." And listen to the amazing declaration of the former Russian Commissar of Education, Anatole Lunarcharsky: "We hate Christians and Christianity. Even the best of them must be considered our worst enemies. Christian love is an obstacle to the development of the revolution. Down with love of one's neighbor! What we want is hate . . . Only then will we conquer the universe!"[3]

I am sure you would agree that when men like these rise to positions of power in the earth it is indeed a challenge to the youth of the free world. When Karl Marx was asked what his object in life was, he said, "To dethrone God and destroy capitalism!"

In a declared war against morals, ethics, and spiritual values among the people, Marx and his associates resolved to completely eliminate the worship of the Almighty among men. Heinrich Heine declared: "Our hearts are filled with compassion for it is . . . Jehovah Himself who is making ready to die,"[4] and Nietzsche, so successful in the atheistic campaign, said: let the "death of God" be boldly proclaimed.[5] Ludwig Feuerbach announced that: "The turning point of history will be the moment man becomes aware that the only God of man is man himself."[6]

Pirates of Science and Religion

The strategy of the materialists was to appropriate to themselves the toga of "science" and take credit for all scientific accomplishments. Then they determined to ridicule and

---

[3] "U. S. CONGRESSIONAL RECORD," *Vol. 77, pp. 1539-1540.*
[4] "REVUE DES DEUX-MONDES," *1834, Vol. 4, p. 408.*
[5] *Quoted in* "ATHEIST HUMANIST," *by Henri deLubac, p. 20.*
[6] *Quoted in* "ATHEIST HUMANIST," *by Henri deLubac, p. 10.*

Secret Weapon of Communism

rationalize away all the things which they opposed by pronouncing them "unscientific." Thus they attacked the Bible, called themselves higher critics, and attempted to explain it away. They explained the worship of God as being merely the effort of man to project the qualities of his own better nature into some fictitious superior being. They called Jesus Christ an itinerant preacher whose life and writings were effeminate and weak. They ridiculed the possibility of his resurrection. They denied the immortality of human life or the existence of the spirit or soul. They said that man was nothing but a graduate beast and that human life—especially the other man's life—was no more sacred than that of a centipede, a caterpillar, or a pig. In other words, the materialists turned their backs on six thousand years of human history and achievement. As Marx and Engels boasted in their *Manifesto*: Our program "abolishes eternal truths; it abolishes all religion, and all morality . . . it therefore acts in contradiction to all past historical experience."

Men Who Worship Themselves

But having denounced God, the scriptures, morals, immortality, eternal judgment, the existence of the spirit, and the sanctity of individual human life, the materialists turned to worship themselves. They decided that man, collectively speaking, was the epitome of perfection among nature's achievements and therefore the center of the universe. This gave Nietzsche an excellent opportunity to teach his concept of "superman." As Nietzsche exalted himself and all other men as the most superior of all existing things he burst forth into statements like this: "Now this God (of the Bible) is dead! You higher men, this God was your greatest danger. . . . Do you understand this saying, Oh my brothers? You are frightened? Do your hearts fail you? Does the abyss yawn at your feet? . . . What of it? Forward, higher men! Now at last the mountain of man's future is about to give birth. God is dead; now it is our will that superman shall live!"[7]

In the egotistical tunnel vision of these men who sought to dethrone God there flamed the phantom hope that somehow they may have made the discovery of the ages. Nietzsche made a studied attempt to assume the proper humility which he felt was becoming to such a genius as himself. Said he, "Great heavens! Who has any idea of the burden that weighs upon me and the strength that it takes to endure myself! I don't know why it should fall upon me of all people—but it may be that I am the first to light upon an idea which will divide the history of mankind in two. . . . It takes some courage to face that thought."

The Fruits of Materialism

But it took more courage than Nietzsche realized. His writings groaned with the burden: "Since there ceased to be a God, loneliness has become intolerable." But then he bolstered his timidity by reminding himself that after all he was a superman and resolved that he, as "the man who overtops the rest must set to work."[8]

But if there is no God, no design, and nothing for the future but an accidental destiny, what is there to work for? In the dark hours of his anti-theistic reasoning and just a short time before he went insane, Nietzsche could not help asking himself: "How did we come to do that? How did we manage to empty the sea? Who gave us a sponge to wipe out the whole horizon? What were we about when we undid the chain which linked this earth to the sun? . . . Are we not wandering through an endless nothingness? Do we not feel the breath of the void in our faces? Isn't it growing colder? Is not night always coming on, one night after another, more and more?"[9]

---

[7] *Quoted in* "ATHEIST HUMANIST," *by Henri deLubac, p. 26.*
[8] *Quoted in* "ATHEIST HUMANIST," *by Henri deLubac, p. 25.*
[9] *Quoted in* "ATHEIST HUMANIST," *by Henri deLubac, pp. 23-24.*

Secret Weapon of Communism

Such was the final, fearful lamentation of the men who started the chain-reaction of pure materialism.

Now we have reached an interesting point in the history of the United States when the word "Communism" has become universally unpopular. If the label of Communism is placed upon a person or an institution it may bring ruin overnight. The disgraceful conduct of Communist leaders has given their name a deep-dyed stigma in the United States.

Communists without Labels

But how many Americans could recognize a Communist without his label? What does a Communist really believe? Most people identify Communism as "state-ownership of property" or Socialism. It is interesting, however, that the economics of Communism are primarily for propaganda purposes. The idea of sharing the wealth appeals to the masses. However, when the Communists took over in Russia you will recall that the first thing they did was impose upon the Russian people a form of economics which we got rid of back in the feudal days. It is a system where a privileged few dispense the necessities of life to the serfs who work for them and rely upon them for protection and leadership.

But if Communist economics are primarily propaganda, what, then, does the Communist believe?

In the interest of time I have endeavored to reduce the basic belief of these people to four fundamental concepts which turn out to be the basis for their philosophy. These beliefs are the heart and soul of dialectical materialism. They pretend to provide a complete explanation for the whole universe. They provide the reasoning which gives an excuse to the Communist for his revolutionary violence and amoral conduct. They are the things which convert a few intellectual people to this foreign ideology, and they are the things which even make a few wealthy people think that Communism is the last great hope of the modern world. Understanding these beliefs helps to evaluate the actions of the Communists when we sit down with them to discuss world problems.

First Major Premise of Communism

Their first major premise is this: *"Everything in existence came about as a result of ceaseless motion among the forces of nature."* Everything is a product of accumulated accident. There is no design. There is no law. There is no God. There is only force, the force of nature. Force is right, force is good, force is natural.

The idea of "dialectics" as propounded by the Communist intellectual is that "conflict in nature" is the womb of all creation; that out of fierce, writhing forces in the elements we obtained all that now is—stars, solar system, plants, animals and the intelligence of man.

When these dialectical materialists first tried to tell me that everything in the universe was the result of force and accident, I could not help but recall the teachings of my high school chemistry professor who said that the major premise of science is a recognition of the fact that there is order in the universe resulting from intelligent design. He pointed out that the mission of the scientist is to explore and discover the engineering principles followed by the Master Architect so that these can be used as a blessing for mankind. In other words, the very foundation of science is the recognition of an intelligent designer who used principles which we ourselves can discover and use.

The followers of Marx are so desperately anxious to overthrow the recognition of God that they have denied that there is any design in the universe. They refuse to admit that there is order, law, or an intelligent creator behind the phenomena of nature. They say all of these things are the product of accumulated accident. I wonder what my chemistry professor would say to that? These materialists claim to glorify the name of science and to march under its banner, but, in their anxiety to discredit and repudiate God, they have openly denied the very things which science has demonstrated.

Second Major Premise

Now here is their second major premise: *"Human beings are only graduate beasts,"* and therefore human life is no more sacred than that of a centipede, a caterpillar or a pig. The completely reckless disregard for human life is the most striking, single characteristic of "materialism in action." For many Americans, the things which were experienced in the Korean War have brought a rude awakening. It means a big difference when we are dealing with people who look upon all humanity as merely "graduate beasts."

Third Major Premise

The third major premise of Communism is this: *"There is no such thing as innate right or wrong."* As one of their leaders pointedly declared, "To lie, is that wrong? Not for a good cause. To steal, is that wrong? Not for a good cause. To kill, is that wrong? Not for a good cause." We call that pragmatism—that the end justifies the means. The dialectical materialists look upon ethics and morals as superficial and fraudulent. V. I. Lenin declared: "The upbringing of Communist youth must not consist of all sorts of sentimental speeches and precepts." And in the same volume he states that "Morality is that which serves to destroy the old exploiting society. . . . Communist morality is the morality which serves this struggle."[10]

It is highly important to Communist discipline to have every person obey blindly. To obey blindly is considered good and therefore morally right. But a system of morals which

---

[10] *Lenin, V. I.,* "SELECTED WORKS," *Vol. IX, p. 477-478.*

The Naked Communist

controls conduct in terms of right and wrong makes each individual a moral free agent. This, Communism cannot stand.

Fourth Major Premise

The fourth major premise of Communism is *"That all religion must be overthrown because it inhibits the spirit of world revolution."* It was the feeling of Marx, Engels and their fellow travelers that the deep spiritual convictions of the people hindered their acceptance of Communist philosophy and Communist rule. It kept them from capturing the revolutionary spirit. It kept them from lying and stealing and killing when leaders commanded it. As one of their writers declared: "Religion does not fit into a dialectical materialist system of thought. It is the enemy of it. One cannot be a thorough materialist, that is, a dialectical materialist, and have any remnants of religious beliefs."[11] Marx said: "Religion is the opium of the people," and as we have pointed out previously, it became a prime objective of the Communist Manifesto to overthrow "all religions."

The Communist founders were not satisfied to have their disciples merely ignore religion. They felt it was highly essential that religion be methodically replaced with militant atheism.

One of their writers declared: "Atheism is a natural and inseparable part of Marxism . . . consequently, a class-conscious Marxist party must carry on propaganda in favor of atheism."[12] In one of their youth magazines the following instruction appeared: "If a Communist youth believes in God and goes to Church, he fails to fulfill his duties. This means that he has not yet rid himself of a religious superstition and has not yet become a fully conscious person."[13]

The Communists have written volumes against religion,

[11] *Browder, Earl,* "COMMUNISM IN THE UNITED STATES," *p. 339.*
[12] *Yaroslavsky, E.,* "RELIGION IN THE USSR," *p. 53.*
[13] "YOUNG BOLSHEVIK," *5-6, 1946, p. 56.*

Secret Weapon of Communism

but this is sufficient to demonstrate that atheism and the rejection of all religions is a very important part of the Communist program.

Can Communist Beliefs Hurt Us?

So there you have the four major premises of Communism. Some people will say, "Well, if that's what it takes to make a Communist—so what? What they believe cannot hurt me." Such attitudes have practically been our undoing. These beliefs *can* hurt us. For example, let me tell you briefly of an important event which occurred toward the conclusion of World War II.

This incident began in June, 1943, when a young Russian by the name of Igor Gouzenko arrived by plane in Ottawa, Canada. He was immediately assigned to the military attache of the Russian Embassy as a cipher clerk. This was the first time Igor Gouzenko had ever been outside of Russia. He later wrote: "I was surprised during the first days by the complete freedom of the individual which exists in Canada, but which does not exist in Russia."[14]

He observed that even during war time, the people enjoyed comparative freedom, that they were a happy people and that the government served the people rather than vice versa. He vicariously enjoyed their freedom just by watching them. As he himself said: "I saw the evidence of what a free people can do. What the Canadian people have accomplished and are accomplishing here under conditions of complete freedom, the Russian people, under the conditions of the Soviet Regime of violence and suppression of all freedom, cannot accomplish even at the cost of tremendous sacrifices, blood and tears."[15]

He was impressed by the vast quantities of goods that were on sale in the stores and he was amazed to find they could be purchased by anyone. He was impressed by the lack

---

[14] "REPORT OF THE ROYAL COMMISSION," *638*.
[15] "REPORT OF THE ROYAL COMMISSION," *639*.

of fear and the lack of chaos, which the Russian propaganda machine claimed existed. Most impressive of all was the way democracy worked. He said: "The last elections which took place recently in Canada, especially surprised me. In comparison with them, the system of elections in Russia appears as a mockery of the conceptions of free elections."[16]

What Puzzled Gouzenko Most?

But while Igor Gouzenko was working for the military attache of the Soviet Embassy, he noticed something else. He observed that contact was being made with top Canadian scientists and sometimes with important Canadian officials. Often they were actually cooperating in furnishing highly secret Government data to the Communist military agents. Gouzenko was further puzzled by the fact that he knew these important officials and scientists were aware that the ultimate aim of the Communists was a world-wide revolution which would destroy the Canadian Government as well as all others.

After watching these developments for a period of two years, Igor Gouzenko decided that he would warn the Canadian people of what was happening. Already he had made up his mind that he would never go back to Russia and raise his own child the way he had been raised. He told his wife that he intended to leave the Russian Embassy and warn the Canadian Government of the espionage network in its midst.

To prove his story he secreted a lot of espionage documents in his clothing and then went to the Canadian officials. He thought, of course, that he would be welcomed with open arms—that the Canadians would be delighted to have the inside story. But as he watched the expressionless face of the first person he contacted, Gouzenko realized he had exposed himself to great danger. *The man did not believe him!* Only at the last moment, when Gouzenko was actually in danger of being recaptured by the Russian N.K.V.D. did it finally dawn

---

[16] "REPORT OF THE ROYAL COMMISSION," *p. 639.*

on some of the officials that perhaps this Soviet code clerk's story might be true. He was therefore immediately taken into protective custody so he could tell his story to the world.

Treason in High Places

The Canadians wondered if the people named by Gouzenko actually would collaborate with a potential enemy. The list included such men as Dr. Raymond Boyer, wealthy faculty member of McGill University, who was a senior supervisor in the National Research Council and co-inventor of the explosive RDX in World War II; Eric Adams, graduate of McGill and Harvard, serving in a top position in the Industrial Development Bank; Israel Halperin, professor of mathematics at Queen's University in Ontario and doing highly technical research for the Directorate of Artillery; David Gordon Lunin, editor of *Canadian Affairs;* Dr. David Shugar, employed by Research Enterprises Limited, doing advanced research on radar; Harold Gerson, holding a top administrative position in the Allied War Supply; F. W. Poland, an officer in the Directorate of Intelligence of the Royal Canadian Air Force; and there was Kathleen Mary Willsher, who held a confidential position with the High Commissioner of the United Kingdom in Canada.

These and other persons on the list were promptly arrested and investigated by a Royal Canadian Commission. This Commission later reported: "Perhaps the most startling single aspect of the entire fifth column network is the uncanny success with which the Soviet Agents were able to find Canadians who were willing to betray their country and to supply to agents of a foreign power secret information to which they had access—in spite of oaths of allegiance, oaths of office, and oaths of secrecy which they had taken;"[17]

What the Royal Commission wanted to know was why

---

[17] "REPORT OF THE ROYAL COMMISSION," *p. 56.*

these high Canadian officials would deliberately turn against the interest of their native land. They asked these people if they had been bribed and one of them replied, "If they had offered me money, I would have been insulted."

When the Commission inquired into the background of these people, they found they were casualties in the ideological war which is being waged between the materialists and the free world. These people had been raised in freedom. They had gone to Canadian and American schools, yet, when asked why they collaborated with the Soviet Agents, one of them made a typical reply: "I thought I was helping humanity."

How were these men and women, raised in a free world, converted by Communist agents to believe that if they collaborated they would be helping humanity? Supposing you were a scientist and one of these agents came to you. How would you react? Supposing he said, "My friend, you know that there is no divine intelligence guiding the human race; you know there is no Providential destiny for humanity; you know that if superior intelligences like yourself do not help us gain control of the human race it will destroy itself." Can you even imagine yourself giving this reply: "I must confess that, in my heart of hearts, I do not believe that there is any God or divine intelligence guiding the human race. Therefore, I suppose I should feel it my duty as one of the superior intelligences of my generation—and for the sake of humanity—to collaborate with your movement which is destined to take over and save the race from itself."

This was not only typical of the statements which many of the Soviet-converted Canadians admitted making, but they verified their complete devotion to such ideas by deliberately engaging in subversive activities against their own country.

The Secret Weapon of Communism

Now what do we deduct from this? Simply that these people were home-grown materialists! As Igor Gouzenko pointed out, there is a defect in your culture when your own people can grow up in your midst without gaining on appreciation of the difference between freedom and slavery, between idealism and atheism, between faith and doubt, or between order and chaos.

Somehow we failed to provide these people with the necessary ammunition to protect them in that critical moment when they were contacted by the agents of a foreign ideology. And we should be quick to recognize that if *our* culture and system of education is producing materialists, then this is the greatest secret weapon the Communists possess!

This means that we can spend two billion dollars developing the atomic bomb and the Communists can sit back and wait until we have succeeded. Then, they can drain off the information from some of our top security personnel. In fact, that is exactly what they did.

The greatest mistake that is being made in the free world today is the fact that we are mixing iron and clay. We are fighting for freedom but allowing some of our boys and girls to grow up believing in things which turn out to be basic Communistic concepts. Materialism is not Americanism but Communism. Every time we produce a boy or girl who is trained to believe that the universe is the product of accumulated accident, that human beings are only graduate beasts, that there is no such thing as innate right or wrong or that deep spiritual convictions are old-fashioned and unnecessary, then we have caused a casualty among our own ranks in the field of ideological warfare.

Without his ever knowing it, a young American is thereby trained to be a potential Red ally. This is indeed the great secret weapon of Communism.

Home-Made Materialism

Now where does an American boy or girl pick up the teachings of materialism? I think I can answer part of that question from a personal experience in an American institution of learning.

I was in my second year—a sophomore—and was taking my first course in philosophy. One morning the Professor said: "Now you young people are sufficiently mature so that your minds should be cleansed from the barnacles of superstition which probably accumulated during your youth. When you were children you were told about Santa Claus. Now you know the truth about Santa Claus. When you were children you were told about the stork. Now you know the truth about that." He then stated that he was about to clarify our thinking in another field which had been cluttered up with childhood fairy tales. "Today," he said, "I will tell you where the ideas about God came from and also about religion." All of us sat back to absorb the gems of knowledge we were about to receive.

"Now in the beginning," said the professor, "men worshipped things which they created with their own hands. It was called idolatry. Later, men imagined that there were a great many unseen gods—a god of war, a god of love, a god of rain, etc., and all these gods required sacrifices in order to keep them happy. Otherwise they showed forth their wrath. Therefore they were frequently called gods of vengeance."

The professor then stated that the Bible is an excellent history of the evolution of religion. He said that it is clear from Bible study that the practice of idolatry prevailed among ancient peoples and that the Hebrews finally rose above it to worship Jehovah as a God of Vengeance. He said the people of Israel made sacrifices to Jehovah to keep him happy.

"Then," he said, "Jesus came along and declared that God was a God of Love possessing the attributes of all the Platonic ultimates. Jesus taught that God was kind, just and forgiving. He taught the higher concepts of the Beatitudes, the Sermon on the Mount, and the Golden Rule."

"Now," he continued, "This is the God men worship today. A God of Love as taught by Jesus. And it is good to go to church and worship this concept of God because it elevates the mind and stimulates the higher senses."

Secret Weapon of Communism

"But," he continued emphatically, "I want you young people to remember this: The idea of God is exactly like other human creations—like a great symphony someone has written, or a great poem; you don't have to fear God, *because we made him up!*"

The professor finished by saying, "There is nothing watching over you—answering your prayers, or directing the human race toward some divine destiny. You young people are on your own."

As the lecture concluded, I looked around at my fellow classmates. On the faces of some there seemed to be an expression of considerable relief. It was as though they were saying "Well, what do you know? Nobody's watching me after all! So that's what God is—something we made up—like a great symphony. . . ."

Conversation between a Student and a Professor

After the class I went to the professor and said, "Doctor, have you ever had an opportunity to read the Old Testament?"

"Well," chuckled the professor, "only parts of it. I never had time to read all of it. But I studied the history and philosophy of the Bible under a well known authority."

The following conversation then took place between the student and the professor. The student told the professor that when he read the Bible he did not find the story in it which the professor said was there. The professor looked puzzled, "What do you mean? What story isn't there?"

"Well," said the student, "the story that religion started out as idolatry, evolved to the worshiping of a God of Vengeance, and then culminated in the worshiping of a God of Love—as taught by Jesus."

"Tell me," asked the professor, "what did *you* find in the Bible?"

The student said that as far as he was able to determine

The Naked Communist

the nature and identity of God had been taught to men from the very beginning. He said he thought the Bible taught that God had raised up prophets and special witnesses from earliest times and these were each given a scientific experience so that they would know for themselves the nature of God and be able to teach it to the people.

Then he continued, "The second thing I understood the Bible taught is that in the beginning God revealed a pattern for happy living which we call religion. He taught us not to steal, not to lie, not to cheat, to serve our fellow men, to remain morally clean.

"Finally," he concluded, "I thought the Bible said idolatry and heathen religious practices were set up to compete with revealed religion because a large percentage of the people refused to subscribe to the things God had revealed. I thought it said manmade religion came long after God had revealed His will to man and that idolatry was a substitute and degenerate form of worship sponsored by men who reveled in the violation of God's commandments."

The professor looked down at his desk for a moment and then said: "I am afraid you are a little naive. Religion was not revealed, it evolved. Certainly you will have to admit that Jehovah was a typical 'God of Vengeance' who made the people offer sacrifices to keep him happy."

"That is another thing," the student replied. "The Bible does not say that the sacrifices in the Old Testament were to make God happy. It says that they were for the benefit of the people—a teaching device. Or, as Paul says, they were a 'school master.' It says that God is the same yesterday, today and forever, and that he was as much a God of Love in the Old Testament as he was in the New Testament."

"I'm afraid I will have to challenge that," said the professor. "I think every authority would have to agree that sacrifices in the Old Testament were simply to make Jehovah happy."

The student asked, "Would you like to hear what Jehovah himself said about sacrifices, and what they represented in the Old Testament?" The professor agreed, so a copy of the

Secret Weapon of Communism

Bible was secured from the library. It was opened to the first chapter of Isaiah and the professor and student read the following verses together.

The Bible Provides Its Own Rebuttal

"To what purpose is the multitude of your sacrifices unto me? saith the Lord: I am full of the burnt offerings of rams, and the fat of fed beasts; I delight not in the blood of bullocks or of lambs, or of he goats. . . . Bring me no more *vain* oblations. . . . ('If these sacrifices were not successful in making better people then they apparently were in vain,' commented the student.) When ye spread forth your hands, I will hide mine eyes from you: yea, when you make your many prayers I will not hear: your hands are full of blood!"

Then the student asked the professor if he thought the next two or three verses reflected the personality of a so-called God of Vengeance or a God of Love:

"Wash you, make you clean; put away the evil of your doing from before mine eyes! Cease to do evil; learn to do well; seek judgment, relieve the oppressed, judge the fatherless, plead for the widow. Come now, and let us reason together, saith the Lord: though your sins be as scarlet, they shall be as white as snow; though they be red like crimson, they shall be as wool, If ye are willing and obedient, ye shall eat the good of the land."[18]

The professor was silent for a moment, and so the sophomore gained the courage to ask the final, crucial question. "Professor, am I wrong in concluding that these passages reflect the same spirit as the Beatitudes, the Sermon on the Mount and the Golden Rule? Am I wrong in concluding that God has always been a God of Love?"

The professor took the Bible, placed a card in the first

---

[18] *Isaiah 1:11-19.*

chapter of Isaiah and said, "Have the librarian transfer this Book to me."

The student appreciated his professor's willingness to re-evaluate what he had been teaching. And he also appreciated something else—a mother and father, Sunday School teachers and others who had encouraged him to get acquainted with the Bible. They did not tell him what he had to believe out of the Bible; they just wanted him to get acquainted with it. He was glad that he had read it sufficiently so that when someone misrepresented what it said he was able to draw his own conclusions.

Sometimes Students Puzzle Parents

Now students who come home from a lecture such as the one I have just described are frequently an enigma to their parents. A boy may come home from a philosophy class, sit down to dinner with his family and say, "Dad, are we monoists or dualists?" His father is likely to look quizzically at the boy and say, "Son, eat your soup."

Frequently parents are unaware that their son or daughter may be coming to grips with important philosophical problems. Of course, some parents are deeply confused themselves about the fundamental values of life and therefore they find it difficult to give much assistance to their children when they first meet the challenge of materialism.

I think my professor was sincere. He was teaching what he had been taught. He was teaching materialism because he had come to believe it was true. I am sure he would have been shocked if someone had told him that in the process of teaching materialism he was also laying the foundation for one of the most important concepts in Communism. If George Washington had been sitting in that class he would have said, "Professor, I think you are wrong." Jefferson would have said, "You are wrong." And Lincoln would have said, "You are

Secret Weapon of Communism

wrong." Those men established this country on the premise
that there is a Divine Intelligence guiding human destiny, a
God in whom we can trust. They believed the Bible and the
testimony of the witnesses who said that if we follow the
principles taught by the prophets, we would find happiness in
them. The founding fathers had such great confidence in
the way of life described in the scriptures that they built the
framework of the American Government and the principles
for happy living which it guarantees, on the precepts and
teachings of the Bible.

What About Atomic-Bomb Security?

The disclosures of Igor Gouzenko in the Canadian spy
case taught us that freedom is not insured by atomic bombs
alone. As long as we are teaching materialism to our boys
and girls we stand in danger of having them grow up to be
vulnerable targets in the East-West war of ideologies.

I have already quoted to you a statement by the former
Commissioner of Education in the Soviet Union indicating that
they despise Christian principles because "Christian love is an
obstacle to the development of the revolution." In fact the
Communist leaders have indicated time and again that our
greatest strength in resisting their efforts to conquer our
minds with dialectical materialism is our belief and understanding of the Judaic-Christian code.

About three years ago I was invited to speak to a convention on the West Coast. During the discussion it was pointed
out that one of the things which the followers of Marx despise
about the American culture is the Judaic-Christian code. So
I asked the members of the convention, "What is this thing
we have which frightens Communists; someone tell us what
the Judaic-Christian code contains." There was a long pause.
No one wanted to suggest a definition for this part of America's strength. Finally an elderly gentleman in the back of the

auditorium raised his hand, "Well," he said, "I'm not sure I know what the Judaic-Christian code is, but I do know this— if they're scared of it, I'm for it!"

Would the Ten Commandments
Frighten a Communist?

In this brief discussion there is not sufficient time to treat the entire Judaic-Christian code, but perhaps we can cover part of it. The Judaic code, for example, is built primarily around the Ten Commandments. Let us discuss each one of them briefly and see if we can discover what there is about them that would frighten a Communist.

In the first commandment God simply asks mankind to recognize Him as the Creator and Master Architect of the universe. He wants us to understand that the remarkable planet on which we live is not the result of accumulated accident. The pleasant environment which we enjoy is not the product of fortuitous happenstance. Nor is it the result of ceaseless motion among the forces of nature. He wants us to know that all of this is a product of design and careful engineering; that it is built on a system of law and order; that He rules in the heavens and that all things are moving toward purposeful goals.

In the second commandment God requires that we shall not create or worship false gods. When He has revealed his identity and purposes to mankind these teachings are not to be perverted, distorted, or changed. As we have already mentioned, the dialectical materialists not only tried to destroy the worship of the Almighty, but they replaced the one true God with a false god. As one of them said, "The turning point of history will be when man becomes aware that the only god of man is man himself."[19] The history of the dialectical materi-

---

[19] "ATHEIST HUMANISM," *Henri deLubac, p. 20.*

Secret Weapon of Communism

alists will reveal that they follow the ancient pagan practice of worshiping one another.

Who Has Seen God?

Now, the Communist says, "If there is a God, show him to me! Have *you* seen God? Has your brother, your sister?" It is interesting to find that some of the early Communist leaders actually went forth in search of God, but their biographies reveal that they went forth with a blowtorch in one hand and a sledge hammer in the other. They were men who defied the Almighty to keep himself hidden from their all-searching scrutiny; and when they failed in their search, they returned savagely angry, convinced that since they did not find God, it proved that there just was not any God to find.

To all of this the Bible gives an answer. It may be found in the 19th chapter of Exodus. There God points out to Moses that it is not difficult for him to appear before men but it is difficult for men to be able to stand it. He points out that only certain ones have been sufficiently prepared so that He can bring them into His presence. He told Moses that if men were not adequately prepared the impact of the experience would destroy them. Moses attempted to prepare the people of Israel so they could enjoy the great scientific experience which he had already received, but their preparation was insufficient. The Lord said "Go down. Charge the people lest they break through unto the Lord to gaze and many of them perish."[20]

Later on, however, some were actually allowed to ascend Mount Sinai and gaze. In fact, the Lord authorized Moses to bring up Aaron, Nadab, Abihu, and seventy of the Elders of Israel to behold the glory of his person. These 73 men were not only allowed to enjoy this remarkable experience, but there is a record of what they saw.[21]

---

[20] *Exodus, 19:21.*
[21] *Exodus 24:9-10.*

370   From generation to generation similar witnesses have been raised up. In fact the Apostle John predicted that eventually every man who ever lived will see his Creator and stand in his presence to be judged by Him.[22]

Now you can see that the first two commandments are a direct contradiction of the first major premise of Communism. The Communist says that the universe is a product of chaos and accident. In the Judaic code God taught that it is a product of careful design; that He is the designer, and He should be acknowledged as such; that we should not attribute these achievements to false forces or false gods.

How Important Is an Oath?

The third commandment says, "Thou shalt not take the name of the Lord thy God in vain." Many people have thought that this merely means that the name of God should not be used in profanity—but this is not what frightens the materialist. There is a far deeper meaning in this commandment. For example, the sanctity of the judicial oath of the United States of America is circumscribed by this third commandment in the Judaic code.

When a man stands in a court room or appears before a Congressional committee and says: "I swear to tell the truth, the whole truth, and nothing but the truth, so help me God," he is under the injunction of the Almighty that the name of God is not to be taken in vain. The American founding fathers believed that we should hold these oaths and covenants sacred and conscientiously fulfill them or the judgment of the Almighty would hold us responsible. Honoring every oath taken in the name of God is a source of great strength to the American pattern of free government and Communists have learned that if they take this oath in vain there is a serious

---

[22] *Revelation 20:12.*

Secret Weapon of Communism

penalty attached to it for "perjury." However, even among loyal Americans I fear the name of God is taken in vain far too often. I believe—and I feel sure you would agree—that if each man honored every sacred promise made in the name of Deity our courts would provide a hundred times more justice, our business life would be a great deal more honest and the administration of public affairs would be more efficient.

The Fourth Commandment

The fourth commandment says we shall perform all necessary labors during six days of the week, but the seventh shall be set aside for attending Church, serving our fellow men in need, and studying the word of God. These are the things which make the Sabbath Day a holy day. We may not appreciate it, but the followers of Marx know that it is the institution of Sabbath-Day-worship which keeps the Hebrew and Christian cultures healthy. Therefore, one of the first things the Marxian materialists did when they came into power was to abolish the observance of the Sabbath Day.

But the effectiveness of the Sabbath can also be lost by just simply changing it from a holy day to a holiday.

By adopting the ancient heathen practice of using the Sabbath exclusively for hunting, fishing, feasting, and entertaining we completely nullify its design and purpose.

The Lord might well say, "I want you to remember this, in the world today I have old people, I have sick people, I have lonely people and poor people. My whole system depends upon your ministering to one another and inasmuch as you do it unto the least of these you do it unto me. This is my method, this is my pattern, this is my program. I could send angels, but I do not. I send you!"

This should always be a part of the American way of life, but frequently we are too busy. We forget the sick and fail to visit our neighbors. We only go to the hospital when it is the boss's wife who is sick. To that extent the American way of life is destroyed, because it ignores the pattern for happy living on which the American social order was originally built.

A Vacuum in the Training of Youth

And because of our failure to reserve any part of the Sabbath to study the word of God, we are rapidly becoming a nation of ignorant Christians. We know so little about the evidence which has been recorded from generation to generation that many have no real basis for their beliefs. Somebody picks up a Bible, holds it aloft and says, "Fairy tales!" Then we are surprised when some of our young people who know very little about the Bible say, "Oh, is that so! Three bears stuff, eh?" And the man says, "Sure, something people made up."

Or a boy who has been raised in a Christian home but is entirely unfamiliar with the proof found in the Bible comes back from school some evening completely confused. At family devotions his father asks him to say grace and he says, "No, Dad, I don't want to." Later his father talks to him and says, "Son, what's the matter? What's happened?" And the boy may reply, "Well, Dad, I don't like to pray to something we made up—something like a piece of music or a poem. I just found out that we made God up."

It is really quite a simple thing to destroy the beliefs of a boy or girl when they are not supported by a knowledge of the evidence which proves the validity of such beliefs.

Are Elderly People Important?

The fifth commandment was designed by God to sustain the integrity of the family. In it the Lord commanded: "Honor thy father and thy mother."

Secret Weapon of Communism

Life is a strange combination of circumstances. When children are tiny, helpless and dependent, their parents are in a position to give them love or abuse, nourishment or neglect, depending upon their inclinations. In later years those same parents may feel the ravages of time and become as little children themselves. Then it is their offspring who are in a position to love or neglect, depending upon *their* inclinations.

So, God was wise. He counseled children to honor their parents and parents to honor their children. Each in their time are dependent upon the other.

Strong family solidarity is part of our religious strength and part of our national strength, but it is despised by the materialist. Marx and Engels wrote in their *Manifesto* that they stood for "the abolition of the family." Immediately after the revolution, Lenin attempted to wipe out the family pattern of life, but social disease and social disorder forced the regime to reverse itself.

What About Communist Purges?

The sixth commandment says, "Thou shalt not kill." The Mosaic code made the sanctity of human life extremely important. That is why a person who believes and practices the Judaic-Christian code does not make a good Communist. He will not kill on command. He cannot believe that a cause is just which depends upon blood purges, concentration camps, and cruel exploitation of human life for its existence.

This explains why we have such statements as this from Joseph Stalin: "Have we suppressed the reactionary clergy? Yes, we have. The unfortunate thing is that it has not been completely liquidated. Anti-religious propaganda is a means by which the complete liquidation of the reactionary clergy must be brought about. Cases occur when certain members of the party hamper the complete development of anti-religious propaganda. If such members are expelled it is a good thing because there is no room for such Communists in the ranks of the party."[23]

Significance of Marital Integrity

The seventh commandment says, "Thou shall not commit adultery." Fundamentally the strength of the American home is rooted in an exchange of confidence between a mother and father, between parents and children. God might well say to us. "I give you nothing except that which is for your ultimate happiness. My commandments are not to take away happiness but to preserve it. I want you to be able to be honest with each other in your marriage covenants. If you want a happy family, if you want to share complete confidence with your mate, then thou shalt not commit adultery."

And moral integrity does not *begin* with marriage. It finds its strength in careful self-discipline over the years. When two young people come to the marriage altar, I do not personally know of any greater insurance for a life of happiness and trust than for each of them to be able to say in their hearts as they kneel together, "Even before I knew you I honored you and kept myself circumspect for you." As a law enforcement officer I learned that when young people approach marriage with this spirit of devotion and personal discipline, then purity, peace and happy families are usually the result.

The Thief and the Character Assassin

The eighth commandment says, "Thou shalt not steal." The Communist commandment says, "Thou shalt not get *caught* stealing."

The ninth commandment says, "Thou shalt not bear false witness." Igor Gouzenko stated that the national pastime in his native land is tearing down the man just above you so you

---

[23] *Stalin, Joseph, "*LENINISM*," Vol. I, p. 387.*

can take his place after he is discredited and gone. In our country we have a few people like that but it is not the American Way. One of the favorite Communist tricks is character assassination. American boys and girls should be taught that when they work for a man they should try and be loyal to him. Surely he is just a human being and he will have his faults, but he should be supported in every good thing he is trying to do. This is what builds communities. It builds industry, it builds schools. It builds a nation.

The Sanctity of Work

Then last of all we come to the tenth commandment which says we should gain wealth through our own industry. If we see a house, a car, or something else which another man owns, we are not supposed to sit down and try to figure out how we can cheat him out of them. That is what God calls, "Coveting our neighbor's goods." Instead, we should go out and work for the things we desire.

To desire good things and work for them is not a sin, but to acquire them by cheating or exhorting them from a neighbor is. While God says to respect the property of others, the materialists have taught for over a century that the object of human existence is the acquisition of loot and power; that the strong man should never be content, never be satisfied; whatever good thing the other man has he should want it and strive to obtain it. The gaining of spoils, the accumulation of others' wealth and the concentration of power has been their constant goal.

The Christian Code

Last of all may I say just a few words about the Christian Code. Here are additional principles which—if understood and practiced—prevent a person from being a good Communist. As I go down the list see if you can determine why the former Soviet Commissioner of Education would say, "We hate Christians and Christianity."

Here are a number of concepts typical of the teachings of Jesus:

DO UNTO OTHERS AS YOU WOULD HAVE THEM DO UNTO YOU.[24]

BLESSED ARE THE PEACEMAKERS.[25]

IT IS BETTER TO GIVE THAN TO RECEIVE.[26]

DO NOT HATE YOUR ENEMIES BUT DO GOOD UNTO THEM.[27]

BE AS HUMBLE AND TEACHABLE AS A LITTLE CHILD.[28]

BE WISE, AGGRESSIVE AND ALERT TO PROMOTE GOOD AND PRESERVE PEACE.[29]

PERFECT YOURSELF BY OVERCOMING PERSONAL WEAK-NESSES.[30]

FOLLOW THE COMMANDMENTS OF GOD TO INCREASE THE VALUE OF YOUR LIFE AND BLOT OUT THE SCARS OF PAST MISTAKES.[31]

THE GREATEST HAPPINESS COMES THROUGH THE GREATEST SERVICE.[32]

DO GOOD SECRETLY AND GOD—WHO SEETH IN SECRET—WILL REWARD YOU OPENLY.[33]

Christianity also teaches that we are responsible to God for our daily conduct, even for our thoughts.[34] It also teaches the reality of human immortality and the resurrection. We are given the scientific declaration of Paul, Peter, Mary Mag-

---

[24] *Matthew 7:12.*
[25] *Matthew 5:9.*
[26] *Acts 20:35.*
[27] *Matthew 5:44.*
[28] *Matthew 18:4.*
[29] *Matthew 10:16.*
[30] *Matthew 5:48.*
[31] *Luke 24:47; Acts 2:38.*
[32] *Luke 10:29-37.*
[33] *Matthew 6:4.*
[34] *Galatians 6:7; Matthew 5:28.*

Secret Weapon of Communism

dalene, the eleven Apostles and five-hundred members of the **377**
Church who saw the resurrected Christ. It is good to know
that after we pass from this life we too will eventually receive
a perfected physical embodiment.

In his teachings Jesus affirmed what the prophets had
taught—that beyond this life we will launch forward into an-
another great pattern of existence. He taught that our next
estate has been carefully engineered and will allow us a great
variety of new experiences as we pass upward along the endless corridors of the future.

Like the Judaic Code these Christian principles give great
strength to any free people. It is not difficult to understand
why Communists seek to discredit these concepts. On the
other hand, if we teach our children that there is no God, that
men are only graduate beasts, that the end justifies the means,
and that religious convictions are not scientific, then we will
hear a resounding "Amen" from across the ocean.

A New Dynamic Trend in Education

In closing let me say that I have never had a more thrilling experience than that which has come to me during the
past year-and-a-half while serving on the faculty of Brigham
Young University. I have been permitted to participate in
a pattern of education where several thousand students are
being taught citizenship along with their scholarship; where
science, philosophy, and religion all find their proper places
in the personalities of these boys and girls. I get a great satisfaction watching these young people crossing the campus,
loaded down with their textbooks—chemistry, physics, fine
art, geology, sociology, history, economics, political science—
and mixed in among those textbooks you will generally find
a copy of the Bible. A great variety of religious subjects is
offered to the student and he may chose those in which he
has the most interest.

Across the country many universities are building chapels

and emphasizing religious participation. They are doing it because there is an increased appreciation that this is a most important part of the American ideal and the source for much of our strength.

Each Tuesday on the BYU campus approximately 5,000 students voluntarily attend the weekly devotional where they have a chance to catch the inspiration of some of the finest religious leaders in the nation.

If the challenge to our youth today is a war of ideologies, then it is time for us to take the offensive. We should not sit back and wait for our boys and girls to be indoctrinated with materialistic dogma and thereby make themselves vulnerable to a Communist conversion when they are approached by the agents of force and fear who come from across the sea. For two generations an important phase of American life has been disintegrating. As parents and teachers we need to recognize that if this pillar of our culture collapses our own children will be the casualties. This disintegration must stop. George Washington knew what makes us strong; Jefferson knew, Lincoln knew: "This nation, under God, cannot fail!"

Of course we must do more than merely teach correct principles—certainly we must practice them. I therefore close with the words of Francis Bacon who said: "It is not what you eat, but what you *digest* that makes you strong. It is not what you earn, but what you *save* that makes you rich. It is not what you preach, but what you *practice* that makes you a Christian!"

Bibliography

Adler, M., "WHAT MAN HAS MADE OF MAN," Longmans Green, N. Y., 1934.

Adoratsky, V., "DIALECTICAL MATERIALISM," M. Lawrence, London, 1934.

Aveling, E., "THE STUDENT'S MARX," Charles Scribner's Sons, N. Y., 1902.

Basseches, N., "STALIN," E. P. Dutton Co., N. Y., 1952.

Barbusse, H., "STALIN," John Lane Co., London, 1935.

Beer, M., "THE LIFE AND TEACHINGS OF MARX," Parsons Co., London, 1921.

Belloc, H., "THE RESTORATION OF PROPERTY," Sheed and Ward, N. Y., 1936.

Belyaev, M., "EVOLUTION," State Pub. House, Moscow, 1934.

Bentley, Elizabeth, "OUT OF BONDAGE," The Devin-Adair Company, New York, 1951.

Berdyaev, N., "THE RUSSIAN REVOLUTION," Sheed and Ward, N. Y., 1933.

Bivort, J., "COMMUNISM AND ANTI-RELIGION," Burns, Oates & Washbourne, London, 1938.

Blodgett, Ralph H., "COMPARATIVE ECONOMIC SYSTEMS," MacMillan Co., New York, 1949.

Bober. M., "KARL MARX'S INTERPRETATION OF HISTORY," Harvard University Press, Cambridge, 1927.

Bohm-Bawerk, E., "KARL MARX AND THE CLOSE OF HIS SYSTEM," T. Union Co., London, 1898.

Boudin, L., "THE THEORETICAL SYSTEM OF KARL MARX," Charles H. Kerr Co., Chicago, 1907.

Brameld, T., "A PHILOSOPHIC APPROACH TO COMMUNISM," University of Chicago Press, Chicago, 1933.

Briefs, G., "THE PROLETARIAT," McGraw-Hill, N. Y., 1938.

Browder, E., "WHAT IS COMMUNISM?" Workers Library Publ., N. Y., 1936.

Bukharin, N., "THE A B C OF COMMUNISM," Communist Party Press, London, 1922.

Bukharin, N., "HISTORICAL MATERIALISM," International Publishers, N. Y., 1925.

Burnham, James, "THE WEB OF SUBVERSION," John Day Co., N. Y., 1954.

Burns, E., "A HANDBOOK OF MARXISM," Gollancz, London, 1935.

Byrnes, James F., "SPEAKING FRANKLY," Harpers, New York, 1947.

Carr, E., "KARL MARX," Dent & Sons, London, 1934.

Bibliography

380

Carr, E., "MICHAEL BAKUNIN," *Macmillan Co., London, 1937.*

Chamberlain, "THE RUSSIAN REVOLUTION," *Macmillan Co., N. Y., 1935.*

Chamberlain, "SOVIET RUSSIA," *Little, Brown & Co., Boston, 1935.*

Chambers, Whittaker, "WITNESS," *Random House, New York, 1952.*

Chang, S., "THE MARXIAN THEORY OF THE STATE," *University of Pennsylvania Press, Philadelphia, 1931.*

Cole, G., "WHAT MARX REALLY MEANS," *Alfred A. Knopf, N. Y., 1934.*

"CONSTITUTION OF THE U.S.S.R.," *International Publishers, N. Y., 1936.*

Conze, E., "DIALECTICAL MATERIALISM," *N.C.L.C. Society, London, 1936.*

Cooper, R., "THE LOGICAL INFLUENCE OF HEGEL ON MARX," *Washington University Press, Seattle, 1925.*

Croce, B., "HISTORICAL MATERIALISM AND THE ECONOMICS OF MARX," *Macmillan, N. Y., 1914.*

Dobb, M., "ON MARXISM TODAY," *Hogarth Press, London, 1932.*

Eastman, M., "MARX, LENIN, AND THE SCIENCE OF REVOLUTION," *Allen and Unwin, London, 1926.*

Eddy, G., "THE MEANING OF MARX (A SYMPOSIUM)," *Farrar and Rinehart, N. Y., 1934.*

Ellwood, C., "MARX'S ECONOMIC DETERMINISM IN THE LIGHT OF MODERN PSYCHOLOGY," *American Journal of Sociology, Vol. XVII, 1911, pp. 35-46.*

Engels, F., "MARX-ENGELS, HISTORISCH-KRITISCHE GESAMTAUSGABE," *edited by D. Rjazanov. 9 Vols. Frankfurt, 1927-1932.*

Engels, F., "MARX-ENGELS: SELECTED CORRESPONDENCE," *M. Lawrence, London, 1934.*

Engels, F., "LUDWIG FEUERBACH," *International Publishers, N. Y., 1934.*

Engels, F., "HERR DUHRING'S REVOLUTION IN SCIENCE (ANTI-DUHRING)," *International Publishers, N. Y., 1935.*

Engels, F., "SOCIALISM: UTOPIAN AND SCIENTIFIC," *International Publishers, N. Y., 1935.*

Engels, F., "ON 'CAPITAL'," *International Publishers, N. Y., 1937.*

Engels, F., "DIE HEILIGE FAMILIE," *Rüten, Frankfurt, 1845.*

Engels, F., "THE ORIGIN OF THE FAMILY, PRIVATE PROPERTY AND THE STATE," *Charles H. Kerr Co., Chicago, 1902.*

Foster, William Z., "TOWARD SOVIET AMERICA," *International Publishers, New York, 1932.*

Fox, R., "LENIN," *Gollancz, London, 1933.*

Freehof, S., "MARX, FREUD AND EINSTEIN," *Argus Co., Chicago, 1933.*

Goldendach, D., "KARL MARX: MAN AND THINKER," *International Publishers, N. Y., 1927.*

Goldendach, D., "KARL MARX AND FRIEDRICH ENGELS," *International Publishers, N. Y., 1927.*

Graham, S., "STALIN," *E. Benn Co., London, 1931.*

Gurian, W., "BOLSHEVISM: ITS THEORY AND PRACTICE," *Sheed and Ward, London, 1932.*

Gurian, W., "THE FUTURE OF BOLSHEVISM," *Sheed and Ward, N. Y., 1936.*

Gurian, W., "THE RISE AND DECLINE OF MARXISM," *Burns, Oates & Washbourne, London, 1938.*

Bibliography

Halm, George N., "ECONOMIC SYSTEMS," Rinehart and Co., N. Y., 1951.

Hanschell, H., "'HISTORY AND CLASS WAR,' ARENA," Dec., 1937. pp. 187-194.

Harper, S., "THE GOVERNMENT OF THE SOVIET UNION," Van Nostrand Co., N. Y., 1938.

Hawkins, D., "'DIALECTICAL MATERIALISM,' ARENA," Dec. 1937, pp. 167-175.

Hearnshaw, F., "A SURVEY OF SOCIALISM," Macmillan, London, 1929.

Hecker, J., "RELIGION UNDER THE SOVIETS," Vanguard Press, N. Y., 1927.

Hecker, J., "THE COMMUNIST ANSWER TO THE WORLD'S NEEDS," Chapman and Hall, London, 1935.

Hecker, J., "COMMUNISM AND RELIGION," Chapman and Hall, London, 1933.

Herbigny, M., "MILITANT ATHEISM," Society for the Promotion of Christian Knowledge, London, 1934.

Hill-Mudie, "THE LETTERS OF LENIN," Chapman and Hall, London, 1937.

Hook, S., "'FROM HEGEL TO MARX,' MODERN QUARTERLY," Vol. VI, 1932.

Hook, S., "'FROM HEGEL TO MARX,' DIALECTICAL MATERIALISM,' JOURNAL OF PHILOSOPHY," Vol. XXV, 1928.

Hook, S., "TOWARDS AN UNDERSTANDING OF KARL MARX," John Day Co., N. Y., 1933.

Hyma, A., "CHRISTIANITY, CAPITALISM AND COMMUNISM," (publ. by author), Ann Arbor, 1938.

Jackson, T., "DIALECTICS: THE LOGIC OF MARXISM," M. Lawrence Co., London, 1936.

Jordan, George Racey, "FROM MAJOR JORDAN'S DIARIES," Harcourt, Brace and Co., N. Y., 1952.

Joseph, H., "THE LABOUR THEORY OF VALUE IN KARL MARX," Oxford University Press, London, 1923.

Kautsky, K., "ETHICS AND THE MATERIALIST CONCEPTION OF HISTORY," Charles H. Kerr, Chicago, 1907.

Kautsky, K., "THE ECONOMIC DOCTRINES OF KARL MARX," Black Co., London, 1925.

Kologrivof, I., "GOD, MAN AND THE UNIVERSE," Coldwell Co., London, 1937.

Krivitsky, W. G., "IN STALIN'S SECRET SERVICE," Harper Brothers, N. Y., 1939.

La Pira, Giorgio, "THE PHILOSOPHY OF COMMUNISM," Fordham University Press, N. Y., 1952.

Laski, H., "COMMUNISM," T. Butterworth Co., London, 1935.

Laski, H., "KARL MARX," League for Industrial Democracy, N. Y., 1933.

Lenin, V., "MATERIALISM AND EMPIRIO - CRITICISM," International Publishers, N. Y., 1927.

Lenin, V., "THE FOUNDATION OF THE COMMUNIST INTERNATIONAL," International Publishers, N. Y., 1934.

Lenin, V., "THE DECEPTION OF THE PEOPLE," M. Lawrence, London, 1935.

Lenin, V., "THE PROLETARIAN REVOLUTION AND THE RENEGADE KAUTSKY," International Publishers, N. Y., 1934.

Lenin, V., "THE TEACHINGS OF KARL MARX," International Publishers, N. Y., 1930.

Lenin, V., "TWO TACTICS OF SOCIAL DEMOCRACY IN THE DEMOCRATIC

Bibliography

382   REVOLUTION," *International Publishers, N. Y., 1935.*

Lenin, V., "THE REVOLUTION OF 1905," *International Publishers, N. Y., 1931.*

Lenin, V., "ON BRITAIN," *M. Lawrence Co., London, 1934.*

Lenin, V., "THE PARIS COMMUNE," *International Publishers, N. Y., 1934.*

Lenin, V., "MARX, ENGELS, MARXISM," *International Publishers, N. Y., 1935.*

Lenin, V., "THE JEWISH QUESTION," *International Publishers, N. Y., 1934.*

Lenin, V., "A LETTER TO AMERICAN WORKERS," *International Publishers, N. Y., 1934.*

Lenin, V., "THE SPEECHES OF LENIN," *International Publishers, N. Y., 1928.*

Lenin, V., "THE LETTERS OF LENIN," *(edited by Hill-Mudie), Chapman-Hall, London, 1937.*

Lenin, V., "THE STATE AND REVOLUTION," *International Publishers, N. Y., 1932.*

Lenin, V., "LEFT-WING COMMUNISM," *International Publishers, N. Y., 1934.*

Lenin, V., "IMPERIALISM: THE HIGHEST STAGE OF CAPITALISM," *International Publishers, N. Y., 1933.*

Lenin, V., "TOWARD THE SEIZURE OF POWER," *International Publishers, N. Y., 1927.*

Lenin, V., "THE ISKRA PERIOD," *International Publishers, N. Y., 1927.*

Lenin, V., "THE IMPERIALIST WAR," *International Publishers, N. Y., 1927.*

Lenin, V., "THE REVOLUTION OF 1917," *International Publishers, N. Y., 1927.*

Lenin, V., "THE STRUGGLE FOR THE BOLSHEVIK PARTY *(1900-1904)*," *International Publishers, N. Y., 1934.*

Lenin, V., "THE PRE-REQUISITES FOR THE FIRST RUSSIAN REVOLUTION *(1894-1899)*," *International Publishers, N. Y., 1934.*

Lenin, V., "FROM THE BOURGEOIS TO THE PROLETARIAN REVOLUTION," *International Publishers, N. Y., 1934.*

Lenin, V., "THE RUSSIAN REVOLUTION," *International Publishers, N. Y. 1938.*

Lenin, V., "AFTER THE SEIZURE OF POWER *(1917-1920)*," *International Publishers, N. Y., 1934.*

Lenin, V., "THE PERIOD OF 'WAR COMMUNISM' *(1918-1920)*," *International Publishers, N. Y., 1934.*

Lenin, V., "RELIGION," *International Publishers, N. Y., 1933.*

Levy, H., "ASPECTS OF DIALECTICAL MATERIALISM," *Watts and Co., London, 1935.*

Lindsay, A., "KARL MARX'S 'CAPITAL'," *Oxford University Press, London, 1925.*

Lippmann, W., "THE GOOD SOCIETY," *Little, Brown & Co., Boston, 1937.*

Loria, A., "KARL MARX," *T. Seltzer Co., N. Y., 1920.*

Maritain, J., "FREEDOM IN THE MODERN WORLD," *Charles Scribner's Sons, N. Y., 1936.*

Marx, K., "MARX-ENGELS, HISTORISCH-KRITISCHE GESAMTAUSGABE," *edited by D. Rjazanov. 9 Vols. Frankfurt, 1927-1932.*

Marx, K., "AUS DEM LITERARISCHEN NACHLASS VON KARL MARX, FRIEDRICH ENGELS," *Edited by F. Mehring. 3 Vols. Stuttgart, 1902.*

Bibliography

Marx, K., "DER BRIEFWECHSEL ZWISCHEN FRIEDRICH ENGELS UND KARL MARX, 1844-1883," edited by Bebel and Bernstein. 4 vols. Dent & Sons, London, 1930.

Marx, K., "A CONTRIBUTION TO THE CRITIQUE OF POLITICAL ECONOMY," International Publishers, N. Y., 1904.

Marx, K., "CRITIQUE OF THE GOTHA PROGRAMME," International Publishers, N. Y., 1933.

Marx, K., "LETTERS OF DR. KUGELMANN," International Publishers, N. Y., 1934.

Marx, K., "SELECTED ESSAYS," International Publishers, N. Y., 1926.

Marx, K., "THE POVERTY OF PHILOSOPHY," International Publishers, N. Y., 1936.

Marx, K., "MARX-ENGELS: SELECTED CORRESPONDENCE," M. Lawrence Co., 1934.

Marx, K., "THE CIVIL WAR IN FRANCE," International Publishers, N. Y., 1933.

Marx, K., "THE COMMUNIST MANIFESTO," (with Engels) International Publishers, N. Y., 1935.

Marx, K., "CLASS STRUGGLES IN FRANCE," International Publishers, N. Y., 1935.

Marx, K., "THE CIVIL WAR IN FRANCE," International Publishers, N. Y., 1937.

Marx., K., "THE EIGHTEENTH BRUMAIRE OF LOUIS BONAPARTE," International Publishers, N. Y., 1935.

Marx, K., "WAGE, LABOUR, CAPITAL; VALUE, PRICE, PROFIT," International Publishers, N. Y., 1935.

Marx, Karl, "CAPITAL," Random House, N. Y., 1932.

McFadden, Charles J., "THE PHILOSOPHY OF COMMUNISM," Benziger Brothers, N. Y., 1939.

Mehring, F., "KARL MARX," John Lane Co., London, 1936.

Murry, J., "THE NECESSITY OF COMMUNISM," T. Seltzer Co., N. Y., 1933.

Nicolaievsky, N., "KARL MARX," J. B. Lippincott Co., Philadelphia, 1936.

Olgiati, F., "CARLO MARX," Milan, 1922.

Osbert, R., "FREUD AND MARX: A DIALECTICAL STUDY," Gollancz, London, 1937.

Parce, L., "ECONOMIC DETERMINISM," Charles H., Kerr and Co., Chicago, 1913.

Perchik, L., "KARL MARX," International Publishers, N. Y., 1934.

Petersen, A., "KARL MARX AND MARXISM," Labor News Co., N. Y., 1933.

Postgate, R., "KARL MARX," H. Hamilton Co., London, 1933.

Prenant, M., "BIOLOGY AND MARXISM," International Publishers, N. Y., 1939.

"PROGRAM OF THE COMMUNIST INTERNATIONAL," Workers Library Publishers, N. Y., 1936.

Rappoport, C., "LA PHILOSOPHIE DE L'HISTOIRE," Riviere, Paris, 1925.

"REPORT OF THE ROYAL COMMISSION," Edmond Cloutier Co., Ottawa, Canada, 1946.

Report of the Subversive Activities Control Board Dated April 20, 1953.

Ruhle, Otto, "KARL MARX," Viking Press, New Home Library Edition, N. Y., 1943.

Russel, B., "BOLSHEVISM: PRACTICE AND THEORY," Bruce and Howe, N. Y., 1920.

Bibliography

384

Russel, B., "THE MEANING OF MARX," (a symposium) Farrar and Rinehard, N. Y., 1931.

Salter, F., "KARL MARX AND MODERN SOCIALISM," Macmillan Co., London, 1921.

Schmidt, W., "THE ORIGIN AND THE GROWTH OF RELIGION," Methuen Co., London, 1931.

Seligman, E., "THE ECONOMIC INTERPRETATION OF HISTORY," Columbia University Press, N. Y., 1924.

Seton-Watson, Hugh, "FROM LENIN TO MALENKOV," Frederich A. Praeger, N. Y., 1953.

Sheed, F., "COMMUNISM AND MAN," Sheed and Ward, London, 1938.

Shirokov-Moseley, "A TEXTBOOK OF MARXISM," Gollancz, London, 1937.

Spargo, J., "KARL MARX," B. Huebsch Co., N. Y., 1910.

Stalin, J., "THE FOUNDATION OF LENINISM," International Publishers, 1934.

Stalin, J., "THE PROBLEMS OF LENINISM," International Publishers 1934.

Stalin, J., "THE OCTOBER REVOLUTION," International Publishers., N. Y., 1934.

Stalin, J., "LENINISM," (2 vols.), Allen and Unwin, London, 1933.

Stalin, J., "MARXISM AND THE NATIONAL AND COLONIAL QUESTION," International Publishers, N. Y., 1935.

Stalin, J., "FROM THE FIRST TO THE SECOND FIVE-YEAR PLAN," International Publishers, N. Y., 1934.

Stalin, J., "ON THE NEW CONSTITUTION," International Publishers, N. Y., 1936.

Stuart, John Leighton, "FIFTY YEARS IN CHINA," Random HOUSE, N. Y., 1955.

Trotsky, L., "THE HISTORY OF THE RUSSIAN REVOLUTION," Simon and Schuster, N. Y., 1936.

Wade, W., "U. N. TODAY," H. W. Wilson Company, New York, 1954.

White, W., "LENIN," Smith and Haas, N. Y., 1936.

Wilson, Edmund, "TO THE FINLAND STATION," Doubleday and Co., N. Y., 1953.

Wood, H., "CHRISTIANITY AND COMMUNISM," Round Table Press, N. Y., 1933.

Yaroslavsky, E., "RELIGION IN THE U.S.S.R.," International Publishers, N. Y., 1934.

Zetkin, C., "REMINISCENCES OF LENIN," International Publishers, N. Y., 1934.

Index

Index

Index

Index

Index

389

Index

Index

Index

Index

Index

Index

Index

Index

Index

Index

Index

Index

Index

Index

Index

Index

Index

Index

407

Index